Microwave and Antenna System in Medical Applications

Microwave and Antenna System in Medical Applications

Editors

Hoi-Shun Antony Lui
Mikael Persson

MDPI Basel • Beijing • Wuhan • Barcelona • Belgrade • Novi Sad • Cluj • Manchester

Editors

Hoi-Shun Antony Lui
University of Tasmania
Sandy Bay
Australia

Mikael Persson
Chalmers University of Technology
Gothenburg
Sweden

Editorial Office
MDPI
St. Alban-Anlage 66
4052 Basel, Switzerland

This is a reprint of articles from the Special Issue published online in the open access journal *Sensors* (ISSN 1424-8220) (available at: https://www.mdpi.com/journal/sensors/special_issues/MASMA).

For citation purposes, cite each article independently as indicated on the article page online and as indicated below:

Lastname, A.A.; Lastname, B.B. Article Title. *Journal Name* **Year**, *Volume Number*, Page Range.

ISBN 978-3-7258-0341-5 (Hbk)
ISBN 978-3-7258-0342-2 (PDF)
doi.org/10.3390/books978-3-7258-0342-2

Contents

sensors

Editorial

Microwave and Antenna Systems in Medical Applications

Hoi-Shun Lui [1,*] and Mikael Persson [2]

1 College of Sciences and Engineering, University of Tasmania, Sandy Bay, TAS 7005, Australia
2 Division of Signal Processing and Biomedical Engineering, Department of Electrical Engineering, Chalmers University of Technology, SE-41296 Gothenburg, Sweden
* Correspondence: lui@ieee.org

The non-ionizing nature of microwave radiation and the low cost of microwave electronics offer innovative solutions for medical diagnosis, treatment, and health monitoring [1,2]. Researchers in antennas, microwave electronics, computational electromagnetics, imaging, and signal processing are working collaboratively with medical practitioners to enhance our lives by developing next-generation healthcare technologies. A well-known example would be the prospect of utilizing microwave sensors for stroke detection such that prehospital diagnosis can be facilitated in ambulances using a portable system [3–5]. In regional areas in Sweden and Australia, stroke patients and the elderly who are located remotely from hospitals will benefit. Clinical trials of microwave stroke detection and breast screening are currently in place across Europe, North America, and Oceania. Another example would be the use of microwave radiation for breast screening, providing alternatives to existing ionizing X-ray mammography for cancer diagnosis [6–8].

The recent boom in artificial intelligence (AI) and machine learning (ML) is opening new avenues that accelerate technical development in microwave-based techniques for medical applications. These developments cover signal processing, imaging processing, as well as microwave and antenna system optimization [9,10].

In this Special Issue, we present a comprehensive exploration of microwave and antenna systems, showcasing their transformative impact on diverse medical applications, including medical diagnosis, treatment, and patient monitoring. This collection features nine cutting-edge original research articles followed by two insightful reviews incorporating microwave imaging and sensing into digital pulmonology and digital gastroenterology. The titles and authors of the articles are listed in Table 1.

Table 1. List of articles included in this Special Issue.

	Title	Authors
(i)	Evaluation of the Resolution in Inverse Scattering of Dielectric Cylinders for Medical Applications	Ehsan Akbari Sekehravani, Giovanni Leone
(ii)	Microwave Antenna System for Muscle Rupture Imaging with a Lossy Gel to Reduce Multipath Interference	Laura Guerrero Orozco, Lars Peterson, Andreas Fhager
(iii)	On the Role of Training Data for SVM-Based Microwave Brain Stroke Detection and Classification	Tomas Pokorny, Jan Vrba, Ondrej Fiser, David Vrba, Tomas Drizdal, Marek Novak, Luca Tosi, Alessandro Polo, Marco Salucci
(iv)	Comparison of Microwave Hyperthermia Applicator Designs with Fora Dipole and Connected Array	Gulsah Yildiz, Iman Farhat, Lourdes Farrugia, Julian Bonello, Kristian Zarb-Adami, Charles V. Sammut, Tuba Yilmaz, Ibrahim Akduman

Citation: Lui, H.-S.; Persson, M. Microwave and Antenna Systems in Medical Applications. *Sensors* **2024**, *24*, 1059. https://doi.org/10.3390/s24041059

Received: 25 January 2024
Accepted: 5 February 2024
Published: 6 February 2024

Table 1. *Cont.*

	Title	Authors
(v)	Thermal Evaluation of Multi-Antenna Systems Proposed to Treat Bone Tumors: Finite Element Analysis	Citlalli Jessica Trujillo-Romero, Juan Dionisio Merida, Texar Javier Ramírez-Guzmán, Raquel Martínez-Valdez, Lorenzo Leija-Salas, Arturo Vera-Hernández, Genaro Rico-Martínez, José Jesús Agustín Flores-Cuautle, Josefina Gutiérrez-Martínez, Emilio Sacristán-Rock
(vi)	Microwave Ablation of Liver, Kidney, and Lung Lesions: One-Month Response and Manufacturer's Charts' Reliability in Clinical Practice	Julien Frandon, Philippe Akessoul, Tarek Kammoun, Djamel Dabli, Hélène de Forges, Jean-Paul Beregi, Joël Greffier
(vii)	Walking Step Monitoring with a Millimeter-Wave Radar in Real-Life Environment for Disease and Fall Prevention for the Elderly	Xuezhi Zeng, Halldór Stefán Laxdal Báruson, Alexander Sundvall
(viii)	Wearable Sensor Based on Flexible Sinusoidal Antenna for Strain Sensing Applications	Mehran Ahadi, Mourad Roudjane, Marc-André Dugas, Amine Miled, Younès Messaddeq:
(ix)	Brain Implantable End-Fire Antenna with Enhanced Gain and Bandwidth	Lisa Sapari, Samnang Hout, and Jae-Young Chung
(x)	Digital Pulmonology Practice with Phonopulmography Leveraging Artificial Intelligence: Future Perspectives Using Dual Microwave Acoustic Sensing and Imaging	Arshia K. Sethi, Pratyusha Muddaloor, Priyanka Anvekar, Joshika Agarwal, Anmol Mohan, Mansunderbir Singh, Keerthy Gopalakrishnan, Ashima Yadav, Aakriti Adhikari, Devanshi Damani, Kanchan Kulkarni, Christopher A. Aakre, Alexander J. Ryu, Vivek N. Iyer, Shivaram P. Arunachalam
(xi)	Practicing Digital Gastroenterology through Phonoenterography Leveraging Artificial Intelligence: Future Perspectives Using Microwave Systems	Renisha Redij, Avneet Kaur, Pratyusha Muddaloor, Arshia K. Sethi, Keirthana Aedma, Anjali Rajagopal, Keerthy Gopalakrishnan, Ashima Yadav, Devanshi N. Damani, Victor G. Chedid, Xiao Jing Wang, Christopher A. Aakre, Alexander J. Ryu, Shivaram P. Arunachalam

1. Original Research Articles

Medical Diagnosis: There are three articles (i–iii) that deal with the use of microwave imaging and sensing for medical diagnosis of breast cancer, hamstring muscle injuries, and stroke detection. Sekehravani and Leone et al. (i) address the inverse scattering problem for dielectric cylinders, providing insights into achievable resolution for medical imaging and highlighting the potential impact of microwave breast cancer imaging on cancer diagnosis. In (ii), researchers from Sweden propose a semicircular microwave imaging array with a novel antenna design for imaging hamstring muscle injuries. The inclusion of a lossy gel in the imaging domain proves instrumental in reducing multipath signals, enhancing imaging quality for more accurate diagnostics. Pokorny et al. (iii) investigate microwave brain stroke detection and classification using support vector machines, emphasizing the importance of training data in achieving high accuracy. The study showcases the potential for microwave technology in diagnosing cerebral conditions.

Disease Treatment: There are three articles about microwave cancer treatment using microwave hyperthermia (iv) and microwave ablation (v,vi). Yildiz et al. (iv) evaluate the effectiveness of different fractal octagonal ring antenna designs. Their research emphasizes the critical role of applicator design in optimizing the specific absorption rate for breast tumor hyperthermia applications. Examining microwave ablation in bone tumors, Trujillo-Romero et al. (v) evaluate the thermal performance of multi-antenna arrays. Using the finite element method, their study presents various antenna configurations, demonstrating the feasibility of treating bone tumors with a specific focus on ablated tissue volume. Frandon et al. (vi) investigate the early response and reliability in treating liver, kidney, and lung lesions using a commercial microwave ablation system in a clinical setting. Their findings underscore the system's potential in patient monitoring through reliable ablations.

Patient Monitoring: There are two papers on patient monitoring using antenna systems (vii,viii), and one paper on implantable antenna design for brain–machine communication applications (ix). Zeng et al. (vii) utilize millimeter-wave radar for gait analysis in a real-life environment. Their research showcases the method's reliability in measuring step time, offering potential applications in fall prevention for the elderly. In (viii), a flexible sinusoidal-shaped antenna sensor is proposed, and its application in strain sensing is explored. Their study demonstrates improved sensitivity and flexibility for wearable sensors, opening avenues for patient monitoring in various medical scenarios. Sapari et al. (ix) introduce an end-fire radiating implantable antenna for brain–machine interfaces; this research emphasizes high-data-rate wireless communication. Their study highlights the antenna's enhanced gain and broadband operation (3 to 5 GHz), showcasing the potential of implanting antennas in the skull during brain surgery.

2. Review Articles

This Special Issue includes two review articles on the potential integration of microwave sensing into the medical diagnosis of respiratory disorders (x) and digestive system disorders (xi). The review in (x) delves into the integration of AI with dual microwave acoustic sensing and imaging for the analysis of lung sounds. The exploration of AI models opens avenues for real-time respiratory sound analysis, potentially revolutionizing clinical pulmonology practice. The review in [xi] focuses on digital gastroenterology, investigating the potential of a bowel sound recording and analysis device—the phonoenterogram. With a spotlight on microwave-based digital phonoenterography, the review envisions a future where AI-driven analysis of bowel sounds becomes an accessible, cost-effective, and versatile diagnostic tool.

3. Conclusions

This Special Issue highlights the multifaceted contributions of microwave and antenna systems to revolutionizing healthcare. The original research presents innovative approaches to various technical challenges, showcasing the potential of microwave technology in diverse applications. The review papers pave the way for integrating microwave sensing and imaging solutions, opening avenues for novel diagnostic applications.

Conflicts of Interest: The authors declare no conflict of interest.

References

1. Chandra, R.; Zhou, H.; Balasingham, I.; Narayanan, R.M. On the Opportunities and Challenges in Microwave Medical Sensing and Imaging. *IEEE Trans. Biomed. Eng.* **2015**, *62*, 1667–1682. [CrossRef] [PubMed]
2. Chiao, J.-C.; Li, C.; Lin, J.; Caverly, R.H.; Hwang, J.C.M.; Rosen, H.; Rosen, A. Applications of Microwaves in Medicine. *IEEE J. Microw.* **2023**, *3*, 134–169. [CrossRef]
3. Persson, M.; Fhager, A.; Trefna, H.D.; Yu, Y.; McKelvey, T.; Pegenius, G.; Karlsson, J.-E.; Elam, M. Microwave-Based Stroke Diagnosis Making Global Prehospital Thrombolytic Treatment Possible. *IEEE Trans. Biomed. Eng.* **2014**, *61*, 2806–2817. [CrossRef] [PubMed]
4. Fhager, A.; Candefjord, S.; Elam, M.; Persson, M. Microwave Diagnostics Ahead: Saving Time and the Lives of Trauma and Stroke Patients. *IEEE Microw. Mag.* **2018**, *19*, 78–90. [CrossRef]

5. Mohammed, B.J.; Abbosh, A.M.; Mustafa, S.; Ireland, D. Microwave System for head imaging. *IEEE Trans. Instrum. Meas.* **2014**, *63*, 117–123. [CrossRef]
6. Fear, E.C.; Bourqui, J.; Curtis, C.; Mew, D.; Docktor, B.; Romano, C. Microwave Breast Imaging With a Monostatic Radar-Based System: A Study of Application to Patients. *IEEE Trans. Microw. Theory Tech.* **2013**, *61*, 2119–2128. [CrossRef]
7. Preece, A.W.; Craddock, I.; Shere, M.; Jones, L.; Winton, H.L. MARIA M4: Clinical evaluation of a prototype ultrawideband radar scanner for breast cancer detection. *J. Med. Imaging* **2016**, *3*, 033502. [CrossRef] [PubMed]
8. Shea, J.D.; Kosmas, P.; Hagness, S.C.; Van Veen, B.D. Three-dimensional microwave imaging of realistic numerical breast phantoms via a multiple-frequency inverse scattering technique. *Med. Phys.* **2010**, *37*, 4210–4226. [CrossRef] [PubMed]
9. Bolomey, J.-C. Advancing Microwave-Based Imaging Techniques for Medical Applications in the Wake of the 5G Revolution. In Proceedings of the 2019 13th European Conference on Antennas and Propagation (EuCAP), Krakow, Poland, 31 March–5 April 2019.
10. Jafarifarmand, A.; Yilmaz, T.; Akduman, I. Microwave Medical Diagnosis System With a Framework to Optimize the Antenna Configuration and Frequency of Operation Using Neural Networks. *IEEE Trans. Microw. Theory Tech.* **2022**, *70*, 5095–5104. [CrossRef]

sensors

MDPI

Article

Evaluation of the Resolution in Inverse Scattering of Dielectric Cylinders for Medical Applications

Ehsan Akbari Sekehravani * and Giovanni Leone

Department of Engineering, University of Campania "Luigi Vanvitelli", I-81031 Aversa, Italy; giovanni.leone@unicampania.it
* Correspondence: ehsan.akbarisekehravani@unicampania.it

Abstract: The inverse scattering problem has numerous significant applications, including in geophysical explorations, medical imaging, and radar imaging. To achieve better performance of the imaging system, theoretical knowledge of the resolution of the algorithm is required for most of these applications. However, analytical investigations about the resolution presently feel inadequate. In order to estimate the achievable resolution, we address the point spread function (PSF) evaluation of the scattered field for a single frequency and the multi-view case both for the near and the far fields and the scalar case when the angular domain of the incident field and observation ranges is a round angle. Instead of the common free space condition, an inhomogeneous background medium, consisting of a homogeneous dielectric cylinder with a circular cross-section in free space, is assumed. In addition, since the exact evaluation of the PSF can only be accomplished numerically, an analytical approximation of the resolution is also considered. For the sake of its comparison, the truncated singular value decomposition (TSVD) algorithm can be used to implement the exact PSF. We show how the behavior of the singular values and the resolution change by varying the permittivity of the background medium. The usefulness of the theoretical discussion is demonstrated in localizing point-like scatterers within a dielectric cylinder, so mimicking a scenario that may occur in breast cancer imaging. Numerical results are provided to validate the analytical investigations.

Keywords: linear inverse scattering; number of degrees of freedom; point spread function; inhomogeneous medium; resolution; TSVD inversion; localization; breast cancer imaging

Citation: Akbari Sekehravani, E.; Leone, G. Evaluation of the Resolution in Inverse Scattering of Dielectric Cylinders for Medical Applications. *Sensors* **2023**, *23*, 7250. https://doi.org/10.3390/s23167250

Academic Editors: Antonio Lázaro, Mikael Persson and Hoi-Shun Antony Lui

Received: 1 June 2023
Revised: 5 August 2023
Accepted: 15 August 2023
Published: 18 August 2023

1. Introduction

The inverse scattering problem requires determining the physical and geometric characteristics of an unknown object from scattered field data provided via the induced perturbation of known incident fields. Since the inverse scattering problem is nonlinear, approximations such as the Born [1] or Rytov [1,2] ones for dielectric objects and physical optics (PO) [3,4] approximation for metallic objects can provide a linear relationship between the scattered field data and the scattering object.

The imaging method based on inverse scattering has gained significant interest and has been thoroughly researched. This is because of its flexibility and appropriateness for various applications, such as radar imaging [5], through-the-wall imaging [6,7], ground penetration radar (GPR) applications [8,9], biological imaging applications [10,11], breast cancer imaging [12–15], brain stroke detection [16,17], and medical imaging [18]. Far and near field data can be available according to the application; in particular, medical imaging can be accomplished in the near zone, which may provide better-resolution benefits compared with far-field imaging.

The full view is a typical case in inverse scattering, which arises as the incident fields illuminate the object from all angles, and the scattered fields are observed at all angles. This case is suitable for various industrial applications or medical imaging applications like head and breast imaging.

The achievable resolution refers to the ability to accurately distinguish and locate small features or details within an object or scene being imaged. It is related to the smallest resolvable distance or size of the features that can be distinguished with the imaging system and has raised much interest in microwave imaging.

In [19], based on nonlinear modelling and inversion, a super resolution was demonstrated for a near-field experimental microwave tomography system; however, in nonlinear inverse scattering, the results depend on the scattering scenario and cannot be investigated a priori. In [20], the resolution within a linear scattering model was considered; however, since the internal field is numerically computed as the exact one instead of being approximated by the incident one as in the Born approximation, no analytical discussion can be performed and it should be computed numerically. In [21], an alternative definition of resolution was introduced, but a numerical computation is always required for a comparison of different scenarios. An approach based on deep learning has been proposed in [22] to improve the spatial resolution for microwave imaging. Therefore, all these approaches achieve results about resolution based on numerical computations.

Instead, in linear scattering, the achievable resolution can be defined in terms of the point spread function (PSF) of the system and it represents the reconstruction of a point-like object. For a compact linear operator, singular value decomposition (SVD) can be used to introduce the PSF. The concept of PSF has found extensive usage in [23–27], showing its broad applicability and relevance in various fields.

The analytical evaluation of the exact PSF can be performed for a limited number of scattering geometries. For most scenarios, numerical methods are the only option. The truncated SVD (TSVD) [28] algorithm can be used to obtain the exact PSF. To compute the exact main lobe width of the PSF, an appropriate truncation value must be chosen, as using an incorrect value may affect the main lobe width and the side lobes. An appropriate truncation choice could be the number of degrees of freedom (NDF) of the scattering object, which is defined as the number of significant singular values of the pertinent scattering operator as they usually decay exponentially.

The NDF evaluation of the scattered field has been addressed in [29] for simple strip geometries for the full-view case in the far zone. That study has demonstrated that the same NDF can be obtained through the use of different variables. One way to provide an analytical expression of the PSF is by evaluating an approximation of the exact PSF to eliminate the limitations of the exact PSF. For instance, in [30], the evaluation of the approximated PSF has been considered for strip source/scatterer geometries for the full view. Those authors used the NDF as a truncation value in the TSVD algorithm. The results showed that the resolution is constant for the full-view case, the approximation worked well in the main lobe, and the NDF was a good choice for truncation. The same analysis is available in [31] for circumference source/scatterer geometries, and the analytical estimation of the NDF was also evaluated.

The NDF of the radiated field was considered in [32] for square sources, and the authors showed that the NDF of a full 2D square is equal to the NDF of a void square source. Sometimes, the analytical estimation of the NDF cannot be evaluated and it should be computed numerically. For the aspect-limited case, the NDF of the scattered field was computed numerically in [33] for curve geometries in different modalities. The analytical approximation of the PSF was also evaluated to estimate the resolution, and it was shown that the resolution is not constant.

A theoretical study on the achievable resolution and image quality of microwave imaging systems has been addressed in [34]. That study clarifies the relationship between resolution and limited-view versus full-view antenna array geometry, monostatic versus multistatic configuration, single-frequency versus wideband operation, and near-field versus far-field imaging. The theoretical relations of image resolution have been addressed in [35] for both the full-view and aspect-limited cases.

Most of the scattering scenarios assume the free space as being in the background, i.e., a homogeneous medium. In subsurface imaging for GPR applications, a two-layered medium has been taken into consideration [36–38] because the closed-form analytical expression of the scattered field can be found. In this circumstance, the available data are inherently aspect-limited to a half-space. Less attention has been paid to other layered geometries, although the closed-form expression of the pertinent scattered field can be available. In this paper, we are interested in a two-layered cylindrical medium composed of a homogeneous dielectric cylinder with a circular cross-section, embedded in the free space. This scenario can provide a theoretical reference for those applications, such as breast cancer/tumor imaging when scattering objects are located within a dielectric medium of known parameters. In this paper, we address the evaluation of the PSF of the scattered field for the single-frequency case and the multi-view sensing configuration for the full-view case to estimate the achievable resolution for both the far and near fields. We investigate how the permittivity of the dielectric can affect the truncation level and the resolution. In addition, an analytical approximate of the exact PSF is evaluated. Furthermore, a localization application that can be used in breast cancer/tumor imaging is provided. Numerical comparisons for the truncation index and two PSFs are provided to validate the theoretical discussion.

The plan for this paper is as follows: In Section 2, the problem statement, a PSF evaluation, and a discussion about how to choose the truncation level for a general scattering geometry are presented. Section 3 introduces and investigates the approximated PSF. Section 4 provides some numerical examples to validate the theoretical discussions. In Section 5, a numerical application to a localization problem is shown. Finally, in Section 6, conclusions are provided.

2. Statement of the Problem

The general geometry of the problem is depicted in Figure 1. An unknown scatterer with relative permittivity $\varepsilon_s(\underline{r})$ is located within a domain referred to as the investigation domain (ID), which is embedded in a homogeneous dielectric cylinder (region 1) with a circular cross-section, radius r_a, and relative permittivity ϵ_{r_a}, centered at the origin. The dielectric cylinder is located in a free space (region 2) with permittivity $\epsilon = \epsilon_0$ and both regions are nondispersive, while the magnetic permeability everywhere is equal to μ_0. (The external medium can be also assumed to be different, though always homogeneous, provided that the appropriate dielectric permittivity is accounted for within the electromagnetic scattering model.) Accordingly, the background medium is inhomogeneous, as it consists of a cylindrically stratified medium.

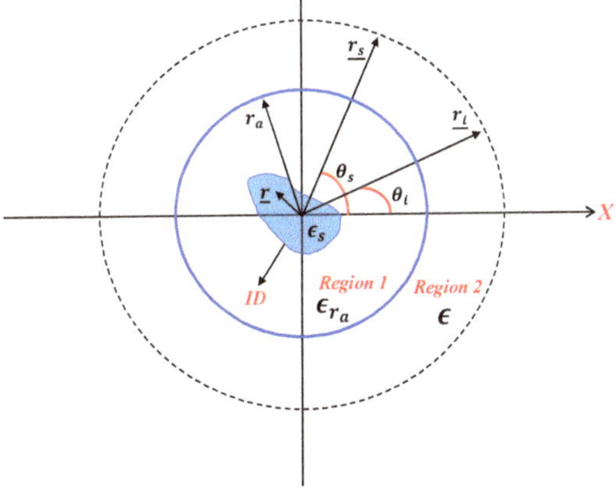

Figure 1. A pictorial view of the geometry of the problem. The dotted line indicates the positions of the source and receivers.

Let us define as $\underline{r} = (\rho, \phi)$, $\underline{r_i} = (r_i, \theta_i)$, and $\underline{r_s} = (r_s, \theta_s)$ as the position vectors spanning the scattering object, the source point (transmitter), and observation point (receiver), respectively. Hereafter, r_i and r_s are also assumed to be constant, i.e., they are circumference. In this paper, we consider the full-view case where the angular ranges of the excitation and observation angles are 2π wide, i.e., $-\pi < \theta_i, \theta_s < \pi$.

Under the Born approximation, in the scalar case, the only component of the scattered field is defined by

$$E_s(\underline{r_s}, \underline{r_i}) = \iint_{ID} \chi(\underline{r})\, G_s(\underline{r}, \underline{r_s}) E_i(\underline{r_i}, \underline{r})\, d\underline{r} = \mathcal{T}(\chi(\underline{r})) \tag{1}$$

apart from some inessential factors, where $\chi(\underline{r}) = \frac{\epsilon_s(\underline{r})}{\epsilon_{ra}} - 1$ and $\mathcal{T}$ are a contrast function and the pertinent linear operator for our multi-view and single-frequency scattering configurations of interest. Moreover, G_s is the Green function pertinent to the inhomogeneous background medium and E_i is the incident field radiated by a filamentary line source within the background medium, that is, in the presence of the dielectric cylinder.

In particular, the Green function can be computed in closed form as a series [39] as

$$G_s(\underline{r}, \underline{r_s}) = \sum_n d'_n H_n^{(2)}(\beta r_s)\, J_n(\beta \sqrt{\epsilon_{r_a}}\, \rho)\, e^{jn(\theta_s - \phi)} \tag{2}$$

where $H_n^{(2)}(\cdot)$ is the Hankel function of the second kind and n-th order and $J_n(\cdot)$ is the Bessel function of the first kind and n-th order. In addition, the wavenumber and wavelength are denoted by β and λ, respectively. The generalized transmission $d_n^{'}$ coefficients are provided by

$$d'_n = \frac{\frac{2j}{\pi \beta r_a}}{J_n(\beta \sqrt{\epsilon_{r_a}}\, r_a)\, H_n^{(2)'}(\beta r_a) - \sqrt{\epsilon_{r_a}}\, J'_n(\beta \sqrt{\epsilon_{r_a}}\, r_a)\, H_n(\beta r_a)} \tag{3}$$

where $H_n^{(2)'}$ and J'_n are the derivative of the Hankel function and the derivative of the Bessel function, respectively.

Because of the reciprocity theorem, the incident field E_i in (1) is equal to the Green function G_s (apart from an inessential constant factor), i.e., $G_s(\underline{r}, \underline{r_i}) = E_i(\underline{r_i}, \underline{r})$ (see Appendix A for more details).

Note that the series in (2) can apparently be approximated using a finite summation of $2N + 1$ terms, where N is equal to $[\beta \sqrt{\epsilon_{r_a}} \max(\rho)]$, with $[\cdot]$ representing the nearest integer. This approximation arises due to the asymptotic behavior of the Bessel function for order larger than the argument. However, the issue of the truncation of (2) will be further considered in Section 3 and in Appendix B.

2.1. PSF Evaluation

In this subsection, we first recall the definition of the exact PSF as the impulse response of an imaging system to a point-like scatterer and express it as the cascade of $\mathcal{T}^{-1}$, i.e., the regularized inverse operator of $\mathcal{T}$ and the forward operator. In other words, the response of the system to a Dirac delta function δ is the PSF of the system. Mathematically, the exact PSF is provided by

$$PSF(\underline{r}, \underline{r_0}) = \mathcal{T}^{-1} \mathcal{T} \delta(\underline{r} - \underline{r_0}) \tag{4}$$

When it is observed at $(\underline{r})$ and the point-like scatterer is located at $(\underline{r_0})$, SVD is applied to (2) because the $\mathcal{T}$ operator is linear and compact. Its singular system consists of the triple $\{v_n, \sigma_n, u_n\}$ [28], where u_n and v_n are the singular functions, which span the data and the scatterer contrast function spaces, respectively, and σ_n is the singular values, arranged under a decreasing order. We can rewrite (4) in terms of the completeness relation truncated to the retained singular function v_n. This is because the minimum–norm solution to the inverse scattering problem is a projection of the actual contrast function onto the singular function having non-zero singular values.

$$PSF(\underline{r}, \underline{r_0}) = \sum_{n=1}^{N_t} v_n(\underline{r})\, v_n^*(\underline{r_0}) \tag{5}$$

where $*$ indicates the conjugation operation. Equation (5) states that the exact PSF is dependent on the number of retained singular values, which is related to the accuracy of the solution. Hence, knowledge of the singular functions and the choice of N_t are required to compute (5), and it can only be calculated in closed form for a limited number of scatterer geometries. The truncation value N_t can be chosen in terms of the NDF, whenever the singular values exhibit a rather flat behavior before the exponentially fast decay. Then, N_t is chosen in correspondence with the knee of the singular value curve, and it is rather independent of the noise on the data. If this is not the case, the correct choice of N_t can be performed once the uncertainties on the data are available, as the choice of N_t can vary and it depends on those uncertainties. Additionally, the inversion results depend on the knowledge available a priori about uncertainties on the data. Therefore, it is worth investigating the behavior of the SVD of (1) to understand what is the typical behavior of singular values for the present inhomogeneous medium geometry.

To numerically calculate the SVD of the pertinent operator, a sufficiently fine discretization of the integral Equation (1) is employed and the resulting matrix equation is processed in the MATLAB environment.

Figures 2 and 3 show the behavior of the singular values for $\epsilon_{r_a} = 4$ and $r_a = 2\lambda$ in the far and near fields, respectively. It is apparent that their behavior is not very different. However, in contrast to the homogeneous background medium case, where a step-like behavior can be expected due to the possibility to recast (1) as a Fourier transform [29,31], the singular value behavior now depends on ϵ_{r_a}. Hence, it is worthwhile to examine how the truncation level of the singular values, which determines the value of N_t in (5), impacts the behavior of PSF.

By observing Figures 4 and 5, which pertain to far and near fields (with $r_i = r_s = r_a + \lambda$), respectively, it can be appreciated that a high truncation level does not affect the main lobe of the PSF, while a low level considerably reduces its side lobe level. Consequently, when the main lobe of the PSF is the primary focus, as it defines the resolution of the inversion algorithm, a rather high truncation level of the singular values can be tolerated. On the contrary, when reconstructing a more complex object, such as a collection of closely located point-like scatterers, it is important to employ a low truncation level (and consequently, a low uncertainty level on data) to prevent adverse effects from high side lobes on the resulting image.

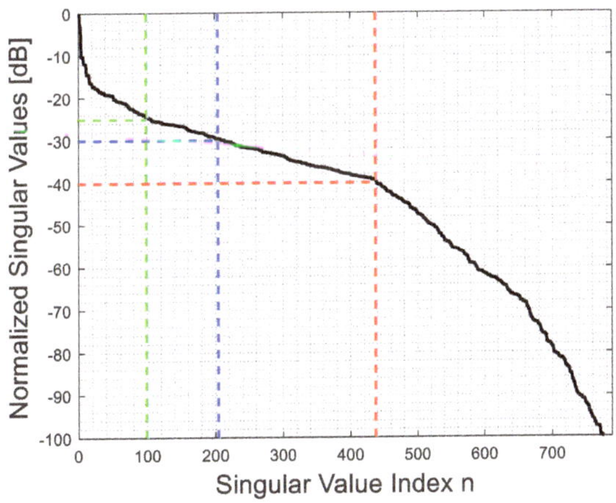

Figure 2. The behavior of the singular values for $\epsilon_{r_a} = 4$ and $r_a = 2\lambda$ for the far field.

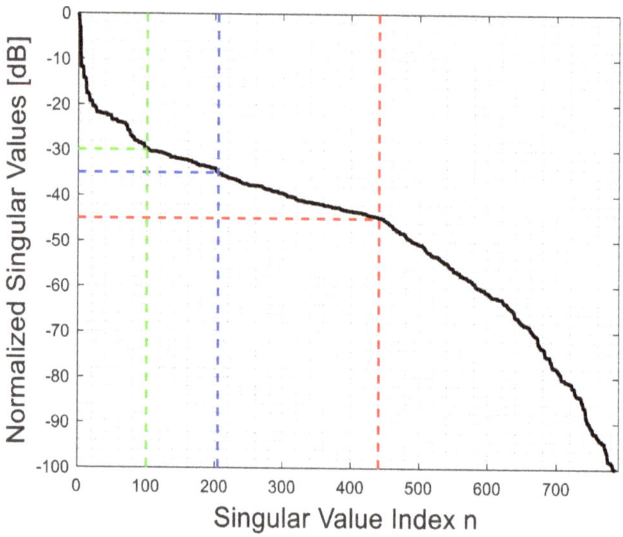

Figure 3. The behavior of the singular values for $\epsilon_{r_a} = 4$ and $r_a = 2\lambda$ for the near field.

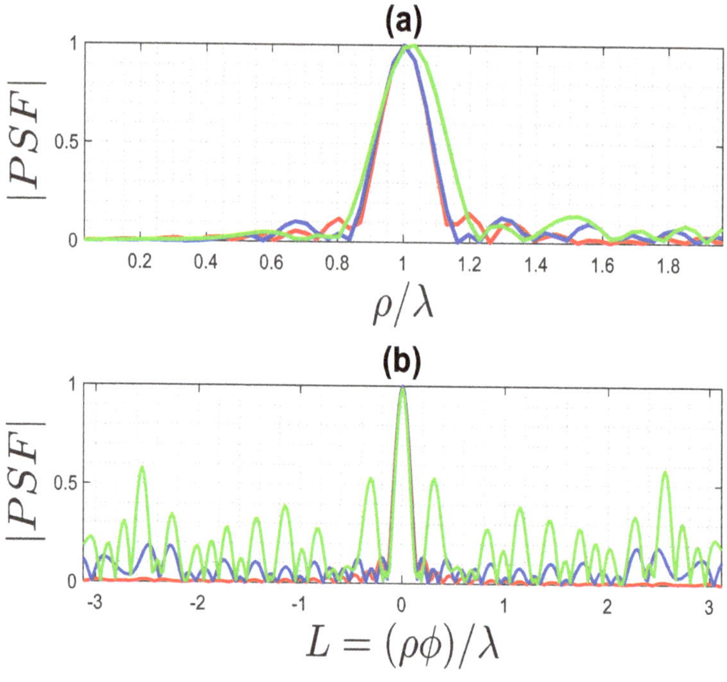

Figure 4. The exact PSF for far field achieved using different truncation levels, where the green line is 25 dB, the blue line is 30 dB, and the red line is 40 dB: (**a**) PSF along ρ-cut, (**b**) PSF along ϕ-cut.

In this paper, the achievable resolution is estimated based on the general behavior of such functions, specifically the main lobe. The resolution R is defined as half of the width W of the main lobe of the PSF function.

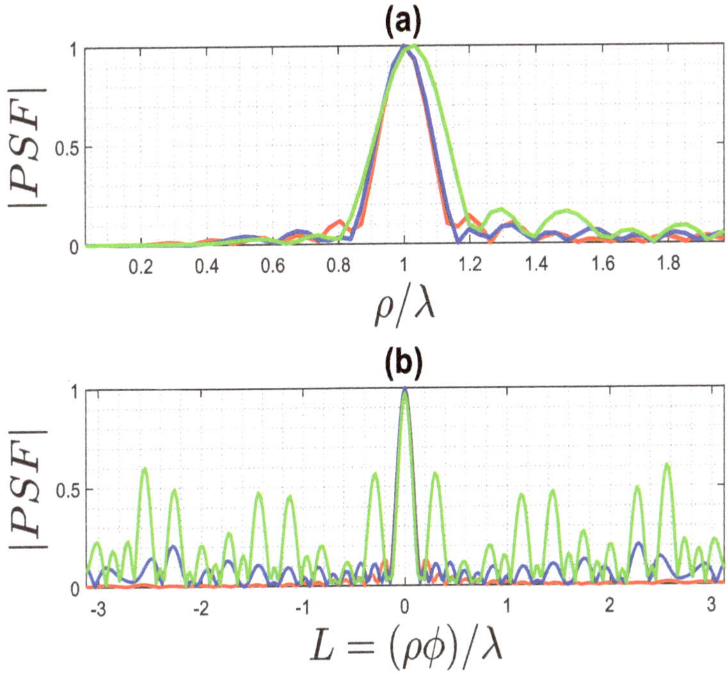

Figure 5. The exact PSF for the near field for different truncation levels, where the green line is 30 dB, the blue line is 35 dB, and the red line is 45 dB: (**a**) PSF along ρ-cut, (**b**) PSF along ϕ-cut.

2.2. Approximate PSF

According to [30,31,33], the adjoint operator may approximate the inverse operator in (4) if the singular values of the relevant operator have a nearly constant behavior before the knee of its curve. Consequently, it is possible to replace the inverse operator with the adjoint one in (4) to introduce a good approximation of the exact PSF to overcome the abovementioned limitation. Notwithstanding, this is not true for the case at hand; hereafter, we adopt the same approximation since it provides a simple analytical function to define the resolution.

Then, the approximated $\widetilde{PSF}$ is defined by

$$\widetilde{PSF}(\underline{r},\underline{r_0}) = \mathcal{T}^{+}\mathcal{T}\delta(\underline{r}-\underline{r_0}) \tag{6}$$

The analytical evaluation of (6) is performed as follows. First, we define the adjoint operator of (1) by

$$\mathcal{T}^{+}E_s = \int_0^{2\pi}\int_0^{2\pi} E_s(\underline{r_s},\underline{r_i})\ G_s^{*}(\underline{r_0},\underline{r_s})E_i^{*}(\underline{r_i},\underline{r_0})\ d\theta_s\ d\theta_i \tag{7}$$

as the source and observation domains are assumed to be the circumference. Then, the spectral theorem for compact self-adjoint operators is applied to $\mathcal{T}^{+}\mathcal{T}$:

$$\begin{gathered}\mathcal{T}^{+}\mathcal{T}\delta(\underline{r}-\underline{r_0}) = \\ \iint_{ID}\chi(\underline{r})\left[\int_0^{2\pi}\int_0^{2\pi} G_s(\underline{r},\underline{r_s})\ E_i(\underline{r_i},\underline{r})\ G_s^{*}(\underline{r_0},\underline{r_s})E_i^{*}(\underline{r_i},\underline{r_0})\ d\theta_s\ d\theta_i\right] d\underline{r}\end{gathered} \tag{8}$$

By using the addition theorem for the Hankel function and interchanging the integrals and the summations, because of (2), (8) becomes a four-fold summation, which, in turn, can be factored as the product of two identical functions with different arguments:

$$\widetilde{PSF}(\rho,\rho_0,\phi,\phi_0) = \mathcal{F}_s(\rho,\rho_0,\phi,\phi_0,r_s)\cdot\mathcal{F}_i(\rho,\rho_0,\phi,\phi_0,r_i) \tag{9}$$

where $\mathcal{F}_s(\rho,\rho_0,\phi,\phi_0,r_s)$ and $\mathcal{F}_i(\rho,\rho_0,\phi,\phi_0,r_i)$ pertain to the observation and incident field, respectively, and are symmetric functions of the arguments. For the full-view case, for instance, the $\mathcal{F}_s$ function can be written as a double summation:

$$\begin{gathered}\mathcal{F}_s(\rho,\rho_0,\phi,\phi_0,\ r_s) = \int_0^{2\pi} G_s(\underline{r},\underline{r_s})G_s^*(\underline{r_0},\underline{r_s})d\theta_s = \\ \left(\begin{array}{c}\int_0^{2\pi} \sum\limits_{n=-N}^{N} d'_n\, H_n^{(2)}(\beta r_s)\, J_n(\beta\sqrt{\epsilon_{r_a}}\,\rho)\, e^{jn(\theta_s-\phi)}\ \cdot \\ \left(\sum\limits_{l=-L}^{L} d'_l\, H_l^{(2)}(\beta r_s)\, J_l(\beta\sqrt{\epsilon_{r_a}}\,\rho_0)\, e^{jl(\theta_s-\phi_0)}\right)^* d\theta_s\end{array}\right)\end{gathered} \tag{10}$$

Then, since the observation domain is a circumference, so that r_s is constant, by performing the simple closed form integration, (10) becomes

$$\mathcal{F}_s(\rho,\rho_0,\phi,\phi_0,r_s) = \sum_{n=-N}^{N} |d'_n|^2 \left|H_n^{(2)}(\beta r_s)\right|^2 J_n(\beta\sqrt{\epsilon_{r_a}}\,\rho)\, J_n(\beta\sqrt{\epsilon_{r_a}}\,\rho_0)\, e^{jn(\phi-\phi_0)} \tag{11}$$

The evaluation of $\mathcal{F}_i$ proceeds in the same way as $\mathcal{F}_s$. Finally, the evaluation of (9) is given by

$$\begin{gathered}\widetilde{PSF}(\rho,\rho_0,\phi,\phi_0) = \left[\sum_{n=-N}^{N} |d'_n|^2 \left|H_n^{(2)}(\beta r_s)\right|^2 J_n(\beta\sqrt{\epsilon_{r_a}}\,\rho)\, J_n(\beta\sqrt{\epsilon_{r_a}}\,\rho_0)\, e^{jn(\phi-\phi_0)}\right]\cdot \\ \left[\sum_{m=-M}^{M} |d'_m|^2\, J_m(\beta\sqrt{\epsilon_{r_a}}\,\rho)\, \left|H_m^{(2)}(\beta r_i)\right|^2 J_m(\beta\sqrt{\epsilon_{r_a}}\,\rho_0)\, e^{jm(\phi-\phi_0)}\right]\end{gathered} \tag{12}$$

which provides the searched analytical evaluation of the approximated $\widetilde{PSF}$. Although (12) provides a closed-form expression under a finite series, further simplifications are considered hereafter.

3. Discussion about the Approximated $\widetilde{PSF}$

In this section, we provide a further discussion about the approximated $\widetilde{PSF}$ (12) to simplify it and to demonstrate that the resolution is the same for both the near and far scattered fields. In particular, we assume that the ID coincides with the whole circular section or region 1 in Figure 1, so that $\max(\rho,\rho_0) = r_a$. Therefore, we consider the influence of $\left|H_n^{(2)}(\beta r_s)\right|^2$, $|d'_n|^2$ and $c_n = |J_n(\beta\sqrt{\epsilon_{r_a}}\, r_a)|^2$ in (12) on the resolution.

3.1. Far Field

For the far field, due to the asymptotic behavior of the Hankel functions for arguments much larger than the order, $\left|H_n^{(2)}(\beta r_s)\right|^2$ can be approximated by $\frac{\pi}{2(\beta r_s)}$, which becomes a constant. Next, the influence of $|d'_n|^2$ on the behavior of the Fourier coefficients in (12) needs to be examined. To this end, Figure 6b shows a typical behavior of $|d'_n|^2$ for $r_a = 3\lambda$ $\epsilon_{r_a} = 3$. It can be observed that they decay for large n (for an explanation, see Appendix B) and that their amplitude is mostly close to 1. On the other hand, as discussed in Section 2 and confirmed by Figure 6a, the c_n coefficients decay asymptotically for $n > N$. Therefore, it is interesting to examine the behavior of the product $\left|d'_n\, J_n(\beta\sqrt{\epsilon_{r_a}}\, r_a)\right|$ (as $\max(\rho,\rho_0) = r_a$).

In the Appendix B, it is shown that this term decays asymptotically for $|n| > N' = [\beta\, r_a]$. Consequently, the Fourier series in (12) can be truncated to $2N' + 1$ terms as

$$\widetilde{PSF}(\rho, \rho_0, \phi, \phi_0) \cong \left(\sum_{n=-N'}^{N'} J_n(\beta\sqrt{\epsilon_{r_a}}\,\rho)\; J_n(\beta\sqrt{\epsilon_{r_a}}\,\rho_0)\; e^{jn(\phi-\phi_0)} \right)^2 \quad (13)$$

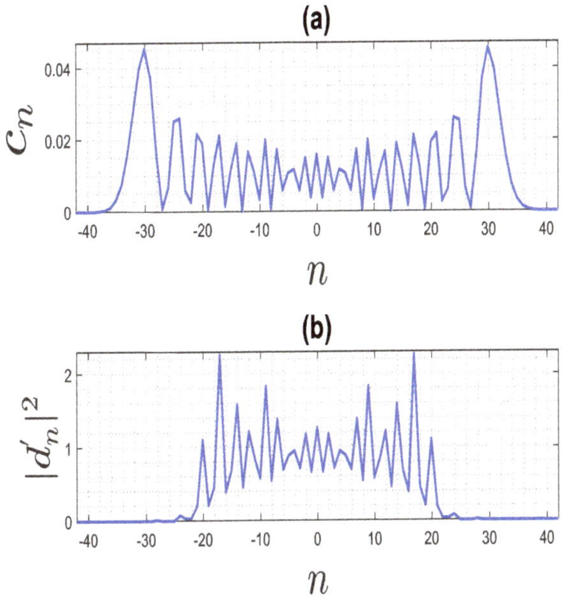

Figure 6. The behavior of two coefficients in (12): (**a**) the behavior of c_n, (**b**) the behavior of $|d_n'|^2$.

But, in virtue of the addition theorem of the Bessel functions, (13) is approximately equal to

$$\widetilde{PSF}(\rho, \rho_0, \phi, \phi_0) \cong \left(J_0(\beta\sqrt{\epsilon_{r_a}}\,|\underline{r} - \underline{r_0}|)\right)^2 \quad (14)$$

A comparison between (12) and (14) is provided in Figure 7 for $\rho_0 = 1.52\lambda$ and $\phi_0 = 0$. The results confirm that the two approximations are completely overlapped.

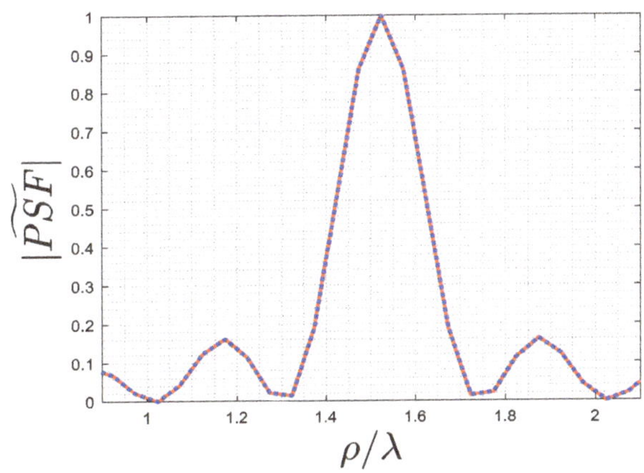

Figure 7. The comparison of the normalized amplitude of (12) (solid blue line) and (14) (dotted red line) PSFs along ρ-cut for $\rho_0 = 1.525\lambda$ and $\phi_0 = 0$.

3.2. Near Field

The results obtained for $|d'_n|^2$ are also valid for the near field as they are independent of r_s. Therefore, the influence of the $\left|H_n^{(2)}(\beta r_s)\right|^2$ factor needs to be considered. Figure 8 shows a comparison of $\left|H_n^{(2)}(\beta r_s)\right|^2$ for different r_s. It is observed that while the curve remains flat for large r_s values, this is not the case for smaller values. However, even when $r_s = a + \lambda$, it can still be considered flat for $|n| < N\prime$, thereby having a negligible impact on (12), and (13) and (14) still hold. Consequently, it can be concluded that the approximate PSF is the same for both the near and far fields, except for cases where $r_s < r_a + 0.5\lambda$, i.e., very close to the dielectric ID. In such cases, it becomes necessary to consider more terms for the convergence of the Fourier series and to account for the close proximity effects of the reactive near field, which become significant.

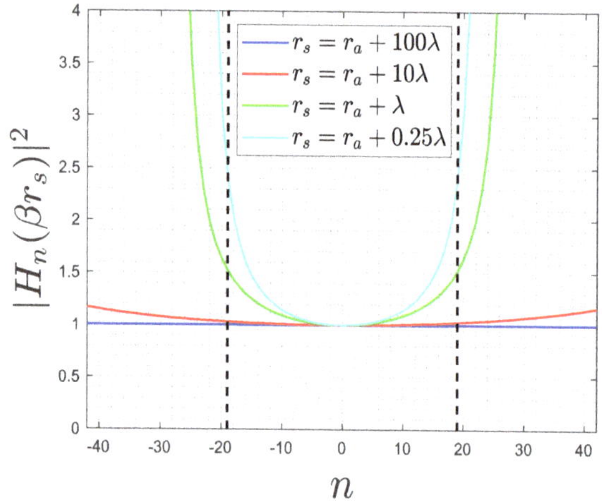

Figure 8. The behavior of $\left|H_n^{(2)}(\beta r_s)\right|^2$ for different r_s (dashed lines shows the value of N').

Figure 9 shows a comparison of Equations (12)–(14) for $\rho_0 = 1.52\lambda$ and $\phi_0 = 0$. The results verify that the three approximations coincide with each other, as expected. Based on the results obtained from the two subsections, it can be concluded that (14) can serve as a reliable approximation for the exact PSF instead of (12). Additionally, it is notable that the resolution remains the same for both the far and near fields. Further numerical examples will be provided in the next section.

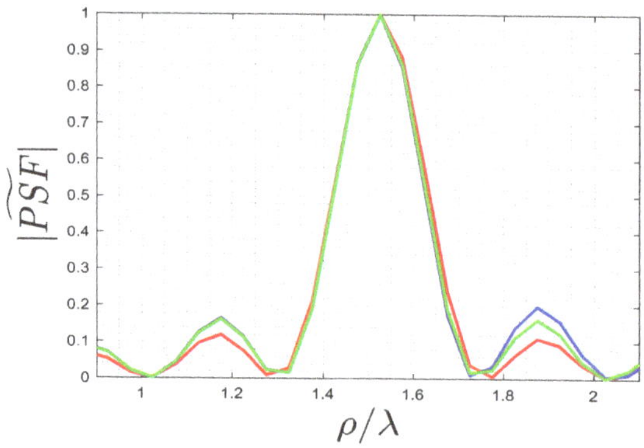

Figure 9. The comparison of the normalized amplitude of (12) (red line), (13) (blue line), and (14) (green line) PSFs along ρ-cut for $\rho_0 = 1.525\lambda$ when $\phi_0 = 0$.

4. Numerical Validation

In this section, various numerical examples are presented to validate the theoretical discussions from the previous sections. We consider a cylinder with a radius of $r_a = 3\lambda$, where the ID coincides with the cylinder. To highlight the focusing properties, only the main lobe of the PSF is taken into account, and the amplitudes of both PSFs are normalized to 1. For all subsequent numerical examples, r_i and r_s are set to $r_a + \lambda$ for the near field.

Firstly, we compare the behavior of singular values of (1) for the far and near fields with different ϵ_{r_a}. Figure 10 illustrates the behavior of normalized singular values of the relevant operators (1) for the near and far fields with varying ϵ_{r_a}. The analytical estimation of the NDF for a free space was provided in [40,41] for the far field, and it is provided using $NDF = \frac{\Sigma A}{(2\pi)^2}$, where A and Σ are the spectral domain area and the measure of the area of the function to be transformed, respectively. For the full-view case, A is $\pi(2\beta)^2$ [41] and Σ is equal to $\pi {r_a}^2$ for the considered ID, and the NDF estimation is confirmed via the blue solid line. The results provide evidence that the singular value behavior is approximately the same for the far and near fields. In addition, the singular value behavior is not flat, indicating that higher values of ϵ_{r_a} result in a faster overall decay.

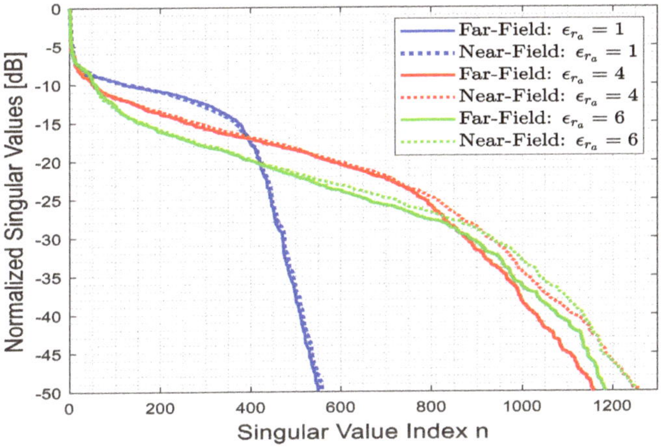

Figure 10. The behavior of the normalized singular values of the linearized inverse scattering for different ϵ_{r_a} for the far and near fields.

A comparison between the exact PSF (12) and the approximated (14) one is performed for both the far and near fields to further evaluate the performance of the achievable resolution and to validate the accuracy of the approximated $\widetilde{PSF}$. Figure 11 illustrates the normalized amplitude of both PSFs along the ϕ-cuts when $\rho_0 = 1.5\lambda$ and $\phi_0 = 0$. It is observed that the resolution is the same for both the far and near fields for different ϵ_{r_a}, as the main lobe width of the PSF becomes slimmer as ϵ_{r_a} increases. Therefore, the resolution R for $\epsilon_{r_a} = 1$, $\epsilon_{r_a} = 4$, and $\epsilon_{r_a} = 6$ is equal to 0.38λ, 0.19λ, and 0.15λ, respectively, as it can be predicted using (14) according to the first zero of the Bessel function of *0*-th order. The space-invariance of the PSF being achieved for the full-view case means that the resolution is constant. This result confirms that two PSFs are approximately overlapped.

To check out the performance of the exact PSF (12) and the approximated (14) along a ρ-cut for the far and near fields, a comparison between two PSFs is provided in Figure 12 for $\rho_0 = 1.5\lambda$ when $\phi_0 = 0$. The resolution is again the same for both the far and the near fields for different ϵ_{r_a}, as expected. In addition, it is confirmed that the approximated $\widetilde{PSF}$ works well. As a result, the resolution is proportion to $\frac{1}{\sqrt{\epsilon_{r_a}}}$.

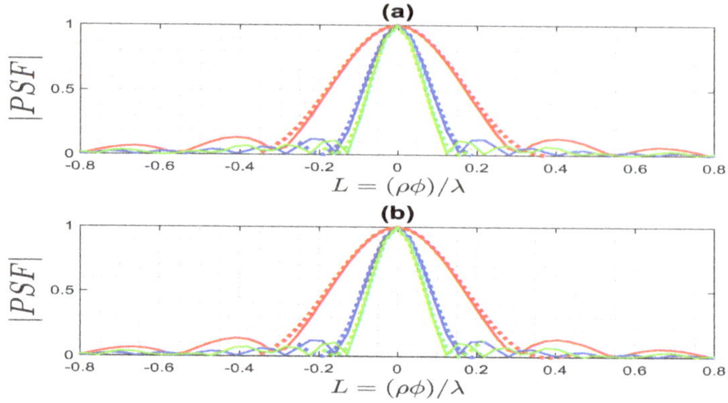

Figure 11. The comparison of the normalized amplitude of the exact (solid lines) and approximated (dashed lines) PSFs along a ϕ-cut for $\phi_0 = 0$ and $\rho_0 = 1.5\lambda$, for $\epsilon_{r_a} = 1$ (red lines), $\epsilon_{r_a} = 4$ (blue lines) $\epsilon_{r_a} = 6$ (green lines): (**a**) far field, (**b**) near field.

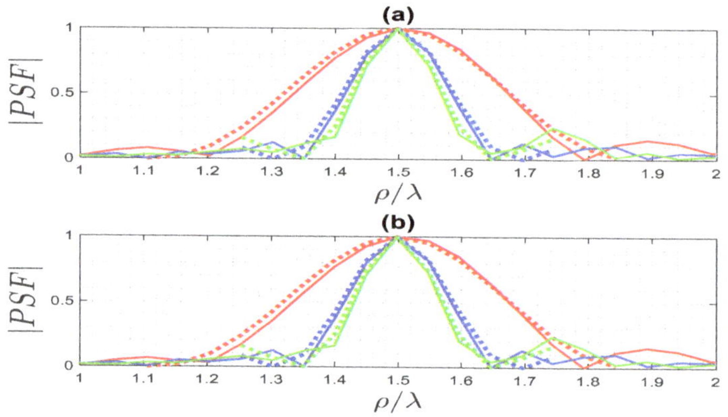

Figure 12. The comparison of the normalized amplitude of the exact (solid lines) and approximated (dashed lines) PSFs along a ρ-cut for $\rho_0 = 1.5\lambda$ when $\phi_0 = 0$, for $\epsilon_{r_a} = 1$ (red lines), $\epsilon_{r_a} = 4$ (blue lines) $\epsilon_{r_a} = 6$ (green lines): (**a**) far field, (**b**) near field.

5. Application to Breast Cancer Scenario

This section provides an application of the aforementioned theoretical discussions to reconstruct a set of point-like scatterers located within an ID (blue circle) with $r_a = 1.5\lambda$ and $\epsilon_{r_a} = 12$ from the near-field scattered data ($r_i = r_s = a + \lambda$). We are aware that actual breast cancer scenarios are more complicate, with strongly inhomogeneous background media, which prevent any analytical work and require numerical modelling. However, in this paper, the goal is to provide an analytical discussion of the resolution and some simplifications are required, such as assuming a dielectric homogenous cylindrical circular investigation domain and modeling tumors as point-like scatterers. For this case, the truncation level of the singular values is selected at 40 dB. As discussed in Section 3, this choice ensures a low side lobe level for the exact PSF without affecting its main lobe. The ID is chosen to mimic a breast cancer scenario, where the dielectric background consists of a medium with high dielectric permittivity, approximating a circular shape. Breast imaging aims to identify the presence of breast cancer or tumors, and it has been extensively studied in the field of microwave sensing and imaging. In particular, breast tumors exhibit relatively high contrast compared with the predominating fat tissue in the breast [42] and can be modelled as point-like scatterers. Therefore, this approach can be used for localizing or detecting breast cancer/tumors, as accurate detection is the first step in classifying cancer/tumors.

In this application, we consider three point-like scatterers on a circumference (the ϕ-cut) with a radius of $\rho_0 = 0.26\lambda$ located in the ID, representing a typical size of the array for breast imaging. Figure 13 shows the geometry of the application.

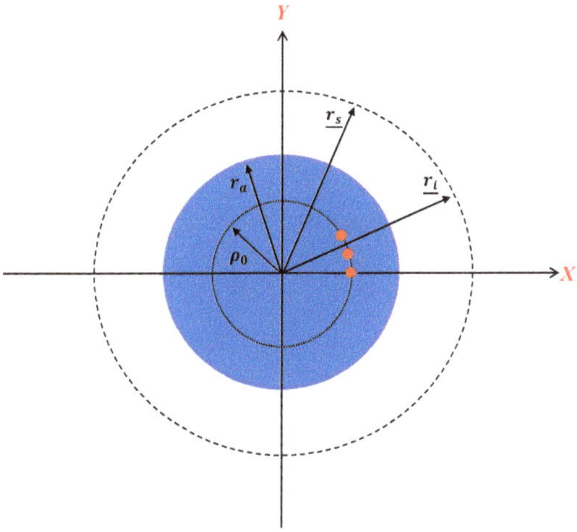

Figure 13. The geometry of the application. The red dots indicate the position of the point-like scatterers. The dotted line indicates the positions of source and receivers.

Figure 14 shows a normalized reconstruction of the considered point-like scatterers, computed via inversion of (1), compared with the result of the summation of three functions (14) as centered at the scatterers positions. As can be seen in Figure 14a, if the distance between point-like scatterers is equal to the width $W = 0.2\lambda$, they can be distinguished from each other, as the predicted resolution is $R = 0.1\lambda$. However, when the distance is less than R, they are not resolvable and appear as a single scattering point, as shown in Figure 14b. The findings indicate that both reconstructions yield similar results.

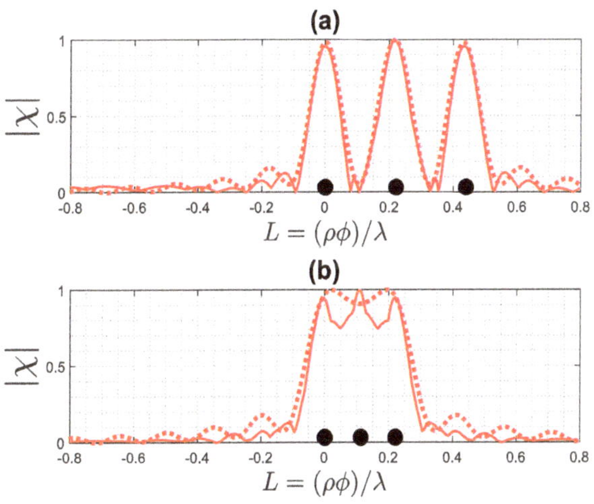

Figure 14. The exact (solid line) and approximated (dotted line) reconstruction of three point-like scatterers: (**a**) the distance between them is equal to the resolution, (**b**) the distance between them is less than the resolution. The black dots indicate the position of the point-like scatterers.

Now, we consider an example where the three point-like scatterers are arranged along the radius of the ID when $\phi_0 = 0$, as shown in Figure 15.

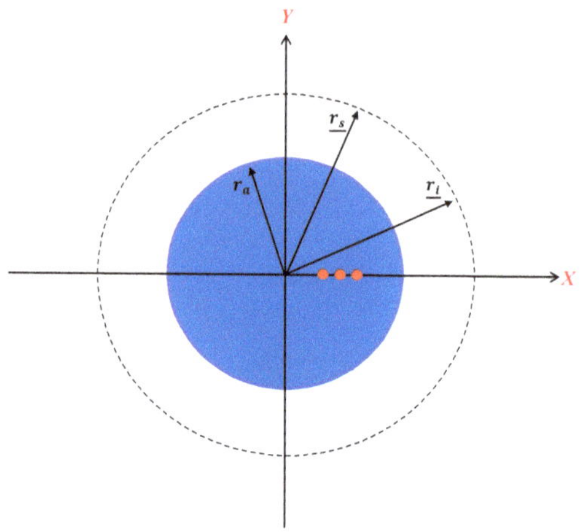

Figure 15. The geometry of the application. The red dots indicate the position of the point-like scatterers. The dotted line indicates the positions of source and receivers.

Figure 16 displays the normalized reconstruction of the point-like scatterers under examination computed via inversion of (1), compared with the result of the summation of three functions (14). Figure 16a demonstrates that, if the distance between the scatterers is the same as the width $W = 0.2\lambda$, they can be identified separately. On the other hand, if the distance is smaller than the resolution, with $R = 0.1\lambda$, they are not distinguishable and appear as a single scattering point, as depicted in Figure 16b. These results once again highlight that both reconstructions produce comparable outcomes.

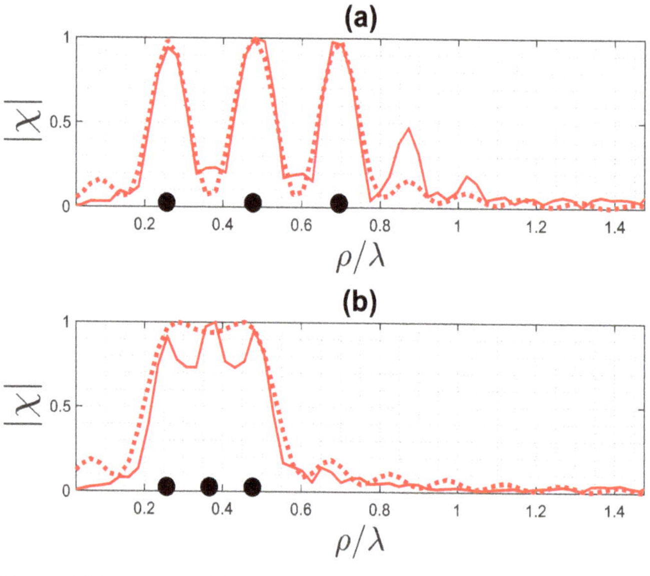

Figure 16. The exact (solid line) and approximated (dotted line) reconstruction of three point-like scatterers: (**a**) the distance between them is equal to the width, and (**b**) the distance between them is equal to the resolution. The black dots indicate the position of the point-like scatterers.

6. Discussion and Conclusions

We have evaluated the PSF of the linear inverse scattering problem for a dielectric cylinder background to estimate the achievable resolution for the full-view case for both the far and near fields. Our main goal has been to provide an analytical approximation of the resolution because the exact evaluation of the PSF can be accomplished only numerically and its accuracy is dependent on the truncation value. First, we have discussed the behavior of the singular values and showed that the singular value behavior is approximately the same for both fields. However, since their behavior is not flat, the accuracy of the result can depend on the number of singular values to be retained, which, in turn, depends on the uncertainties on data. It has been pointed out that the choice of the truncation level for the PSF computation affects only its side lobe level, while the main lobe remains mostly unchanged. Then, an approximate analytical PSF has been introduced and some numerical simulations have validated the accuracy of the approximated PSF against the exact PSF. In particular, the results have shown that there is good agreement in the main lobe region of both PSFs for different permittivities, which is sufficient for predicting actual resolution in a sensing configuration. The analytical and the numerical results have also demonstrated that the resolution is the same for both fields and remains unchanged along the whole ID, i.e., it is space-invariant. Additionally, both results clearly have highlighted that the resolution changes by varying the permittivity of the ID in both fields and is inversely proportional to $\sqrt{\epsilon_{r_a}}$.

Finally, we have presented an application for reconstructing point-like scatterers located within the ID from the near field, which is valuable for detecting breast cancer/tumors. The application demonstrates that when the distance between two point-like scatterers equals the width of the main lobe PSF, they can be distinguished from each other. Conversely, if the distance is less than the width, they cannot be differentiated. The results once again have shown that both reconstructions achieved similar results. Indeed, the approach suffers from a limitation. In fact, the approximate evaluation of the PSF is shown to be accurate in the main lobe, while the behavior of the side lobes is less predictable. This means that the reconstruction of the isolated point-like scatterers, even if randomly located, can be expected to be accurate. On the contrary, if there are many point-like scatterers and they are close to each other, it may not be possible to reconstruct all of them correctly due to the effect of the side lobes of the corresponding approximate PSF.

For microwave imaging systems designed to operate up to 2GHz, for a reasonable value of the relative permittivity of human tissues as $\epsilon_{r_a} = 6$, a resolution of 2.25 cm can be predicted. Of course, from the imaging point of view, this figure can provide unsatisfactory results in actual complicated scenarios with many tumors with smaller separations. However, for detection purposes, especially in the very initial stage, the results of the presented analysis can provide the minimum detection distance for isolated tumors. In any case, the resolution at microwave frequencies is connected to the free space wavelength because of the wave scattering interaction.

Author Contributions: Conceptualization, G.L.; methodology, G.L.; software, E.A.S.; validation, E.A.S. and G.L.; formal analysis, E.A.S. and G.L.; investigation, E.A.S. and G.L.; resources, E.A.S.; data curation, E.A.S.; writing—original draft preparation, E.A.S.; writing—review and editing, G.L. and E.A.S.; visualization, G.L.; supervision, G.L.; project administration, G.L.; funding acquisition, E.A.S. All authors have read and agreed to the published version of the manuscript.

Funding: This research received no external funding.

Data Availability Statement: Data supporting the reported results were generated during the study.

Conflicts of Interest: The authors declare no conflict of interest.

Appendix A

In this appendix, we demonstrate the connection between the Green function and the incident field by starting from equations (7-32a) in [43], which provide an integral relating the file radiated in the region 2 by sources occupying region 1 to the field radiated in region 1 by sources occupying region 2. In the scalar case, where both electric sources and fields have only the z-component, if we assume no magnetic sources and electric filamentary line sources with a constant current, the integrals can be evaluated straightforwardly.

Then, the source 1, $J_1 = I\delta(\underline{r}' - \underline{r_S})$, located in $\underline{r}' = \underline{r_S}$, radiates the field $E_1(\underline{r}') = E_i(\underline{r_S}, \underline{r}')$, while the source 2 , $J_2 = \delta(\underline{r}' - \underline{r})$, located in $\underline{r}' = \underline{r}$, radiated the field $E_2(\underline{r}') = G_s(\underline{r}, \underline{r}')$. Consequently, the left-hand side of equations (7-32a) becomes $IG_s(\underline{r}, \underline{r_S})$ and the right-hand side becomes $E_i(\underline{r_S}, \underline{r})$, and the two functions are proportional when the argument variables are exchanged.

Appendix B

In this appendix, we examine the asymptotic behavior for large n of the Fourier coefficients of (12) in the far-field case. In particular, we consider the factor $\left|d_n' \, J_n\left(\beta\sqrt{\epsilon_{r_a}}\,\rho\right)\right|$, which is common to all summations. We make use of the following asymptotic expansion of the Bessel and Hankel functions for orders larger than the arguments:

$$J_n(z) \sim \frac{1}{\sqrt{2\pi n}}\left(\frac{ez}{2n}\right)^n \tag{A1}$$

and

$$H_n^{(2)}(z) \sim j\sqrt{\frac{2}{\pi n}}\left(\frac{ez}{2n}\right)^{-n} \tag{A2}$$

where e is Euler's number.

We start from the denominator of (3), to be rewritten as

$$J_n(\beta\sqrt{\epsilon_{r_a}}\, r_a)H_{n-1}^{(2)}(\beta r_a) - \sqrt{\epsilon_{r_a}}\, J_{n-1}(\beta\sqrt{\epsilon_{r_a}}\, r_a)\, H_n(\beta r_a) \tag{A3}$$

in virtue of the Bessel functions. Then, via substitution of (A1) and (A2), we obtain

$$\frac{\sqrt[n]{\epsilon_{r_a}}}{\pi}\frac{2}{e\beta r_a}\frac{n^n}{(n-1)^{n-1}}\left\{\left[\frac{e\beta r_a}{2}\left(\frac{n-1}{n}\right)^n\frac{1}{n-1}\right]^2 - 1\right\} \tag{A4}$$

which can be simplified to

$$\frac{\sqrt[n]{\epsilon_{r_a}}}{\pi}\frac{2}{e\beta r_a} \tag{A5}$$

This provides

$$\left|d_n'\right| \sim \frac{e}{\sqrt[n]{\epsilon_{r_a}}} \tag{A6}$$

When we multiply this factor by the asymptotic expansion of the Bessel function, we obtain

$$\left|d_n' J_n(\beta\sqrt{\epsilon_{r_a}}\,\rho)\right| \sim \frac{e}{\sqrt{2\pi n}}\left(\frac{e\beta\rho}{2n}\right)^n \sim e\left|J_n(\beta\,\rho)\right| \tag{A7}$$

This means that the product decays asymptotically for $|n| > \max(\beta\,\rho) = [\beta r_a] = N'$.

References

1. Oristaglio, M.L.; Blok, H. *Wavefield Imaging and Inversion in Electromagnetics and Acoustics*; Cambridge University Press: Cambridge, UK, 2004.
2. Habashy, T.M.; Groom, R.W.; Spies, B.R. Beyond the Born and Rytov approximations: A nonlinear approach to electromagnetic scattering. *J. Geophys. Res. Space Phys.* **1993**, *98*, 1759–1775. [CrossRef]
3. Mager, R.; Bleistein, N. An examination of the limited aperture problem of physical optics inverse scattering. *IEEE Trans. Antennas Propag.* **1978**, *26*, 695–699. [CrossRef]
4. Pierri, R.; Liseno, A.; Soldovieri, F. Shape reconstruction from PO multifrequency scattered fields via the singular value decomposition approach. *IEEE Trans. Antennas Propag.* **2001**, *49*, 1333–1343. [CrossRef]
5. Soldovieri, F.; Solimene, R.; Ahmad, F. Sparse tomographic inverse scattering approach for through-the-wall radar imaging. *IEEE Trans. Instrum. Meas.* **2012**, *61*, 3340–3350. [CrossRef]

6. Fedeli, A.; Pastorino, M.; Ponti, C.; Randazzo, A.; Schettini, G. Through-the-wall microwave imaging: Forward and inverse scattering modeling. *Sensors* **2020**, *20*, 2865. [CrossRef]
7. Barzegar, A.S.; Cheldavi, A.; Sedighy, S.H.; Nayyeri, V. 3-D through-the-wall radar imaging using compressed sensing. *IEEE Geosci. Remote Sens. Lett.* **2021**, *19*, 1–5. [CrossRef]
8. Ambrosanio, M.; Bevacqua, M.T.; Isernia, T.; Pascazio, V. Performance analysis of tomographic methods against experimental contactless multistatic ground penetrating radar. *IEEE J. Sel. Top. Appl. Earth Obs. Remote Sens.* **2020**, *14*, 1171–1183. [CrossRef]
9. Alani, A.M.; Soldovieri, F.; Catapano, I.; Giannakis, I.; Gennarelli, G.; Lantini, L.; Ludeno, G.; Tosti, F. The use of ground penetrating radar and microwave tomography for the detection of decay and cavities in tree trunks. *Remote Sens.* **2019**, *11*, 2073. [CrossRef]
10. Semenov, S. Microwave tomography: Review of the progress towards clinical applications. *Philos. Trans. R. Soc. A Math. Phys. Eng. Sci.* **2009**, *367*, 3021–3042. [CrossRef]
11. Caorsi, S.; Massa, A.; Pastorino, M. Numerical assessment concerning a focused microwave diagnostic method for medical applications. *IEEE Trans. Microw. Theory Tech.* **2000**, *48*, 1815–1830.
12. Poplack, S.P.; Tosteson, T.D.; Wells, W.A.; Pogue, B.W.; Meaney, P.M.; Hartov, A.; Kogel, C.A.; Soho, S.K.; Gibson, J.J.; Paulsen, K.D. Electromagnetic breast imaging: Results of a pilot study in women with abnormal mammograms. *Radiology* **2007**, *243*, 350–359. [CrossRef] [PubMed]
13. Casu, M.R.; Vacca, M.; Tobon, J.A.; Pulimeno, A.; Sarwar, I.; Solimene, R.; Vipiana, F. A COTS-based microwave imaging system for breast-cancer detection. *IEEE Trans. Biomed. Circuits Syst.* **2017**, *11*, 804–814. [CrossRef] [PubMed]
14. Fear, E.C.; Li, X.; Hagness, S.C.; Stuchly, M.A. Confocal microwave imaging for breast cancer detection: Localization of tumors in three dimensions. *IEEE Trans. Biomed. Eng.* **2002**, *49*, 812–822. [CrossRef]
15. Bond, E.J.; Li, X.; Hagness, S.C.; Van Veen, B.D. Microwave imaging via space-time beamforming for early detection of breast cancer. *IEEE Trans. Antennas Propag.* **2003**, *51*, 1690–1705. [CrossRef]
16. Ireland, D.; Bialkowski, K.; Abbosh, A. Microwave imaging for brain stroke detection using Born iterative method. *IET Microw. Antennas Propag.* **2013**, *7*, 909–915. [CrossRef]
17. Bisio, I.; Fedeli, A.; Lavagetto, F.; Luzzati, G.; Pastorino, M.; Randazzo, A.; Tavanti, E. Brain stroke detection by microwave imaging systems: Preliminary two-dimensional numerical simulations. In Proceedings of the 2016 IEEE International Conference on Imaging Systems and Techniques (IST), Chania, Greece, 4–6 October 2016; pp. 330–334.
18. Larsen, L.E.; Jacobi, J.H. *Medical Applications of Microwave Imaging*; IEEE Press: Piscataway, NJ, USA, 1986.
19. Bayat, N.; Mojabi, P. A mathematical framework to analyze the achievable resolution from microwave tomography. *IEEE Trans. Antennas Propag.* **2016**, *64*, 1484–1489. [CrossRef]
20. Gilmore, C.; Mojabi, P.; Zakaria, A.; Pistorius, S.; LoVetri, J. On super-resolution with an experimental microwave tomography system. *IEEE Antennas Wirel. Propag. Lett.* **2010**, *9*, 93–396. [CrossRef]
21. Simonov, N.; Son, S.H.; Kim, B.R.; Jeon, S.I. Investigation of spatial resolution in a microwave tomography system. In Proceedings of the 2014 International Conference on Electronics, Information and Communications (ICEIC), Kota Kinabalu, Malaysia, 15–18 January 2014; pp. 1–2.
22. Shah, P.; Moghaddam, M. Super resolution for microwave imaging: A deep learning approach. In Proceedings of the 2017 IEEE International Symposium on Antennas and Propagation & USNC/URSI National Radio Science Meeting, Boston, MA, USA, 9–14 July 2017; pp. 849–850.
23. Den Dekker, A.J.; Van den Bos, A. Resolution: A survey. *JOSA A* **1997**, *14*, 547–557. [CrossRef]
24. Miller, C.R.; Routh, P.S. Resolution analysis of geophysical images: Comparison between point spread function and region of data influence measures. *Geophys. Prospect.* **2007**, *55*, 835–852. [CrossRef]
25. Nakahara, H.; Haney, M.M. Point spread functions for earthquake source imaging: An interpretation based on seismic interferometry. *Geophys. J. Int.* **2015**, *202*, 54–61. [CrossRef]
26. Amineh, R.K.; McCombe, J.J.; Khalatpour, A.; Nikolova, N.K. Microwave holography using point-spread functions measured with calibration objects. *IEEE Trans. Instrum. Meas.* **2014**, *64*, 403–417. [CrossRef]
27. Leone, G.; Munno, F.; Solimene, R.; Pierri, R. A PSF Approach to Far Field Discretization for Conformal Sources. *IEEE Access* **2022**, *10*, 23394–23407. [CrossRef]
28. Bertero, M.; Boccacci, P. *Introduction to Inverse Problems in Imaging*; IOP Publishing: Bristol, UK, 1998.
29. Sekehravani, E.A.; Leone, G.; Pierri, R. NDF of Scattered Fields for Strip Geometries. *Electronics* **2021**, *10*, 202. [CrossRef]
30. Sekehravani, E.; Leone, G.; Pierri, R. PSF Analysis of the Inverse Source and Scattering Problems for Strip Geometries. *Electronics* **2021**, *10*, 754. [CrossRef]
31. Sekehravani, E.A.; Leone, G.; Pierri, R. NDF and PSF analysis in inverse source and scattering problems for circumference geometries. *Electronics* **2021**, *10*, 2157. [CrossRef]
32. Sekehravani, E.A.; Leone, G.; Pierri, R. NDF of the far zone field radiated by square sources. In Proceedings of the 2021 XXXIV General Assembly and Scientific Symposium of the International Union of Radio Science, URSI GASS, Rome, Italy, 28 August–4 September 2021; pp. 1–4.
33. Sekehravani, E.A.; Leone, G.; Pierri, R. Resolution of born scattering in curve geometries: Aspect-Limited observations and excitations. *Electronics* **2021**, *10*, 3089. [CrossRef]

34. Naghibi, A.; Attari, A.R. Near-field radar-based microwave imaging for breast cancer detection: A study on resolution and image quality. *IEEE Trans. Antennas Propag.* **2020**, *69*, 1670–1680. [CrossRef]
35. Brancaccio, A.; Leone, G.; Pierri, R. Information content of Born scattered fields: Results in the circular cylindrical case. *J. Opt. Soc. Am. Part A* **1998**, *15*, 1909–1917. [CrossRef]
36. Cui, T.J.; Chew, W.C.; Yin, X.X.; Hong, W. Study of Resolution and Super Resolution in Electromagnetic Imaging for Half-Space Problems. *IEEE Trans. Antennas Propag.* **2004**, *52*, 1398–1411.
37. Maisto, M.A.; Pierri, R.; Solimene, R. Sensor arrangement in monostatic subsurface radar imaging. *IEEE Open J. Antennas Propag.* **2020**, *2*, 3–13. [CrossRef]
38. Ludeno, G.; Gennarelli, G.; Lambot, S.; Soldovieri, F.; Catapano, I. A comparison of linear inverse scattering models for contactless GPR imaging. *IEEE Trans. Geosci. Remote Sens.* **2020**, *58*, 7305–7316. [CrossRef]
39. Harrington, R.F. *Time-Harmonic Electromagnetic Fields*; McGraw-Hill College: New York, NY, USA, 1961.
40. Gori, F.; Guattari, G. Shannon number and degrees of freedom of an image. *Opt. Commun.* **1973**, *7*, 163–165. [CrossRef]
41. Sekehravani, E.A.; Leone, G.; Pierri, R. Performance of the Linear Model Scattering of 2D Full Object with Limited Data. *Sensors* **2022**, *22*, 3868. [CrossRef] [PubMed]
42. Chandra, R.; Zhou, H.; Balasingham, I.; Narayanan, R.M. On the opportunities and challenges in microwave medical sensing and imaging. *IEEE Trans. Biomed. Eng.* **2015**, *62*, 1667–1682. [CrossRef]
43. Balanis, C.A. *Advanced Engineering Electromagnetics*; John Wiley & Sons: Hoboken, NJ, USA, 2012.

sensors MDPI

Article

Microwave Antenna System for Muscle Rupture Imaging with a Lossy Gel to Reduce Multipath Interference

Laura Guerrero Orozco [1,2,*], Lars Peterson [3] and Andreas Fhager [1,2]

1 Department of Electrical Engineering, Chalmers University of Technology, 41296 Gothenburg, Sweden; andreas.fhager@chalmers.se
2 MedTech West, Sahlgrenska University Hospital, 41345 Gothenburg, Sweden
3 Sahlgrenska Academy, University of Gothenburg, 40530 Gothenburg, Sweden; peterson.lars@telia.com
* Correspondence: laurag@chalmers.se

Abstract: Injuries to the hamstring muscles are an increasing problem in sports. Imaging plays a key role in diagnosing and managing athletes with muscle injuries, but there are several problems with conventional imaging modalities with respect to cost and availability. We hypothesized that microwave imaging could provide improved availability and lower costs and lead to improved and more accurate diagnostics. In this paper, a semicircular microwave imaging array with eight antennae was investigated. A key component in this system is the novel antenna design, which is based on a monopole antenna and a lossy gel. The purpose of the gel is to reduce the effects of multipath signals and improve the imaging quality. Several different gels have been manufactured and evaluated in imaging experiments. For comparison, corresponding simulations were performed. The results showed that the gels can effectively reduce the multipath signals and the imaging experiments resulted in significantly more stable and repeatable reconstructions when a lossy gel was used compared to when an almost non-lossy gel was used.

Keywords: microwave imaging; medical diagnosis; antenna system; muscle rupture; prototype; multipath signal; image reconstruction

Citation: Guerrero Orozco, L.; Peterson, L.; Fhager, A. Microwave Antenna System for Muscle Rupture Imaging with a Lossy Gel to Reduce Multipath Interference. *Sensors* **2022**, *22*, 4121. https://doi.org/10.3390/s22114121

Academic Editor: James F. Rusling

Received: 13 April 2022
Accepted: 26 May 2022
Published: 29 May 2022

1. Introduction

Microwave imaging techniques are beginning to see an increase in clinical research for different applications. These techniques include breast cancer imaging [1,2], stroke detection [3–5] and others. In sports, muscle injuries are an increasing problem, especially injuries to the four hamstring muscles (the biceps femoris caput longum, biceps femoris caput breve, semimembranosus and semitendinosus muscles) on the back of the thigh that act as extensors in the hip joint and flexors in the knee joint. Hamstring injuries are the most common muscle injuries among athletes because they are non-contact injuries [6] and take place during exercises when the muscle develops tension while lengthening [7]. They have been reported in numerous different sports, such as sprinting, running, soccer and gymnastics [8,9]. The prevalence of hamstring tears in recreational sports and non-sporting situations are not well defined [10]; however, some cases have been reported among the general population [11,12]. These injuries represent a major cause of time lost in sports [13]. The rehabilitation process can be frustrating for the patient because the symptoms often persist for a long time (healing time can reach up to 12 months in serious cases) and re-injuries are common [14].

The biggest problem is that there are no scientific studies that objectively follow the muscle healing process over time, from injury through all phases of muscle healing from the inflammation phase to the regeneration phase and the remodeling-maturation phase. Consequently, there is no general consensus on the time that the patient needs to wait until it is safe to exercise again [15]. Some studies have reported that almost one out of three hamstring strains recur and that many happen within 2 weeks of returning to sports [16], a time frame that would likely decrease if it were better understood when it would be safe to return to physical activity.

Imaging plays a key role in the diagnosis and management of athletes with muscle injuries. Magnetic resonance imaging and ultrasonography are the imaging modalities of choice [17]. However, magnetic resonance imaging is a scarce resource that is expensive and has long measurement times that can be uncomfortable for some patients [18]. The portability and availability of ultrasound imaging systems make them an attractive imaging modality that can be used for functional tests. A disadvantage of these systems is that their effectiveness is dependent on the operator experience [12]. The operator should be skilled in the technique and have detailed knowledge of compartmental muscle anatomy, as well as experience in assessing normal and abnormal muscle tissue during the healing phases. For this reason, the microwave imaging system could be a breakthrough. This system can be portable and low cost, meaning that it could even be used on-site by the medical team where athletes are training, which would lead to a faster and safer diagnosis without the need for a skilled operator. Moreover, there is a future prospective with which microwave imaging could be used to follow the injury healing process to allow the athlete a safe return to sports and to prevent recurring injuries or complications.

Microwave imaging diagnostic techniques exploit the dielectric contrast between tissues. This particular work aimed to exploit this contrast for muscle rupture detection. A ruptured muscle causes a bleed inside the muscle and the detection of the rupture can be performed by assessing the dielectric contrast between the blood and the surrounding muscle tissue [19,20]. The tissue contrast is visualized by reconstructed images that represent the dielectric tissue properties using microwaves that are transmitted through the muscle.

There are two main microwave image reconstruction techniques: tomographic and radar-based imaging. In tomographic imaging systems, quantitative images of the following dielectric properties are generated: permittivity ε and conductivity σ. Image reconstruction requires the solution of an inverse scattering problem, usually with computationally demanding methods [21]. Many groups have generated simulation results using tomographic techniques [22,23]. Furthermore, several approaches have advanced to phantom and clinical investigations [24–27].

Radar-based microwave imaging does not generate quantitative images of dielectric properties, but instead identifies and localizes strong scatterers. These systems exploit a time of flight analysis of measured signals in either mono-, bi- or multistatic antenna system configurations. Many different confocal microwave imaging algorithms have been proposed to solve this imaging problem, such as the Delay and Sum (DAS) [28,29] and Delay, Multiply and Sum (DMAS) [30] algorithms, are commonly used. In these methods, received signals from the object are synthetically focused, creating an image of the strong scatterers. The confocal microwave imaging technique has been studied in simulations and in phantom and patient examinations. For example, the works of Fear and Stuchly [31] show examples of the monostatic technique. A group led by Craddock at the University of Bristol showed image reconstruction in clinical trials [32]. The technique has also been studied clinically by other groups [33].

A particular challenge with the radar-based algorithms is that the measured microwave signals include early-time and late-time content: the early-time content is dominated by reflections from the skin and the late-time content contains the desired object response. Before any imaging is attempted, the early-time content must be removed as it usually has a significantly larger amplitude than the late-time object response. Otherwise, the desired object response easily drowns in the much larger skin reflection. Different methods can be applied to reduce the early-time content. The most common is the use of a priori measurements of a tissue, such as phantom, lesion-free or healthy tissue [30], and the use of adaptive filtering algorithms [34,35]. The use of a priori data for patient measurement may not always be possible as it requires measurements to be taken before and after the injury and subtracting the latter from the former. In that case, a filtering algorithm may be more suitable. For experimental investigations on tissue phantoms, it is usually possible to perform before and after measurements. All of these algorithms are similar in that they attempt to estimate the early-time skin response so it can be removed from the signals before reconstructing the image. Consequently, they are sensitive to measurement variability and noise in the scattering data. Even a small variability creates errors or uncertainties in the estimation and removal of the early-time signal that could also corrupt the late-time object response to be preserved. One important step to help mitigate these problems is to reduce the variability in the measurement data and to keep the signals free from undesired scattering that originates from sources other than the skin and the inside of the body. Signal artifacts could occur as reflections from other parts of the antenna system and the surrounding environment, direct coupling and multipath signals between antennae, etc. As these signals also tend to be large in amplitude, even very small variations from measurement to measurement can introduce somewhat unpredictable inconsistencies in the estimation of the early-time signals and result in the poor removal of skin reflections. As a result, image reconstruction becomes prone to containing artifacts, which is shown and discussed in this article.

In the works by Meaney et al. [36], they found that multipath signals are the most significant factor in the corruption of the measured microwave signals in their imaging system. In this context, "multipath signals" is a uniting term that refers to all parts of the signals that do not originate from the signals propagating through the object under investigation. Instead, these are contributions from waves taking alternative routes (such as surface waves), reflections and scattering from the antennae themselves, supporting structures, cables or the surrounding environment. It also includes cross-channel leakage in the electronic system [37]. Multipath signals cannot be filtered out easily as they all originate from the same signal source as the desired signals, are at the same frequency and only appear as interference. The problem with multipath signals is most pronounced in near-field applications in which the signals are heavily attenuated by tissue [37].

By immersing the antennae and objects under investigation in lossy coupling baths, consisting of saline–glycerine mixtures, unwanted multipath signals can be attenuated [38–40]. At the same time, the coupling medium provides impedance matching between the antennae and the objects to maximize the energy coupled into the object. The lossy bath also has an advantageous effect on the operating bandwidth of the antennae, which is broadened due to increased resistive loading. This enables the use of simple and low-profile antennae, such as monopoles or dipoles, in a wide frequency band [41].

A somewhat different approach to maximizing the energy that is coupled into the object and, at the same time, minimize the power radiating in other directions is to design both off-body and on-body antennae with a high directivity. With the main radiation lobe directed toward the body, multipath effects from waves traveling outside and around the imaging target are minimized. Sometimes, this property is quantified by the front to back ratio and in this case, a high front to back ratio was desired. There are several examples of such antenna designs [2,3,42–46]. These antennae usually have many advantages, such as broader bandwidths, unidirectional radiating patterns with high gain and small sizes so there is space for a sufficient number of antennae within the imaging system. Unfortunately, these antennae also come with the disadvantage of increased complexity and, with that complexity, a finer meshing and more computationally demanding simulation models [47,48]. Typically, this means that this type of antenna is less suited for quantitative tomographic algorithms, for which accurate numerical models are needed, and more suited for radar-based algorithms.

Simpler monopole antennae seem to be effective in applications that aim for quantitative image reconstruction [48–50] and recently, we developed a fast reconstruction algorithm based on the 2D discrete dipole approximation [48]. This algorithm exploits the use of low-profile monopole antennae, which are modeled very efficiently using the analytical expressions of a line source. A lossy coupling bath ensures a reduction in unwanted multipath signals, for example, in the form of scattering from the wall of the imaging tank and the antenna elements themselves.

In this work, one of the goals was to investigate the design principles of an antenna system that is adapted for muscle rupture imaging and, at the same time, use a lossy matching medium to minimize multipath signals so that monopole antennae can be used. In this paper, we present a new antenna design that makes use of a semisolid gel consisting of a mix of saline water and agar to recreate the effects of antennae in a lossy bath [38,40] without having to immerse the entire leg, for example, in a tank filled with liquid. The idea of using a gel as a coupling medium is not new. Previously, regular ultrasound gel has been used for microwave simulations of bone density in the leg [51]. This gel, however, is almost lossless and, therefore, it does not dampen multipath signals. Furthermore, it is not solidified, making it a bit messier to handle. On the other hand, to the best of our knowledge, the idea to use a lossy and semisolid gel to eliminate multipath signals is novel. The goal was not to completely eliminate multipath signals but to attenuate them sufficiently to avoid corruption in the measured signals and image reconstruction. An additional feature of using a lossy gel is the shielding effect that they have on antennae against external disturbances. We used the DMAS radar-based imaging method to investigate the effects of reduced multipath signals on image reconstruction.

The overall goal of this work was to show the proof of principle of this novel antenna design. However, we did not attempt to optimize the antenna performance, nor the imaging accuracy for different shapes, sizes and positions of the leg and blood tissue phantoms. These questions will be addressed in future work.

This paper is organized as follows. Section 2 describes the proposed antennae and antenna system design, together with the measurement and simulation setup. Section 3 shows the simulated numerical results and the results from phantom experiments, as well as image reconstructions using the phantom measurements. Finally, the results are discussed in Section 4 and the conclusions are presented in Section 5.

2. Materials and Methods

In this section, we describe the simulation model and experimental setup that were used to investigate the antenna design, which was based on monopoles immersed in a semisolid lossy gel. The antennae and antenna system design are explained and we describe the investigations that were performed to determine their effects on the wave propagation and the reduction in multipath signals using different conductivity in the gel. The aim was to determine what is needed to achieve sufficient multipath signal reduction in order to facilitate accurate and consistent image reconstruction. We also investigated how the signal levels inside the leg were affected by the conductivity of the gel and the method that was used to investigate these effects is also described in this section. Lastly, the image reconstruction method is described, together with the experiments and simulations that were used to assess the imaging performance.

2.1. Dielectric Properties of Tissue, Phantom Materials and Simulation Models

The experiments and simulations were performed in a simplified environment consisting of only two tissues: muscle and blood. Muscle tissue was used to model the leg of a patient and blood was used to model the bleeding caused by a muscle rupture. Other tissues in the leg, such as bone, fat and skin, were omitted for simplicity. This simplified scenario should still be sufficient to show the proof of principle for the use of a lossy gel to mitigate the effects of multipath signals. Dielectric data for muscle tissue and blood tissue were obtained from [20] and are shown in Figure 1. For the experiments, muscle and blood phantoms were manufactured using water as a solvent, salt to control the conductivity, sugar to control the permittivity and agar to solidify the phantom [52]. The goal was to manufacture phantoms with properties that were as close as possible to published dielectric tissue data. However, with these substances, it was not possible to accurately mimic the dispersive behavior of real tissue over a wide frequency band. There are many other different substances with which to fabricate tissue-mimicking phantoms, such as oil in gelatin mixtures [53] and Triton X-100-based liquid mixtures [54], but these also come with the problem of inaccurately mimicking dispersive behavior compared to the tissue data. We decided to use water, salt and sugar because the manufacturing process is simple, the ingredients are harmless and the dielectric properties are good enough for a proof of concept. The permittivities and conductivities of the phantom and gel materials were measured using SPEAG's Dielectric Assessment Kit (DAK). The dielectric properties used in the simulations were the same as the measured dielectric properties of the phantom material.

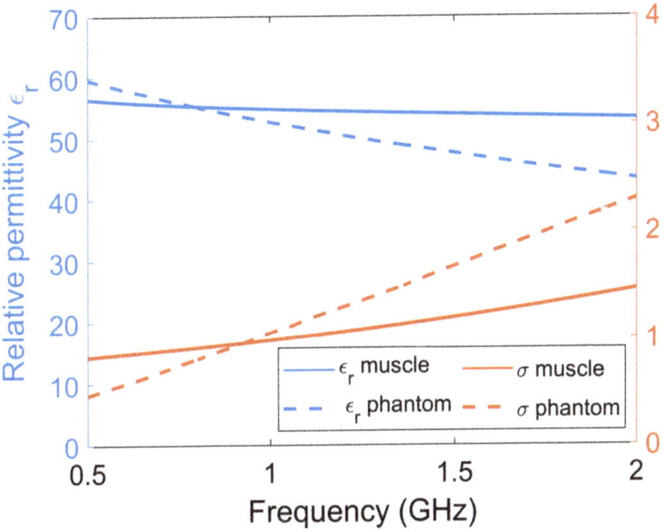

(**a**)

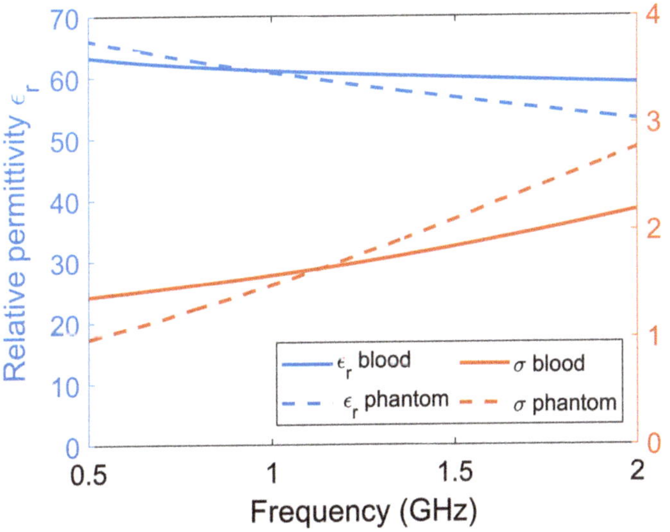

(**b**)

Figure 1. The dielectric data for (**a**) muscle tissue and (**b**) blood tissue. Each plot contains the permittivity and conductivity data from the literature, the measured dielectric values of the phantoms and the corresponding data that were used in the simulations.

The antennae consisted of rectangular containers filled with lossy gel. Three different gels were manufactured to investigate the effects of the different attenuating properties of the gel: Gel #1 was made from regular tap water and 1.5 weight percent (wt%) agar; Gel #2 was made from a mixture of tap water, 1.5 wt% agar and 4 wt% NaCl (table salt); Gel #3 was made from a mixture of tap water, 1.5 wt% agar and 10 wt% NaCl. Figure 2 shows the measured dielectric properties of the gels, together with the corresponding properties that were used for the simulations. The measured properties of the gels are almost constant over the frequency band of interest. To simplify the numerical modeling, we used constant dielectric values that were equal to the measured properties at 1 GHz. This should not affect the validity of our conclusions.

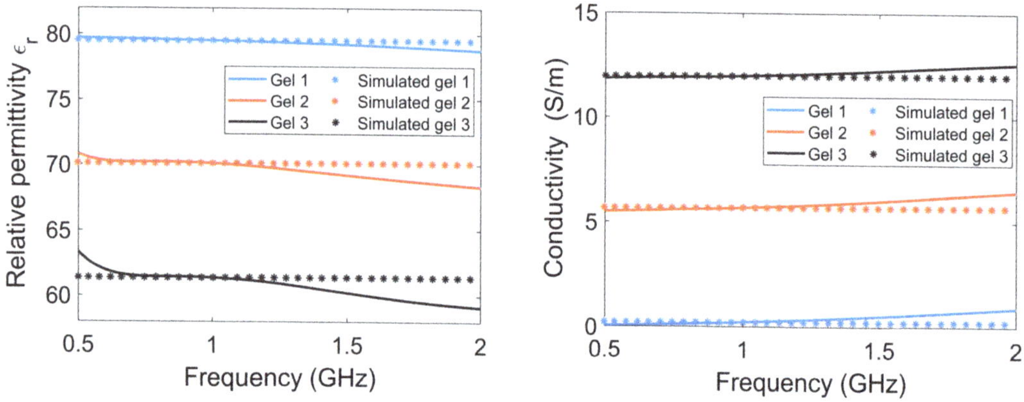

Figure 2. The relative permittivity and conductivity of the three lossy gels. The measured data of the gels, as well as the corresponding properties that were used in the simulations, are shown.

2.2. *Antennae, Antenna Array and Experimental Setup*

The antennae that we proposed for the muscle rupture detection application are shown in Figure 3a,b. The monopole antennae were manufactured by peeling off the outer conductor from a semirigid coaxial cable. The resulting radiating element had a length of 35 mm. The monopole was bent 90°, such that it could be mounted through a hole in the back of the plastic container, as seen in Figure 3b. The plastic containers had inner dimensions of 20 × 60 mm. The thickness of the plastic wall was 5 mm. The figure also shows the gel present inside the container. During the measurements, the antennae were applied in direct contact with the surface of the muscle phantom, such that the monopole elements were also in direct contact with the phantom. For the sake of maximizing the transmission into the leg, we did not want any lossy gel between the antenna and the skin, only behind and beside the skin to attenuate the outgoing multipath signals.

Figure 4a shows the measurement system with the eight transmitting/receiving antennae. The antennae were mounted in a semicircular array with a 16-cm diameter and an angular spacing of 20° between the individual antennae. The antennae were connected to a Rohde & Schwarz ZNBT8 16-channel vector network analyzer via flexible coaxial cables. This VNA has a dynamic range of up to 140 dB and operates within the frequency range of 9 kHz to 8.5 GHz, even though we only measured within the range of 0.5 GHz to 2.0 GHz. The measurements were taken using each antenna as a transmitter while the remaining antennae acted as receivers. In Figure 4b, the muscle phantom can be seen inside the antenna array. The phantom was slightly smaller than the array, with a diameter of 15.6 cm.

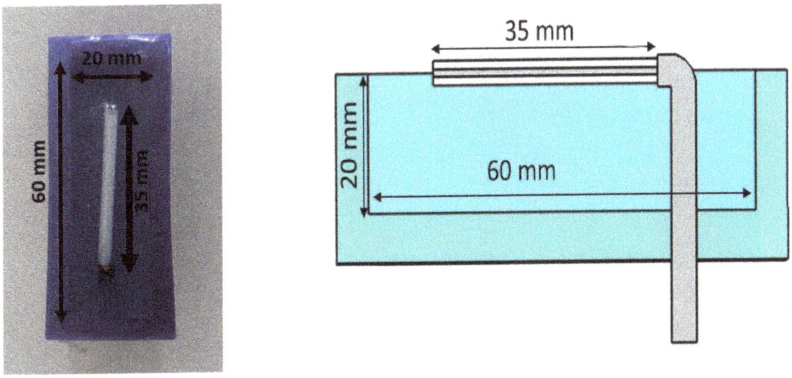

(**a**) (**b**)

Figure 3. Monopole antenna with cup full of gel: (**a**) top view of antenna; (**b**) side view of antenna.

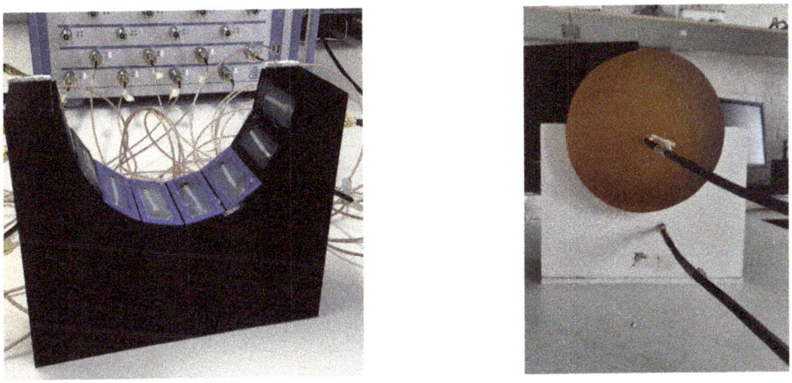

(**a**) (**b**)

Figure 4. Measurement setup for probe measurements and image reconstruction: (**a**) semicircular antenna array consisting of 8 antennae; (**b**) muscle phantom in the antenna array, with probes.

As already mentioned, the idea of this antenna design was to reduce multipath signals traveling outside the phantom, for example, surface waves. However, we did not want to sacrifice field strength inside the phantom, as this constituted the useful probing field. One set of experiments was conducted to investigate the amplitude of the fields, both outside and inside the muscle phantom, using different gels in the antennae. For this experiment set, two additional monopole antennae were used as field probes, both with lengths of 19 mm. The experiments were performed such that one antenna in the array transmitted, whereas the field probes were used to measure the amplitudes inside and outside the phantom, i.e., the transmission coefficients. The antenna and field probe arrangement that was used for both simulations and measurements is sketched in Figure 5. For both measurements and simulations, we chose to use the lowest antenna position within the array as the transmitter since this was where the phantom rested directly on the transmitting antenna and thus, had the best contact. Antenna #5 was used as the transmitting antenna and one of the two field probes was placed just behind Antenna #3, marked (a) in the figure. The other field probe was placed in the center of the muscle phantom, marked (b) in the figure. With these probes, we could determine how the field strengths inside and outside the phantom were affected by different gel properties. The measurements and simulations with Gel #1, Gel #2 and Gel #3 were conducted using this setup.

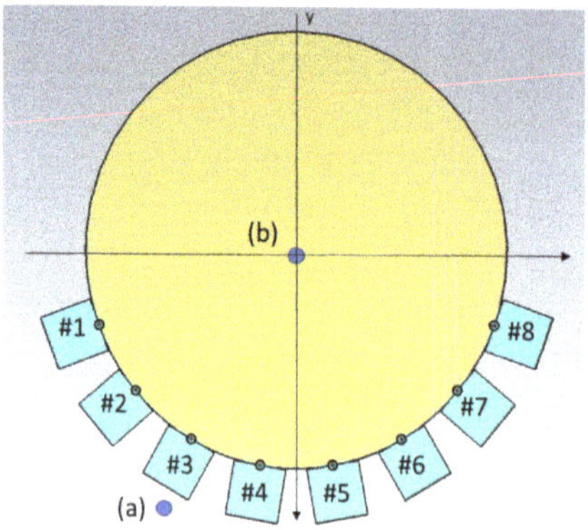

Figure 5. Schematic illustration of the simulation model, including the positions of the two field probes (**a**,**b**). Antennae are numbered #1–#8.

Another set of experiments was carried out for the purpose of image reconstruction. For this, a hole was carved into the muscle phantom to allow for the insertion of a blood phantom. The hole went 13 cm deep from the top of the phantom, as sketched in Figure 6. This hole was filled with a liquid muscle phantom of the same properties as the solid muscle phantom. This hole made it easy to make a priori measurements without the blood phantom being present. The blood phantom had a diameter of 4 cm and is shown in Figure 7a. Figure 7b shows the hole through which the blood phantom was inserted into the muscle phantom. A wooden stick was attached to the muscle phantom to facilitate the insertion and extraction of the blood phantom. The measurements were taken with and without the blood phantom present.

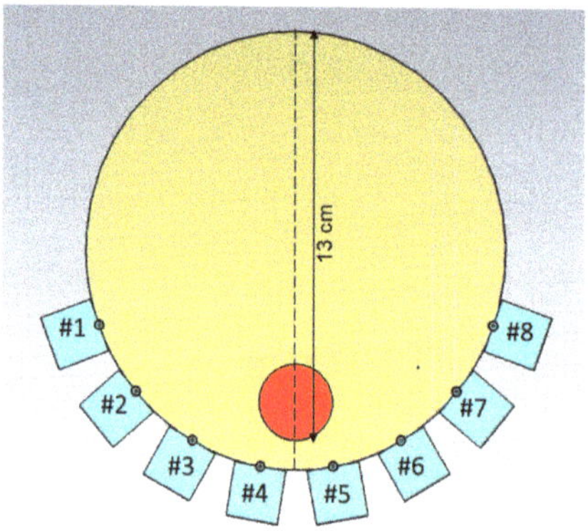

Figure 6. Schematic illustration of the measurement setup, including the position of the blood phantom, as well as the position of the transect cutting through the middle of the phantom. Antennae are numbered #1–#8.

For the image reconstruction, the measurements were conducted such that the muscle phantom was placed in the antenna array and the measurements were repeated 15 times. Efforts were made not to touch or move anything within the setup between measurements. Then, the blood phantom was inserted into the hole in the muscle phantom until it touched the bottom and then 15 more measurements were taken. This procedure was repeated for both Gel #1 and Gel #3, amounting to a total of 60 measurements and 30 reconstructed images: 15 reconstructions with Gel #1 and 15 with Gel #3.

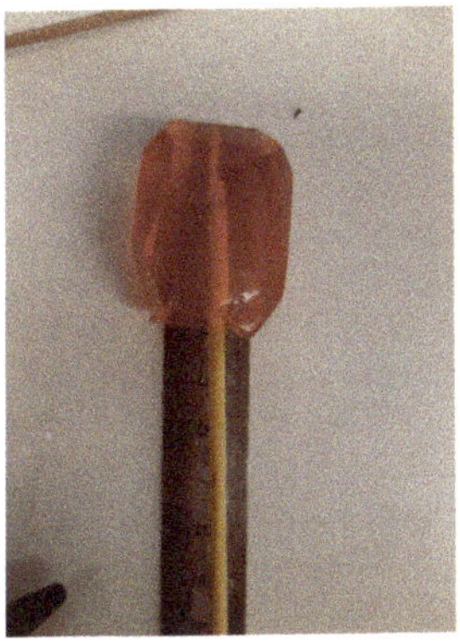

(a)

(b)

Figure 7. The blood phantom and muscle phantom that were used in the image reconstruction experiments: (**a**) blood phantom; (**b**) top view of the muscle phantom.

2.3. Simulations

Simulations corresponding to the field probe measurements were performed. The simulations were carried out in 3D and a cross-sectional image of the model is shown in Figure 5. In this figure, the muscle phantom is represented by a cylinder with a 16-cm diameter and the eight antennae, numbered #1–#8, are shown at the bottom of the image. The monopoles are shown as circles touching the muscle phantom and behind them are the quadratic-shaped gels. The plastic material of the containers was not included in this model. The dielectric properties of the simulated Gel #1, Gel #2 and Gel #3 are shown in Figure 2. The monopole antennae had the same dimensions as those in the measurements. The simulations were performed using the CST Studio Suite, Release Version 2020.07, in the frequency range of 0.5–3 GHz. In the same way as in the previous experiments, the simulations were performed using the two field probe antennae: one placed in the center of the phantom (a) and one placed just behind Antenna #3 (b).

2.4. Image Reconstruction Algorithm

The DMAS beamforming algorithm [30] was used to reconstruct the images. We used a multistatic configuration in which the signals between all possible antenna pairs were measured. To remove the early-time content, i.e., skin reflections, the measurements of the homogeneous muscle phantom were subtracted from the corresponding measurements with the blood phantom present.

3. Results

In this section, the results from the simulations and phantom experiments are presented. The results showed the effects of the conductivity in the antenna gels. Firstly, the simulation results are described in Section 3.1. We show the results of wave propagation inside and outside the muscle phantom using different lossy gels within the antennae. We also show examples of the simulations of S-parameter transmission data for Gel #1 and Gel #3. Secondly, the results from the experiments are shown and compared to the results from the simulations. Finally, the image reconstruction results are shown, based on the experimental data.

3.1. Wave Propagation Patterns Inside and Outside the Muscle Phantom

The magnitude of the electric field distribution was investigated using the simulation model shown in Figure 5 but without the field probes present. To elaborate, the cross-sectional images of the field patterns are shown for the frequencies of 0.7 GHz and 1.65 GHz in Figure 8. Antenna #1 was acting as transmitter. These images illustrate that it was possible to decrease the magnitude of the waves propagating outside the muscle phantom and around the antennae with a more lossy gel. For the lowest conductivity cases for Gel #1, as shown in Figure 8a,d, the wave patterns inside the phantom were rather chaotic and the field amplitudes outside the phantom were prominent. This effect was especially evident for the 0.7 GHz case. With increasing conductivity in the gel for Gel #2, as shown in Figure 8b,e, and the even higher conductivity in Gel #3, as shown in Figure 8c,f, it was seen that the field strengths outside the muscle phantom decreased and the wave fronts inside the phantom became more regularly shaped as semicircular wave fronts. We interpreted these results as meaning that the lossy gels helped to attenuate the multipath signals outside of the muscle phantom model. With weaker field strengths outside the muscle phantom, weaker fields were also coupled back into the phantom from directions other than the transmitting antenna itself and, therefore, less interference with the straight path propagation from the transmitting antenna occurred inside of the model. The effects of the multipath signal propagation were more apparent at 0.7 GHz than at 1.65 GHz due to the higher attenuation at higher frequencies.

Traditional radiation diagrams are not relevant to illustrate the directional properties of the antennae as they show far-field characteristics, so to further illustrate the damping effect of the gels, something similar to a radiation diagram was generated. The simulations were carried out as above at frequencies of 0.7 GHz and 1.65 GHz, but with only one transmitting antenna present and the other seven antennae removed. The magnitude of the electric field was sampled on a circle that was centered in the monopole element and had a radius of one wavelength (1λ) at the corresponding frequency. This field was then plotted in the radial diagram in Figure 9. The geometry was such that the plot corresponded to the H-plane of a radiation pattern and the angular coordinate was oriented so that 0° in the plot was pointing in the same direction as the surface normal of the antenna at the antenna–phantom interface. For Gel#1 (Figure 9a,c), the field strengths behind the antennae were even higher than those in the muscle tissue in front of the antenna. Figure 9b,d show that for Gel #3, the E-field behind the antennae was significantly lower than that for Gel #1. In front of the antenna, the field was stronger; in fact, it was almost the same amplitude as for Gel # 1. This verified that the lossy Gel #3 effectively attenuated the waves traveling backward and sideways from the antenna.

3.2. Field Probe Simulations and Measurements

The magnitude of the transmission coefficients that represented the electric field strengths at one point inside the muscle phantom and one point outside the phantom were measured and simulated. The positions are indicated in Figure 5. One antenna in the array was transmitting and the two field probes recorded the received data. Figure 10a shows the simulated magnitudes at probe location (A) as a function of frequency when Antenna #1 was acting as transmitter with the three different gels. Interestingly, the attenuation of the electric field (measured transmission coefficient) was not a linear function of the conductivity of the coupling gel. The decrease in signal level was much greater from Gel #1 to Gel #2 than from Gel #2 to Gel #3, indicating that it might approach a saturation point at which increased conductivity in the gels does not provide ever-increasing attenuation. Figure 10b shows the corresponding measured signals that were obtained from the field probe antenna positioned behind Antenna 3. For these measurements, the field strength around the muscle phantom decreased in magnitude as the conductivity of the material increased. Even though the levels were not exactly the same as in the simulations, the attenuation trend was similar, except at the frequencies in the range of 0.5 GHz to about 0.75 GHz, at which hardly any difference was seen between Gel #1 and Gel #2. However, for most of the frequency bands, the attenuation increased with increasing loss in the gel. Both the simulations and measurements agree that the more the conductivity in the gels increased, the more the leaking to the surrounding phantom decreased. Possible explanations for these differences include imperfections in the experimental setup and the computational model being overly simplified and not including any supporting structures, antenna cables, etc. The antenna gels had perfect contact with the curved surface of the muscle phantom in the simulations. In the experiments, there might be small air gaps between the edges of the flat antennae and the curved phantom surface. When the monopole element rose even slightly above the surface of the gel, this effect could be even more pronounced. The larger amplitudes in the field probe measurements than in the simulations suggested that this might be a plausible explanation.

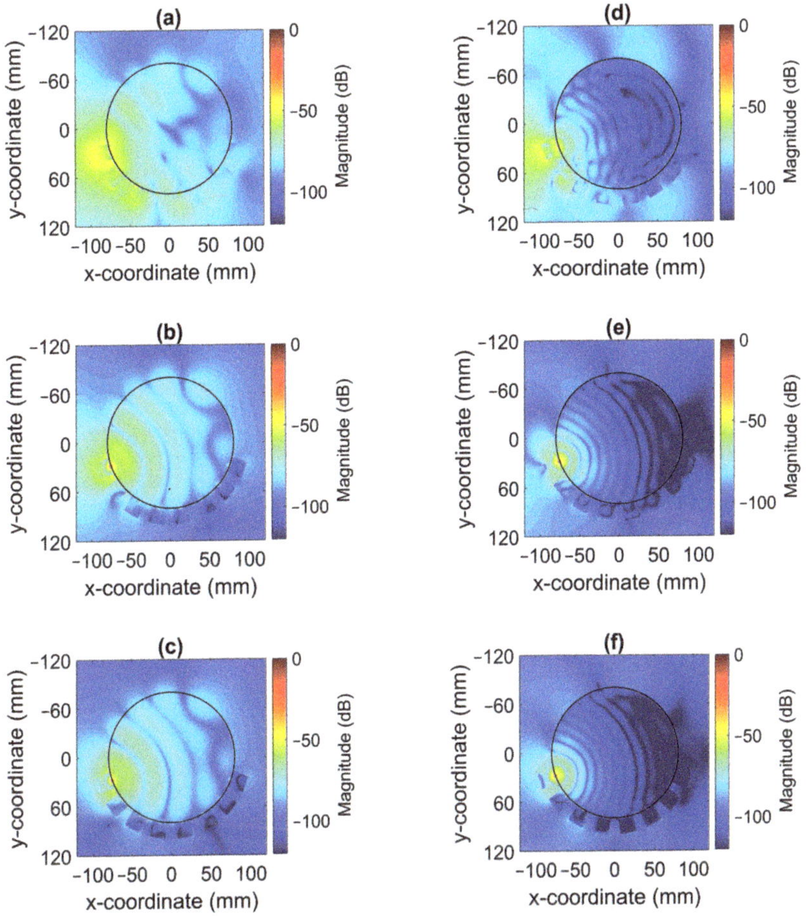

Figure 8. Simulated radiation patterns for a monopole antenna surrounded by coupling gels in contact with a muscle phantom for different conductivity values at 0.7 GHz ((**a**) Gel #1; (**b**) Gel #2; (**c**) Gel #3) and at 1.65 GHz ((**d**) Gel #1; (**e**) Gel #2; (**f**) Gel #3).

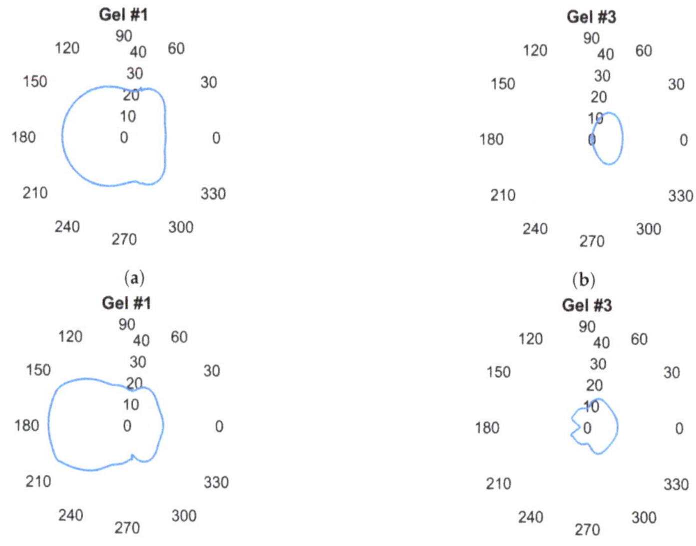

(a) (b) (c) (d)

Figure 9. E-field sampled at a circle with radius λ around a single transmitting antenna: (**a**,**b**) at 0.7 GHz; (**c**,**d**) at 1.65 GHz.

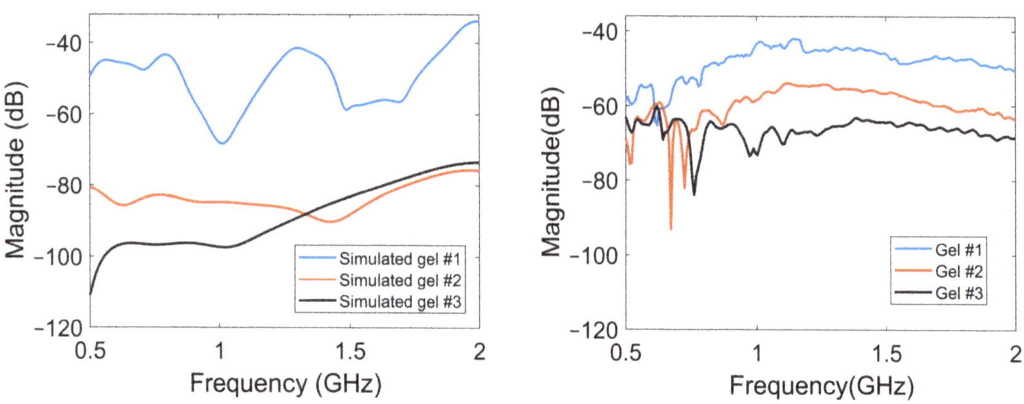

(a) (b)

Figure 10. Magnitude of transmission coefficients between the transmitting antenna and Probe A for Gel #1, Gel #2 and Gel #3: (**a**) simulated transmission coefficients; (**b**) measured transmission coefficients.

Another complication was that the probe was placed in air and rather close to the transmitting antenna, where strong interference patterns could arise. This made the measurements more sensitive to misalignment between the simulations and experiments, for example.

The amplitude of the electric field was also measured using a field probe in the center of the muscle phantom, as shown in Figure 5 with probe location (B). The purpose was to study whether the field strength inside the muscle phantom could also be attenuated by increasingly lossy gels. The waves inside the muscle phantom were the actual probing fields that were used to sense the scattering environment. Keeping them as high in amplitude as possible was therefore favorable from a measurement point of view. Figure 11a shows the simulated magnitudes of the electric fields at probe location (B). Here, Antenna #1 was also used as transmitter. A notable difference in the field strength outside the phantom was that the overall magnitude of attenuation between the different gels decreased to a much lesser degree, except in the region of 0.5–0.6 GHz. This meant that the increase in the conductivity of the gels could be implemented without greatly affecting the field strength inside the muscle phantom. Figure 11b shows the results of the measurements with the antenna in the middle of the muscle phantom. The measurement results agreed well with the simulated results for the field strength. These results indicate that this antenna design could be effective in attenuating multipath waves while preserving a high field amplitude inside the tissue.

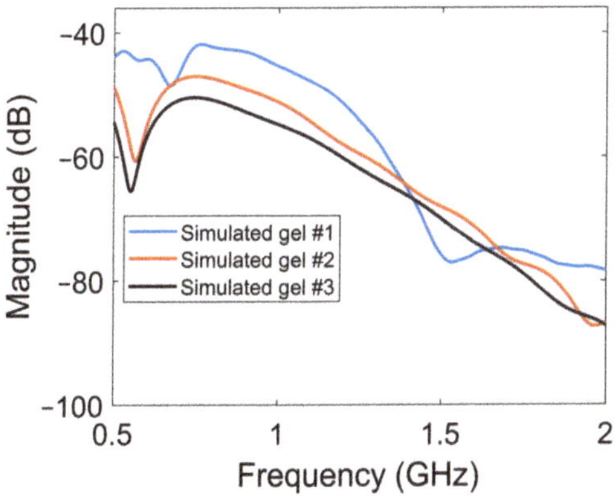

(a)

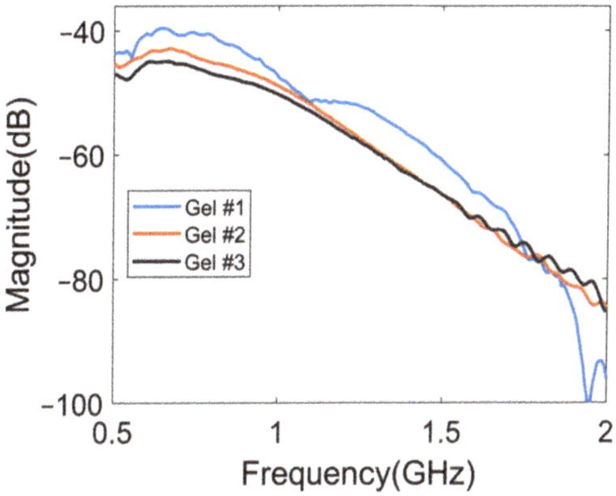

(b)

Figure 11. Magnitude of transmission coefficients between the transmitting antenna and Probe B for Gel #1, Gel #2 and Gel #3: (**a**) simulated transmission coefficients; (**b**) experimental transmission coefficients.

S-Parameters

Figure 12 shows a few examples of the transmission coefficients (S21 and S41) for two of the previous cases with Gel #1 and Gel #3. Both measured and simulated data are shown. The first notable observation was that the overall amplitude for Gel #3 was lower than that for Gel #1 for both S21 and S41. Additionally, this figure shows the same behavior as that shown in Figures 10 and 11, with the curve for Gel #3 being much smoother than that for Gel #1. Both the simulated and measured cases for Gel #1 showed a strongly alternating amplitude that appeared to be caused by the multipath waves interfering with the desired object response. As mentioned already, the amplitudes for Gel #3 were, in general, much lower in amplitude than those for Gel #1. As shown by the previous results, the field amplitudes inside the muscle phantom were preserved while the surrounding multipath signals were dampened. The lower amplitude was therefore a sign that the multipath signals had been removed and the scattering amplitudes from within the phantom had been preserved, which should be favorable in the subsequent signal processing and image reconstruction.

As shown in Figure 12, there were significant differences between the simulated and experimental data for Gel #1. Gel #1 had a low conductivity and, therefore, did not dampen the backward waves effectively. As a result, significant levels of multipath signals around the system that interfered with each other could be expected. The measured S-parameters, therefore, became quite unpredictable as even small changes in the experimental setup could lead to large fluctuations in the measured signals, making it difficult to obtain a good agreement between experimental and simulation data. To some extent, this also illustrated the importance of using a lossy gel, which reduced the levels of multipath signals and made the measurements more predictable. With Gel #3, the multipath signals were attenuated to a much larger degree, resulting in a better agreement between the measurement and simulation results.

3.3. *Image Reconstruction Experiments*

In the imaging reconstruction experiments, two datasets were used, i.e., measurements with Gel #1 and those with Gel #3. Figures 10 and 11 show that the results for Gel #2 were between those for Gel #1 and Gel #3 and in the spirit of keeping the rest of the paper as concise as possible, we chose to only use them in the imaging experiment. For each gel, 15 measurements were taken as a priori measurements and 15 measurements were taken with the blood phantom inserted into the muscle phantom. For each gel, 15 differential signals could then be calculated, i.e., the input signals for the DMAS algorithm. These are shown in Figure 13: Figure 13a shows the results for Gel #1 and Figure 13b shows the results for Gel #3. The two upper figures show the results for S21 and the two lower figures show the results for S41. As can be clearly seen, the results for Gel #3 were more stable but had an increasing level of noise with the increasing frequency. The results for Gel #1, however, showed a much more random variability, also for the lower frequencies. It was rather intuitive to conclude that a stable and repeatable input signal for the DMAS algorithm created a stable and repeatable image reconstruction. Figure 14 shows a few selected reconstructions that were obtained with the measured data for Gel #1 and Gel #3. The reconstructions from the measured data for Gel #3 showed fewer artifacts in the background, the three images were very similar, as can be seen by a visual inspection of the figure, and the blood phantom was reconstructed in the correct position. The reconstructions from the measured data for Gel #1, however, showed a much greater variability between the images. As can be seen in the figure, the upper image looked qualitatively quite good but with stronger artifacts close to the bottom edge compared to the images from the Gel #3 data. The other two images looked significantly different and some of the artifacts were even larger in amplitude than the reconstructed blood phantom target. To visualize all 15 image reconstructions, plots of the reconstructed amplitudes were drawn at the vertical line crossing through the center of the muscle phantom, see the dashed line in Figure 6. The reconstructed amplitudes are shown in Figure 15.

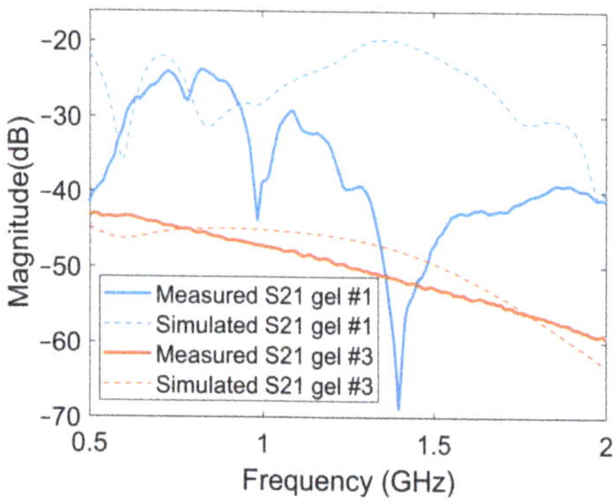

(**a**)

Figure 12. *Cont.*

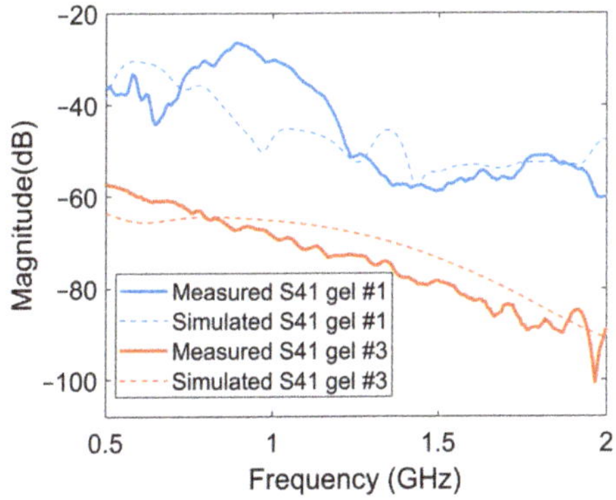

(b)

Figure 12. Comparison of transmission coefficients obtained from simulated and measured data for Gel #1 and Gel #3: (**a**) results for S21; (**b**) results for S41.

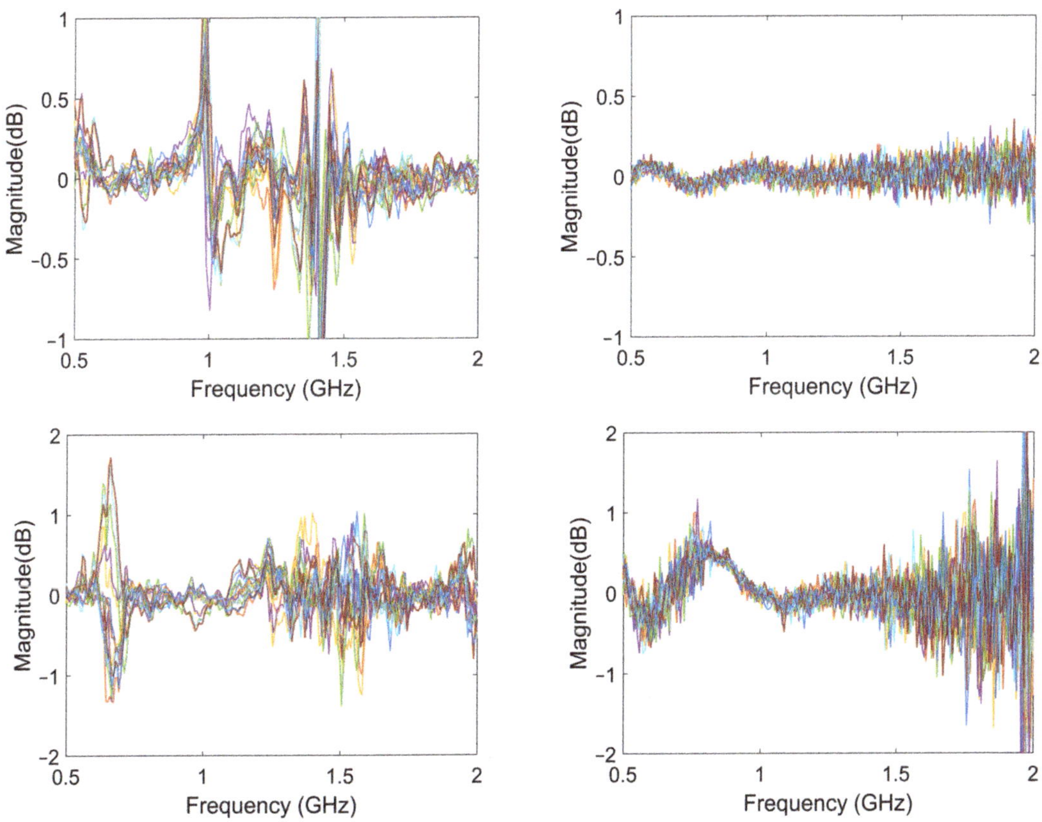

Figure 13. Differences between the object and baseline for 15 measurements: (**a**) results using Gel #1; (**b**) results using Gel #3. The upper images show the results for S21 and the lower images show the results for S41.

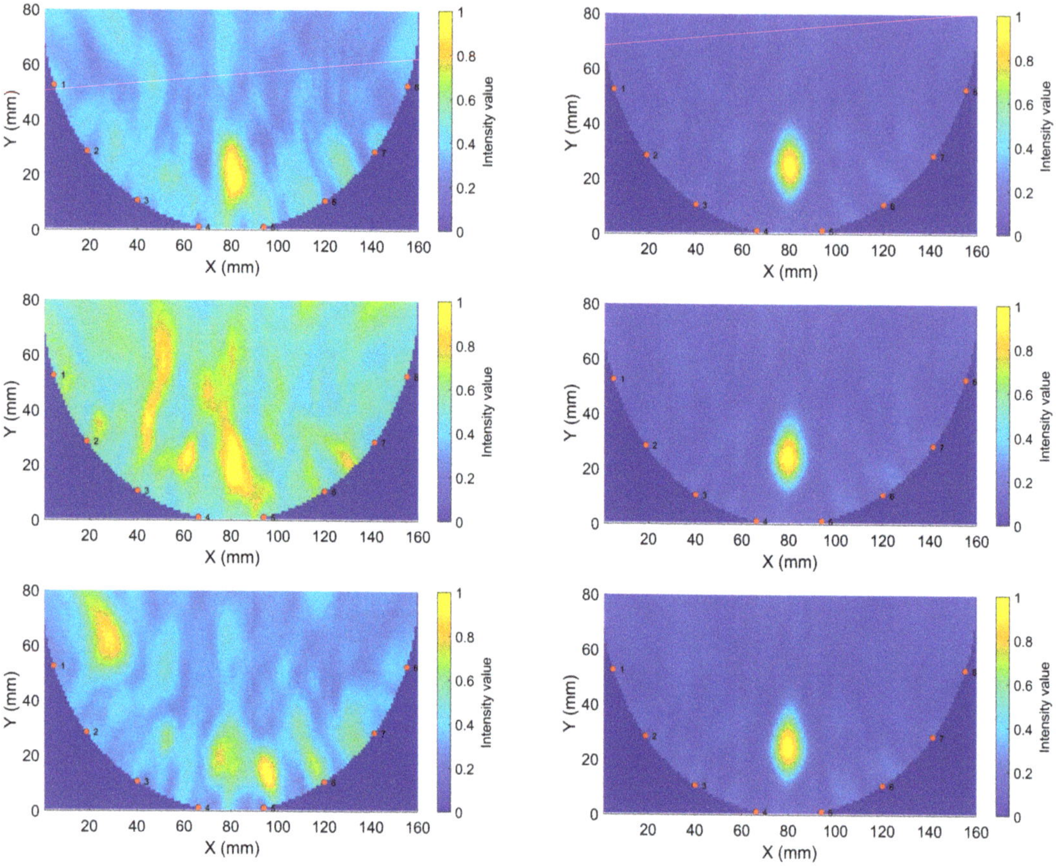

(a) (b)

Figure 14. Sample reconstructions using phantom measurements: (**a**) Gel #1; (**b**) Gel #3.

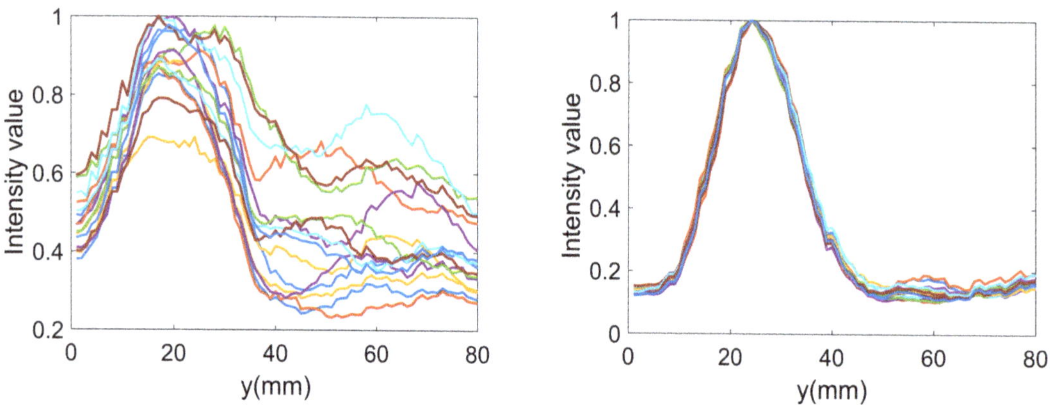

(a) (b)

Figure 15. Reconstructed data along the line through the center of the imaging domain for 15 images: (**a**) Gel #1; (**b**) Gel #3.

4. Discussion

In the work by Meaney et al. [36], it was demonstrated how multipath signals corrupt measured data within a microwave imaging system. By exploiting a lossy coupling bath, they successfully reduced the multipath signals and implemented a consistent imaging procedure. In the present work, the aim was to develop an imaging system for muscle rupture detection and diagnosis because of the need to immerse the entire leg in a big tank of lossy liquid is not practical and, in fact, prevents the widespread use of this technique as the system becomes too bulky and impractical to use. With our new design of a monopole antenna in front of a lossy gel to somewhat mimic the features of a lossy bath, the system becomes easier to handle. Antennae can be arranged in configurations that can be attached directly to the skin and allow the gels to dampen outgoing multipath signals that otherwise would cause artifacts in the measured data. In this work, both the simulated and measured data prove that the gels can successfully be used to reduce outgoing multipath signals. We noted some inconsistencies within the field probe data outside the antenna array, as shown in Figure 10. This was possibly due to imperfections in the experimental arrangement and an overly simplified simulation model. Further studies are needed to fully understand the sources of these discrepancies. However, the trend is clear and in agreement with the simulations that lossy gels do attenuate the outgoing signals.

A technique using directive antennae was suggested to maximize the energy that is coupled into the body while minimizing the energy that travels sideways and backward away from the body. In principle, this may also serve the same purpose of reducing multipath interference within the measurements. However, antenna designs are usually more complex and sophisticated compared to those for monopole antennae, which also suggests the need for a corresponding increase in the numerical modeling complexity. In the quest for fast quantitative imaging, a reconstruction method based on the discrete dipole method has been shown to exploit the simplicity of modeling a monopole antenna in a lossy bath [48]. A muscle rupture diagnostic method could very well be based on an efficient confocal imaging algorithm. However, as a long-term strategy, it seems reasonable to seek a solution that also works for fast quantitative imaging as the dielectric properties may contain important information with respect to diagnosing a patient. Therefore, a design that is based on monopoles is desired. The image reconstructions that were made using a lossy gel showed a significant improvement in the imaging quality over an almost lossless gel. We took great effort in performing the measurements on the muscle phantom without touching or moving anything within the experimental setup, yet the underlying microwave data, as well as the reconstructed images, showed a significant variability in the 15 reconstructed images. Performing measurements with the lossy gels, however, resulted in a very stable reconstruction of the 15 images, with the images looking almost identical. The only plausible explanation is that multipath signals were attenuated, which resulted in a significantly more stable imaging system.

5. Conclusions

We presented and investigated a novel design for antennae and an antenna array that is intended for the microwave imaging of the leg with the purpose of detecting and diagnosing muscle ruptures. The antennae consist of containers filled with a lossy gel and a monopole antenna mounted at the surface of the gel. During experimental measurements, the antennae were placed in direct contact with the muscle phantom and, consequently, the radiating elements were also in contact with the phantom. The reason for using the lossy gel on the back and side of the antennae was to attenuate the outgoing and sideways-moving waves and contribute to a reduction in multipath signals. The results showed that the field strengths outside the phantoms and antennae were significantly reduced when a lossy gel was used compared to when an almost lossless gel was used. The results also showed that the amplitudes of the transmission coefficients between the antennae decreased with increasing lossy in the gel; however, the field strength inside the muscle phantom only changed slightly. These results prove that the antennae are effective in reducing unwanted multipath signals while effectively preserving the amplitudes of the probing fields inside the object under investigation. The results obtained for the simulated and experimental data were in good agreement.

In repeated image reconstruction experiments using the DMAS, the lossy antennae resulted in significantly more stable and repeatable reconstructions than when an antenna with an almost lossless gel was used. We can conclude that a reduction in multipath signals made the signals less corrupted with unpredictable artifacts due to unwanted multipath scattering, particularly those from the region outside the muscle phantom, i.e., the antennae, cables, supporting structures, etc.

These results are promising, but the fine-tuning and optimization of the antenna characteristics may further improve the reduction in multipath signals and result in enhanced imaging capability. The implementation of a skin reflection removal algorithm that does not require a priori measurements of healthy tissue is also needed to make the technique more practically usable on patients. Future work should also include the use of more realistic phantoms or patients to investigate how image reconstruction is affected by other tissues, such as bone and fat, as well as how well blood phantoms of different sizes, shapes and locations can be reconstructed.

Author Contributions: The following summarizes the author contributions: conceptualization, L.G.O., L.P. and A.F.; methodology, L.G.O. and A.F.; software, L.G.O. and A.F.; validation, L.G.O. and A.F.; formal analysis, L.G.O. and A.F.; investigation, L.G.O. and A.F.; resources, A.F.; writing—original draft preparation, L.G.O., L.P. and A.F.; writing—review and editing, L.G.O., L.P. and A.F.; visualization, L.G.O. and A.F.; supervision, A.F.; project administration, A.F.; funding acquisition, A.F. All authors have read and agreed to the published version of the manuscript.

Funding: This work was partly financed by the "Strengthened Collaboration Environments under MedTech West" project (project ID: 20201637), with funding from the European Regional Development Fund through the Swedish Agency for Economic and Regional Growth (Tillväxtverket). This work was partly financed by internal funds at Chalmers University of Technology.

Conflicts of Interest: The authors declare no conflict of interest.

Abbreviations

The following abbreviations are used in this manuscript:

2D	Two dimensional
3D	Three dimensional
DAS	Delay and Sum
DMAS	Delay, Multiply and Sum

References

1. Fear, E.; Low, A.; Sill, J.; Stuchly, M. Microwave system for breast tumor detection: Experimental concept evaluation. In Proceedings of the IEEE Antennas and Propagation Society International Symposium (IEEE Cat. No.02CH37313), San Antonio, TX, USA, 16–21 June 2002; Volume 1, pp. 819–822. [CrossRef]
2. Meaney, P.; Fanning, M.; Li, D.; Poplack, S.; Paulsen, K. A clinical prototype for active microwave imaging of the breast. *IEEE Trans. Microw. Theory Tech.* **2000**, *48*, 1841–1853. [CrossRef]
3. Persson, M.; Fhager, A.; Trefná, H.D.; Yu, Y.; McKelvey, T.; Pegenius, G.; Karlsson, J.E.; Elam, M. Microwave-Based Stroke Diagnosis Making Global Prehospital Thrombolytic Treatment Possible. *IEEE Trans. Biomed. Eng.* **2014**, *61*, 2806–2817. [CrossRef] [PubMed]
4. Semenov, S.Y.; Corfield, D.R. Microwave Tomography for brain imaging: Feasibility assessment for stroke detection. *Int. J. Antennas Propag.* **2008**, *2008*, 254830. [CrossRef]
5. Sohani, B.; Tiberi, G.; Ghavami, N.; Ghavami, M.; Dudley, S.; Rahmani, A. Microwave Imaging for Stroke Detection: Validation on Head-mimicking Phantom. In Proceedings of the 2019 PhotonIcs Electromagnetics Research Symposium—Spring (PIERS-Spring), Rome, Italy, 17–20 June 2019; pp. 940–948. [CrossRef]
6. Lempainen, L.; Banke, I.; Johansson, K.; Brucker, P.; Sarimo, J.; Orava, S.; Imhoff, A.B. Clinical principles in the management of hamstring injuries. *Knee Surg. Sports Traumatol. Arthrosc. Off. J. ESSKA* **2014**, *23*, 2449–2456. [CrossRef]
7. Kujala, U.M.; Orava, S.; Järvinen, M. Hamstring injuries. *Sports Med.* **1997**, *23*, 397–404. [CrossRef]

8. Volpi, P.; Melegati, G.; Tornese, D.; Bandi, M. Muscle strains in soccer: A five-year survey of an Italian Major League team. *Knee Surg. Sports Traumatol. Arthrosc.* **2004**, *12*, 482–485. [CrossRef]
9. Askling, C.M.; Tengvar, M.; Saartok, T.; Thorstensson, A. Acute first-time hamstring strains during high-speed running. *Am. J. Sports Med.* **2007**, *35*, 197–206. [CrossRef]
10. Mica, L.; Schwaller, A.; Stoupis, C.; Penka, I.; Vomela, J.; Vollenweider, A. Avulsion of the hamstring Muscle Group: A follow-up of 6 adult non-athletes with early operative treatment: A brief report. *World J. Surg.* **2009**, *33*, 1605–1610. [CrossRef]
11. Kuske, B.; Hamilton, D.F.; Pattle, S.B.; Simpson, A.H.R.W. Patterns of Hamstring Muscle Tears in the General Population: A Systematic Review. *PLoS ONE* **2016**, *11*, e0152855. [CrossRef]
12. Koulouris, G.; Connell, D. Hamstring muscle complex: An imaging review. *RadioGraphics* **2005**, *25*, 571–586. [CrossRef]
13. Chu, S.K.; Rho, M.E. Hamstring injuries in the athlete. *Curr. Sports Med. Rep.* **2016**, *15*, 184–190. [CrossRef] [PubMed]
14. Petersen, J. Evidence based prevention of hamstring injuries in Sport. *Br. J. Sports Med.* **2005**, *39*, 319–323. [CrossRef] [PubMed]
15. Ramos, A.; Arliani, G.G.; Astur, D.C.; Pochini, A.D.; Ejnisman, B.; Cohen, M. Rehabilitation of hamstring muscle injuries: A literature review. *Rev. Bras. Ortop.* **2017**, *52*, 11–16. [CrossRef]
16. Heiderscheit, B.C.; Sherry, M.A.; Silder, A.; Chumanov, E.S.; Thelen, D.G. Hamstring strain injuries: Recommendations for diagnosis, rehabilitation, and injury prevention. *J. Orthop. Sports Phys. Ther.* **2010**, *40*, 67–81. [CrossRef]
17. Yamada, A.F.; Godoy, I.R.; Pecci Neto, L.; Taneja, A.K.; Hernandez Filho, G.; Skaf, A.Y. Diagnostic imaging of muscle injuries in Sports Medicine: New Concepts and radiological approach. *Curr. Radiol. Rep.* **2017**, *5*, 27. [CrossRef]
18. Lee, J.C.; Mitchell, A.W.; Healy, J.C. Imaging of muscle injury in the elite athlete. *Br. J. Radiol.* **2012**, *85*, 1173–1185. [CrossRef] [PubMed]
19. Gabriel, C.; Gabriel, S.; Corthout, E. The dielectric properties of biological tissues: I. Literature survey. *Phys. Med. Biol.* **1996**, *41*, 2231–2249. [CrossRef]
20. Gabriel, S.; Lau, R.W.; Gabriel, C. The dielectric properties of biological tissues: III. Parametric models for the dielectric spectrum of tissues. *Phys. Med. Biol.* **1996**, *41*, 2271–2293. [CrossRef]
21. Aldhaeebi, M.A.; Alzoubi, K.; Almoneef, T.S.; Bamatraf, S.M.; Attia, H.; Ramahi, O.M. Review of Microwaves Techniques for Breast Cancer Detection. *Sensors* **2020**, *20*, 2390. [CrossRef]
22. Shea, J.D.; Kosmas, P.; Hagness, S.C.; Van Veen, B.D. Three-dimensional microwave imaging of realistic numerical breast phantoms via a multiple-frequency inverse scattering technique. *Med. Phys.* **2010**, *37*, 4210–4226. [CrossRef]
23. Fhager, A.; Persson, M. Using a priori Data to Improve the Reconstruction of Small Objects in Microwave Tomography. *IEEE Trans. Microw. Theory Tech.* **2007**, *55*, 2454–2462. [CrossRef]
24. Meaney, P.M.; Fanning, M.W.; Paulsen, K.D.; Li, D.; Pendergrass, S.A.; Fang, Q.; Moodie, K.L. Microwave thermal imaging: Initial in vivo experience with a single heating zone. *Int. J. Hyperth.* **2003**, *19*, 617–641. [CrossRef] [PubMed]
25. Karadima, O.; Rahman, M.; Sotiriou, I.; Ghavami, N.; Lu, P.; Ahsan, S.; Kosmas, P. Experimental Validation of Microwave Tomography with the DBIM-TwIST Algorithm for Brain Stroke Detection and Classification. *Sensors* **2020**, *20*, 840. [CrossRef] [PubMed]
26. Meaney, P.M.; Kaufman, P.A.; Muffly, L.S.; Click, M.; Poplack, S.P.; Wells, W.A.; Schwartz, G.N.; di Florio-Alexander, R.M.; Tosteson, T.D.; Li, Z.; et al. Microwave imaging for Neoadjuvant Chemotherapy Monitoring: Initial Clinical experience. *Breast Cancer Res.* **2013**, *15*, R35. [CrossRef] [PubMed]
27. Janjic, A.; Cayoren, M.; Akduman, I.; Yilmaz, T.; Onemli, E.; Bugdayci, O.; Aribal, M.E. SAFE: A Novel Microwave Imaging System Design for Breast Cancer Screening and Early Detection—Clinical Evaluation. *Diagnostics* **2021**, *11*, 533. [CrossRef]
28. Li, X.; Hagness, S. A confocal microwave imaging algorithm for breast cancer detection. *IEEE Microw. Wirel. Compon. Lett.* **2001**, *11*, 130–132. [CrossRef]
29. Fear, E.; Li, X.; Hagness, S.; Stuchly, M. Confocal microwave imaging for breast cancer detection: Localization of tumors in three dimensions. *IEEE Trans. Biomed. Eng.* **2002**, *49*, 812–822. [CrossRef]
30. Been Lim, H.; Thi Tuyet Nhung, N.; Li, E.P.; Duc Thang, N. Confocal Microwave Imaging for Breast Cancer Detection: Delay-Multiply-and-Sum Image Reconstruction Algorithm. *IEEE Trans. Biomed. Eng.* **2008**, *55*, 1697–1704. [CrossRef]
31. Fear, E.; Stuchly, M. Microwave system for breast tumor detection. *IEEE Microw. Guid. Wave Lett.* **1999**, *9*, 470–472. [CrossRef]
32. Preece, A.W.; Craddock, I.; Shere, M.; Jones, L.; Winton, H.L. MARIA M4: Clinical evaluation of a prototype ultrawideband radar scanner for breast cancer detection. *J. Med. Imaging* **2016**, *3*, 033502. [CrossRef]
33. Moloney, B.M.; McAnena, P.F.; Abd Elwahab, S.M.; Fasoula, A.; Duchesne, L.; Gil Cano, J.D.; Glynn, C.; O'Connell, A.; Ennis, R.; Lowery, A.J.; et al. Microwave Imaging in Breast Cancer—Results from the First-In-Human Clinical Investigation of the Wavelia System. *Acad. Radiol.* **2022**, *29*, S211–S222. [CrossRef] [PubMed]
34. Maklad, B.; Curtis, C.; Fear, E.C.; Messier, G.G. Neighborhood-based algorithm to facilitate the reduction of skin reflections in radar-based Microwave Imaging. *Prog. Electromagn. Res. B* **2012**, *39*, 115–139. [CrossRef]
35. Elahi, M.A.; Glavin, M.; Jones, E.; O'Halloran, M. Artifact removal algorithms for microwave imaging of the breast. *Prog. Electromagn. Res.* **2013**, *141*, 185–200. [CrossRef]
36. Meaney, P.M. Addressing multipath signal corruption in microwave tomography and the influence on system design and algorithm development. *Open Access J. Biomed. Eng. Biosci.* **2018**, *1*, 102. [CrossRef] [PubMed]
37. Meaney, P.M.; Shubitidze, F.; Fanning, M.W.; Kmiec, M.; Epstein, N.R.; Paulsen, K.D. Surface wave multipath signals in near-field microwave imaging. *Int. J. Biomed. Imaging* **2012**, *2012*, 697253. [CrossRef] [PubMed]

38. Meaney, P.M.; Fox, C.J.; Geimer, S.D.; Paulsen, K.D. Electrical Characterization of Glycerin: Water Mixtures: Implications for Use as a Coupling Medium in Microwave Tomography. *IEEE Trans. Microw. Theory Tech.* **2017**, *65*, 1471–1478. [CrossRef]
39. Chang, J.; Paulsen, K.; Meaney, P.; Fanning, M. Non-invasive thermal assessment of tissue phantoms using an active near field microwave imaging technique. *Int. J. Hyperth.* **1998**, *14*, 513–534. [CrossRef]
40. Bourqui, J.; Garrett, J.; Fear, E. Measurement and analysis of microwave frequency signals transmitted through the breast. *Int. J. Biomed. Imaging* **2012**, *2012*, 562563. [CrossRef]
41. Fox, C.J.; Meaney, P.M.; Shubitidze, F.; Potwin, L.; Paulsen, K.D. Characterization of an implicitly resistively-loaded monopole antenna in lossy liquid media. *Int. J. Antennas Propag.* **2008**, *2008*, 580782. [CrossRef]
42. Li, X.; Jalilvand, M.; Sit, Y.L.; Zwick, T. A Compact Double-Layer On-Body Matched Bowtie Antenna for Medical Diagnosis. *IEEE Trans. Antennas Propag.* **2014**, *62*, 1808–1816. [CrossRef]
43. Bahramiabarghouei, H.; Porter, E.; Santorelli, A.; Gosselin, B.; Popović, M.; Rusch, L.A. Flexible 16 Antenna Array for Microwave Breast Cancer Detection. *IEEE Trans. Biomed. Eng.* **2015**, *62*, 2516–2525. [CrossRef] [PubMed]
44. Tommer, M.; Kjelgård, K.G.; Lande, T.S. Body coupled wideband monopole antenna. In Proceedings of the 2016 Loughborough Antennas Propagation Conference (LAPC), Loughborough, UK, 14–15 November 2016; pp. 1–5. [CrossRef]
45. De Oliveira, A.M.; de Oliveira Neto, A.M.; Perotoni, M.B.; Nurhayati, N.; Baudrand, H.; de Carvalho, A.; Justo, J.F. A Fern Antipodal Vivaldi Antenna for Near-Field Microwave Imaging Medical Applications. *IEEE Trans. Antennas Propag.* **2021**, *69*, 8816–8829. [CrossRef]
46. Li, X.; Zwirello, L.; Jalilvand, M.; Zwick, T. Design and near-field characterization of a planar on-body UWB slot-antenna for stroke detection. In Proceedings of the 2012 IEEE International Workshop on Antenna Technology (iWAT), Tucson, AZ, USA, 5–7 March 2012; pp. 201–204. [CrossRef]
47. Fhager, A.; Padhi, S.K.; Persson, M.; Howard, J. Antenna Modeling and reconstruction accuracy of Time Domain-based image reconstruction in Microwave Tomography. *Int. J. Biomed. Imaging* **2013**, *2013*, 343180. [CrossRef] [PubMed]
48. Hosseinzadegan, S.; Fhager, A.; Persson, M.; Geimer, S.D.; Meaney, P.M. Discrete Dipole Approximation-Based Microwave Tomography for Fast Breast Cancer Imaging. *IEEE Trans. Microw. Theory Tech.* **2021**, *69*, 2741–2752. [CrossRef]
49. Meaney, P.; Paulsen, K.; Chang, J. Near-field microwave imaging of biologically-based materials using a monopole transceiver system. *IEEE Trans. Microw. Theory Tech.* **1998**, *46*, 31–45. [CrossRef]
50. Gilmore, C.; Zakaria, A.; Pistorius, S.; LoVetri, J. Microwave imaging of human forearms: Pilot study and image enhancement. *Int. J. Biomed. Imaging* **2013**, *2013*, 673027. [CrossRef]
51. Alkhodari, M.; Zakaria, A.; Qaddoumi, N. Monitoring Bone Density Using Microwave Tomography of Human Legs: A Numerical Feasibility Study. *Sensors* **2021**, *21*, 7078. [CrossRef]
52. Duan, Q.; Duyn, J.H.; Gudino, N.; de Zwart, J.A.; van Gelderen, P.; Sodickson, D.K.; Brown, R. Characterization of a dielectric phantom for high-field magnetic resonance imaging applications. *Med. Phys.* **2014**, *41*, 102303. [CrossRef]
53. Porter, E.; Fakhoury, J.; Oprisor, R.; Coates, M.; Popović, M. Improved tissue phantoms for experimental validation of microwave breast cancer detection. In Proceedings of the Fourth European Conference on Antennas and Propagation, Barcelona, Spain, 12–16 April 2010; pp. 1–5.
54. Romeo, S.; Di Donato, L.; Bucci, O.M.; Catapano, I.; Crocco, L.; Scarfì, M.R.; Massa, R. Dielectric Characterization Study of liquid-based materials for mimicking breast tissues. *Microw. Opt. Technol. Lett.* **2011**, *53*, 1276–1280. [CrossRef]

sensors

MDPI

Article

On the Role of Training Data for SVM-Based Microwave Brain Stroke Detection and Classification

Tomas Pokorny [1,*], Jan Vrba [1], Ondrej Fiser [1], David Vrba [1], Tomas Drizdal [1], Marek Novak [1], Luca Tosi [2], Alessandro Polo [2] and Marco Salucci [2]

1 Department of Biomedical Technology, Faculty of Biomedical Engineering, Czech Technical University in Prague, 166 00 Prague, Czech Republic
2 ELEDIA Research Center (ELEDIA@UniTN—University of Trento), DICAM—Department of Civil, Environmental, and Mechanical Engineering, Via Mesiano 77, 38123 Trento, Italy
* Correspondence: tomas.pokorny@fbmi.cvut.cz

Abstract: The aim of this work was to test microwave brain stroke detection and classification using support vector machines (SVMs). We tested how the nature and variability of training data and system parameters impact the achieved classification accuracy. Using experimentally verified numerical models, a large database of synthetic training and test data was created. The models consist of an antenna array surrounding reconfigurable geometrically and dielectrically realistic human head phantoms with virtually inserted strokes of arbitrary size, and different dielectric parameters in different positions. The generated synthetic data sets were used to test four different hypotheses, regarding the appropriate parameters of the training dataset, the appropriate frequency range and the number of frequency points, as well as the level of subject variability to reach the highest SVM classification accuracy. The results indicate that the SVM algorithm is able to detect the presence of the stroke and classify it (i.e., ischemic or hemorrhagic) even when trained with single-frequency data. Moreover, it is shown that data of subjects with smaller strokes appear to be the most suitable for training accurate SVM predictors with high generalization capabilities. Finally, the datasets created for this study are made available to the community for testing and developing their own algorithms.

Keywords: SVM; brain stroke; microwave devices; numerical model

Citation: Pokorny, T.; Vrba, J.; Fiser, O.; Vrba, D.; Drizdal, T.; Novak, M.; Tosi, L.; Polo, A.; Salucci, M. On the Role of Training Data for SVM-Based Microwave Brain Stroke Detection and Classification. *Sensors* **2023**, *23*, 2031. https://doi.org/10.3390/s23042031

Academic Editors: Mikael Persson and Hoi-Shun Antony Lui

Received: 10 January 2023
Revised: 4 February 2023
Accepted: 7 February 2023
Published: 10 February 2023

1. Introduction

Microwave (MW) technology enables the development of an affordable, non-invasive, compact, lightweight, and therefore, a portable diagnostic system suitable for pre-hospital care. In contrast to standard medical imaging methods such as computed tomography (CT) and magnetic resonance imaging (MRI), MW stroke diagnostic systems could thus be included in ambulance vehicles. This could reduce the time to stroke classification and thus speed up the initiation of treatment reducing the lasting effects of strokes on patients [1].

MW detection and classification of strokes is based on measuring changes in dielectric properties of the brain during stroke progression [2]. For this purpose, an antenna array is placed around the patient's head and the reflection and transmission coefficients at the antenna ports are measured. In supervised machine learning approaches [3,4], the algorithm is trained using data for known ("labeled") scenarios (i.e., the existence of a stroke and, eventually, its type). Training data can be obtained either synthetically using numerical simulations or by measurements of phantoms or human subjects. However, this is almost impossible, as it requires at least data from hundreds of patients who are in life-threatening danger at any given time [5,6].

In [7,8], two brain stroke types are classified using inverse FFT transformation S-matrix. In [9,10], a human head model with intracranial hemorrhage was used to investigate the ability of a machine learning-based classification algorithm to distinguish healthy individuals from subjects with intracranial hemorrhage, depending on the number of subjects for training.

In [11], the first version of a laboratory MW system developed in our group in 2015, a homogeneous head phantom was used in experimental measurements, which demonstrated the potential of MW systems for brain stroke classifications/diagnostics. In [12], the SVM algorithm was used to detect the presence of a stroke on a simplified head phantom. Very high stroke detection accuracy was achieved even with a limited amount of data used for learning the algorithm. A follow-up work [13] dealt with the distinction between ischemic and hemorrhagic cerebrovascular events. From [14,15], where the classification results using different machine learning algorithms (Support Vector Machines, Nearest Neighbors, Discriminant analysis, Naïve Bayes classifier and Classification Tree) were compared, it suggests that SVM might be the most suitable for this application.

The aim of this study was to test the influence of the variability of the training data sets on the detection and classification accuracy using the SVM algorithm. Further, based on these results, we want to be able to recommend suitable properties of the training dataset. For this purpose, several 2D numerical models were created and experimentally verified consisting of an antenna array surrounding reconfigurable geometrically and dielectrically realistic human head models including virtually embedded stroke phantoms. The human head models were based on 10 different real subject heads. Thus, a large database of training and test datasets was created. The SVM-based algorithm was tested for the detection of the stroke presence and the classification of its type. For the SVM-based classification of strokes, we tested the following hypotheses:

Hypothesis 1 (H1). *The most suitable training data are from subjects with small strokes.*

Hypothesis 2 (H2). *Single-frequency and multi-frequency training data lead to the same classification accuracy.*

Hypothesis 3 (H3). *A SVM trained on data from subjects with small strokes can accurately classify randomly sized strokes.*

Hypothesis 4 (H4). *A SVM trained on data from patients with small strokes can accurately classify randomly sized strokes at random positions.*

2. Materials and Methods

2.1. Numerical Simulations

In this study, COMSOL Multiphysics [16] was used to create 2D synthetic training and test data in the form of transmission and reflection coefficients (called scattering parameters or, shortly, S-parameters). The corresponding 2D numerical models consist of a fixed antenna array surrounding reconfigurable geometrically and dielectrically realistic human head models. The geometry of the antenna array model corresponds to a cross-section of a laboratory prototype of a microwave imaging system described in [11].

2.2. Numerical Model

The geometry of one numerical model is depicted in Figure 1.

The 2D geometry was created from the cross-section of the laboratory prototype 3D numerical model in 100 mm z-coordinates. Absorption boundary conditions are set around the entire outer perimeter of the computational domain. The antenna elements used in this study are inspired by the slot antenna from [17]. An antenna 2D equivalent model consists of a rectangle representing a conductive cavity and a slot was used in simulations (see Figure 2). A slot segment was created on the perimeter of the rectangle facing the displayed area and the boundary condition of the port ("User defined", Ez) was assigned to it. The rest of the perimeter of the rectangle antenna was assigned a perfect electric conductor boundary condition. The sizes of the antenna segments representing the slots were changed to find the global minimum of a cost function using the genetic algorithm. We minimized the transmission parameter differences between the optimized 2D model and the reference experimental measurement for the entire 10-port system. The inner part of the antenna array was filled only with the matching medium. The maximum possible agreement between the transfer coefficients for 2D numerical simulation and experimental measurement was achieved. Relative magnitude differences were calculated according to Equation (1). Antennas operate in the frequency range from 0.8 GHz to 2 GHz. A triangular mesh was used, where the maximum value of the side length was set to 1/8 of the transverse electromagnetic wavelength in the given environment and for the highest frequency equal to 2 GHz.

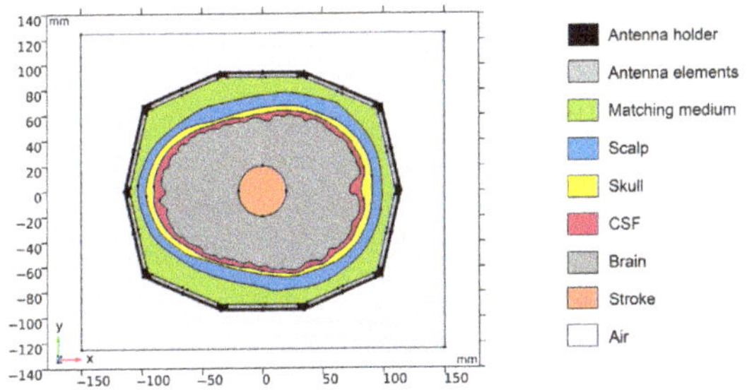

Figure 1. Geometry of the 2D numerical model. Antenna holder and antenna elements surrounding a realistic human head model. XY-plane corresponds to the cross-section at z = 100 mm of the laboratory prototype 3D numerical model.

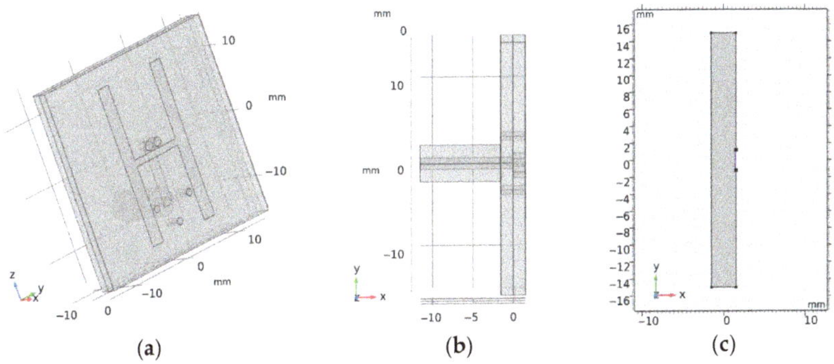

Figure 2. (**a**,**b**) is the 3D geometry of the antennas and (**c**) is the final 2D equivalent antenna model, where segments representing the slots (marked in blue) were changed to achieve maximum agreement to the measured transmission parameters within laboratory system.

The 2D geometries of the models of all 10 human heads used here are based on 3D head models from the IT'IS Foundation's "The Population Head Model V1.0" database [18]. In Materialize 3-matic software [19], the mesh of the models was modified so that it could be imported and used for FEM simulations in COMSOL Multiphysics. 2D models were created from a section of 3D models in the brain part of the head. The models contain layers representing the scalp, skull, cerebrospinal fluid, and brain (white matter and grey matter). For completeness, the geometries of the 10 head phantoms are depicted in Appendix A. The stroke locations are represented by a circle with diameters from 20 to 40 mm placed in different positions in the brain domain shown in Figure 3.

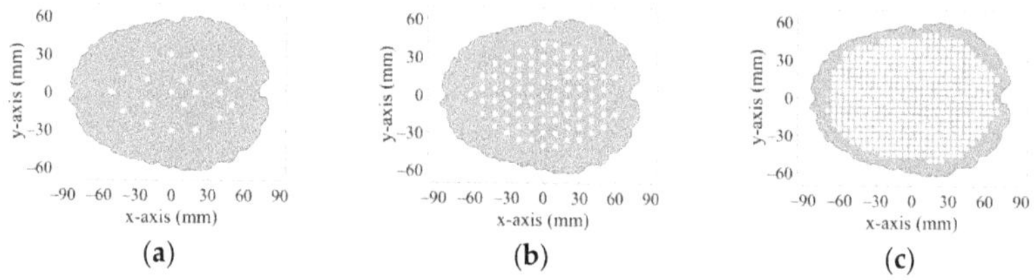

Figure 3. 20 positions (**a**), 83 positions (**b**), and 456 positions (**c**) in the brain where strokes of various sizes were placed.

2.3. Dielectric Properties of Biological Tissues

Realistic dielectric properties values were assigned to the Individual domains of the human head models, which represents different biological tissues. These values were determined using the frequency-dependent 4-pole Cole–Cole model [20]. Specifically, for the skull, CSF, and hemorrhagic stroke represented by the blood, the 4-pole Cole–Cole model parameters were directly adopted from the database [21]. For the brain dielectric properties, we used average values of white matter, gray matter and cerebellum and for the scalp average values of skin and fat. The dielectric properties of the individual domains at 1 GHz are shown in Table 1.

Table 1. Dielectric properties of the domain in the human head modes at 1 GHz [21].

Tissue Layer	ε_r (−)	σ (S/m)
Scalp †	35.68	0.66
Skull	12.34	0.16
CSF	68.44	2.46
Brain ‡	40.00	1.00
Ischemic stroke	34.00	0.85
Hemorrhagic stroke	61.07	1.58
Matching Medium *	40.00	1.00

† Average parameters of skin and fat. ‡ Average parameters of grey matter, white matter, and cerebellum.
* Matching medium dielectric properties are given by the IEEE standard [22].

2.4. Numerical Models Validation

Validation of the numerical models was done in two steps. First, we directly compared the (synthetic) S-parameters obtained from simulations using 2D and 3D models (the geometries of these models are shown in Figures 1 and 4) and measurements using the laboratory prototype of a MW imaging system [11] shown in Figure 5.

For the 2D and 3D simulations and measurements, the inner part of the antenna array was filled only with the matching medium, which allowed us idealized comparisons of all these scenarios.

Relative magnitudes differences are defined as:

$$\Delta M_{ij} = 20 \cdot \log_{10}\left(\left|\frac{S_{ij}^A}{S_{ij}^B}\right|\right), \tag{1}$$

where S_{ij}^A and S_{ij}^B denote the scattering parameters in the presence or absence of a stroke, respectively, for each i, j antennas pair.

Magnitudes differences of S-parameters are listed in Appendix C.

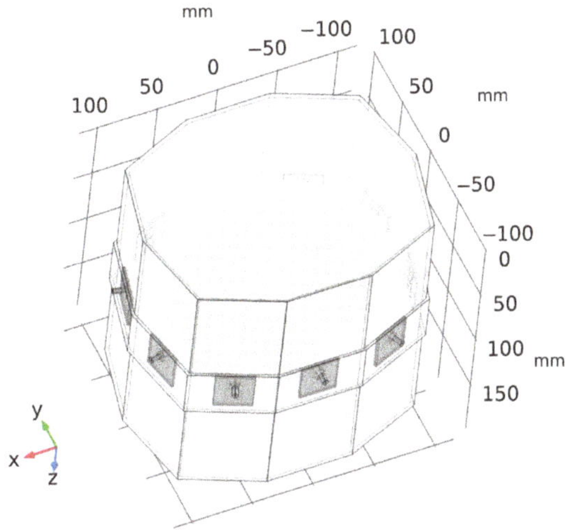

Figure 4. A geometry of a 3D numerical model of the laboratory prototype of microwave imaging system. For clarity, the air surrounding the antenna array is omitted in the figure.

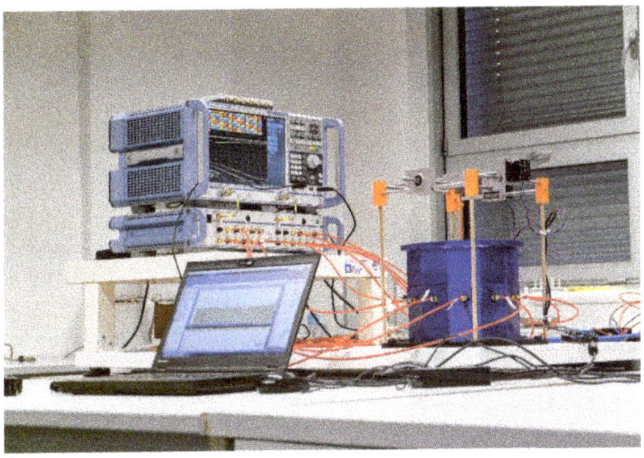

Figure 5. A laboratory prototype of the microwave imaging system [11] consisting of an in-house designed antenna array and a positioning system for stroke models, and commercial measuring devices: a vector network analyzer ZNB8, and a switching matrix ZN-Z84, both Rohde Schwartz, Germany.

2.5. Acquisition, Nature, and Variability of Training and Testing Data Sets

The datasets were automatically generated using the reconfigurable numerical model described in Section 2.2 and 2D simulations done in COMSOL Multiphysics controlled with in-house written MATLAB scripts. These scripts specifically set the operating frequency, stroke type, size and position, head phantom size scaling, and saved the resulting S-matrices together with the numerical model settings to a MATLAB structure matrix file.

According to studies [5,13], the most suitable operating frequencies for MW imaging are around 1 GHz. Our datasets contain simulation results for 25 equidistant frequency points ranging from 0.8 to 2 GHz.

The head models were based on 10 different patient-specific geometries. To increase the variability of tested datasets, the geometries of the head models were scaled to 95–105% of their original size independently in the x and y directions. The scaling factors were determined for each data point using a uniform probability density random number generator. We used 2 types of strokes: Ischemic stroke (iStroke) caused by blockage of a blood vessel by a clot and hemorrhagic stroke (hStroke) caused by intracranial bleeding, also the scenario without stroke (noStroke) was used. Three datasets have been generated as summarized in the text below and Table 2.

Table 2. Model parameters in the DataSets.

DataSet (–)	Stroke Type (–)	Stroke Sizes (mm)	Stroke Positions (–)	Head Phantoms (–)	Head Scaled (%)	Frequency Points (–)
1	hStroke iStroke noStroke	20, 25, 30, 35, 40	Fixed 20 + 83 + 456	10	95–105 †	25
2	hStroke iStroke noStroke	20–40 †	Fixed 20	10	95–105 †	25
3	hStroke iStroke noStroke	20–40 †	Random 20 †	10	95–105 †	25

† Uniform probability density random number generator.

DataSet 1 includes 2D simulation results for subjects with five different stroke sizes (20, 25, 30, 35 and 40 mm in diameter) of both stroke types placed at 20 predefined positions within randomly chosen and scaled head models. In total, 1000 simulations were for each stroke type, and 1000 simulations of randomly scaled head models without stroke. Therefore, 3000 calculations of S–matrices were done for one frequency point. DataSet1 was subsequently supplemented with data generated in the same way for 83 and 456 different stroke positions.

DataSet 2 includes the simulations' results for subjects with ischemic and hemorrhagic strokes of random size (ranging from 20 to 40 mm in diameter determined using uniform probability density random number generator) placed at 20 predefined positions within randomly chosen and scaled head models. In total, 200 simulations were computed for each type of stroke and 200 simulations for randomly scaled head models without stroke.

DataSet 3 includes the simulations' results for subjects with ischemic and hemorrhagic strokes of random size (range from 20 to 40 mm and determined using uniform probability density random number generator) placed at random positions within randomly chosen and scaled head models. In total, 200 simulations were calculated for each type of stroke and 200 simulations for randomly scaled head models without stroke.

2.6. Feature Selection and Extraction

As previously mentioned, the numerical models contain, in total, 10 antenna elements. For each simulation, we thus obtain a complex S-matrix with dimensions of 10×10. Thanks to the Lorentz principle of reciprocity $\left(S_{ij} = S_{ji}\right)$ there are only 55 independent elements of the S-matrix. We divided the complex values of these S-parameters into real and imaginary parts and thus obtained 110 observed features which give us 110 dataset dimensions for one frequency point [15].

The training and test data were centered and normalized to a range from 0 to 1. For training data, we calculate the principal component coefficients using Principal Component Analysis (PCA) through Singular Value Decomposition (SVD). The principal component coefficient was used to reduce the dimension for training and test data sets. The most appropriate number of data dimensions (i.e., of PCA-extracted features) was chosen based on the classification accuracy for different dimension sizes.

2.7. Stroke Classification

For stroke detection and classification, we used a non-linear SVM with kernel function [22]. The kernel function maps the data to a higher-dimensional space, where the classes are easier to separate. For the classification between head phantom with ischemic stroke (iStroke), hemorrhagic stroke (hStroke), and head phantom without stroke (noStroke) classes, we constructed a multiclass classifier by combining multiple binary classifiers [13].

To improve the performance of the algorithm, we searched for the best settings of the SVM algorithm by optimizing hyper parameters based on Bayesian optimization.

To train the algorithm, an input matrix of a known set of input samples (TrainData) and an input matrix of known responses to the samples (TrainDataClass) were prepared according to the tested hypothesis. The input matrix of known samples consisted of a predefined number of rows in which every row was filled with a single-measured S-matrix, normalized, and dimensionality reduced by PCA. The input matrix with the response to the samples was prepared by assigning a number to every class in the input matrix of known samples.

A trained model was used to classify the data matrix of unknown samples (Data). A matrix of unknown samples (Data) was created from all samples that correspond to all stroke types, sizes, and positions according to the hypothesis tested. Different data were always used to train and test the algorithm to verify its generalization capabilities. Additional information for analysis (stroke size and position, phantom scale in x-axes and y-axes) contains an equivalent info matrix (DataInfo). Data from this matrix were used exclusively for the evaluation of problematic classifications.

The classification accuracy (CL-accuracy) and cross-validation error (CV-error) were calculated. A confusion matrix was used to determine which type of stroke was problematic for classification.

2.8. Hypothesis

Hypothesis 1 (H1). *The most suitable training data are from subjects with small strokes.*

Data corresponding to patients with small ischemic and hemorrhagic stroke sizes show the smallest deviation from data for healthy subjects. It can be expected that they represent the worst case for classification and therefore may be the most relevant for determining support vectors. We trained the SVM algorithm with datasets including successively only 20, then 30, and finally, 40 mm iStrokes and hStrokes placed at 20 positions in 10 randomly scaled phantoms (in total, 600 for each stroke type for testing). The SVM algorithm classified the remaining data (DataSet 1). Dimensionality reduction using PCA was not used in this case. For simplification, only data for 1 GHz were used. The data used for training and testing are described in Table 3.

Table 3. Training and testing data parameters for hypothesis H1.

	TrainData	**TestData**
DataSet (−)	No. 1	No.1
Stroke type (−)	hStroke, iStroke, noStroke	hStroke, iStroke, noStroke
Stroke sizes (mm)	20 or 30 or 40	20, 25, 30, 35, 40
Stroke positions (−)	Fixed 20	Fixed 20
Head phantoms (−)	10	10
Frequency points (−)	1	1
DataSet size † (−)	600	3000
DataSet dimensions ‡ (−)	110	110

† The single measured S-matrices, ‡ The number of S-parameters from S-matrix.

Hypothesis 2 (H2). *Single-frequency and multi-frequency training data lead to the same classification accuracy.*

For a smaller number of frequency points, the algorithm works with a smaller amount of data. On the other hand, for a higher number of frequency points, we can reduce the dimensionality to only useful information. Classification results were compared for the SVM algorithm trained on data for a single frequency point (1 GHz), five frequency points (from 0.8 GHz, step 0.1 GHz, to 1.2 GHz), fifteen frequency points (from 0.8 GHz, 0.05 GHz step, up to 1.5 GHz) data and twenty-five frequency points (from 0.8 GHz, 0.05 GHz step, up to 2 GHz) data. We train the SVM algorithm for 20 mm iStroke and hStroke sizes located at 20 positions in 10 random scaled phantoms. The SVM algorithm classified the remaining data (DataSet 1). The data used for training and testing are described in Table 4. Complete graphs of classification accuracy and cross-validation error for different dimension reductions are provided in Appendix B.

Table 4. Training and testing data parameters for hypothesis H2.

	TrainData	TestData
DataSet (−)	No. 1	No. 1
Stroke type (−)	hStroke, iStroke, noStroke	hStroke, iStroke, noStroke
Stroke sizes (mm)	20	20, 25, 30, 35, 40
Stroke positions (−)	Fixed 20	Fixed 20
Head phantoms (−)	10	10
Frequency points (−)	1 or 5 or 15 or 25	1
DataSet size † (−)	600	3000
DataSet dimensions ‡ (−)	110 or 550 or 1650 or 2750	110 or 550 or 1650 or 2750

† The single measured S-matrices, ‡ The number of S-parameters from S-matrix.

Hypothesis 3 (H3). *SVM trained on data of subjects with small strokes can accurately classify randomly sized strokes.*

We trained the SVM algorithm using data on subjects with 20 mm iStroke and hStroke located at 20 positions in 10 randomly scaled phantoms (DataSet 1). We used training data for a frequency of 1 GHz and 90 dimensions reduced by PCA. The SVM algorithm classified the data of subjects with random stroke sizes (DataSet 2). The data used for training and testing are described in Table 5.

Table 5. Training and testing data parameters for hypothesis H3.

	TrainData	TestData
DataSet (−)	No. 1	No. 2
Stroke type (−)	hStroke, iStroke, noStroke	hStroke, iStroke, noStroke
Stroke sizes (mm)	20	20–40
Stroke positions (−)	Fixed 20	Fixed 20
Head phantoms (−)	10	10
Frequency points (−)	1	1
DataSet size † (−)	600	600
DataSet dimensions ‡ (−)	90	90

† The single measured S-matrices, ‡ The number of S-parameters from S-matrix.

Hypothesis 4 (H4). *SVM trained on data of subjects with small strokes can accurately classify randomly sized strokes at random positions.*

We trained the SVM algorithm using data for 20 mm iStroke and hStroke sizes located at 20, 83, and 456 positions in 10 randomly scaled phantoms (DataSet 1). We used training data for a frequency of 1 GHz and 90 dimensions reduced by PCA. The SVM algorithm classified data for random stroke sizes and random stroke positions (DataSet 3). The data used for training and testing are described in Table 6.

Table 6. Training and testing data parameters for hypothesis H4.

	TrainData	TestData
DataSet (−)	No.1	No.3
Stroke type (−)	hStroke, iStroke, noStroke	hStroke, iStroke, noStroke
Stroke sizes (mm)	20	20–40
Stroke positions (−)	Fixed 20 or 83 or 456	Random 20
Head phantoms (−)	10	10
Frequency points (−)	1	1
DataSet size † (−)	600 or 2490 or 1368	600
DataSet dimensions ‡ (−)	90	90

† The single measured S-matrices, ‡ The number of S-parameters from S-matrix.

3. Results

3.1. Numerical Model Validation

Numerical model validation was done by direct comparison of measured S-parameters from laboratory prototype of the microwave imaging system and S-parameters from 2D and 3D numerical simulations (see Figure 6).

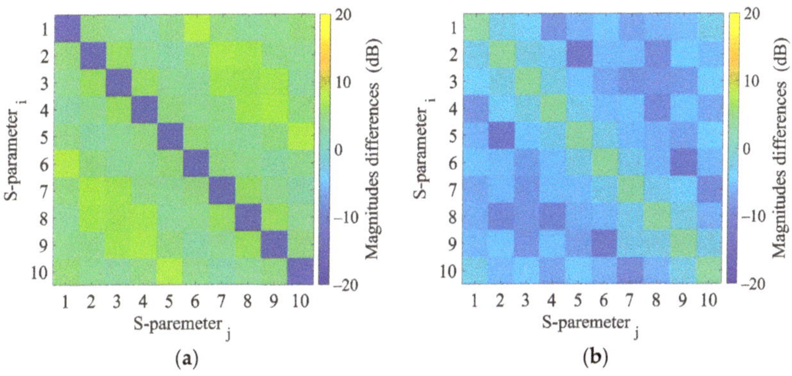

Figure 6. Magnitudes differences of 2D numerical model and 3D numerical model (**a**) and magnitudes differences of 3D numerical model and experimental measurement (**b**).

Results of 2D and 3D numerical analysis of the changes in S-parameters induced by the virtual presence of the stroke model are listed in Appendix C. The reflection coefficients did not change when the stroke was inserted. Changes in the transmission coefficients were observed and were different for ischemic and hemorrhagic stroke and therefore applicable for the given purpose. Results in the 2D model cause more significant changes in the transmission coefficients than in the 3D model.

3.2. Principal Component Analysis

The variance of DataSet 1 determined by principal component analysis (PCA) is shown in Figure 7. Around the 90th dimension, the variance begins to decrease more rapidly. Several higher principal components show significantly lower variance than others. Based on Figures 7 and A2, where the classification accuracy was the highest and the cross-validation error the lowest, we decided to set 90 dimensions for a frequency of 1 GHz.

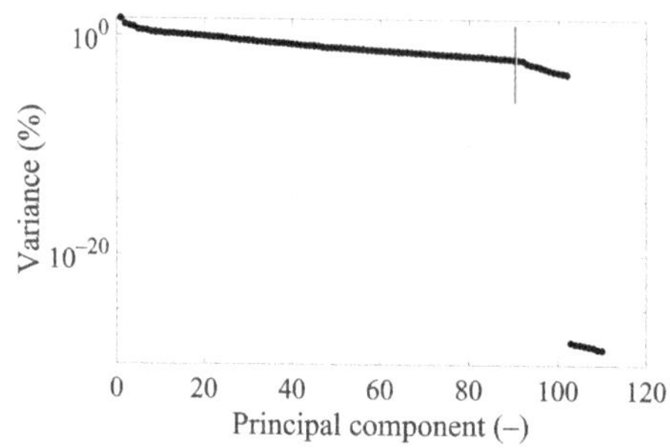

Figure 7. Principal components' variance graph for DataSet 1 at 1 GHz. The red line indicates data reduction to 90 dimensions.

3.3. *Hypothesis*

Hypothesis 1 (H1). *The most suitable training data are from subjects with small strokes.*

SVMs were successively trained with data for different stroke sizes and then classified the remaining strokes (Training and testing data are described in Table 3). By training the algorithm with data corresponding to the smallest considered stroke sizes (with a diameter of 20 mm), the highest classification accuracy was achieved (see Table 7), even when classifying strokes up to the maximum considered diameter (40 mm). Thus, the hypothesis that the training data for small stroke sizes is the most suitable for training the SVM algorithm for stroke classification was confirmed.

Table 7. Effect of stroke sizes on classification accuracy for DataSet1 at 1 GHz.

Stroke Size (mm)	CV-Error (%)	CL-Accuracy (%)
20	11.8	95.7
30	7.0	85.3
40	5.5	65.5

Hypothesis 2 (H2). *Single-frequency and multi-frequency training data lead to the same classification accuracy.*

Graphs of classification accuracy and cross-validation error for different values of dimensionality and different numbers of frequency points are in Appendix B. From Table 8, we conclude that for SVM training, it turns out to be most appropriate to use 1 or 5 frequency points, where the classification accuracy and cross-validation error were almost identical. For 15 and 25 frequency points the results are significantly worse and only after dimensionality reduction using PCA do the results reach similar classification accuracy as with a lower number of frequency points. Thus, the hypothesis that the training data for one frequency point is sufficient for an accurate classification of stroke using the SVM algorithm was confirmed.

Table 8. The effect of number of frequency points and dimension reduction on the classification accuracy.

Frequency Points (–)	Frequencies (GHz)	Total Dimensions (–)	CL-Accuracy CV-Error (%)	Reduced Dimensions (–)	CL-Accuracy CV-Error (%)
1	1.00	110	94.6 14.9	90	96.9 10.4
5	0.80 1.00 1.20 1.40 1.50	550	77.0 17.3	80	96.8 10.2
15	0.80–1.50 step 0.05	1650	87.2 21.1	70	96.3 11.1
25	0.80–2.00 step 0.05	2750	33.3 28.6	150	92.2 8.4

Hypothesis 3 (H3). *SVM trained on data of subjects with small strokes can accurately classify randomly sized strokes.*

The confusion matrix in Figure 8 shows that the classification between the iStroke and the hStroke class was accurate, only a 6.5% strokes were classified as the noStroke class, and 6.0% noStrokes were classified as the iStroke class. The hypothesis that the SVM algorithm for stroke classification trained on small strokes can classify random-size strokes was confirmed.

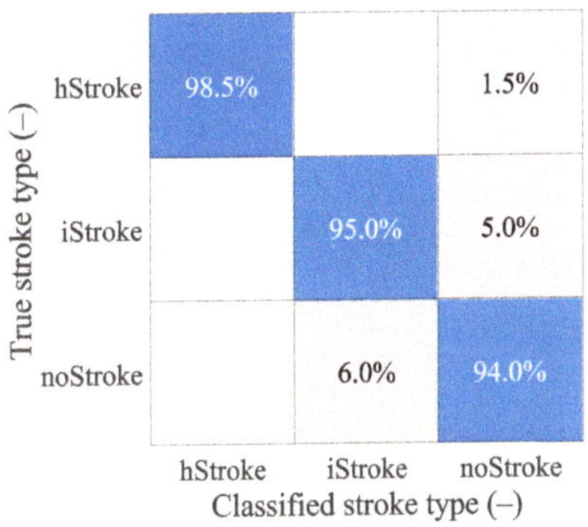

Figure 8. The confusion matrix for the classification of random ischemic and hemorrhagic stroke sizes.

Hypothesis 4 (H4). *SVM trained on data of subjects with small strokes can accurately classify randomly sized strokes at random positions.*

From Table 9 we see that even for a larger amount of data, the algorithm cannot classify random data accurately and reach a maximum at around 70% classification accuracy. From the confusion matrixes in Figure 9, we can observe the correct and incorrect classification of iStroke, hStroke, and noStroke classes. The hypothesis that the SVM algorithm for stroke classification trained on small strokes can classify random size and random position strokes was not confirmed.

Table 9. The SVM algorithm classification of random stroke sizes and random stroke positions with different amounts of training data (different number of 20 mm stroke positions in the head).

Training Data Stroke Positions (–)	Training Data Number of Phantoms (–)	CV-Error (%)	CL-Accuracy (%)	Hyperparameters Optimalization Settings (–)
20 hStroke 20 iStroke	10	11.3	64.3	Box Constraint = 912.92 Kernel Function = Gaussian Kernel Scale = 17.8
83 hStroke 83 iStroke	10	8.9	70.5	Box Constraint = 212.97 Kernel Function = Gaussian Kernel Scale = 11.41
456 hStroke 456 iStroke	1 randomly selected from 10 phantoms	11.3	70.2	Box Constraint = 385.03 Kernel Function = Gaussian Kernel Scale = 19.74

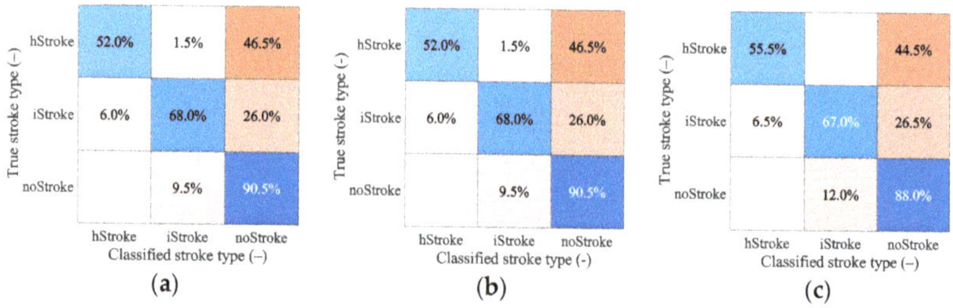

Figure 9. The confusion matrixes for classification of random stroke sizes and random stroke positions. In total, 200 samples for iStroke, 200 samples for hStroke and 200 samples for noStroke. SVM algorithm was trained for (**a**) 20 and (**b**) 83 ischemic and hemorrhagic strokes in 10 scaled phantoms and (**c**) for 456 ischemic and hemorrhagic strokes in 1 randomly selected phantom from 10 scaled phantoms.

4. Discussion

The results of this work are for a large dataset for the training and testing of machine learning algorithms for MW detection and classification of cerebrovascular events. The dataset can be used to optimize the setting and study the performance and limits of the algorithms for the considered application. As part of this work, the aforementioned dataset was used to test selected hypotheses. The second result of this work is hypothesis testing, where it was proven that (a) the data of subjects with strokes of sizes and distributed throughout the brain are the most suitable for training SVM algorithms, (b) the SVM algorithm can reliably detect and classify iStrokes and hStrokes at a single frequency, and multi-frequency data do not bring an increase in classification accuracy, (c) a large amount of data of subjects with small strokes must be used to train the SVM algorithm.

4.1. Comparison of S-Parameters Obtained by 2D and 3D Simulations and Measurements

In general, the 2D numerical model does not consider the propagation of EM waves in the 3rd dimension. In this work, a global optimization method was used to find the size of the boundary condition of the antenna port, which guarantees a good match between the measured and simulated transmission coefficients. Therefore, the magnitudes of the transmission parameters calculated and measured are in agreement; see Figure 6. On the other hand, the agreement in the reflection coefficients is worse. The calculated S-parameters are symmetric according to its main diagonal, while the measurements S-parameters show slight symmetry in the second decimal place in dB. These differences can be caused by noise or temperature fluctuations and must be considered when detecting a stroke.

4.2. S-Parameter Variability due to the Presence of Strokes

Changes in S-parameter values induced by the presence of ischemic and hemorrhagic stroke were studied using 2D and 3D numerical simulations. While the reflection coefficients did not change when the stroke was inserted, changes in the transmission coefficients were observed even for the worst-case scenario with the stroke located in the middle of the brain. The changes in transmission coefficients were different for ischemic and hemorrhagic stroke and therefore applicable for the given purpose. It is also possible to observe changes in the transmission parameters for the stroke location (−20, 30).

When comparing the calculated changes in the transmission coefficients in 2D and 3D, it is evident that not considering the EM wave propagation in the 3rd dimension causes more significant changes in the transmission coefficients than in the 3D model. Stroke detection and classification on 2D data can perform better than on real data or data obtained through 3D numerical simulations.

4.3. PCA

Based on the knowledge of the measured data and the information that the s-matrix from numerical simulations and measurements is symmetric, only the independent S-parameters of the matrix were selected, which resulted in the first reduction in the data dimension. Dimensionality reduction was tested using PCA for different frequency points.

With 25 frequency points, it is necessary to strongly reduce the data using PCA to achieve good classification accuracy results (see Figure A5), but we still did not achieve a higher classification accuracy or lower cross-validation error compared to a smaller number of frequency points (see Table 8). For five frequency points it is again necessary to strongly reduce the data using PCA to achieve good classification accuracy results (see Figure A3). The classification accuracy and cross-validation error for five frequency points are almost identical to one frequency point (see Figure A2), where only a small data reduction from 110 to 90 dimensions is needed to achieve the best classification accuracy results. This result is also suggested by the variance of the data (see Figure 7), where around 90 dimensions, the principal component starts to radically lose variance, and even a few principal components reach a significantly lower variance than most of the data. We decided to set 90 dimensions for extraction using PCA, where the data contain 99.9% variance.

4.4. Hypothesis H1

From Table 7, we can conclude that when training the algorithm only on the data of subjects with the smallest strokes (diameter 20 mm), the SVM algorithm achieved the highest classification accuracy of subjects with larger strokes up to a diameter of 40 mm. On the other hand, the cross-validation error increased from 5.5% to 11.8%. We assume that data of subjects with larger strokes contain higher variability; therefore, it is easier to classify them, and the algorithm achieves a smaller cross-validation error when training for larger strokes. Useful information for creating a support vector is provided by small-stroke subjects; however, they are more difficult to divide, which is why the Cross-validation error is higher than for larger strokes.

4.5. Hypothesis H2

SVM trained on data containing one and five frequency points showed almost identical classification accuracy and cross-validation error. They also outperformed an SVM trained with data containing a larger number of frequency points, even though the performance of the latter was enhanced by dimensionality reduction using PCA. This means that for this particular application, it would be enough to use a narrowband imaging system.

4.6. Hypothesis H3

The confusion matrixes in Figure 8 shows that the classification between ischemic and hemorrhagic stroke was accurate and only 6.5% of strokes were classified as non-stroke scenario and 6.0% of no strokes were classified as ischemic stroke.

Pre-hospital MW detection and classification of cerebrovascular events have the following specifics. Ischemic strokes need to be detected because they can be treated immediately with thrombolytic therapy. A situation where a hemorrhagic stroke is classified as ischemic is completely unacceptable. Thrombolytic therapy in case of hemorrhagic stroke causes hematoma enlargement and increases the risk of mortality [23]. In our study, unacceptable misclassification was observed only when we classify random stroke sizes and random stroke positions (DataSet 3), but the training dataset is extended by more stroke positions to eliminate misclassifications. It is, therefore, possible to consider only a 2-class classification into ischemic cerebrovascular events and the rest.

4.7. Hypothesis H4

The hypothesis that the SVM algorithm for stroke classification trained on data of the subjects with small strokes can accurately classify random size and random position strokes were not confirmed. From Table 9, we can conclude that only 20 iStroke and hStroke positions were not enough and the SVM algorithm only achieved a 63.5% classification accuracy. For 83 and 456 iStroke and hStroke positions SVM algorithm achieved only classification accuracy of 70% and 71%, respectively. Furthermore, we observed that the box constraint, which was determined by the optimization of the hyper-parameters, reaches high values. High box constraint values suggest good separation and fewer misclassifications, but unknown data for random stroke size and random stroke positions, the SVM algorithm is not able to classify correctly, and achieves only 70% classification accuracy. We also checked which samples were misclassified, but no pattern was discovered. From the confusion matrixes in Figure 9 we conclude that most of the inaccurate classifications belonged to the category without stroke, and these stroke patients will be taken to the hospital anyway. The biggest problem in the treatment of stroke patients is the classification of hemorrhagic strokes into the ischemic category. The use of anticoagulation in hemorrhagic stroke causes hematoma enlargement and increases the risk of mortality [23]. For this situation, there were no misclassifications for the 456 iStroke and hStroke positions used for SVM algorithm training.

4.8. Comparison with Published Studies

The results are partially comparable to [10], where a study of the feasibility of subdural hematoma classification by the SVD-based algorithm was performed on synthetic data from 2D numerical simulations. The authors achieved 82–96% classification success rate, considering only a two-class classification of healthy subjects and subjects with subdural hematomas. Ischemic stroke cases were not considered. Subdural hematoma is distinct from intracerebral hemorrhage, which is the most common type of hemorrhage in stroke patients. Intracerebral hemorrhage is located within the brain tissue and is usually of spherical shape and is generally characterized by a smaller volume than subdural hematoma; hence, the subdural hematoma may be classified with lower error. The 2D model is a significant simplification; therefore, a 3D numerical study was presented in [9]. Again, a two-class classification is performed. In our study, the results of classification into three classes are presented.

In [24], an alternative and efficient method was proposed to create the training dataset, based on the distorted Born approximation, to obtain a linear scattering operator from the dielectric contrast space to the scattering parameters' one. A dataset containing 10,000 samples was created in a relatively short time and with low computational effort. On the other hand, a single 3D CAD model of a human head was used and scaled to obtain a total of 10 head models. In our study, a higher data variability was considered because all 10 different head models were scaled randomly in each numerical simulation.

The algorithms were tested in [24] on a large amount of data obtained from the linear dispersion operator. An evaluation of the suitability of different datasets for training was not carried out. In our study, the effect of multi-frequency data on classification accuracy was tested, but the results show and agree with the statement in [24] that single-frequency data is sufficient for this application.

Classification using the SVM algorithm with a different data processing approach was performed in [7]. Data were obtained for 10 head models without scaling and only for ellipsoid strokes of 10 mm^3 to 35 mm^3. A total of 100 stroke head models were created. A two-class classification was performed between iStroke and hStroke classes. NoStroke class was not included. Inverse FFT was used to convert these signals to time series signals. Data variability was increased by adding noise, which also significantly reduced the classification success rate from 94% to 77%. In [8], dimensionality reductions by PCA led to classification success rate increase to 99%. The increase in the classification success using PCA also confirms our results, even though it was a different data processing approach.

4.9. Further Plans

Training data for machine learning algorithms should ideally be obtained from measurements performed in subjects with acute strokes. However, these patients are in a life-threatening situations. Using 2D numerical simulations, we obtained the large amount of data needed to train and test machine learning algorithms and to optimize their settings. We can test various hypotheses to understand well the performance and limits of this application. In future, we plan to perform 3D numerical simulations for a larger number of human heads and a more realistic MW imaging system with up to 24 antennas. Algorithms trained on the data obtained from numerical simulations would probably fail in the real world. Therefore, we plan to test the algorithm on experimentally obtained measurement data using a MW system [25] and anatomically and dielectrically realistic phantoms of the human head such as those proposed in [26]. Machine learning algorithms do not provide the position or magnitude of the stroke in the human head; therefore, in the future, we propose to combine the SVM algorithm with the TSVD Born approximation to obtain an image of the observed area. Both algorithms can be used on the same device.

5. Conclusions

Machine learning algorithms appear to be a promising method for MW stroke detection and classification. A large dataset for the training and testing of machine learning algorithms for MW detection and classification of cerebrovascular events was created. We demonstrated that the SVM algorithm is able to detect the presence of the stroke and classify it as ischemic and hemorrhagic classes. Data from a single frequency point (1 GHz) are sufficient for training the accurate SVM predictors. Further, it was shown that the data of subjects with smaller strokes appear to be the most suitable for training accurate SVM predictors with high generalization capabilities for stroke-trained position placement. The study indicate that it is difficult to find suitable training data to accurately detect and classify the type of stroke located at an arbitrary position in the head.

Author Contributions: Conceptualization, T.P., J.V. and M.S.; methodology, T.P., J.V., O.F., M.S., L.T. and A.P.; software, T.P., D.V., T.D. and M.N.; validation, T.P., J.V. and M.S.; formal analysis, T.P., J.V. and M.N.; investigation, T.P., T.D. and O.F.; resources, T.P.; data curation, T.P.; writing—original draft preparation, T.P. and J.V.; writing—review and editing, T.P., J.V., M.S., D.V., T.D., M.N., O.F., L.T. and A.P.; visualization, T.P. and O.F.; supervision, J.V., D.V. and M.S.; project administration, T.P. and D.V.; funding acquisition, J.V. and D.V. All authors have read and agreed to the published version of the manuscript.

Funding: This research was funded by the research program of the Czech Science Foundation, Project no. 21-00579S and by the Grant Agency of the Czech Technical University in Prague, grant name: Microwave Imaging Methods for Medical Applications.

Data Availability Statement: DataSets from 2D numerical simulations can be downloaded after filling out the form: https://forms.gle/K2WPhfsXgTmgJCnh6 (accessed on 9 February 2023).

Conflicts of Interest: The authors declare no conflict of interest. The funders had no role in the design of the study; in the collection, analyses, or interpretation of data; in the writing of the manuscript; or in the decision to publish the results.

Appendix A

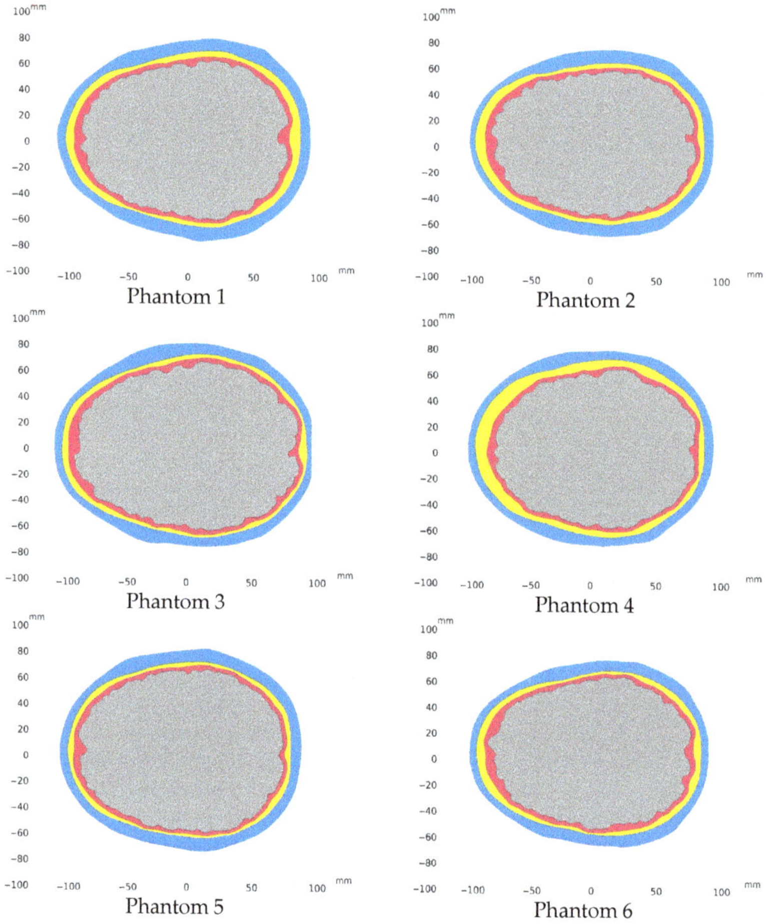

Figure A1. *Cont.*

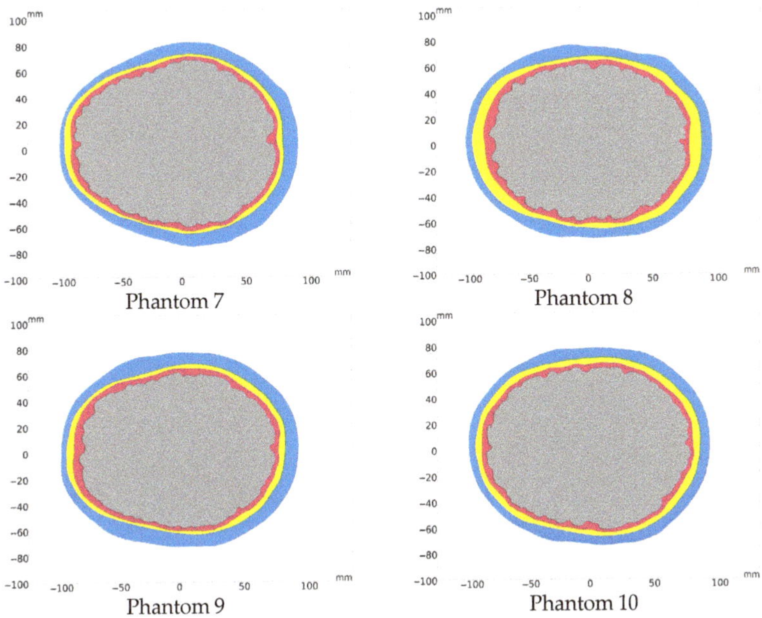

Figure A1. 10 different human head model geometries based on real subjects.

Appendix B

Graphs of classification accuracy and cross-validation error for different dimensionality reductions for different numbers of frequency points.

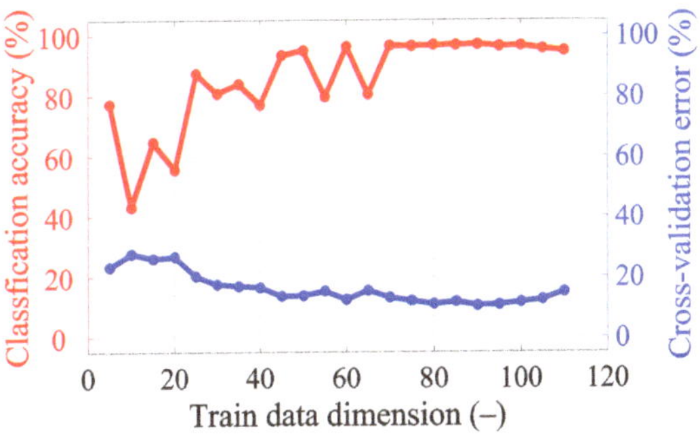

Figure A2. Classification accuracy and cross-validation error for different dimensionality reductions in data for a single frequency point (1 GHz).

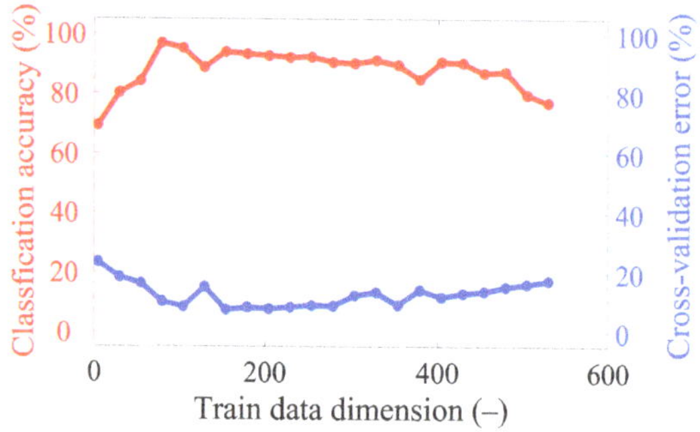

Figure A3. Classification accuracy and cross-validation error for different dimensionality reductions in the data for five frequency points (from 0.8 GHz, step 0.1 GHz, to 1.2 GHz).

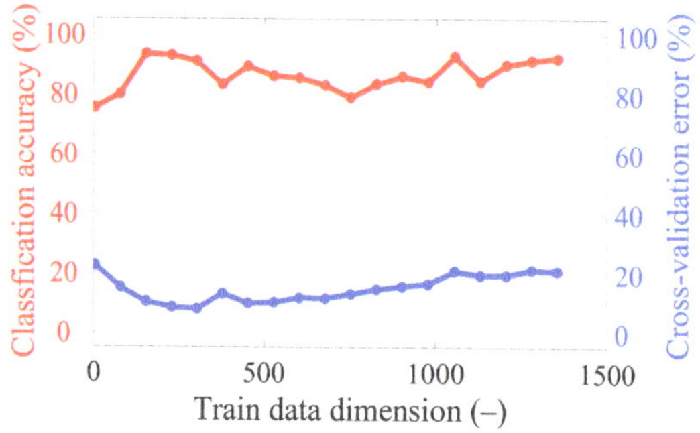

Figure A4. Classification accuracy and cross-validation error for different dimensionality reductions in data for 15 frequency points (from 0.8 GHz, step 0.05 GHz, to 1.5 GHz).

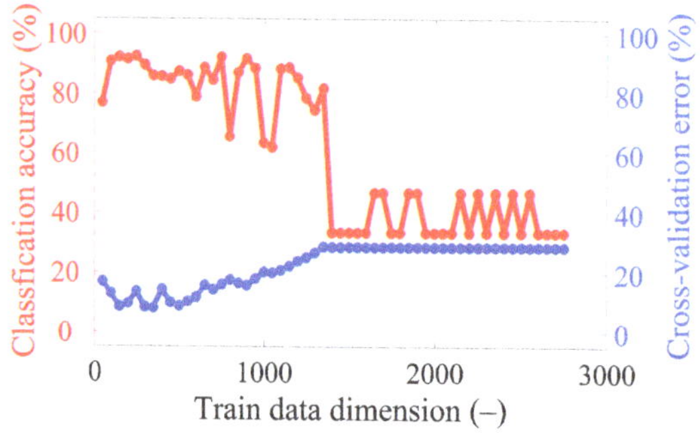

Figure A5. Classification accuracy and cross-validation error for different dimensionality reductions in the data for 25 frequency points (from 0.8 GHz, step 0.05 GHz, to 2 GHz).

Appendix C

This appendix presents the S-parameter changes induced by the virtual presence of ischemic and hemorrhagic strokes calculated using 2D and 3D numerical models. These changes were calculated by subtracting the S-parameters for the case when the inner part of the antenna system was filled only with the matching medium ($\varepsilon r = 40$, $\sigma = 1$ S/m) from the S-parameters for the case where the stroke model was added virtually.

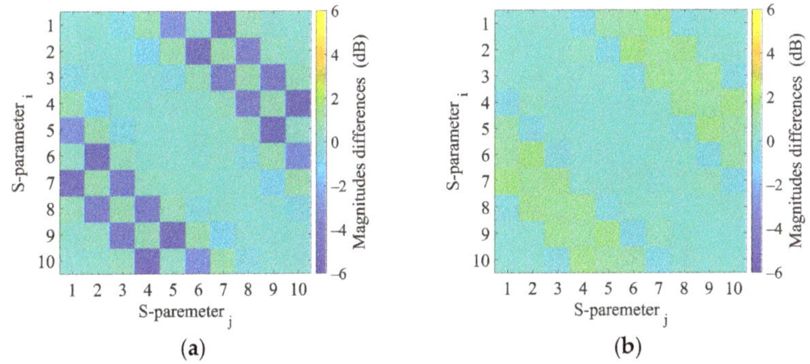

Figure A6. 2D numerical simulations. Magnitudes difference of 2D numerical model induced by the virtual presence of a 4 cm radius (**a**) hemorrhagic and (**b**) ischemic stroke located at position (0, 0).

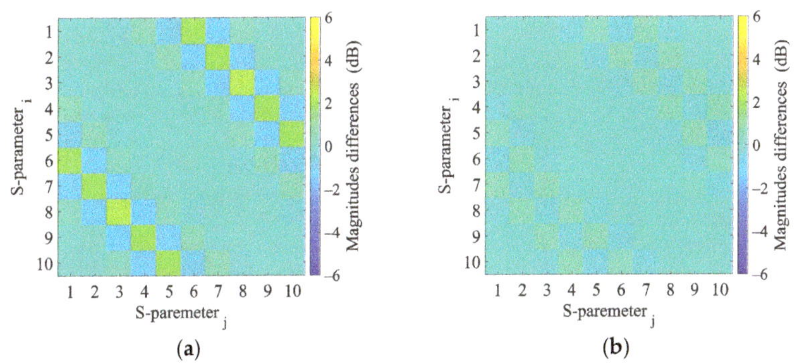

Figure A7. 3D numerical simulations. Magnitudes difference of 3D numerical model induced by the virtual presence of a 4 cm radius (**a**) hemorrhagic and (**b**) ischemic stroke located at position (0, 0).

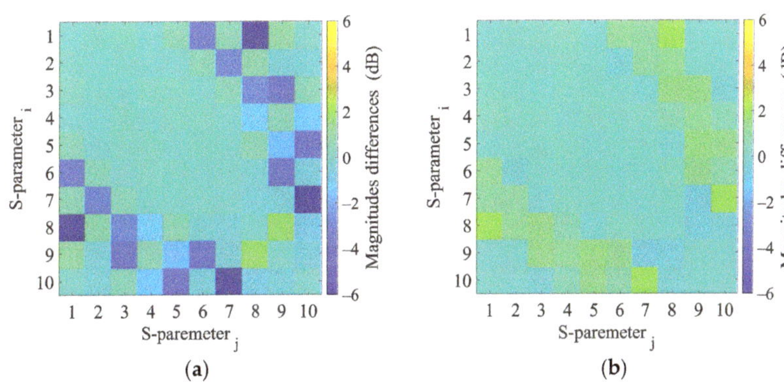

Figure A8. 2D numerical simulations. Magnitudes difference of 2D numerical model induced by the virtual presence of a 4 cm radius (**a**) hemorrhagic and (**b**) ischemic stroke located at position (−20, 30).

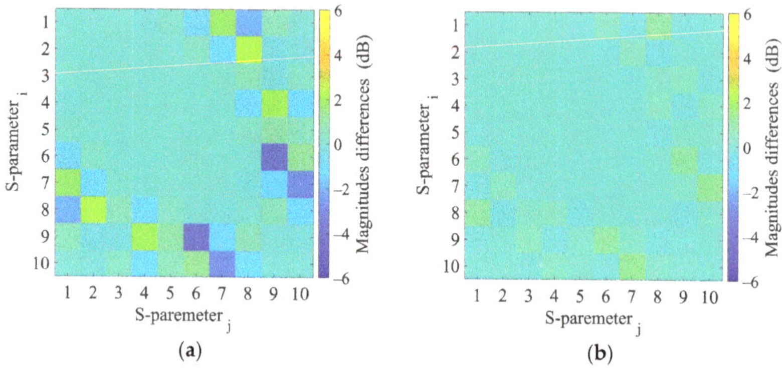

Figure A9. 3D numerical simulations. Calculated differences in S-parameters induced by the virtual presence of a 4 cm radius (**a**) hemorrhagic and (**b**) ischemic stroke located at position (−20, 30).

References

1. Meaney, P.M. Microwave Imaging and Emerging Applications. *Int. J. Biomed. Imaging* **2012**, *2012*, 252093. [CrossRef] [PubMed]
2. Semenov, S.; Huynh, T.; Williams, T.; Nicholson, B.; Vasilenko, A. Dielectric properties of brain tissue at 1 GHz in acute ischemic stroke: Experimental study on swine. *Bioelectromagnetics* **2017**, *38*, 158–163. [CrossRef] [PubMed]
3. Salucci, M.; Arrebola, M.; Shan, T.; Li, M. Artificial Intelligence: New Frontiers in Real-Time Inverse Scattering and Electromagnetic Imaging. *IEEE Trans. Antennas Propag.* **2022**, *70*, 6349–6364. [CrossRef]
4. Massa, A.; Oliveri, G.; Salucci, M.; Anselmi, N.; Rocca, P. Learning-by-examples techniques as applied to electromagnetics. *J. Electromagn. Waves Appl.* **2018**, *32*, 516–541. [CrossRef]
5. Oliveri, G.; Rocca, P.; Massa, A. SVM for Electromagnetics: State-of-art, potentialities, and trends. In Proceedings of the 2012 IEEE International Symposium on Antennas and Propagation, Chicago, IL, USA, 8–14 July 2012; pp. 1–2.
6. Persson, M.; Fhager, A.; Trefná, H.D.; Yu, Y.; McKelvey, T.; Pegenius, G.; Karlsson, J.E.; Elam, M. Microwave-Based Stroke Diagnosis Making Global Prehospital Thrombolytic Treatment Possible. *IEEE Trans. Biomed. Eng.* **2014**, *61*, 2806–2817. [CrossRef]
7. Zhu, G.; Bialkowski, A.; Guo, L.; Mohammed, B.; Abbosh, A. Stroke Classification in Simulated Electromagnetic Imaging Using Graph Approaches. *IEEE J. Electromagn. RF Microw. Med. Biol.* **2021**, *5*, 46–53. [CrossRef]
8. Li, J.; Zhu, G.; Xi, M. Automating Stroke Subtype Classification from Electromagnetic Signals Using Principal Component Methods. In Proceedings of the The 7th International Workshop on Advanced Computational Intelligence and Intelligent Informatics (IWACIII2021), Beijing, China, 31 October–3 November 2021.
9. Fhager, A.; Candefjord, S.; Elam, M.; Persson, M. 3D Simulations of Intracerebral Hemorrhage Detection Using Broadband Microwave Technology. *Sensors* **2019**, *19*, 3482. [CrossRef] [PubMed]
10. Candefjord, S.; Winges, J.; Malik, A.A.; Yu, Y.; Rylander, T.; McKelvey, T.; Fhager, A.; Elam, M.; Persson, M. Microwave technology for detecting traumatic intracranial bleedings: Tests on phantom of subdural hematoma and numerical simulations. *Med. Biol. Eng. Comput.* **2017**, *55*, 1177–1188. [CrossRef] [PubMed]
11. Merunka, I.; Massa, A.; Vrba, D.; Fiser, O.; Salucci, M.; Vrba, J. Microwave Tomography System for Methodical Testing of Human Brain Stroke Detection Approaches. Available online: https://www.hindawi.com/journals/ijap/2019/4074862/abs/ (accessed on 8 April 2019).
12. Salucci, M.; Vrba, J.; Merunka, I.; Massa, A. Real-time brain stroke detection through a learning-by-examples technique—An experimental assessment. *Microw. Opt. Technol. Lett.* **2017**, *59*, 2796–2799. [CrossRef]
13. Salucci, M.; Gelmini, A.; Vrba, J.; Merunka, I.; Oliveri, G.; Rocca, P. Instantaneous brain stroke classification and localization from real scattering data. *Microw. Opt. Technol. Lett.* **2019**, *61*, 808. [CrossRef]
14. Pokorny, T.; Tesarik, J. Microwave Stroke Detection and Classification Using Different Methods from MATLAB's Classification Learner Toolbox. In Proceedings of the 2019 European Microwave Conference in Central Europe (EuMCE), Prague, Czech Republic, 13–15 May 2019; pp. 500–503.
15. Salucci, M.; Polo, A.; Vrba, J. Multi-Step Learning-by-Examples Strategy for Real-Time Brain Stroke Microwave Scattering Data Inversion. *Electronics* **2021**, *10*, 95. [CrossRef]
16. *COMSOL Multiphysics®*; COMSOL AB: Stockholm, Sweden, 2022; Available online: www.comsol.com (accessed on 9 January 2023).
17. Tesarik, J.; Pokorny, T.; Vrba, J. Dielectric sensitivity of different antennas types for microwave-based head imaging: Numerical study and experimental verification. *Int. J. Microw. Wirel. Technol.* **2020**, *12*, 982–995. [CrossRef]
18. Erik, G.; Lee, R.L.H. *Population Head Model Repository V1.0*; IT'IS Foundation: Zurich, Switzerland, 2016. [CrossRef]
19. *Materialize 3-Matic*; Leuven, Belgium. Available online: www.materialise.com (accessed on 9 January 2023).

20. Said, T.; Varadan, V.V. Variation of Cole-Cole model parameters with the complex permittivity of biological tissues. In Proceedings of the 2009 IEEE MTT-S International Microwave Symposium Digest, Boston, MA, USA, 7–12 June 2009; pp. 1445–1448.
21. Hasgall, P.A.; Di Gennnaro, F.; Baumgartner, C.; Neufeld, E.; Lloyd, B.; Gosselin, M.C.; Payne, D.; Klingenböck, A.; Kuster, N. *IT'IS Database for Thermal and Electromagnetic Parameters of Biological Tissues, version 4.0*; IT'IS Foundation: Zurich, Switzerland, 2018. [CrossRef]
22. *IEEE Std 1528-2013 Revis. IEEE Std 1528-2003*; IEEE Recommended Practice for Determining the Peak Spatial-Average Specific Absorption Rate (SAR) in the Human Head from Wireless Communications Devices: Measurement Techniques. IEEE: New York, NY, USA, 2013; pp. 1–246. [CrossRef]
23. McGurgan, I.J.; Ziai, W.C.; Werring, D.J.; Salman, R.A.-S.; Parry-Jones, A.R. Acute intracerebral haemorrhage: Diagnosis and management. *Pract. Neurol.* **2021**, *21*, 128–136. [CrossRef] [PubMed]
24. Mariano, V.; Tobon Vasquez, J.A.; Casu, M.R.; Vipiana, F. Brain Stroke Classification via Machine Learning Algorithms Trained with a Linearized Scattering Operator. *Diagnostics* **2023**, *13*, 23. [CrossRef] [PubMed]
25. Tesarik, J.; Diaz Rondon, L.F.; Fiser, O. Prototype of Simplified Microwave Imaging System for Brain Stroke Follow Up. In Proceedings of the World Congress on Medical Physics and Biomedical Engineering 2018, Prague, Czech Republic, 3–8 June 2018; Lhotska, L., Sukupova, L., Lacković, I., Ibbott, G.S., Eds.; Springer: Singapore, 2019; pp. 771–774.
26. Pokorny, T.; Vrba, D.; Tesarik, J.; Rodrigues, D.B.; Vrba, J. Anatomically and Dielectrically Realistic 2.5D 5-Layer Reconfigurable Head Phantom for Testing Microwave Stroke Detection and Classification. Available online: https://www.hindawi.com/journals/ijap/2019/5459391/ (accessed on 25 November 2019).

sensors

MDPI

Article

Comparison of Microwave Hyperthermia Applicator Designs with Fora Dipole and Connected Array

Gulsah Yildiz [1,*], Iman Farhat [2,*], Lourdes Farrugia [2], Julian Bonello [2], Kristian Zarb-Adami [2], Charles V. Sammut [2], Tuba Yilmaz [1,3] and Ibrahim Akduman [1,3]

[1] Department of Electronics and Communication Engineering, Istanbul Technical University, 34469 Istanbul, Turkey
[2] Department of Physics, University of Malta, MSD 2080 Msida, Malta
[3] Mitos Medical Technologies, 34467 Istanbul, Turkey
* Correspondence: gulsahyildiz@itu.edu.tr (G.Y.); iman.farhat@um.edu.mt (I.F.)

Abstract: In microwave hyperthermia tumor therapy, electromagnetic waves focus energy on the tumor to elevate the temperature above its normal levels with minimal injury to the surrounding healthy tissue. Microwave hyperthermia applicator design is important for the effectiveness of the therapy and the feasibility of real-time application. In this study, the potential of using fractal octagonal ring antenna elements as a dipole antenna array and as a connected array at 2.45 GHz for breast tumor hyperthermia application was investigated. Microwave hyperthermia treatment models consisting of different fractal octagonal ring antenna array designs and a breast phantom are simulated in COMSOL Multiphysics to obtain the field distributions. The antenna excitation phases and magnitudes are optimized using the global particle swarm algorithm to selectively increase the specific absorption rate at the target region while minimizing hot spots in other regions within the breast. Specific absorption rate distributions, obtained inside the phantom, are analyzed for each proposed microwave hyperthermia applicator design. The dipole fractal octagonal ring antenna arrays are comparatively assessed for three different designs: circular, linear, and Cross–array. The 16-antenna dipole array performance was superior for all three 1-layer applicator designs, and no distinct difference was found between 16-antenna circular, linear, or cross arrays. Two-layer dipole arrays have better performance in the deep-tissue targets than one-layer arrays. The performance of the connected array with a higher number of layers exceeds the performance of the dipole arrays in the superficial regions, while they are comparable for deep regions of the breast. The 1-layer 12-antenna circular FORA dipole array feasibility as a microwave hyperthermia applicator was experimentally shown.

Keywords: microwave hyperthermia; cancer therapeutics; fractal octagonal ring array; dipole antenna; connected array; particle swarm optimization

Citation: Yildiz, G.; Farhat, I.; Farrugia, L.; Bonello, J.; Zarb-Adami, K.; Sammut, C.V.; Yilmaz, T.; Akduman, I. Comparison of Microwave Hyperthermia Applicator Designs with Fora Dipole and Connected Array. *Sensors* **2023**, *23*, 6592. https://doi.org/10.3390/s23146592

Academic Editors: Mikael Persson and Hoi-Shun Antony Lui

Received: 29 May 2023
Revised: 3 July 2023
Accepted: 19 July 2023
Published: 21 July 2023

1. Introduction

Hyperthermia (HT) studies have attested that elevated tissue temperature can damage and shrink cancerous cells while causing minimal harm to normal tissues [1]. Moreover, HT makes some of the tumor cells more susceptible to radiation therapy and chemotherapy [2]. Hence, it has been used to treat different types of advanced cancers in combination with various other forms of cancer therapy, including radiation therapy and chemotherapy [3]. HT is a process that artificially elevates tumor temperature to between 40 °C and 45 °C for a sufficient period of time (30–60 min) while maintaining the normal body temperature in the remaining tissue [3]. HT can be delivered using three different modalities, such as ultrasound, thermal conduction, and microwave radiation devices. However, the final effect varies for every tissue depending on its location and constituents, such as fat, water, or bone. This study focuses on a noninvasive system of microwave hyperthermia (HT) to be used in the treatment of breast cancer.

A relatively high proportion of carcinomas arises in the upper outer quadrant of the breasts [4]. However, malignant tissues can develop deep or at any location within the breast, even near the chest wall. Hence, clinical HT applicators should possess controllable power deposition profiles to treat lesions of varying sizes and shapes that may occur at diverse locations within the breast. HT employs beamforming techniques to focus microwave energy on the breast tumor by adjusting the excitation phase and amplitudes of the antenna array. Therefore, the choice of the HT applicator and its array distribution is very important in hyperthermia treatment planning (HTP). Circular-shaped applicators (CA) are the most common applicator type in breast HT [5–7]. The symmetry offered by CA provides good coverage of the breast tissue. Linearly distributed applicator (LA) designs have also been proposed [8–10]; however, their practice has not been appealing because it has low coverage due to non-symmetrical geometry. In a recent study, the physical rotation of the linear array has been proposed to better align LA with the target, and thus enhance the focusing performance [11]. Furthermore, a formation of a hemispherical hyperthermia chamber deploying an antenna array around the breast has been shown to realize selective heating of a tumor in a sample [12–14]. It offers a comfortable and wearable hyperthermia system that can provide complete coverage of the breast. This enables conformal tumor heating by mechanically or electronically scanning a highly focused beam through the target region at various breast locations [12,15]. Moreover, efficient HT focusing can be achieved for small deep-seated breast tumors utilizing radiating elements implemented in a symmetric cross configuration [16,17]. In [18,19] a Cross–array (XA) arrangement of four sub-arrays of corrugated tapered slot antennas for application in three-dimensional (3D) HT was investigated using MRI-derived realistic 3D breast phantoms in full-wave electromagnetic simulations. The results of this array configuration illustrated the possibility of selectively heating a tumor volume of 1 cm^3 in gland tissue.

This paper employs fractal octagonal ring antenna (FORA) elements for a near-field phased array antenna and explores its feasibility for an efficient HT system. FORA is a printable antenna that can be tailored for a wide range of applications [20]. Implementation of FORA under flat and curvature conditions would be valuable for HT therapy systems to follow the patient's body contour. Two types of antenna system were adopted using FORA elements, which are the disconnected dipole arrays and the connected arrays. The FORA dipole array is a standard narrow-band antenna design, intended to keep low mutual coupling between the radiating elements, so as not to unduly alter the performance of each isolated element. On the other hand, a FORA–connected array is a broadband array design in which mutual coupling is intentionally introduced between the array elements in addition to capacitance coupling between the tip ends of each element [21]. This enables almost continuous current flow among the different FORA elements, thus realizing the continuous current sheet proposed by Wheeler [22]. The earlier works of the authors are related to wide-band Vivaldi antennas, tailored especially for imaging applications [8,10,11]. In this work, FORA dipole provides the narrow-band application, while FORA–connected array provides the conformal and wide-band characteristic that can be used in a future wearable hyperthermia device application.

For efficient microwave focusing, global particle swarm optimization (PSO) was used to find the optimum antenna excitations, which enables constructive interference in the desired target region and destructive interference elsewhere. To computationally verify the FORA array performance, a 3D simulation of a cylindrical breast phantom was performed, and two-dimensional (2D) optimization of the antenna excitation parameters was conducted, then the SAR and temperature results were represented in 2D planes.

FORA dipoles were arranged in circular, linear, and Cross–array applicator designs which are compatible with the cylindrical phantom geometry. To assess the applicator design performance in a simple medium, a homogeneous fat phantom was used, and the positions of different applicator designs were pre-adjusted to show their best performance at the investigated target locations. One-layer dipole applicators were investigated for varying antenna numbers and inter-antenna distances. The best-performing designs of the

1-layer applicators were then investigated for two layers, and for the inter-layer distance. The FORA–connected array was investigated for different antenna numbers and layer numbers, and thus different curvatures. Comparisons between the 1- and 2-layer FORA dipole applicators and different designs of FORA–connected arrays are given. Comparisons presented in this paper are based on the target-to-breast SAR ratio and the necessary total antenna power to reach the desired temperature at the target.

An experimental setup with a 1-layer 12-antenna circular FORA dipole array and fat-mimicking phantom is presented. The computed result and the experimental result are compared to each other.

The main contributions of this work can be summarized as follows:

- FORA antenna element is proposed to be used in an HT application.
- FORA element is comparatively assessed in the forms of dipole and connected arrays.
- The FORA dipole arrays are comparatively assessed for three different designs (circular, linear, and Cross–array applicators); the number of constituent antennas; the number of antenna layers; inter-antenna distances; antenna-tissue distances; and inter-layer distances.
- The FORA–connected arrays are comparatively assessed for the number of constituent antennas; number of antenna layers; and antenna-tissue distances.
- The use of the FORA circular array as a hyperthermia applicator was experimentally verified on a fat-mimicking phantom.

The rest of the paper is organized as follows: an introduction to Pennes' bio-heat equation that governs the thermodynamic relation in space and time between the SAR and the tissue temperature is given in Section 1.1. The following methodology is provided in Section 2, where the phantom, the FORA antenna, the HT applicator designs, and the simulation environment are explained in detail. In Section 3, 1- and 2-layer dipole HT applicator design results as well as the connected FORA array design results are provided, and the experimental results are presented. Finally, the authors conclude the work in Section 4.

1.1. Pennes' Bio-Heat Equation

The normal body tissue temperature is $T_0 = 37\ ^\circ\text{C}$. Once heated with an applicator during hyperthermia therapy, the heat transmission process in living tissue includes thermal conduction, blood circulation and perfusion, and metabolic heat output. Pennes [23] was the first to develop a mathematical model that describes heat transfer in human tissue involving the effects of blood flow on tissue temperature on a continuum basis, assuming the venous blood temperature is equivalent to the local tissue temperature. Pennes' bio-heat equation is the most widely used thermal model for studying heat transfer phenomena associated with hyperthermia treatment modalities. For the transient problem, the temperature distribution in the breast phantom is addressed by Pennes' bio-heat model expressed in (1), which allows for a different blood temperature.

$$C_p\rho\frac{\partial T}{\partial t} = \nabla \cdot (K\nabla T) + Q_m + \rho SAR - B(T - T_b) \tag{1}$$

where C_p is tissue-specific heat capacity, ρ is the tissue density, K is thermal conductivity, T is the temperature, T_b is the blood temperature, Q_m is the metabolic heat generation, B is the capillary blood perfusion coefficient. These parameters are tissue-specific. The specific absorption rate (SAR) depends on the external heating source, as well as tissue-specific parameters. SAR can be formulated as:

$$SAR = 0.5\frac{\sigma|E|^2}{\rho} \qquad \text{W/kg} \tag{2}$$

where E is the electric field (V/m) in the tissue and σ (S/m) is the electrical conductivity. By Green's function approach, it was shown in [5] that the maxima of SAR and the temperature are located at the same point, assuming K and B are constants and in a steady state. Based on this result, the approach adopted in the present work was first to focus the maximum SAR on the target tissue and then scale the intensity to reach the desired tissue temperature.

2. Materials and Methods

2.1. Numerical Breast Phantom

We used a numerical homogeneous breast phantom model centered at (0, 0, 0) mm, consisting of fatty breast tissue in the form of a cylinder with a diameter and height of 90 mm. The phantom dielectric properties were taken from the phantom repository of the University of Wisconsin Cross-Disciplinary Electromagnetics Laboratory [24,25]. Fatty-1 tissue was used for the fat cylinder phantom, and the Debye parameters provided by [24,25] are given in Table 1. The constant dielectric parameters were calculated at the frequency of 2.45 GHz as e_r = 3.9095 and σ = 0.339 S/m. Thermal properties provided in Table 1 for breast fat tissue were taken from [26].

Table 1. The Debye parameters of the fat tissue dielectric properties. Thermal properties of the fat tissue.

Debye Model Parameters	ϵ_∞ 2.85	$\Delta\epsilon$ 1.10	σ_s (S/m) 0.01	τ (ps) 13.00
Dielectric Properties at 2.45 GHz	ϵ_r 3.9095	σ (S/m) 0.339		
Thermal Properties	ρ (kg/m^3) 932	C_p (J/kg/K) 2220	k (W/m/K) 0.17	Qm (W/m^3) 458

2.2. FORA

The antenna elements are based on fractal octagonal ring array geometry (referred to as FORA), a form of iterative octagon rings subdivided into sequences such that each sequence is a reduced size of the outer octagonal ring, with a scaling factor of 0.91. Two types of antennas were developed based on the proposed fractal elements, the dipole FORA antenna (Figure 1a) and the connected FORA antenna (Figure 1b). The dipole FORA antenna consists of two identical FORA elements matched to 50 Ω input impedance, such that the inter-element distance between the elements is 0.3 mm and the spacing between dipole arrays is one of the key parameters to balance between the room limitation and the mutual coupling. The dipole is fed through the 0.3 mm feed point between the FORA elements, see Figure 1a. The material of the antennas was selected as a perfectly electric conductor (PEC) throughout the simulations.

The connected FORA antenna is an array of FORA dipoles that are electrically connected, arranged such they are closely packed with an inter-element distance of 4 mm ($<< \lambda/2$ of the highest operating frequency-5 GHz-) between the arrays in one direction. The dimension of a single antenna element in the connected array should always be less than half the wavelength of the operating frequency. Furthermore, it is capacitively coupled in the longitudinal direction using inter-digital capacitors consisting of 6 fingers at each element end. The array in this form is no longer composed of separated resonant elements but can be considered to be a single antenna periodically fed and backed by a ground plane at a distance of ≈20 mm from the array elements [27]. The FORA–connected array is linearly polarized and matched to an input impedance of 180 Ω. The antennas were fed through the 4 mm feed points between the FORA elements, see Figure 1b.

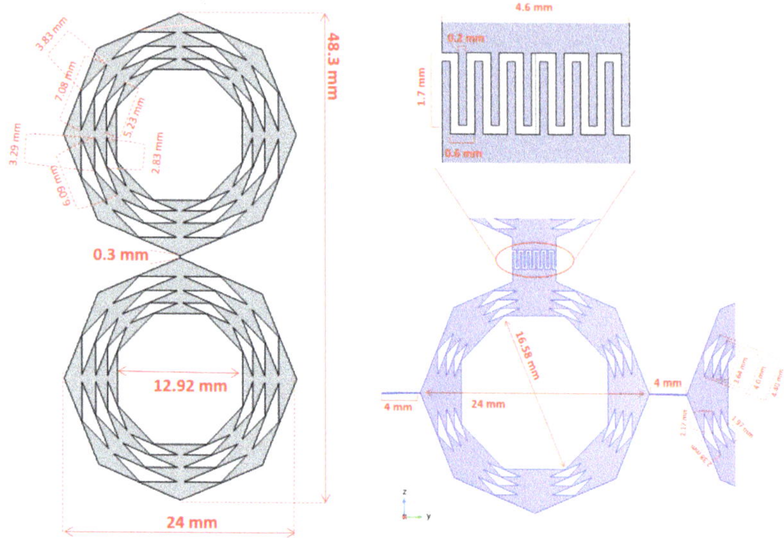

(a) (b)

Figure 1. (**a**) FORA dipole element. (**b**) FORA−connected element and the inter-digital capacitor between the two elements in consecutive layers.

The reflection coefficient performance of the two FORA antennas, namely the FORA dipole array and FORA−connected array, in the vicinity of the fat phantom are illustrated in Figure 2. As can be seen from both Figure 2a,b, the FORA dipole and the FORA−connected array are well matched with a return loss of less than −10 dB at the frequency of 2.45 GHz. This indicates that the incident power is efficiently transferred to the FORA antenna array and in turn, to the breast phantom. Figure 2b illustrates S11 parameters performance for different elements of the FORA−connected array fed at the center (the blue line), at distant from the center of the 3 × 13 FORA connected array (yellow line) and the upper layer of the array just above the central element (orange line). Unlike the FORA−connected array where the S11 depends on the position of the elements in the array, the FORA dipole elements in the array exhibit similar S11 performance in the FORA dipole array deployed linearly, as can be seen in Figure 2a.

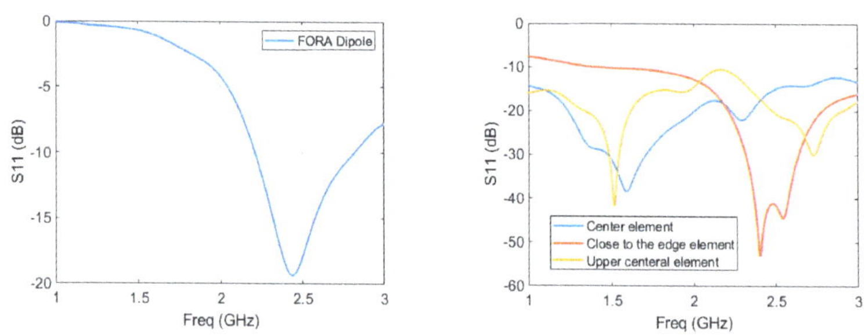

(a) (b)

Figure 2. (**a**) Simulated S11 parameter as a function of frequency for a single FORA Dipole antenna in a linear array configuration, (**b**) and for different FORA−connected array elements.

The FORA dipole element in a linear array consists of four elements and has a 3 dB beam width of 40.5° in the elevation plane whereas 33.3° in the azimuth plane. For the embedded element pattern in the connected array, there is a 3 dB beam width of 39.6° in the elevation plane whereas 39.2° in the azimuth plane. The maximum gains obtained for a single element at the center of the array are 1.7 dBi and 4.75 dBi for the dipole array and connected array, respectively. This is expected since the connected array has a ground plane and therefore has a higher gain that varies between 4 dBi to 8 dBi depending on the position of the element in the array. The bandwidths obtained by the FORA dipole and the connected array middle element are 24.5% and 81.6%, respectively. These bandwidths are enough for narrow-band hyperthermia applications.

2.3. *HT Applicators*

Different HT applicator designs were carefully investigated in this paper. First, a single layer of FORA dipoles was simulated, the results were analyzed, and the 2D, $z = 0$ plane was chosen for this scenario. Linear, circular, and cross arrays were implemented with FORA dipole antennas. Second, the 1-layer applicators which show the best performance were duplicated on the second layer and positioned such that they were symmetrical with respect to the $z = 0$ slice. The 2D evaluation was conducted on the same $z = 0$ plane, and the effect of the layer separation, dz, was investigated for the 2-layer dipole arrays. Finally, the connected FORA array was investigated for multiple layers and the number of antennas. The inter-antenna distances dy and dz are provided as multiples of the free space wavelength, $\lambda_0 \approx 122.45$ mm.

2.3.1. Linear Array

The dipole antennas were placed on two opposite sides of the phantom with the same alignment. The distance between the first and the last antenna is dy, and the distance between the consecutive antennas is $\frac{dy}{N/2-1}$. A linear HT applicator with 8 antennas together with a cylindrical phantom can be seen in Figure 3c. An N−antenna linear array will be referred to as LA^N for convenience. The analyzed parameters for the linear array are as follows:

- Number of antennas (N): 6, 8, 12, 16, 20 antennas
- dx: Distance between the tip of the antennas and the phantom
- dy: Distance between the first and the last antennas

2.3.2. Circular Array

The dipole antennas were arranged in a circle of radius $r_{antenna} = (45 \text{ mm} + \Delta r)$ around the phantom ($r_{phantom} = 45$ mm), and have an angular separation of 360/N degrees. A circular HT applicator with 8 antennas around a cylindrical phantom is shown in Figure 3a. An N−antenna circular array will be referred to as CA^N for convenience. The analyzed parameters for the circular array are as follows:

- Number of antennas (N): 6, 8, 12, 16, 20 antennas
- Δr: Distance between the tip of the antennas and the phantom

2.3.3. Cross−Array

The dipole antennas were situated at the edges of a square centered on the axis of the phantom. The distance between the first and the last antenna is dy, and the distance between the consecutive antennas is $\frac{dy}{N/4-1}$. A cross HT applicator with 16 antennas is depicted in Figure 3b. An N−antenna Cross−array will be referred to as XA^N for convenience. The analyzed parameters for the Cross−array are as follows:

- Number of antennas (N): 8, 12, 16, 20 antennas
- dx: Distance between the tip of the antennas and the phantom
- dy: Distance between the first and the last antennas

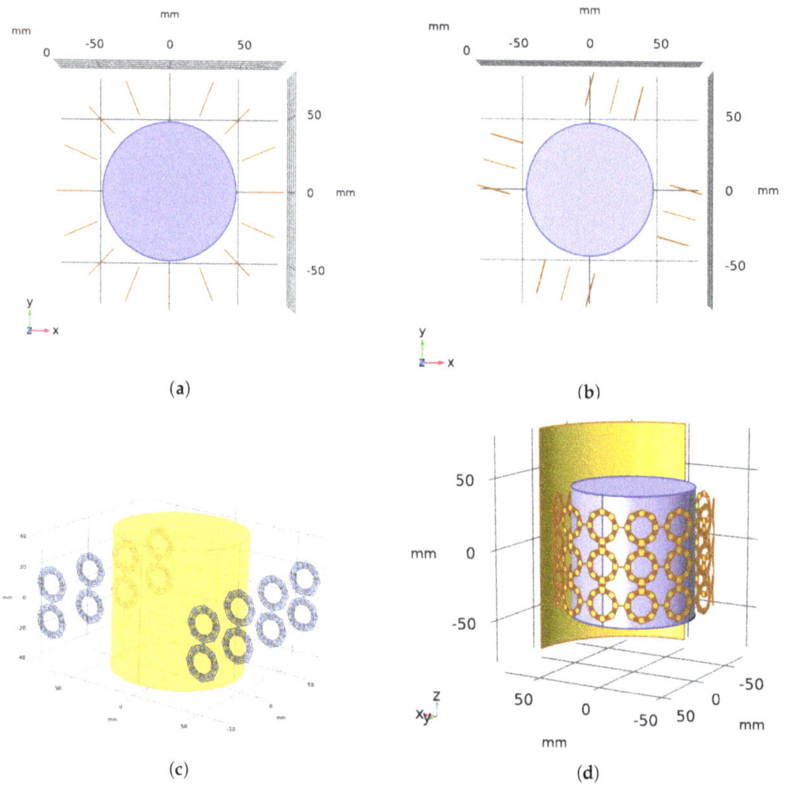

Figure 3. (**a**) Circular array with 16 FORA dipoles (top view). (**b**) Cross–array with 12 FORA dipoles (top view). (**c**) Linear array with eight FORA dipoles (side view). (**d**) Connected array with 39 FORA elements and three layers (side view).

2.3.4. Connected Array

The FORA elements are capacitively coupled via inter-digital capacitors in the longitudinal direction, and connected linearly through lumped ports laterally, as seen in Figures 1b and 3d. A connected array with N antennas will be referred to as $ConA^N$ for simplicity. A total of 11 and 13 elements were analyzed for one layer, and the radii of connected arrays were 4 mm and 12.9 mm for the 11- and 13-element arrays, respectively. The curvature of the elements follows the given cylindrical geometry. Two and three layers for the 11-element and two, three, and five layers for 13-element arrays were investigated, namely 2×11, 2×13, 3×11 and 3×13 finite connected arrays with a backing reflector. The inter-element distances were kept the same and less than $0.5\lambda_0$ of the highest operational frequency (3 GHz). The side element and the middle element have one and two inter-digital capacitor arms in the longitudinal direction, respectively. The 2-layer $ConA$ has two layers of side elements, while the 3-layer $ConA$ has an additional layer of middle elements while the 5-layer $ConA$ has three additional layers of middle elements. Furthermore, an 80 mm long cylindrical ground plane is situated at r = 80 mm to direct the radiation towards the phantom.

2.3.5. Antenna Positions of FORA Dipole Arrays

In this paper, we analyze and compare the behavior of three different FORA dipole applicator designs. First, the effect of the FORA dipole orientation was investigated when the dipole is placed parallel and perpendicular to the phantom. Owing to the dipole symmetry, parallel and perpendicular orientations gave the same radiation pattern in free space and a similar pattern within the vicinity of the phantom. We adopt the perpendicular orientation of the FORA dipole for the rest of the paper since the inter-antenna distance can be adjusted much smaller with this configuration.

Second, each applicator design was optimized to give the best performance. To facilitate design comparison, the target centers were set on the positive x-axis, between (0, 0, 0) and (39, 0, 0) mm with increments of (1, 0, 0) mm. Keeping the target locations fixed, each applicator was axially rotated around the origin [11] and the TBR was analyzed. For the circular and the linear applicators, the positions shown in Figures 3a,c gave the individual best performance. For the cross applicator, it was observed that the best results for these targets were reached when the applicator was $-15°$ rotated around the origin, as shown in Figure 3b, and the Cross–array results were taken from the geometry shown in Figure 3b.

2.4. *Simulation Environment*

The EM simulations and numerical calculations were implemented on Windows 10 Pro operating system with an Intel i7 processor and CPU 7800X with 3.50 GHz and 128 GB RAM. EM simulations were conducted using the finite element method (FEM) multiphysics solver COMSOL Multiphysics v6.0. *Electromagnetic Waves, Frequency Domain* physics inside *Radio Frequency* module was run on a single frequency in a frequency domain [28].

2.4.1. Data Generation

The total electric field vector inside the breast phantom with N antenna excitations can be written as [29]:

$$\vec{E}_{tot}(r) = \sum_{i}^{N} a_i \vec{E}_i(r) e^{j\phi_i} \tag{3}$$

where $\vec{E}_i(r)$ is the electric field vector inside the breast when only ith antenna is excited with unitary excitation and $a_i e^{j\phi_i}$ is the ith excitation coefficient with ϕ_i phase difference and a_i amplitude. For every simulation case, N individual $\vec{E}_i(r)$ fields were exported for each antenna from the EM solver and sent to MATLAB. ϕ_i and a_i are the parameters to be optimized for the desired focal point.

2.4.2. SAR Optimization Metrics

In this section, the evaluation metrics to be used for the comparison are explained. Since the principal aim of this work was to focus the SAR on the desired target region, the metrics were devised based on SAR distributions. First, the 2D average spatial SAR operator is defined as follows:

$$avSAR_{\Omega} = \frac{\sum_{\Omega} SAR}{\text{Area of } \Omega} \qquad \text{W/kg/m}^2 \tag{4}$$

where Ω is the surface of the 2D target region and av represents the averaged SAR over Ω. The main objective of the HT is to increase the SAR intensity at the target, while the healthy tissue SAR is kept to a minimum. To this end, target-to-breast ratio (TBR) and hotspot-to-target quotient (HTQ) [30] metrics were defined as follows:

$$TBR = \frac{avSAR_{target}}{avSAR_{breast}} \tag{5}$$

$$HTQ = \frac{avSAR_{hotspot}}{avSAR_{target}} \tag{6}$$

Defining the resolution as the width of the contour where the SAR intensity falls to half its maximum value, the resolution of the HT system inside the homogeneous fat cylinder phantom was ≈24 mm at 2.45 GHz. The desired target dimension is processed as half of this value: a square of 12 mm × 12 mm. The rest of the phantom region is divided into square grids with 12 mm side and $avSAR_{grid}$ is calculated for each of the grids. The hotspot region is chosen automatically as the grid with the highest $avSAR_{grid}$.

As mentioned before, PSO is prone to converge on a local best value depending on the specified initial conditions, which were random in our study. To obtain the underlying trend for each applicator case and to overcome the local convergence issue, a moving maximum filter with four consecutive points was applied to the obtained TBR values, and then a 6th degree polynomial fitting was applied.

2.4.3. Particle Swarm Optimization

Particle Swarm Optimization was used to optimize the antenna excitation parameters, i.e., the phase and the power of the individual antenna feed. PSO has previously been used as an optimization technique in HT [11,16,18,19]. It is a fast optimization technique, and it enables multi-parameter optimization and multi-objective cost functions. In particular, PSO with an inertia weight was used in this study [31]. It has been known that the random initialization of the parameters can cause local solutions, producing a different optimized parameter set every time PSO is applied. To overcome the sensitivity of the system to this issue, each PSO was conducted for 50 repetitions. For each repetition, a swarm size of 100 was iterated 200 times. The optimization process consists of multiple steps, and the corresponding flowchart is shown in Figure 4.

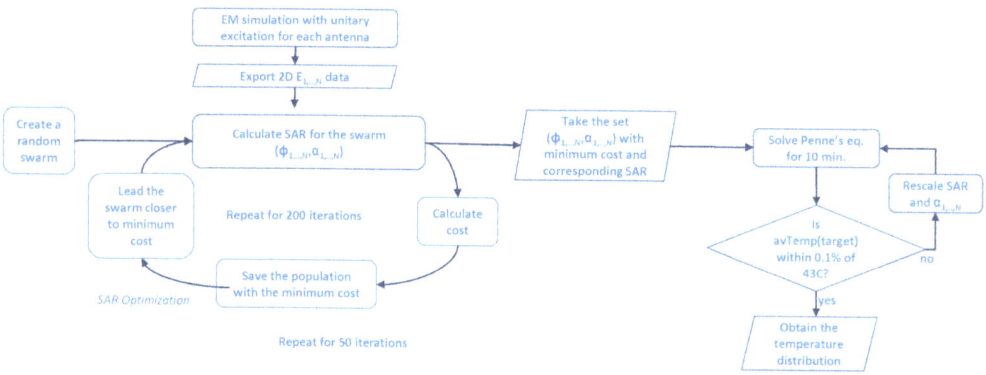

Figure 4. Flowchart of the optimization scheme.

Multi-parameter optimization was implemented: phase difference and amplitude values were optimized together. Initially, the range of values that amplitudes can take was chosen as [0, 1] (V), and the range of values that phase differences can take as $[-\pi, \pi]$ (rad). Cost function to be minimized was chosen as HTQ/TBR. From 50 repetitions, the optimized set of parameters giving the minimum cost was determined to be the solution. Using the optimized SAR distribution, Equation (1) was solved for ten minutes, and the corresponding temperature was calculated. With a feedback algorithm, SAR amplitude values were scaled and Equation (1) was calculated until the temperature level at the desired location increased to 43 °C in ten minutes. With this feedback algorithm, the final optimized amplitudes were recorded for the desired temperature levels.

2.4.4. Temperature Calculation

Pennes' Bio-heat Equation (1) was implemented using a finite difference time domain (FDTD) method in MATLAB. The resulting SAR distribution was fed into this equation to obtain the temperature change as a function of time. The time steps were two seconds and spanned over ten minutes, resulting in 300 time steps. The initial temperature of the phantom was assumed to be 37 °C. Spatial increments in both directions were taken as 1 mm. The Dirichlet boundary condition was used, where the boundary temperatures were equated to 37 °C. Using a feedback loop, the SAR was scaled until the temperature at the desired target reached 43 °C in 10 min. Then, this scaling was used to adjust the antenna excitation amplitudes. The amplitudes were converted into the antenna input power by $P_i[W] = a_i^2[V]/Z[\Omega]$, where a_i was the excitation amplitude of the ith antenna and Z was the port impedance; $Z = 50\ \Omega$ for the dipole and $Z = 180\ \Omega$ for the connected array. The sum of the input powers can be written as $P_{tot} = \sum_i P_i$ [W].

3. Results and Discussion

The results are given first for 1-layer FORA dipole arrays. The best-performing 1-layer HT applicator designs are, then, duplicated to a second layer, and 2-layer FORA dipole array results are provided in Section 3.2. The results from connected FORA arrays are provided in Section 3.3.

A common trend from the resulting data indicates a change in behavior of TBR with position, approximately at x = 8 mm and x = 30 mm. These are indicated with yellow and cyan lines in Figures 5–10. We will refer to targets occurring in the region $0 < x < 8$ mm as deep-seated, those occurring within $8 < x < 30$ mm as the middle region, and those lying beyond x = 30 mm as the superficial region.

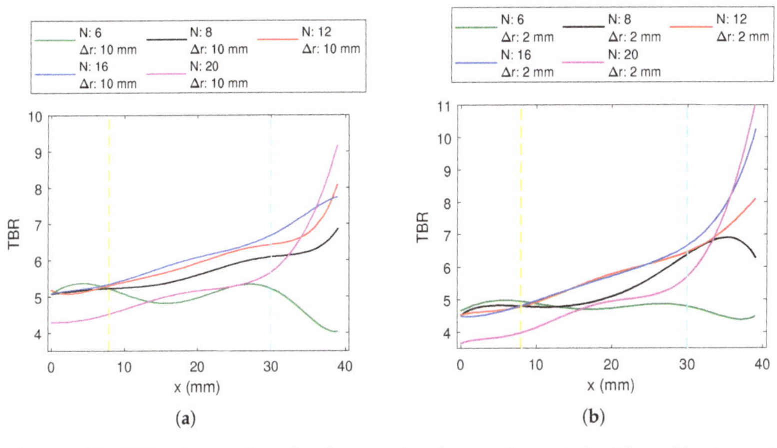

Figure 5. The TBR values evaluated at the target locations on the x-axis for 1-layer N-antenna circular dipole array (CA) with: (**a**) Δr = 10 mm, (**b**) Δr = 2 mm.

3.1. Results of 1-Layer FORA Dipole Arrays

The results of 1-layer circular, linear, and Cross–array HT applicators are presented in this section. The results for each applicator design are presented in separate sub-sections, then the results for N–antenna arrays and the best-performing applicator configuration are grouped and compared.

3.1.1. Circular Applicator

Plots of TBR variation with the target position graphs are shown in Figure 5 for the 1-layer circular array. Figures 5a,b are given for Δr of 10 and 2 mm, respectively. The variation with respect to the number of antennas can be observed. Up to N = 16, the higher the number of antennas, the higher TBR values are obtained. CA^6 has higher TBR for deep-seated targets, and lower TBR for middle and superficial regions. Compared with other antenna numbers, although CA^6 has comparable TBR for deep-seated targets, it gives the lowest value for the remaining target locations. For Δr = 2 mm, CA^{12} and CA^{16} have almost the same values for the deep and the middle-region targets, while CA^{16} provides higher TBR with the superficial regions. CA^{20} has the lowest deep region performance among the investigated antenna numbers for the circular array and has high performance for the superficial regions.

CA with dx = 10 mm have higher TBR at deep and middle regions; however, the performance of CA with dx = 2 mm is better in superficial regions.

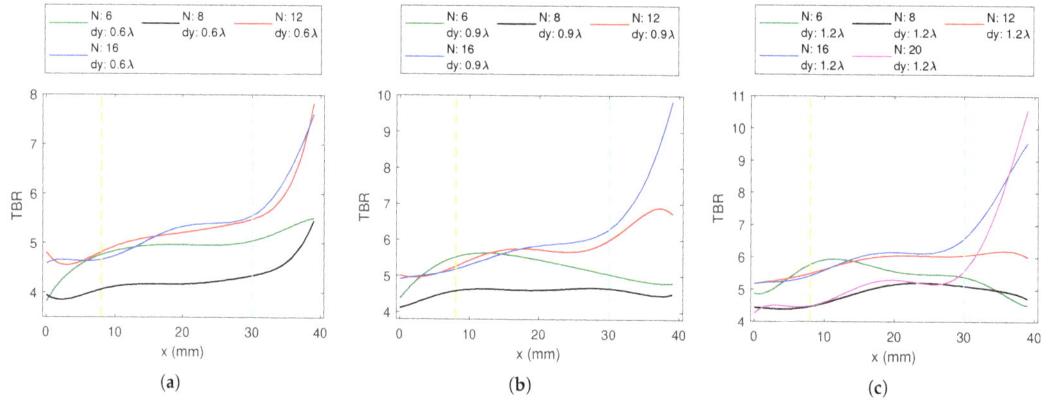

Figure 6. The TBR values evaluated at the target locations on the x-axis for 1-layer N-antenna linear dipole array (LA) with dx = 2 mm and (**a**) $dy = 0.6\ \lambda_0$, (**b**) $dy = 0.9\ \lambda_0$, (**c**) $dy = 1.2\ \lambda_0$.

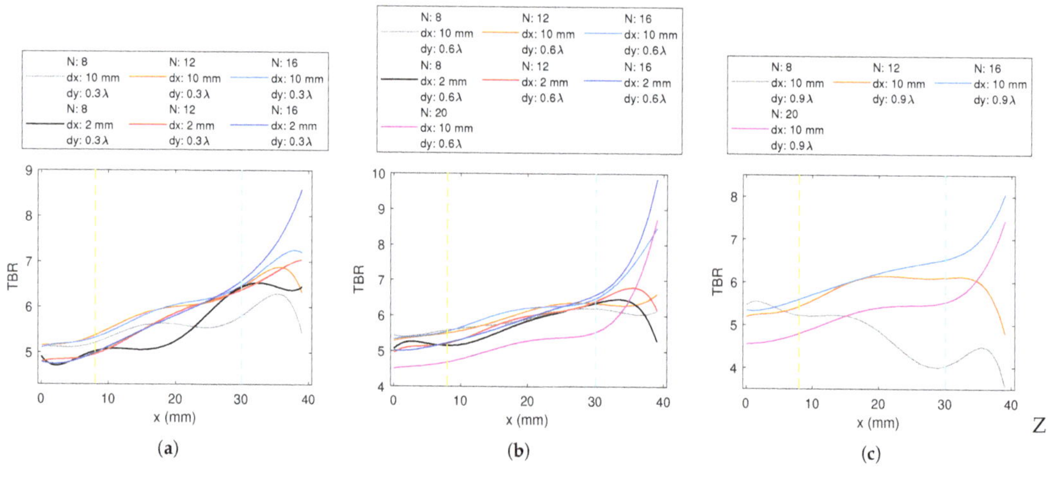

Figure 7. The TBR values evaluated at the target locations on the x-axis for 1-layer N-antenna cross-dipole array (XA) with: (**a**) $dy = 0.3\ \lambda_0$, (**b**) $dy = 0.6\ \lambda_0$, (**c**) $dy = 0.9\ \lambda_0$.

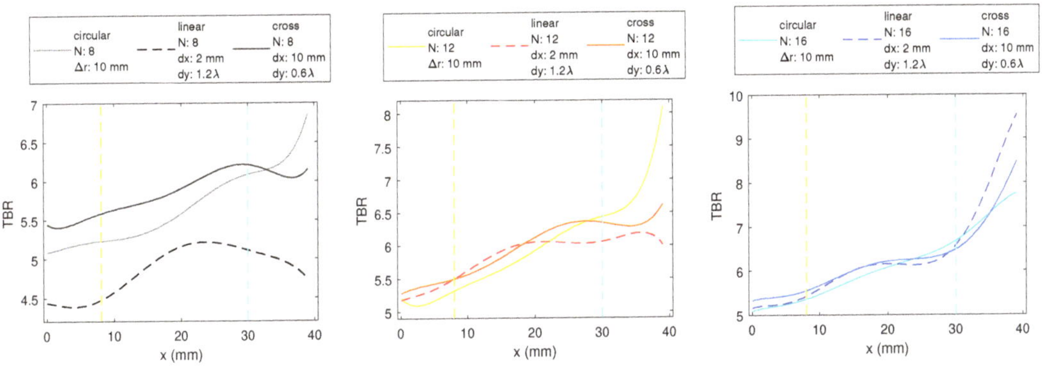

(a) (b) (c)

Figure 8. The *TBR* values evaluated at the target locations on the *x*-axis for: (**a**) 1-layer 8-antenna, (**b**) 1-layer 12-antenna, (**c**) 1-layer 16-antenna circular dipole array (*CA*), linear dipole array (*LA*) and cross-dipole array (*XA*) applicators.

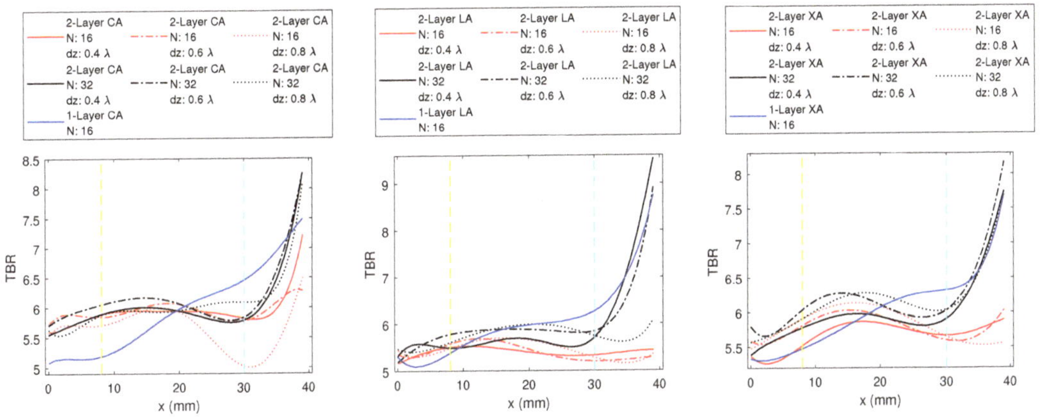

(a) (b) (c)

Figure 9. The *TBR* values evaluated at the target locations on the *x*-axis for: (**a**) 2-layer circular dipole array (*CA*) with Δr = 10 mm and N = 16, N = 32 and 1-layer 16-antenna *CA* with Δr = 10 mm, (**b**) 2-layer linear dipole array (*LA*) with dx = 2 mm and dy = 1.2 λ_0 and N = 16, N = 32 and 1-layer 16-antenna *LA* with dx = 2 mm and dy = 1.2 λ_0, and (**c**) 2-layer cross-dipole array (*XA*) with dx = 10 mm and dy = 0.6 λ_0 and N = 16, N = 32 and 1-layer 16-antenna *XA* with dx = 10 mm and dy = 0.6 λ_0.

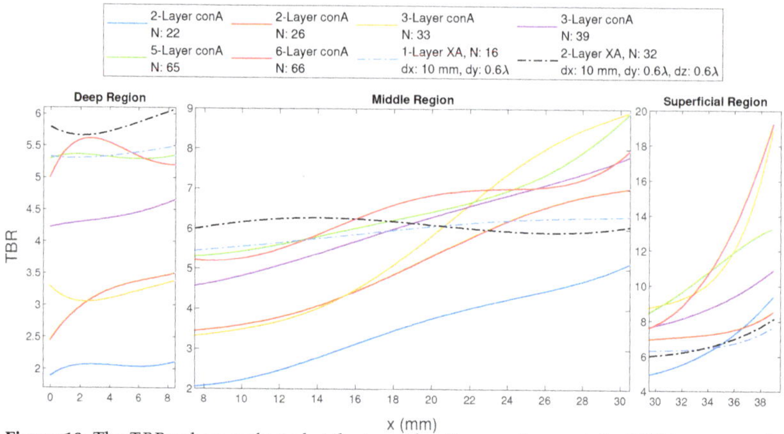

Figure 10. The TBR values evaluated at the target locations on the x-axis for FORA–connected array ($ConA$) with multi-layer, 1-layer 16-antenna cross-dipole array (XA) with dx = 10 mm and $dy = 0.6\ \lambda_0$ and 2-layer 32-antenna cross-dipole array (XA) with dx = 10 mm, $dy = 0.6\ \lambda_0$ and $dz = 0.6\ \lambda_0$.

3.1.2. Linear Applicator

For the 1-layer linear array, dx = 10 mm resulted in smaller TBR than for dx = 2 mm in all cases, and therefore the associated results are omitted. For a fixed dx = 2 mm, TBR plots for different dy values with changing antenna numbers are shown in Figure 6. In contrast with the circular array, the 8-antenna linear array has lower TBR than the 6-antenna array over the phantom for three dy values. LA^{12} and LA^{16} behave similarly for deep and middle targets, while LA^{16} has higher TBR for superficial regions. It can be observed that, in general, as dy increases, TBR also increases. N = 20 was evaluated only for dx = 2 mm and $dy = 1.2\ \lambda_0$ (Figure 6c). LA^{20} has poor deep and middle-region performance but TBR values drastically increase for superficial regions.

3.1.3. Cross Applicator

Figure 7 shows the TBR vs. target location plots of constant dy cases. XA^{16} TBR values are predominantly superior in all the cases, followed by XA^{12}. The slope of XA^{16} increases while the targets become closer to the surface, XA^{12} and XA^{16} follow a very similar trend in the deep and middle regions.

For XA^{8}, dx = 10 mm alignment provided higher TBR than dx = 2 mm in the deep and middle regions. For the same dy values, however, dx = 2 mm shows better performance for the superficial regions. $dy = 0.3\ \lambda_0$ exhibits lower TBR than $dy = 0.6\ \lambda_0$ in the deep and middle regions. For both XA^{8} and XA^{12}, although comparable to others in deep-seated regions, dx = 10 mm and $dy = 0.9\ \lambda_0$ provides much lower TBR in the superficial region (Figure 7c). Up to the superficial region, for XA^{12}, dx = 10 mm was superior to dx = 2 mm, and $dy = 0.6\ \lambda_0$ was superior to $dy = 0.3\ \lambda_0$ (Figures 7a,b). In the superficial region, the performance of dx = 2 mm is superior. All the cases of XA^{16} follow a similar trend. In the deep and middle regions, the combination dx = 10 mm and $dy = 0.6\ \lambda_0$ results in a higher TBR, and $dy = 0.9\ \lambda_0$ was close to $dy = 0.6\ \lambda_0$, contrary to the other antenna numbers. In the superficial regions, the TBR performance with dx = 2 mm increases.

XA^{20} results are given for dx = 10 mm case for both $dy = 0.6\ \lambda_0$ and $0.9\ \lambda_0$ designs. XA^{20} performance was low in the deep and middle regions and above N = 8 and 12 applicators in the superficial regions (Figures 7b,c).

The cases with the highest TBR values for different applicator designs are plotted in Figure 8 for N = 8, 12, and 16. Cross and circular 1-layer applicators with the same N, provide, in general, similar trends of TBR, while the values for circular arrays are slightly inferior to those from cross arrays for deep and middle-region targets, and for N = 8 and 12, much higher in the superficial regions (Figures 8a,c). The linear applicator does not perform as well as the others when $N = 8$ (Figure 8a). The performance of the LA^{12} configuration is comparable to that of XA^{12} in the inner half of the phantom but inferior to the other configurations in the outer half (Figure 8b). For 16 antennas, its performance is better than the others for superficial regions (Figure 8c). For deep and middle regions with $N = 16$, there is no distinct difference between the circular, cross, and linear applicator structures in terms of TBR.

The applicator designs given in Figure 8c were used to focus on four targets and the resulting SAR distributions are shown in Figure 11. The corresponding TBR and P_{tot} values are given in Table 2. The first and the second targets in the table are on the x-axis, and they can be referred to as the deep and the superficial regions. TBR values are consistent with each other such that the linear array has the highest value and the circular array has the lowest value. The deep target TBR was lower than the superficial target values. Although the third target was at the same distance from the origin as the second target, the linear array result changed drastically. This is because the position of the linear array was assumed as stated previously in this paper such that the best performance occurs along the x-axis. Since the third target is rotated 90° rotated from the x-axis, it was expected that the TBR value of the linear array becomes lower. The position of the Cross–array was also arranged for the x-axis, but since it is symmetrical on 4 quarters, there was almost no change in the TBR value. The result of the circular array does not change for the third target due to circular symmetry. The fourth target was in the middle region and has an angle of 25.5° with the x-axis. Cross and linear arrays give higher TBR than the circular for the fourth target.

Table 2. The TBR and total antenna input power (P_{tot}) results of the best-performing 1-layer FORA dipole applicators focused on different target locations.

Applicator \ Target Position (mm)	(10, 0, 0)	(30, 0, 0)	(0, 30, 0)	(20, 10, 0)
		TBR		
CA^{16}, $\Delta r = 10$ mm	5.26	6.45	6.45	5.54
XA^{16}, $dx = 10$ mm and $dy = 0.6\ \lambda_0$	5.56	6.32	6.34	5.80
LA^{16}, $dx = 2$ mm and $dy = 1.2\ \lambda_0$	5.59	6.58	5.76	5.81
		$P_{tot}[W]$		
CA^{16}, $\Delta r = 10$ mm	68	63	78	89
XA^{16}, $dx = 10$ mm and $dy = 0.6\ \lambda_0$	69	109	94	158
LA^{16}, $dx = 2$ mm and $dy = 1.2\ \lambda_0$	162	174	187	219

The circular array has the lowest power requirement to reach 43 °C in 10 min and the linear array has the highest P_{tot}. Please note that power requirements were not optimized in this study, and these values were obtained with the procedure explained in Section 2.4.4. Concerning the 1-layer 16-antenna circular FORA dipole array applicator, with 68 W total input power, after ten minutes of SAR exposure, the temperature at the (10, 0, 0) target point increases to 45.2 °C, and the average temperature at the target region (12 mm × 12 mm region centered at (10, 0, 0) point) becomes 43 °C. The total input power, then, was scaled from 0 W to 136 W with 13.6 W increments and the temperature level at the target point was calculated for the corresponding scaled SAR distributions to show the temperature change for different power levels. The temperature at the target is shown in Figure 12 as a function of exposure time for each input power level (W) provided in the legend.

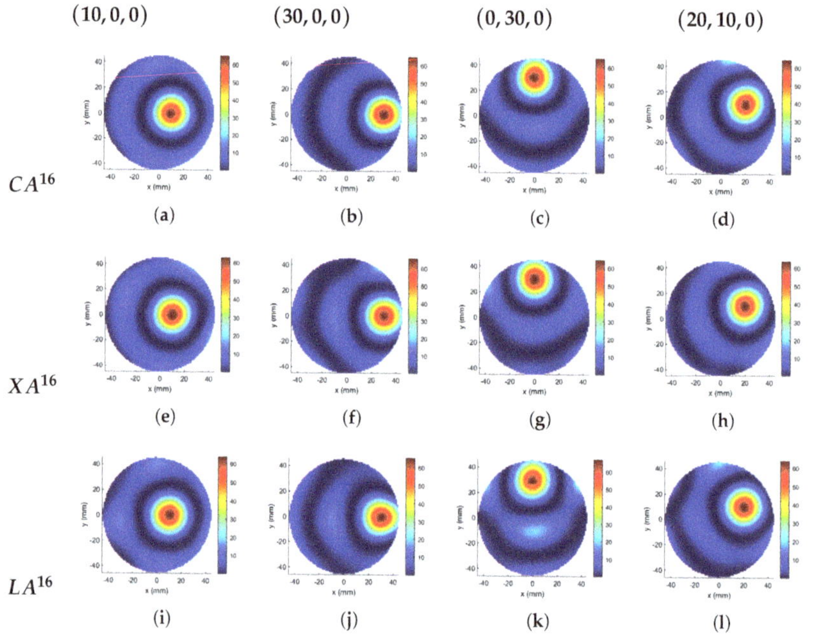

Figure 11. SAR distributions [W/kg] focused at (10, 0, 0), (30, 0, 0), (0, 30, 0), and (20, 10, 0) mm positions, and obtained with 1-layer of FORA dipole elements. (**a–d**) Circular array with 16 antennas and Δr = 10 mm. (**e–h**) Cross–array with 16 antennas, dx = 10 mm, and dy = 0.6 λ_0. (**i–l**) Linear array with 16 antennas, dx = 2 mm, and dy = 1.2 λ_0.

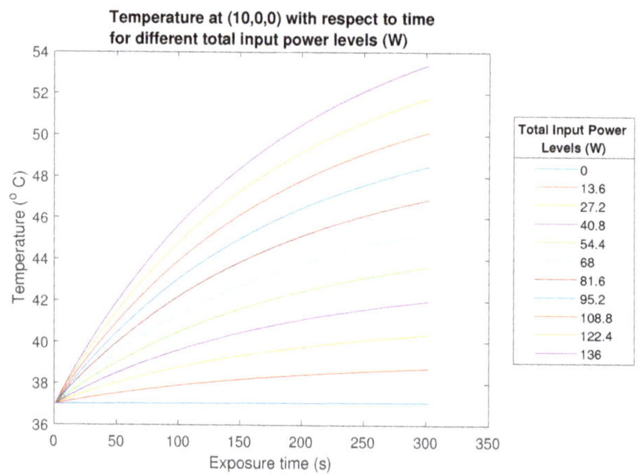

Figure 12. Temperature (°C) at (10, 0, 0) mm target point as a function of exposure time for different total input power levels (W).

For 1-layer arrays, in general, a larger number of antennas gives higher TBR, which was an expected result due to increased optimization sensitivity, directivity, and gain. The number of antennas can be increased until the mutual coupling limits are reached. Arrays with 20 antennas exhibited inferior performance when compared to other applicators with a smaller number of antennas in the array.

3.2. Results of 2-Layer FORA Dipole Arrays

The best HT applicator designs obtained from the 1-layer application were: the 16-antenna circular array with Δr = 10 mm, 16-antenna Cross–array with dx = 10 mm and dy = 0.6 λ_0, and 16-antenna linear array with dx = 2 mm and dy = 1.2 λ_0 (also shown in Figure 8c). This suggests that among the 1-layer applicators, 16-antenna arrays perform the best. In this section, we duplicated these 1-layer antenna arrays to a second layer and set the inter-layer distance to 0.4 λ_0, 0.6 λ_0, and 0.8 λ_0, while maintaining the symmetry around the z = 0 plane. Furthermore, the same procedure was repeated by decreasing the number of antennas in each layer to half to understand whether N = 16 should be maintained as the total number of antennas or as the number of antennas in one layer. Therefore, 2-layer 32-antenna and 2-layer 16-antenna applicators were explored. Figure 9 shows the 2-layer results and the corresponding 1-layer best-case result.

Among the 2-layer CAs, the 32-antenna arrays show superior results to the array with 16 antennas as shown in Figure 9a. For N =16, dz = 0.6 λ_0 provides higher TBR than dz = 0.4 λ_0, while dz = 0.8 λ_0 gives the lowest TBR values. For N = 32, dz = 0.6 λ_0 provides higher TBR than both dz = 0.4 λ_0 and dz = 0.8 λ_0. 2-layer CA^{32} with dz = 0.4 λ_0 has the highest TBR value among the explored designs. The 2-layer CA shows inferior results to the 1-layer best CA up to the middle region and performs better in the superficial region. At the most superficial target that was explored, the 2-layer CA^{32} becomes comparable to the 1-layer CA^{16}.

Comparing 2-layer linear arrays given in Figure 9b, LA^{32} was superior to LA^{16}. dz = 0.8 λ_0 has the lowest and dz = 0.4 λ_0 has the highest superficial performance. dz = 0.6 λ_0 has higher TBR for most of the remaining regions for LA^{32}. LA^{32} has higher TBR values than the 1-layer LA^{16} in the deep region, and comparable results at the most superficial target that was investigated. However, over most of the phantom, the 1-layer LA^{16} has better performance.

In Figure 9c, the 32-antenna array with dz = 0.8 λ_0 has the highest TBR value, followed by dz = 0.6 λ_0. XA^{32} was superior to its counterpart with 16 antennas that have the same dz distance. The 2-layer cross applicators investigated, except XA^{16} with dz = 0.4 λ_0, show better performance than the 1-layer XA^{16} in the deep region and the first half of the middle region, but the 1-layer XA^{16} shows better performance in the outer half of the phantom. The 2-layer XA^{32} catches up with the 1-layer XA^{16} performance at the outermost target regions.

Table 3 provides the TBR values and P_{tot} –the power requirement for the target to reach 43 °C in 10 min.– of 2-layer CA^{32} with Δr = 10 mm and dz = 0.6 λ_0, and the 2-layer XA^{32} with dx = 10 mm, dy = 0.6 λ_0, and dz = 0.8 λ_0 for targets (10, 0, 0) mm and (30, 0, 0) mm. In the deep target, although the TBR values were higher for 2-layer applicators than for the 1-layer, the increase in the P_{tot} values was greater. At the superficial target, 2-layer applicators both exhibit lower performance and higher power demand. Please note that the power requirement was not optimized in this study.

Duplicating the 1-layer array with the best results onto the second layer provided better performance in the inner half of the phantom for circular and cross applicators than their 1-layer counterparts, and only in the deep region for the linear applicator. Although the 32-antenna 2-layer applicators reach and even exceed the performance of the 1-layer arrays in the outermost targets, their performance in the outer half of the phantom was inferior to 1-layer applicators. For a deep-seated target, it was better to use multilayers; however, 1-layer FORA dipole applicators with 16 antennas perform better for the remaining phantom regions.

Table 3. The TBR and total antenna power P_{tot} results of the best-performing 2-layer FORA dipole applicators and FORA–connected array applicators focused on different target locations.

Applicator \ Target Position (mm)	(10, 0, 0)	(30, 0, 0)
	TBR	
2-layer CA^{32}, Δr = 10 mm, $dz = 0.6\ \lambda_0$	6.10	5.84
2-layer XA^{32}, dx = 10 mm, $dy = 0.6\ \lambda_0$, $dz = 0.8\ \lambda_0$	6.02	6.04
3-layer $ConA^{33}$, Δr = 4 mm	4.82	7.72
5-layer $ConA^{65}$, Δr = 12.9 mm	5.44	8.67
6-layer $ConA^{66}$, Δr = 4 mm	5.26	7.76
	P_{tot} [W]	
2-layer CA^{32}, Δr = 10 mm, $dz = 0.6\ \lambda_0$	270	150
2-layer XA^{32}, dx = 10 mm, $dy = 0.6\ \lambda_0$, $dz = 0.8\ \lambda_0$	271	554
3-layer $ConA^{33}$, Δr = 4 mm	197	206
5-layer $ConA^{65}$, Δr = 12.9 mm	332	319
6-layer $ConA^{66}$, Δr = 4 mm	176	189

3.3. *Results of Multi-Layer FORA–connected Arrays*

The connected FORA array results are given in Figure 10. In this plot, TBR values are given separately for three regions, and the sub-plots of each region are scaled to better discern the results. The TBR value was higher for the higher number of layers in the connected array, although the performance of the 3- and 5-layer 13-antenna connected array becomes comparable around x = 20 mm. TBR values were higher for the 13-antenna $ConA$ than the ones with 11 antennas for the same number of layers, except for the outermost targets. This was a similar situation to the dipole circular array, where Δr = 2 mm shows better performance over Δr = 10 mm in the outermost targets. The 5-layer 13-antenna $ConA$ and 6-layer 11-antenna $ConA$ are especially given together in Figure 10 since their number of antennas is close. The 65- and 66-antenna arrays show similar behavior in the inner half of the phantom. The TBR resulting from the 65-antenna array shows a more monotonic increase in the second half of the phantom, while the 66-antenna array shows better performance in the outermost targets. The investigated connected arrays show inferior results compared to the 1-layer CA^{16} with Δr = 10 mm in the deep and the middle regions, except for $ConA^{65}$ and $ConA^{66}$, which resulted in comparable results. In the superficial region, the 3-, 5-, and 6-layer connected arrays show better performance than the dipole circular array.

In Figure 10, the 1- and 2-layer cross-dipole array results as well as the connected array results are shown together. In the deep region, 2-layer XA^{16} is superior and followed by $conA^{66}$, $conA^{65}$ and 1-layer XA^{16}. In the middle region, the behavior of all the applicators changes. In the superficial region, $conA^{66}$ and $conA^{33}$ are superior and followed by $conA^{65}$, and the 1- and 2-layer cross-dipole array performances are inferior to most of the explored connected arrays. The $conA^{66}$ provides the overall better performance, suggesting the high number of antennas constituting the connected array demonstrate better focusing capability. Although the number of antennas within $conA^{65}$ is very close to 66 antennas, one can conclude that the higher number of layers of the connected array also demonstrates better performance. Also, when the distance between the antenna and the phantom is small, the focusing performance at the superficial regions increases as in $conA^{33}$ and $conA^{66}$. Adding higher layers than two was not possible for the given arrangement of the dipole array. Therefore, more layers could not be compared.

Table 3 provides the TBR and P_{tot} values of $ConA^{39}$, $ConA^{65}$ and $ConA^{66}$ at a deep and superficial target. Comparing Tables 2 and 3, 5- and 6-layer $ConA$ have comparable deep target performance with the best-case 1-layer applicators, while $ConA^{39}$ was inferior. In superficial regions, three connected arrays show superior performance to the 1-layer dipole applicators. Power requirements of *ConA* were higher than 1-layer dipole applicators and comparable to 2-layer dipole applicators.

In beamforming studies, the inter-antenna distance is more important than the total area that the antennas span. In a medical application, however, there is limited available space, and the total area that the antenna span becomes an important issue. This is why, in this paper, instead of the inter-antenna distance, dy, the distance between the first and the last antennas, is used as one of the parameters. The effects on the applicator performance of the other parameters, such as the number of antennas, were compared for a fixed antenna space. The total applicator distance on the x-axis was 158 mm when dx = 10 mm and 142 mm when dx = 2 mm and the largest antenna separation that was investigated was $dy = 1.2\,\lambda \approx = 147$ mm in the y-direction. Therefore, for the best-performing 1-layer dipole linear array, the area of the applicator was 147 mm × 142 mm, and it was 158 mm × 158 mm for the circular array. This paper shows a comparison between different FORA element arrays on a cylindrical fat phantom of diameter 90 mm. The results of best-performing HT applicators might be different for a bigger phantom or a realistic breast phantom.

3.4. Experimental Results

The purpose of the experiment was to increase the temperature of the phantom at (9, 21, 0) mm, where the center of the phantom was chosen as the origin. The fat-mimicking phantom has a radius of 45 mm and height of 90 mm and is cut into two equal pieces at $z = 0$ slice. To mimic the fat tissue, 80% oil-in-gelatin mixture was prepared according to the instructions given in [32]. The dielectric properties of the manufactured phantom were measured with a DAK probe to have $\epsilon_r = 3.77$ and $\sigma = 0.035$ S/m at 2.45 GHz. Three measurement points were chosen at $z = 0$ slice as: (30, 0) mm, (25, 25) mm, (9, 21) mm. For each point, three more points were selected 90 degrees apart, symmetrical with respect to the origin. The thirteenth measurement point was selected at the origin.

The HT applicator was comprised of 12 FORA dipole antennas arranged in a circular array and enclosed in expanded polyethylene foam, as shown in Figure 13b. The block diagram of the components of the experimental system is given in Figure 13a. Each antenna was connected to an individual 10W RF power amplifier (HI Microwave Technology, China HIPA02034040) and the corresponding channels of the phase shifter (HI Microwave Technology, China HPS-1700T6000M, with 20 dB loss at each channel) providing a specific relative phase shift. Phase shifter was fed with 16 dBm signal with 2.45 GHz generated by the microwave source (Agilent Technologies, USA E8257D). The excitation parameters were further optimized according to the antenna maximum power inputs allowed by the RF system. Using a Vector Network Analyzer (Keysight, USA M9018A PXIe Chasis), each signal at the antenna input was fine-tuned to overcome any imbalance over each amplifier. Table 4 details the ideal magnitude and phase values required for each element in the array.

Table 4. Optimized antenna excitations values for the experiment.

	Antenna Number											
	1	2	3	4	5	6	7	8	9	10	11	12
Phase (°)	21	132	65	70	42	−103	−130	−90	−138	−60	35	114
Power (W)	0.80	1.61	1.02	1.86	2.27	1.67	3.32	3.73	2.88	0.72	3.09	1.58

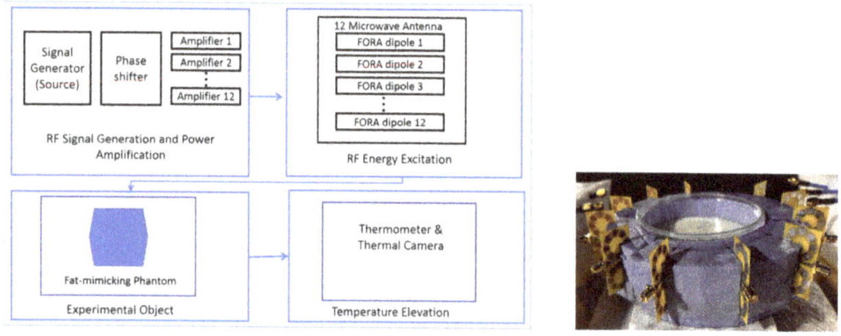

(**a**) (**b**)

Figure 13. (**a**) The block diagram of the experimental system. (**b**) The circular FORA dipole array prototype with the bottom half of the fat-mimicking phantom in the middle.

The maximum available antenna input power was 4 W due to the loss at the phase shifter, while 70 W was required in the simulation results to reach 43 °C from 37 °C in ten minutes. The experiment was run for 60 min when the phantom initial temperature was 18 °C and the room temperature was 20 °C. Computational results are also given for 60 min of treatment. The computed temperature distribution and the thermal camera (Guide ZC04C2001351) image are compared to verify the thermal effect generated by the HT applicator in a 2D plane (XY-plane). Figure 14 shows the optimized SAR distribution of the simulation for the experimental setup, and the associated temperature profile after an hour.

The phantom was taken outside of the applicator after 60 min, the top half of the phantom was put aside, and all the data were taken from the bottom piece at $z = 0$ slice. First, the thermal image was taken and then, thermometer readings were recorded at 13 points, and these 13 values were interpolated in MATLAB to visualize the temperature distribution. Figure 15a shows the temperature profile. The temperature profile from the thermal camera is shown in Figure 15b.

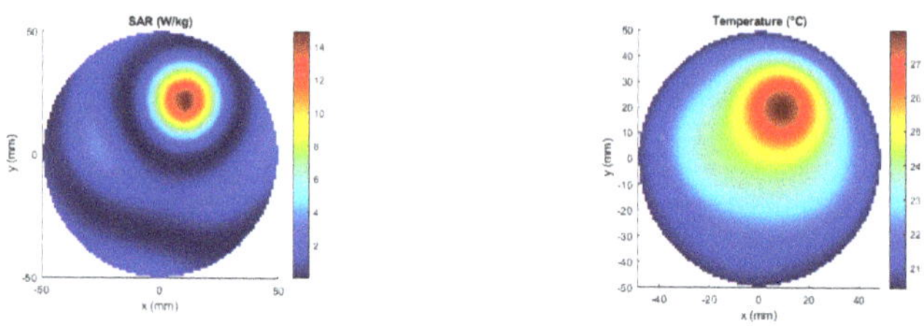

(**a**) (**b**)

Figure 14. Computational results of the experimental setup. (**a**) Optimized SAR distribution (W/kg), (**b**) Temperature profile after 60 min (°C).

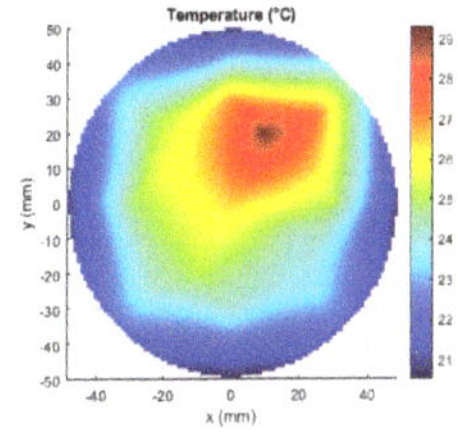

(a)

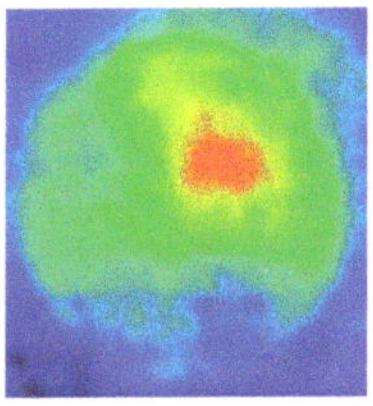

(b)

Figure 15. Experimental results. (**a**) Temperature distribution interpolated from the 13 points of the thermometer readings (°C), (**b**) Thermal camera image.

The utilized thermal camera during the experiment did not provide specific temperature values or color bars. Therefore, the real temperature values could not be obtained. The highest temperature position, on the other hand, was conceivable and well matched with the computed results. To obtain the specific temperature values, thermometer readings were provided from 13 discrete locations and the values of these positions also match well with the expected result. Considering the two data acquisition techniques, both the real temperature values and the surface temperature distribution, the experimental results verify the computational results. The difference between the temperature distributions of the computed and the experimental results can be due to the inhomogeneity of the phantom and the unknown thermal parameters.

4. Conclusions

In this paper, we presented fractal octagonal (FORA) elements adopted for two types of antenna arrays, the sparse array and the connected array. The former is referred to as the FORA dipole array, and the latter is the FORA–connected array. The choice for FORA elements was due to their characteristics, which enable tailoring these elements for such types of arrays. This paper investigated FORA antenna elements as breast hyperthermia applicators for deep and superficial seated targets. The phantom was modeled as a fatty tissue as it provides a homogeneous environment for such a comparative analysis.

FORA elements were used both as 1- and 2-layer dipole arrays and multi-layer connected arrays. First, the 1-layer dipole antenna arrays were analyzed, and the best-performing designs were shown. FORA dipole antenna performance aligned in a linear, cross, and circular array were examined compared to each other's performance to selectively minimize hot spots while focusing the energy on a particular target in the phantom under quest. One-layer 16-antenna dipole arrays were found to be superior to the other one-layer antenna arrays with lower or higher numbers of antennas for all dipole array configurations. Duplicating these best cases showed that the 2-layer dipole array performs better in the deep-seated regions. Two-layer circular and cross arrays performed superior to the two-layer linear array in the deep-seated regions. Based on these results, 1- and 2-layer cross arrays were compared to connected arrays. Then, multi-layer connected FORA arrays were investigated for 2-,3-,5- and 6-layers. It was found that their results were superior to the 1-layer dipole array in the superficial region of the phantom. In terms of target-to-breast SAR ratio TBR performance, one can conclude that the 2-layer dipole FORA array would be a better choice for reaching deep-tissue targets, while the multi-layer connected arrays should be chosen for the superficial regions. However, the power requirements of these multi-layer connected arrays were higher than the examined 1-layer HT dipole applicators. The experimental results verify the use of FORA antenna in microwave hyperthermia application.

Author Contributions: Conceptualization, G.Y. and I.F.; methodology, G.Y. and I.F.; formal analysis, G.Y. and I.F.; investigation, G.Y., J.B., L.F. and T.Y.; resources, K.Z.-A., L.F., C.V.S., T.Y. and I.A.; data curation, G.Y.; writing—original draft preparation, G.Y. and I.F.; writing—review and editing, C.V.S.;

supervision, L.F., C.V.S., T.Y. and I.A.; funding acquisition, L.F., C.V.S., T.Y. and I.A. All authors have read and agreed to the published version of the manuscript.

Funding: This work has received funding from COST Action grant agreement CA17115 and the Scientific and Technological Research Council of Turkey under grant agreement 118S074.

Institutional Review Board Statement: Not applicable.

Informed Consent Statement: Not applicable.

Data Availability Statement: Not applicable.

Conflicts of Interest: The authors do not declare any conflict of interest.

Abbreviations

The following abbreviations are used in this manuscript:

HT	Hyperthermia
SAR	Specific Absorption Rate
FORA	Fractal octagonal ring array
EM	Electromagnetic
TR	Time Reversal
iw-PSO	inertia weighted-Particle Swarm Optimization
HTP	Hyperthermia Treatment Planning
FDTD	Finite Difference Time Domain
FEM	Finite Element Method
ISM	Industrial Scientific Medical
MRI	Magnetic Resonance Imaging
TBR	Target-to-breast ratio
HTQ	Hotspot-to-target quotient
CA	Circular Array
LA	Linear Array
XA	Cross–array
ConA	Connected Array

References

1. van der Zee, J.; González, D.; van Rhoon, G.C.; van Dijk, J.D.; van Putten, W.L.; Hart, A.A. Comparison of radiotherapy alone with radiotherapy plus hyperthermia in locally advanced pelvic tumours: A prospective, randomised, multicentre trial. *Lancet* **2000**, *355*, 1119–1125. [CrossRef] [PubMed]
2. Jha, S.; Sharma, P.K.; Malviya, R. Hyperthermia: role and risk factor for cancer treatment. *Achiev. Life Sci.* **2016**, *10*, 161–167. [CrossRef]
3. Alexander, H. Isolation perfusion. *Cancer Princ. Pract. Oncol.* **2001**, *1*, 2.
4. Lee, A.H. Why is carcinoma of the breast more frequent in the upper outer quadrant? A case series based on needle core biopsy diagnoses. *Breast* **2005**, *14*, 151–152. [CrossRef]
5. Iero, D.A.; Isernia, T.; Morabito, A.F.; Catapano, I.; Crocco, L. Optimal constrained field focusing for hyperthermia cancer therapy: A feasibility assessment on realistic phantoms. *Prog. Electromagn. Res.* **2010**, *102*, 125–141. [CrossRef]
6. Isernia, T.; Di Iorio, P.; Soldovieri, F. An effective approach for the optimal focusing of array fields subject to arbitrary upper bounds. *IEEE Trans. Antennas Propag.* **2000**, *48*, 1837–1847. [CrossRef]
7. Iero, D.A.; Crocco, L.; Isernia, T. Thermal and microwave constrained focusing for patient-specific breast cancer hyperthermia: A robustness assessment. *IEEE Trans. Antennas Propag.* **2013**, *62*, 814–821. [CrossRef]
8. Yildiz, G.; Yasar, H.; Uslu, I.E.; Demirel, Y.; Akinci, M.N.; Yilmaz, T.; Akduman, I. Antenna Excitation Optimization with Deep Learning for Microwave Breast Cancer Hyperthermia. *Sensors* **2022**, *22*, 6343. [CrossRef]
9. Fenn, A.J. An adaptive microwave phased array for targeted heating of deep tumours in intact breast: animal study results. *Int. J. Hyperth.* **1999**, *15*, 45–61. [CrossRef]
10. Altintas, G.; Akduman, I.; Janjic, A.; Yilmaz, T. A Novel Approach on Microwave Hyperthermia. *Diagnostics* **2021**, *11*, 493. [CrossRef]
11. Yildiz, G.; Yilmaz, T.; Akduman, I. Rotationally Adjustable Hyperthermia Applicators: A Computational Comparative Study of Circular and Linear Array Applicators. *Diagnostics* **2022**, *12*, 2677. [CrossRef] [PubMed]
12. Curto, S.; Garcia-Miquel, A.; Suh, M.; Vidal, N.; Lopez-Villegas, J.M.; Prakash, P. Design and characterisation of a phased antenna array for intact breast hyperthermia. *Int. J. Hyperth.* **2017**, *34*, 250–260. [CrossRef] [PubMed]

13. Xu, L.; Wang, X. Focused microwave breast hyperthermia monitored by thermoacoustic imaging: A computational feasibility study applying realistic breast phantoms. *IEEE J. Electromagn. Microwaves Med. Biol.* **2019**, *4*, 81–88. [CrossRef]
14. Li, J.; Xu, L.; Wang, X. A computational study on number of elements in antenna array for focused microwave breast hyperthermia. In Proceedings of the 2019 IEEE MTT-S International Microwave Biomedical Conference (IMBioC), Nanjing, China, 6–8 May 2019; IEEE: Piscataway, NJ, USA, 2019; Volume 1, pp. 1–3.
15. Li, J.; Wang, B.; Zhang, D.; Li, C.; Zhu, Y.; Zou, Y.; Chen, B.; Wu, T.; Wang, X. A preclinical system prototype for focused microwave breast hyperthermia guided by compressive thermoacoustic tomography. *IEEE Trans. Biomed. Eng.* **2021**, *68*, 2289–2300. [CrossRef]
16. Nguyen, P.T.; Abbosh, A.; Crozier, S. Three-Dimensional Microwave Hyperthermia for Breast Cancer Treatment in a Realistic Environment Using Particle Swarm Optimization. *IEEE Trans. Biomed. Eng.* **2017**, *64*, 1335–1344. [CrossRef]
17. Elkayal, H.A.; Ismail, N.E. Efficient focusing of microwave hyperthermia for small deep-seated breast tumors treatment using particle swarm optimization. *Comput. Methods Biomech. Biomed. Eng.* **2021**, *24*, 985–994. [CrossRef]
18. Nguyen, P.T.; Abbosh, A.M.; Crozier, S. 3-D Focused Microwave Hyperthermia for Breast Cancer Treatment With Experimental Validation. *IEEE Trans. Antennas Propag.* **2017**, *65*, 3489–3500. [CrossRef]
19. Nguyen, P.T.; Abbosh, A.; Crozier, S. Microwave Hyperthermia for Breast Cancer Treatment Using Electromagnetic and Thermal Focusing Tested on Realistic Breast Models and Antenna Arrays. *IEEE Trans. Antennas Propag.* **2015**, *63*, 4426–4434. [CrossRef]
20. Farhat, E.O.; Adami, K.Z.; Zhang, Y.; Brown, A.K.; Sammut, C.V. Ultra-wideband tightly coupled fractal octagonal phased array antenna. In Proceedings of the 2013 International Conference on Electromagnetics in Advanced Applications (ICEAA), Turin, Italy, 9–13 September 2013; IEEE: Piscataway, NJ, USA, 2013; pp. 140–144.
21. Farhat, I.O.; Adami, K.Z.; Sammut, C.V. Near-Field to Far-Field pattern measurements for a mid-aperture FR-ORA array. In Proceedings of the 2015 IEEE Conference on Antenna Measurements & Applications (CAMA), Chiang Mai, Thailand, 30 November–2 December 2015; IEEE: IEEE: Piscataway, NJ, USA, 2015; pp. 1–4.
22. Wheeler, H. Simple relations derived fom a phased-array antenna made of an infinite current sheet. *IEEE Trans. Antennas Propag.* **1965**, *13*, 506–514. [CrossRef]
23. Pennes, H.H. Analysis of Tissue and Arterial Blood Temperatures in the Resting Human Forearm. *J. Appl. Physiol.* **1998**, *85*, 5–34. [CrossRef]
24. Zastrow, E.; Davis, S.; Lazebnik, M.; Kelcz, F.; Van Veen, B.; Hagness, S. Development of Anatomically Realistic Numerical Breast Phantoms With Accurate Dielectric Properties for Modeling Microwave Interactions With the Human Breast. *IEEE Trans. Biomed. Eng.* **2008**, *55*, 2792–2800. [CrossRef]
25. Phantom Repository. 2008. Available online: https://uwcem.ece.wisc.edu/phantomRepository.html (accessed on 10 October 2020).
26. Said Camilleri, J.; Farrugia, L.; Curto, S.; Rodrigues, D.B.; Farina, L.; Caruana Dingli, G.; Bonello, J.; Farhat, I.; Sammut, C.V. Review of Thermal and Physiological Properties of Human Breast Tissue. *Sensors* **2022**, *22*, 3894. [CrossRef] [PubMed]
27. Farhat, I.; Cutajar, D.; Adami, K.Z.; Sammut, C.; Abela, J. Characterization of 36 meter square mid-frequency radio astronomy prototype antenna array. In Proceedings of the 2018 IEEE Conference on Antenna Measurements & Applications (CAMA), Vasteras, Sweden, 3–6 September 2018; IEEE: Piscataway, NJ, USA, 2018; pp. 1–3.
28. COMSOL. RF Module User's Guide. Available online: https://doc.comsol.com/5.4/doc/com.comsol.help.rf/RFModuleUsersGuide.pdf (accessed on 10 August 2022).
29. Canters, R.; Wust, P.; Bakker, J.; Van Rhoon, G. A literature survey on indicators for characterisation and optimisation of SAR distributions in deep hyperthermia, a plea for standardisation. *Int. J. Hyperth.* **2009**, *25*, 593–608. [CrossRef] [PubMed]
30. Sumser, K.; Bellizzi, G.G.; van Rhoon, G.C.; Paulides, M.M. The Potential of Adjusting Water Bolus Liquid Properties for Economic and Precise MR Thermometry Guided Radiofrequency Hyperthermia. *Sensors* **2020**, *20*, 2946. [CrossRef] [PubMed]
31. Shi, Y.; Eberhart, R. A modified particle swarm optimizer. In Proceedings of the 1998 IEEE international conference on evolutionary computation proceedings. IEEE world congress on computational intelligence (Cat. No. 98TH8360), Anchorage, AK, USA, 4–9 May 1998; IEEE: Piscataway, NJ, USA, 1998; pp. 69–73.
32. Lazebnik, M.; Madsen, E.L.; Frank, G.R.; Hagness, S.C. Tissue-mimicking phantom materials for narrowband and ultrawideband microwave applications. *Phys. Med. Biol.* **2005**, *50*, 4245. [CrossRef] [PubMed]

sensors

MDPI

Article

Thermal Evaluation of Multi-Antenna Systems Proposed to Treat Bone Tumors: Finite Element Analysis

Citlalli Jessica Trujillo-Romero [1,*], Juan Dionisio Merida [2], Texar Javier Ramírez-Guzmán [3], Raquel Martínez-Valdez [4], Lorenzo Leija-Salas [3], Arturo Vera-Hernández [3], Genaro Rico-Martínez [5], José Jesús Agustín Flores-Cuautle [6], Josefina Gutiérrez-Martínez [1] and Emilio Sacristán-Rock [7]

1 Division of Medical Engineering Research, National Institute of Rehabilitation-LGII, Calz. México Xochimilco No. 289, Arenal de Guadalupe, Mexico City 14389, Mexico
2 Department of Electrical Engineering, Universidad Autonoma Metropolitana, UAM-Iztapalapa, Av. Ferrocarril San Rafael Atlixco, 186, Leyes de Reforma, Mexico City 09310, Mexico
3 Electrical Engineering Department, Bioelectronics Section, CINVESTAV-IPN, Instituto Politécnico Nacional 2508, San Pedro Zacatenco, Mexico City 07360, Mexico
4 Biomedical Engineering Program, Universidad Politécnica de Chiapas, Suchiapa 29150, Mexico
5 Bone Tumors Service, National Institute of Rehabilitation-LGII, Calz. México Xochimilco No. 289, Arenal de Guaudalupe, Mexico City 14389, Mexico
6 CONACYT-National Technological Institute of Mexico/I.T. Orizaba, Posgraduate Studies and Research Division, Oriente 9, No. 852, Orizaba 94320, Mexico
7 National Center for Research in Instrumentation and Medical Imaging, UAM-Iztapalapa, Av. Ferrocarril San Rafael Atlixco, 186, Leyes de Reforma, Mexico City 09310, Mexico
* Correspondence: cjtrujillo@inr.gob.mx

Citation: Trujillo-Romero, C.J.; Dionisio Merida, J.; Ramírez-Guzmán, T.J.; Martínez-Valdez, R.; Leija-Salas, L.; Vera-Hernández, A.; Rico-Martínez, G.; Flores-Cuautle, J.J.A.; Gutiérrez-Martínez, J.; Sacristán-Rock, E. Thermal Evaluation of Multi-Antenna Systems Proposed to Treat Bone Tumors: Finite Element Analysis. *Sensors* **2022**, *22*, 7604. https://doi.org/10.3390/s22197604

Academic Editors: Hoi-Shun Antony Lui and Mikael Persson

Received: 6 September 2022
Accepted: 5 October 2022
Published: 7 October 2022

Abstract: Microwave ablation is commonly used in soft tissue tumors, but its application in bone tumors has been barely analyzed. Antennas to treat bone tissue (~3 cm^2), has been lately designed. Bone tumors at pathological stage T1 can reach 8 cm wide. An antenna cannot cover it; therefore, our goal is to evaluate the thermal performance of multi-antenna arrays. Linear, triangular, and square configurations of double slot (DS) and monopole (MTM) antennas were evaluated. A parametric study (finite element method), with variations in distance between antennas (ad) and bone thickness (bt) was implemented. Array feasibility was evaluated by SWR, ablated tissue volume, etc. The linear configuration with DS and MTM antennas showed SWR $\leq$ 1.6 for ad = 1 mm–15 mm and bt = 20 mm–40 mm, and ad = 10 mm–15 mm and bt = 25 mm–40 mm, respectively; the triangular showed SWR $\leq$ 1.5 for ad = 5 mm–15 mm and bt = 20 mm–40 mm and ad = 10 mm–15 mm and bt = 25 mm–40 mm. The square configuration (DS) generated SWR $\leq$ 1.5 for ad = 5 mm–20 mm and bt = 20 mm–40 mm, and the MTM, SWR $\leq$ 1.5 with ad = 10 mm and bt = 25 mm–40 mm. Ablated tissue was 4.65 cm^3–10.46 cm^3 after 5 min. According to treatment time and array configuration, maximum temperature and ablated tissue is modified. Bone tumors >3 cm^3 can be treated by these antenna-arrays.

Keywords: microwave ablation; bone tumors; thermal ablation; antenna array; FEM modeling

1. Introduction

The most common procedures to treat bone cancer are surgery, radiotherapy, and chemotherapy. The chosen therapy depends on the condition and necessities of the patient; however, it is well-known that radiotherapy and chemotherapy are not totally effective. In radiotherapy, high doses are required due to the fairly low radiosensitivity of the bone; therefore, healthy tissue can be damaged [1]. Chemotherapy is less used because most of the bone tumors are not very sensitive to it [2]. Moreover, both therapies have the disadvantage of producing several side effects that reduce the patient quality of life. In recent years, thermotherapies such as thermal ablation have been proposed to treat bone tumors. Microwave ablation (MWA) is a minimally invasive technique where critical temperatures around 60 °C are reached as an effect of the deposition of electromagnetic (EM) energy [3]. Specifically, MWA is more effective in treating bone tumors because the tissue heats faster, and larger ablation zones are achieved [4–6]. Several authors report that MWA has been successfully used as a complementary treatment for different musculoskeletal tumors [7,8]. Microwave heating applicators work at frequencies in the ISM band (Industrial Scientific and Medical). One of the frequencies, 2.45 GHz, is the most used worldwide in medical practice for thermal ablation. The reported antennas work at 2.45 GHz and reach temperatures higher than 60 °C [9–11] when using more than 50 W as input power [4]. Although this means that thermal ablation is present, high input power levels are necessary because the tested antennas were designed to treat soft tissue instead of bone tissue. To compensate the power loss, the required treatment time and input power level to generate thermal ablation increases.

Lately, researchers at the National Institute of Rehabilitation Luis Guillermo Ibarra Ibarra (INR-LGII) started developing micro-coaxial antennas that were designed to specifically treat bone tissue by MWA [12–17]. Trujillo-Romero et al. firstly designed a single slot antenna to treat bone tumors [15]. A double slot (DS) antenna was also designed for the same purpose; it was modeled, built, and characterized in ex vivo porcine bone. The results showed ablation temperatures (60–100 °C) are reached by applying 10 W per 10 min; moreover, the maximum standing wave ratio (SWR) was 1.8 [16]. Although both antennas were effective in treating bone tissue, their diameter (1.19 mm) allows its deformation. This effect could reduce the antenna lifetime and affect its performance after just a few uses. Therefore, a new set of four different micro-coaxial antennas with a thicker diameter (2.19 mm) was proposed [17]. The antennas were modeled, built, and tested by using phantoms and ex vivo porcine tissue. The antennas showed SWR values lower than 1.7; moreover, just 5 W were applied during 5 min to reach ablation temperatures (60–100 °C). The reduction of input power levels had been possible due to the optimization process of our antennas This process allows to improve the efficiency of the MW system; therefore, ablated temperatures are reached with lower levels of input power (less than 10 W) in a relatively short period of time (minutes). The proposed antennas can cover a tissue region of approximately 3 cm^2. However, according to the pathological stage of cancer, bone tumors at stage T1 can reach no more than 8 cm, while at T2 can be greater than 8 cm wide [18]. This region dimension cannot be covered by using a single micro-coaxial antenna, then, either multiple antenna insertions or a multi-antenna system must be used. The literature reports that some studies were carried out to evaluate multi-antenna arrays; however, most of these studies were implemented in liver tissue [19–22]. Karampatzakis et. al. reported a study that was performed to evaluate the heating characteristics of antenna arrays by using computational modeling [23]. However, in this study the use of triangular and square configurations of double slot (DS) antenna arrays to treat liver tumors was proposed; additionally, a brief analysis of some other tissues, including bone, were also implemented. Furthermore, to our knowledge, our study is the first one completely focused on evaluating the effect of using multi-antenna arrays to treat bone cancer. Therefore, the goal of this work was to evaluate the thermal behavior of different micro-coaxial antenna arrays that were proposed to treat bone cancer by MWA. Our hypothesis is that by using micro-coaxial antenna arrays, it is possible to increase the volume of the treated tumor; moreover, by using different antenna types and treatment time, different shapes of the ablation zones can be generated. The micro-coaxial antennas that were included in the study were the double slot (DS) and the monopole (MTM) antenna. A 3D parametric computational study that was based on the finite element method was proposed. The antenna arrays of two (linear), three (triangular), and four (square) antennas were analyzed. Several scenarios considering relevant parameters such as distance between the antennas (ad) and bone thickness (bt) were evaluated. In order to estimate the thermal effect over the tissues, SWR (standing wave ratio) values, maximum temperatures reached, the volume of tissue at the ablation temperatures, and the thermal distributions were analyzed.

2. Materials and Methods

Figure 1 shows a flow chart to summarize the implemented study step-by-step.

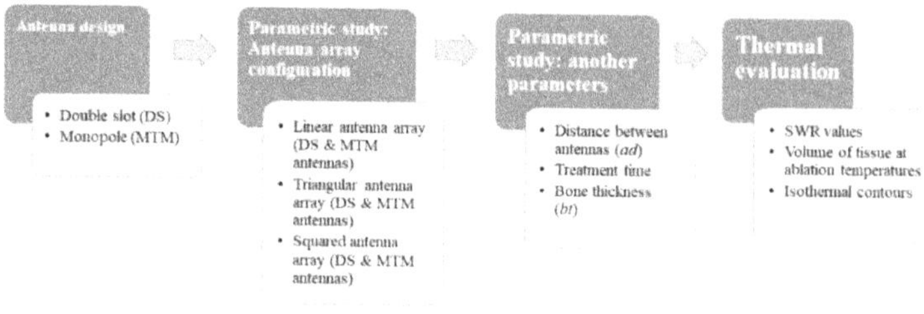

Figure 1. Step by step flow chart that was followed to implement the study.

2.1. Micro Coaxial Antennas

To carry out this study, one of the most commonly used antennas to treat soft tissue (double slot antenna) was proposed. Moreover, as this research was focus on bone tumors, the monopole antenna was also proposed to evaluate the possibility to cover a larger region of bone tissue. The double slot and the monopole antennas were previously modeled, optimized, and tested in multi-tissue phantoms and ex vivo porcine tissue by this research group [17]. The computational models showed SWR values of 1.26 and 1.55 for the double slot (DS) and the monopole (MTM) antennas, respectively. Figure 2 shows the geometrical scheme of each antenna and its dimensions that ensure a maximum energy transmission. The antenna diameters were set in accordance with the geometric characteristics of the semi-rigid micro-coaxial cable UT-085; moreover, each antenna is placed in a catheter to avoid contact with the surrounding tissue.

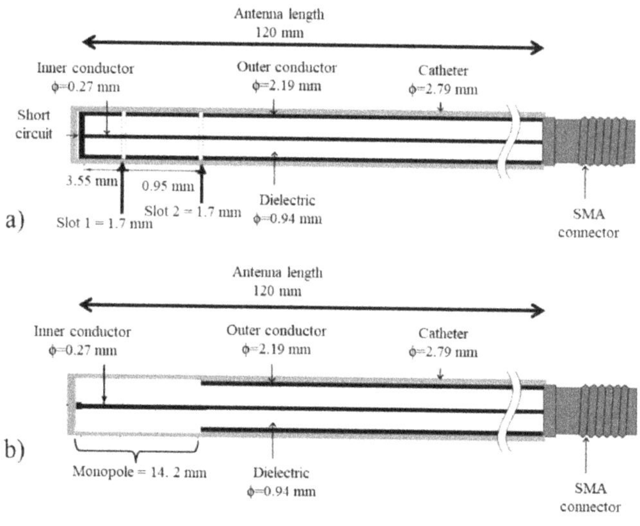

Figure 2. Proposed antennas, (**a**) double slot antenna and (**b**) monopole antenna.

2.2. Finite Element Models (FEM)

Electromagnetic and thermal models of the proposed multi-antenna systems were performed in COMSOL Multiphysics (COMSOL Inc., Burlington, MA, USA). The electromagnetic simulations were implemented in the frequency domain (2.45 GHz) and solved by using the stationary solver (used to find the solution to linear and nonlinear stationary problems). The thermal simulations were implemented as time-dependent by using the time-dependent solver (used to find the solution to time-dependent problems). 3D models that include the multi-antenna system as well as a multi-tissue segment (bone, muscle, fat, and skin) were implemented.

2.2.1. Electromagnetic (EM) Models

To implement the FEM model and to predict the antenna's performance, a current source (J_{imp}) that irradiated an electromagnetic field was considered. Element Model Maxwell's equations, described by Equations (1)–(4), govern the antennas' performance [24].

$$\nabla \times \boldsymbol{E} = -j\omega \overset{\leftrightarrow}{\mu} \cdot \boldsymbol{H} - \boldsymbol{M}_{imp} \tag{1}$$

$$\nabla \times \boldsymbol{H} = -j\omega \overset{\leftrightarrow}{\varepsilon} \cdot \boldsymbol{E} - \boldsymbol{J}_{imp} \tag{2}$$

$$\nabla \cdot \left(\overset{\leftrightarrow}{\varepsilon} \cdot \boldsymbol{E} \right) = -\frac{1}{j\omega} \nabla \cdot \boldsymbol{J}_{imp} \tag{3}$$

$$\nabla \cdot \left(\overset{\leftrightarrow}{\mu} \cdot \boldsymbol{H} \right) = -\frac{1}{j\omega} \nabla \cdot \boldsymbol{M}_{imp} \tag{4}$$

where $\boldsymbol{M}_{imp}$ is the magnetic current density, and $\overset{\leftrightarrow}{\varepsilon}$ and $\overset{\leftrightarrow}{\mu}$ are the permittivity and permeability of the tissues that were irradiated by the antenna, $\boldsymbol{E}$ is the electric field, and H is the magnetic field intensity. The boundary condition for the metallic surfaces, represented by Equation (5) is considered to solve them:

$$\mathbf{n} \times \mathbf{E} = 0 \ \mathrm{r} \ \epsilon \ \mathrm{S_{PEC}} \tag{5}$$

where SPEC represents the antenna body surface as a perfect electric conductor (PEC). Moreover, the feed point of each antenna was modeled as a port (micro coaxial) boundary condition.

The E and H field satisfy the Sommerfeld radiation boundary condition. These equations can be hardly analytical solved; therefore, they are solved by numerical methods. Due to an EM field that is irradiated by the antenna to the infinite, the solution space must be limited (S_0). Therefore, a new boundary condition to describe the EM waves propagation in a finite space is applied. The boundary condition, known as first-order absorbing, described by Equation (6), is applied to approximate this behavior. Moreover, this condition indicates that the EM field can travel in the space without reflections, i.e., the boundary does not disturb the EM field distribution.

$$\hat{\mathbf{n}} \times \nabla \times \begin{pmatrix} \mathbf{E} \\ \mathbf{H} \end{pmatrix} + \mathrm{j}\mathrm{k}_0 \hat{\mathbf{n}} \times \hat{\mathbf{n}} \times \begin{pmatrix} \mathbf{E} \\ \mathbf{H} \end{pmatrix} \approx 0 \ \mathrm{r}\epsilon \mathrm{S}_0 \tag{6}$$

where $\hat{n}$ is the unit vector normal to the surface S_0. Equation (7) is obtained by doing all the mathematical procedures:

$$\begin{aligned} &\iiint_{\mathbf{V}} \left[(\nabla \times \mathbf{T}) \cdot \overset{\leftrightarrow}{\mu}_{\mathbf{r}}^{-1} \cdot (\nabla \times \mathbf{E}) - \mathbf{k}_0^2 \mathbf{T} \cdot \overset{\leftrightarrow}{\varepsilon}_{\mathbf{r}} \cdot \mathbf{E} \right] \mathbf{dV} \\ &= \oiint_{\mathbf{S}_0 \cup \mathbf{S}_{\mathbf{PEC}}} \hat{\mathbf{n}} \cdot \left[\mathbf{T} \times \left(\overset{\leftrightarrow}{\mu}_{\mathbf{r}}^{-1} \cdot \nabla \times \mathbf{E} \right) \right] \mathbf{dS} \\ &- \iiint_{\mathbf{V}} \mathbf{T} \cdot \left[\mathbf{j}\mathbf{k}_0 \mathbf{Z}_0 \mathbf{J}_{\mathbf{imp}} + \nabla \times \left(\overset{\leftrightarrow}{\mu}_{\mathbf{r}}^{-1} \cdot \mathbf{M}_{\mathbf{imp}} \right) \right] \mathbf{dV} \end{aligned} \tag{7}$$

where $\overset{\leftrightarrow}{\mu}_r = \frac{\overset{\leftrightarrow}{\mu}}{\mu_0}$ and $\overset{\leftrightarrow}{\varepsilon}_r = \frac{\overset{\leftrightarrow}{\varepsilon}}{\varepsilon_0}$ are the relative permeability and permittivity tensor, respectively, $k_0 = \omega\sqrt{\mu_0 \varepsilon_0}$ is the wavenumber in free space, $\mathbf{Z}_0 = \sqrt{\frac{\mu_0}{\varepsilon_0}}$ is the intrinsic impedance, V is the volume confined by S_0, and T the testing function.

To describe the EM problem, Equation (8) was obtained by applying the first-order absorbing boundary condition.

$$\begin{aligned} \iiint_V \left[(\nabla \times \mathbf{T}) \cdot \overleftrightarrow{\mu}_r^{-1} \cdot (\nabla \times \mathbf{E}) - k_0^2 \mathbf{T} \cdot \overleftrightarrow{\varepsilon}_r \cdot \mathbf{E} \right] d \\ = \oiint_{S_{PEC}} \left(\hat{\mathbf{n}} \times \mathbf{T} \right) \cdot \overleftrightarrow{\mu}_r^{-1} \cdot (\nabla \times \mathbf{E}) d\mathbf{S} \\ -jk_0 \oiint_{S_0} \left(\hat{\mathbf{n}} \times \mathbf{T} \right) \cdot \left(\hat{\mathbf{n}} \times \mathbf{E} \right) d\mathbf{S} \\ - \iiint_V \mathbf{T} \cdot \left[jk_0 Z_0 \mathbf{J}_{imp} + \nabla \times \left(\overleftrightarrow{\mu}_r^{-1} \cdot \mathbf{M}_{imp} \right) \right] dV \end{aligned} \tag{8}$$

To numerically solve the equation, V is divided in small finite elements.

A transverse electromagnetic field (TEM) describes the wave propagation in a micro-coaxial cable. Equations (9)–(11) describe the antenna wave propagation for a time-harmonic fields [25]:

$$E = e_r \frac{C}{r} e^{j(\omega t - kz)}, \tag{9}$$

$$H = e_\varphi \frac{C}{rR} e^{j(\omega t - kz)}, \tag{10}$$

$$P_{av} = e_z \pi \frac{C^2}{Z} lnln \left(\frac{r_{inner}}{r_{outer}} \right), \tag{11}$$

where z is the direction of propagation; r, φ, and z are the coordinates of the antenna body; P_{av} is the power flow; Z is the wave impedance, r_{inner}, and r_{outer} are the radius of the inner and the outer conductors, respectively; ω is the angular frequency; and k the constant of propagation.

On the other hand, the specific absorption rate (SAR) describes the absorbed energy per unit of mass in a human body when it is exposed to an electromagnetic source, as described by Equation (12):

$$SAR = \frac{\sigma}{2\rho} |E|^2 \tag{12}$$

where E is the propagated electric field, σ and ρ are the conductivity (S/m), and density (kg/m^3) of the irradiated medium, respectively.

2.2.2. Thermal Models

The thermal model is described by the Pennes bioheat transfer equation represented by Equation (13):

$$\rho c \frac{\partial T}{\partial t} = \nabla \cdot (k \nabla T) + \rho Q + SAR - C_b W (T - T_b) \tag{13}$$

where c (J/kg/K) is the heat capacity, ρ (k/m^3) is the tissue density, k (W/m ∗ K) is the thermal conductivity, C_b is the blood heat capacity (J/Kg/K), W ($kg/m^3/s$) is the blood perfusion, T_b (K) is the blood temperature, Q (W/m^3) is the metabolism heat generation, and SAR (W/kg) was previously described by Equation (12).

The FEM model represents the heat-transfer problem in a small section of the multi-tissue domain (bone, muscle, fat, and skin), i.e., the domains were truncated; therefore, an insulation boundary condition was applied as described by Equation (14):

$$n \cdot \nabla T = 0 \tag{14}$$

where T is set as the initial physiological tissue temperature (37 °C). Table 1 presents the tissues and antenna properties that were used in the FEM modeling.

Table 1. Tissues and antenna properties used in the FEM models [26].

Parameter	Value	Parameter	Value
Blood density	1050 (kg/m^3)	$\varepsilon_{r\,fat}$	10.8 (—)
Specific heat	3639 (J/kg·K)	σ_{fat}	0.268 (S/m)
Blood temperature	37 °C	k_{fat}	0.21 [W/(m·K)]
$\varepsilon_{r\,bone}$	18.5 (—)	ρ_{fat}	911 [kg/m^3]
σ_{bone}	0.805 (S/m)	c_{fat}	2348 [J/(kg·K)]
k_{bone}	0.31 [W/(m·K)]	$\varepsilon_{r\,skin}$	38 (—)
ρ_{bone}	1908 [kg/m^3]	σ_{skin}	1.46 [S/m]
c_{bone}	1313 [J/(kg·K)]	k_{skin}	0.37 [W/(m·K)]
$\varepsilon_{r\,muscle}$	52.7 (—)	ρ_{skin}	1109 [kg/m^3]
σ_{muscle}	1.74 (S/m)	c_{skin}	3391 [J/(kg·K)]
k_{muscle}	0.49 [W/(m·K)]	$\varepsilon_{r\,catheter}$	2.6 (—)
ρ_{muscle}	1090 [kg/m^3]	$\varepsilon_{r\,dielectric}$	2.03 (—)
c_{muscle}	3421 [J/(kg·K)]		

2.3. Parametric Study

Bone tumors can be more than 8 cm wide. To cover a more significant volume than the one that was covered by a single antenna, a study to evaluate the antenna arrays performance was proposed. Both antennas (DS and MTM) were evaluated by following the linear (Figure 3a), triangular (Figure 3b), and square (Figure 3c) antenna array configurations. In the study, each antenna was set as A_1 A_2, A_3, and A_4 according to the antenna configuration. A parametric study was performed to obtain the maximum distance between antennas (*ad*) that was needed to enhance the volume of tissue that was affected by the thermal ablation. In order to set the distance between antennas (*ad*), the next specifications, according to previous studies that were done by this research group, were considered [15,17]. The designed antennas reach temperatures higher than 60 °C at approximately 10 mm from the antenna axis, and similar temperatures were reached at approximately 6 mm further to the antenna tip. Therefore, the covered distance ad was set from 1 to 15 mm with steps of 5 mm. These distances were chosen to ensure that the thermal pattern of the antennas will be combined; consequently, larger volumes of tissue at ablation temperatures are expected. Moreover, to evaluate the maximum bone size that can be treated and the thermal effect over the other tissues (muscle, fat, and skin), the bone thickness (*bt*) was also included in the parametric study. Table 2 shows the values that were included in this study.

Table 2. Parameters included in the parametric study.

Parameter	Values
Distance between antennas (*ad*)	1, 5, 10, 15 (mm)
Bone thickness (*bt*)	2, 2.5, 3, 3.5, 4 (cm)

Figure 3d shows an example of a triangular configuration of antennas that was used to implement this study. Moreover, model dimensions, distance between antennas (*ad*), bone thickness (*bt*), and the axes of the observation planes that were used for the antenna performance evaluation, are represented.

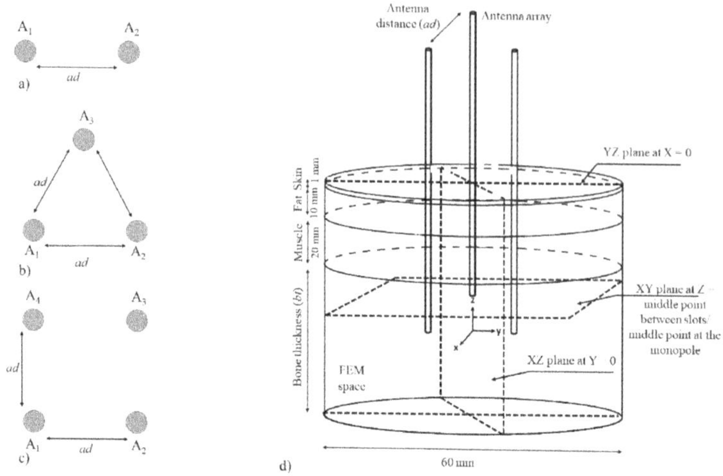

Figure 3. Proposed antenna array configurations to be analyzed, the antennas are depicted as A_1 A_2, A_3, and A_4 according to the antenna configuration, and example of the 3D computational model, (**a**) linear antenna array, (**b**) triangular antenna array, (**c**) square antenna array, and (**d**) example of the geometry that was used to implement this study. The geometry consists of a cylinder of multilayer tissue (bone, muscle, fat, and skin), as well as the evaluated antenna array. The thicknesses of muscle, fat, and skin were 2 cm, 1 cm, and 1 mm, respectively. The observation planes XY, XZ, and YZ that were used for the evaluation are also depicted. As previously described, the distance between antennas (*ad*) was modified from 1 mm to 15 mm and bone thickness (*bt*) from 2 to 4 cm.

2.4. Evaluated Parameters

The standing wave ratio corresponding to each antenna was obtained. The SWR measures the impedance coupling among the load and the transmission line that supplies it. An SWR equal to 1 indicates that the entire power is transmitted to the irradiated medium. The higher the SWR, the greater power loss in the system; therefore, higher levels of power returns to the microwave system and damages either to the equipment or to the patient can be presented. On the other hand, maximum temperatures, tissue volumes at ablation temperatures, and temperature patterns that were generated by the antenna arrays were obtained. It is well-known that thermal damage depends on the reached temperature and the treatment time (energy exposure); temperatures around 50–55 °C reduce the necessary time to generate irreversible cell damage to 4–6 min. Temperatures around 60–100 °C must be reached to produce nearly immediate tissue and cell coagulation [27]. Therefore, in this study, the coagulation of tissue was considered once it reaches 55 °C.

3. Results

3.1. Convergence Analysis

By using an adaptive mesh, a finer mesh in the region of interest was generated; therefore, the number of elements in the mesh can be reduced. An adequate mesh can help to reduce computational cost without an underestimation of the results. A convergence study was implemented to choose the adequate mesh size. Therefore, different mesh sizes were tested to perform the tests. The convergence test was done by analyzing the relationship between SWR and the simulation time versus the number of elements in the mesh. For all the antenna arrays, it was observed that the coarser mesh underestimates the results. For the linear arrays, models with around 625,885 (42 min)–842,209 (60 min) elements generated SWR values around 1.15. For triangular arrays, models with around 262,088 (30 min)–925,835 (80 min) generated stable SWR values around 1.34. Finally, for the square array, models with around 371,124 (60 min)–623,272 (130 min) elements generated

SWR values around 1.4. It is important to address that due to the simplicity of the linear array models, the number of elements in the mesh can be increased without a big impact on the computational time.

3.2. Standing Wave Ratio (SWR)

Figure 4 shows the SWR values for linear, triangular, and square configurations of double slot (DS) and monopole (MTM) antennas. For triangular and square configurations, just the lowest and the highest SWR values (A_1 and A_3) are presented, i.e., the SWR values corresponding to antennas A_2 and A_4 were between the SWR values that are described in Figure 4. Figure 4a depicts the SWR for both antennas (A_1 and A_2) in the linear array that was composed of the DS and the MTM antennas. In all cases (antenna distance ad and bone thickness *bt*), the DS antennas showed better performance, i.e., the SWR was lower than 1.4, which means a better coupling of the antenna with the microwave system. On the other hand, the MTM antennas reached SWR values between 1.3 and 2, being the worst-case scenarios (SWR $\cong$ 2), the ones with *ad* = 1 mm, for all the analyzed bone thickness (*bt*). Figure 4b shows the SWR for the triangular array; the DS antennas generated SWR values that were lower than 1.5, except for those cases where *ad* = 1 mm. The MTM antennas with *ad* = 10 mm and *ad* = 15 mm had SWR values lower than 1.6; however, for *ad* = 1 mm and *ad* = 5 mm, the SWR was between 2 and 3. Finally, Figure 4c shows the SWR for the square array; in this case, the DS antenna shows SWR values between 1.3 and 1.5, except for those cases where *ad* = 1 mm (SWR $\geq$ 2). The MTM array with *ad* = 10 mm and *ad* = 15 mm had SWR values that were lower than 1.6; however, for *ad* = 1 mm and *ad* = 5 mm, the SWR was between 2 and 3.7. Moreover, to use the MTM antenna in multi-antenna arrays, the *bt* must be higher than 20 mm.

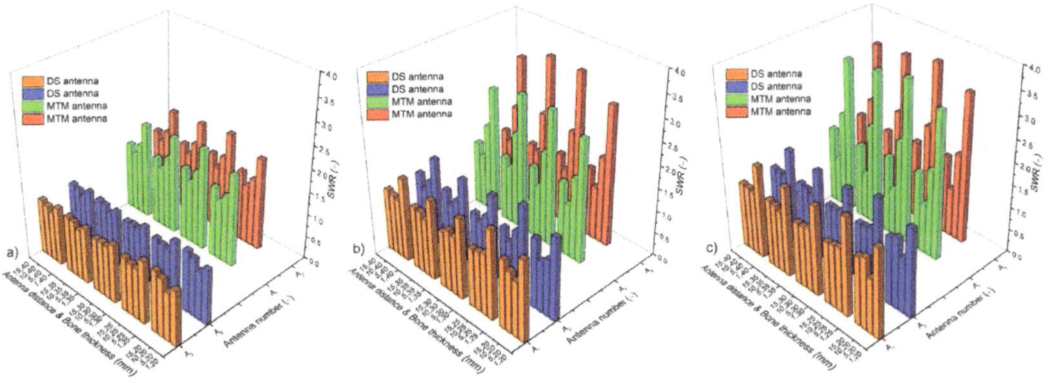

Figure 4. SWR of the antennas that compose the analyzed antenna arrays. (**a**) linear antenna array, (**b**) triangular antenna array (SWR for A_2 is within the values of A_1 and A_3), and (**c**) square antenna array (SWR for A_2 and A_4 is within the values of A_1 and A_3). DS = double slot antenna, MTM = monopole antenna; A_1, A_2, A_3, and A_4 correspond to the antenna number in each antenna array.

3.3. Microwave Heat-Source Density and Thermal Distributions

Figure 5 shows the distributions of the microwave heat source in the observation plane XY, that was generated for the best-case scenarios, as well as the 3D views of the thermal distribution at temperatures higher than 50 °C. Clearly, the temperature field distributions are strongly related with the heat source distribution. Figure 5a,c,e,g,i,k shows how the microwave heat-source density can be modified as a function of the antenna type and antenna distance (ad). It is observed that the fields that are generated by each antenna are combined; therefore, the region of tissue that reaches thermal ablation is bigger. Consequently, the heat distributions are also different for each antenna array, as can be observed in Figure 5b,d,f,h,j,l. It is also observed how the reached temperature is different for each case-scenario. Moreover, the reached temperature also depends on the treatment time; for example, Figure 5b,d represent the thermal distribution after 10 min, Figure 5f,h after 5 min, while Figure 5j,l after 10 and 5 min, respectively. The reached temperatures depend on the antenna type, antenna distance (*ad*), and the treatment time.

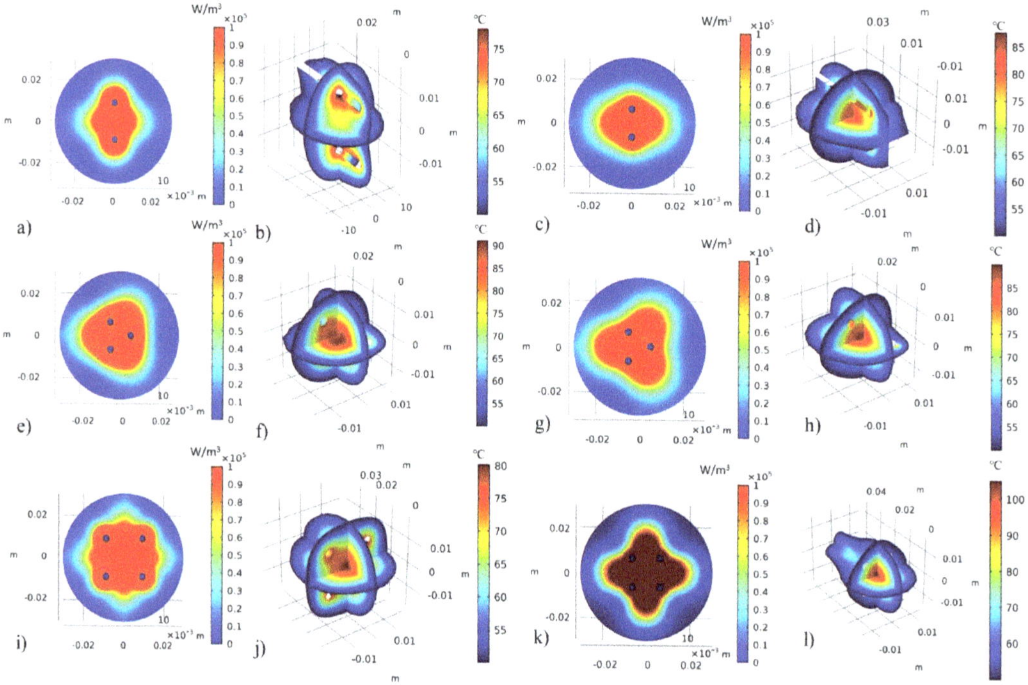

Figure 5. Distributions of the microwave heat source in the observation plane XY (W/cm^3) and 3D views of the thermal distribution at temperatures higher than 50 °C. (**a**) heat source field for a linear array of doble slot antennas (*ad* = 15 mm and *bt* = 30 mm), (**b**) thermal distribution generated by the linear array of doble slot antennas *ad* = 15 mm and *bt* = 30 mm after 5 min, (**c**) heat source field for a linear array of monopole antennas (*ad* = 10 mm and *bt* = 40 mm), (**d**) thermal distribution generated by the linear array of monopole antennas (*ad* = 10 mm and *bt* = 40 mm) after 10 min, (**e**) heat source field for a triangular array of doble slot antennas (*ad* = 10 mm and *bt* = 40 mm), (**f**) thermal distribution generated by the triangular array of doble slot antennas (*ad* = 10 mm and *bt* = 40 mm) after 5 min, (**g**) heat source field for a triangular array of monopole antennas (*ad* = 10 mm and *bt* = 40 mm), (**h**) thermal distribution generated by the triangular array of monopole antennas (*ad* = 10 mm and *bt* = 40 mm) after 5 min, (**i**) heat source field for a square array of doble slot antennas (*ad* = 15 mm and *bt* = 40 mm), (**j**) thermal distribution generated by the square array of doble slot antennas (*ad* = 15 mm and *bt* = 40 mm) after 10 min, (**k**) heat source field for a square array of monopole antennas (*ad* = 10 mm and *bt* = 25 mm), (**l**) thermal distribution generated by the square array of monopole antennas (*ad* = 10 mm and *bt* = 25 mm) after 5 min.

3.4. Linear Antenna Array

Figure 6 shows the volume of bone tissue at ablation temperatures (T > 55 °C) as a function of time, antenna distance (*ad*), and bone thickness (*bt*). According to the SWR values (Figure 5a), all the case scenarios that were analyzed for the DS linear antenna array had a good performance (SWR < 1.4). Therefore, Figure 6a shows the volumes of bone tissue at ablation temperatures that were reached by the DS antenna array. As it was expected, the volume of heating tissue increases a function of time; moreover, the smaller the *ad*, the higher the tissue volume at ablation temperatures. Figure 6b shows the volume of bone tissue at ablation temperatures that was obtained with the linear array of MTM antennas. The best-case scenarios for each analyzed bone thickness (*bt*) were obtained with *ad* = 5 mm and *ad* = 10 mm. Although the rest of the cases for the MTM antenna arrays showed ablation temperatures in bone tissue, the SWR values for those antennas were approximately 2, which means higher power losses that can either overheat the patient or damage the equipment. Moreover, the tissue volumes that were reached by the MTM antenna array were lower than those that were reached with the DS antenna array. As it could be observed, different volumes of bone tissue at ablation temperatures could be reached depending on antenna type, treatment time, antenna distance, and bone thickness.

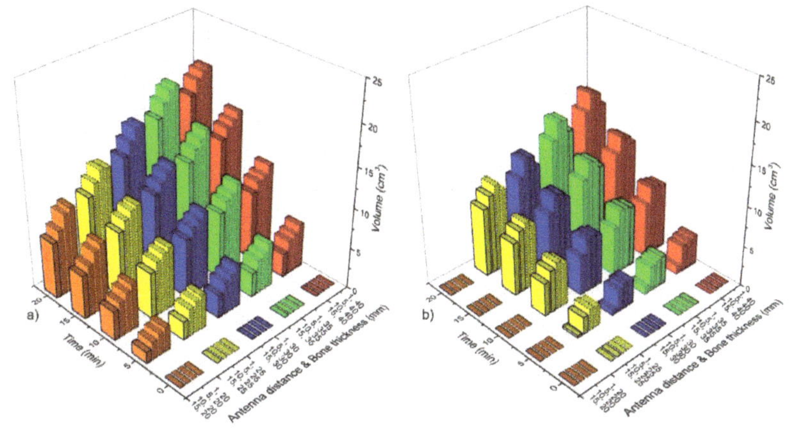

Figure 6. Bone tissue volume at ablation temperatures (T > 55 °C) as a function of time, antenna distance (*ad*), and bone thickness (*bt*). (**a**) Linear array of DS antennas, (**b**) linear array of MTM antennas.

Table 3 shows the performance of the best-case scenarios for each bone thickness (*bt* = 20 mm–40 mm). The SWR, maximum temperature, and volume of bone ($V_{\_bone}$) and muscle ($V_{\_muscle}$) at ablation temperatures (T > 55 °C) are shown. For the DS antenna array, the best antenna distance was 5 mm; except for a *bt* = 30 mm, where *ad* = 15 mm was the best option. In all cases, ablation temperatures were reached after 5 min; however, the tissue volumes under ablation were lower than those that were reached after 20 min. Although the volume of bone tissue at ablation temperatures was between 9.74 cm^3 and 19.15 cm^3 after 20 min, the maximum reached temperatures were greater than 100 °C; moreover, the surrounding muscle tissue was also affected by temperature increases. It must consider that treatment time can be reduced from 20 min to 15 min to reduce the temperature and the effect on muscle. The MTM antenna showed maximum temperatures that were lower than 100 °C even after 20 min. The volume of bone at ablation temperatures goes from 9.81 cm^3 to 16.49 cm^3. After 20 min, the maximum muscle volume at ablation temperatures was 5.02 cm^3, which means that muscle tissue is less affected when the MTM antenna is used. It is important to address that treatment time plays an important role in the volume of tissue (either bone or muscle) that reaches ablation.

Table 3. Linear antenna array performance. Best-case scenarios were obtained for each analyzed bone thickness (*bt*) based on the SWR of the antennas. Maximum reached temperature and tissue volume at temperatures higher than 55 °C are presented.

Antenna Array	*ad* [mm]	*bt* [mm]	SWR		T_max [°C]		V_bone [cm³]		V_muscle [cm³]	
			A_1	A_2	5 min	20 min	5 min	20 min	5 min	20 min
2 double slot antennas (DS)	5	20	1.05	1.05	85.49	106.10	2.69	9.74	1.36	8.13
	5	25	1.11	1.11	88.23	109.00	3.90	13.00	0.28	4.41
	15	30	1.15	1.15	70	85.22	2.85	13.09	0	2.15
	5	35	1.10	1.10	86.76	109.10	4.67	18.58	0	0.08
	5	40	1.09	1.09	87.41	109.50	4.65	19.15	0	0
2 monopole antennas (MTM)	10	25	1.30	1.30	65.60	82.82	2.08	9.81	0.22	5.02
	10	30	1.36	1.36	67.63	84.20	2.71	12.07	0	2.52
	10	35	1.32	1.32	68.7	86.02	3.06	14.83	0	0.48
	10	40	1.29	1.29	68.23	86.01	3.24	16.49	0	0

Figure 7 shows the projections of the ablation zones on three observation planes, as explained below, for treatment times of 5, 10, 15, and 20 min. The isothermal contours at 55 °C that were generated by linear DS and MTM antenna arrays are presented. In these cases, each antenna was fed with 3 W, which means a total power of 6 W. The observation was throughout one transversal and two longitudinal planes. The transversal observation plane (XY) intersects the antenna insertion path at the height between both slots and at the middle point of the monopole. The longitudinal observation plane XZ and YZ crosses the centroid of the geometry of each configuration over the respective axes (See Figure 3). Figure 7a–c show the performance of a linear DS antenna array with *ad* = 15 mm and *bt* = 30 mm, at planes XZ, XY, and YZ, respectively; while Figure 7d–f show the performance of a linear MTM antenna array with *ad* = 10 mm and *bt* = 40 mm at the same planes. It was observed that even after 5 min of treatment time, both configurations were capable of generating continuous ablation zones, which became more extended as a function of treatment time. Both configurations generated different isothermal contours; however, it is observed that the longer the distance between antennas (*ad*), the smaller the ablation zone. Moreover, the DS antenna array shows temperatures higher than 100 °C in plane XY for times above 15 min and in plane YZ for times above 10 min, while the MTM antenna array does not generate overheating even after 20 min. Figure 6 shows how the isothermal contour can be modified by antenna type, antenna distance (*ad*), and bone thickness (*bt*).

Table 4 shows the ablation zone distances along the X, Y, and Z axes for 5 and 20 min. In order to quantify the uniformity of the ablation zone, a sphericity index was calculated. It was the ratio between the ablation zone volume when it is calculated as an ellipsoid by considering the distances (DX, DY, DZ), divided by the volume of a sphere that was generated by considering the longest distance. The distances (DX, DY, DZ) were calculated as the widest distance of the isothermal contour at 55 °C along the three axes.

Table 4. Best-case scenarios of ablation zone dimensions for 5 min and 10 min (6 W) for the linear configurations of DS and MTM antennas.

	DS Antenna Array		MTM Antenna Array	
Antenna distance (*ad*) (mm)	15		10	
Bone thickness (*bt*) (mm)	30		40	
Heating time	5 min	20 min	5 min	20 min
D_X (cm)	0.71	2.45	1.39	2.77
D_Y (cm)	1.91	3.29	2.26	3.76
D_Z (cm)	2.66	3.31	1.49	2.80
Sphericity index	0.19	0.73	0.40	0.54

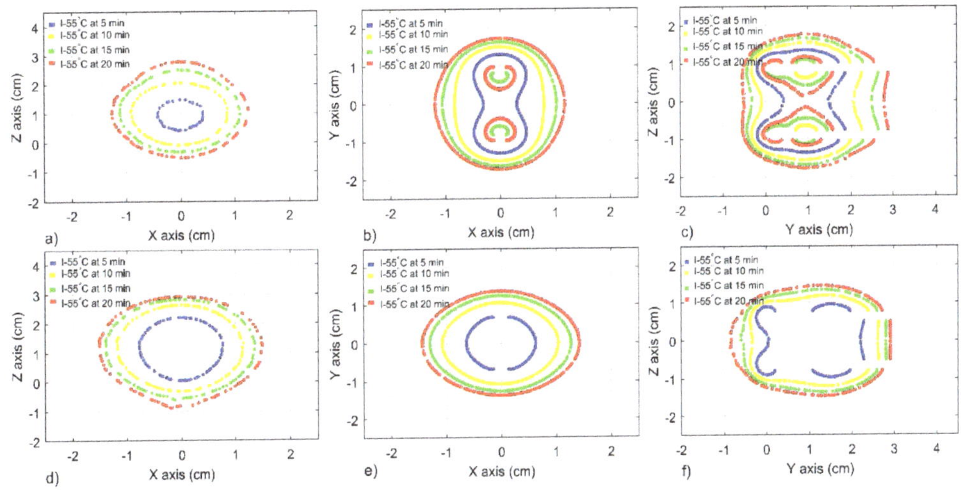

Figure 7. Isotherm contour at 55 °C generated by a linear antenna array over different planes after 5 min, 10 min, 15 min, and 20 min of treatment time. (**a–c**) XZ, XY, and YZ planes for a DS antenna array with ad = 15 mm and bt = 30 mm, respectively (**d–f**) XZ, XY, and YZ planes for a MTM antenna array with ad = 10 mm and bt = 40 mm, respectively.

3.5. Triangular Antenna Array

Figure 8 shows the volume of bone tissue at ablation temperatures that were reached by the triangular antenna array. Figure 8a shows the volumes that were generated by the DS antenna array. In this case, and according to the SWR values (See Figure 4b), all cases, except the ones with *ad* = 1 mm and *bt* = 20 mm–40 mm (SWR $\cong$ 2), had a good performance, i.e., these cases present SWRs values <2 and $V_{\_bone} \cong 4$ cm^3 (5 min)–31 cm^3 (20 min). The MTM antenna array with *ad* = 1 mm and *bt* = 25 mm–40 mm showed SWR values ≥ 3; however, for the rest of the cases, the SWRs <2 and $V_{\_bone} \cong 4$ cm^3 (5 min)–31 cm^3 (20 min). Although the DS antenna array and the MTM antenna array reach similar $V_{\_bone}$ after 20 min, in general, with the MTM antenna array, the $V_{\_bone}$ achieved is lower than those achieved by the DS antenna array, as can be observed in Figure 8a,b. The triangular array, either DS or MTM antennas, produces a more significant temperature effect over the muscle tissue, which means that muscle can also reach ablation temperatures depending on treatment time.

Table 5 shows the best-case scenarios that were obtained with the triangular antenna arrays for each analyzed bone thickness (*bt*). The DS antenna array, *bt* = 20 mm and *ad* = 5 mm generated bone tissue overheating ($T_{\_max}$ > 100 °C) even after 5 min of treatment time ($T_{\_max}$ = 111.20 °C). Therefore, treatment times that are lower than 3 min are recommended; however, the ablated tissue volume will be less than 4 cm^3. An increase in the antenna distance (*ad* = 10 mm) helps to reduce $T_{\_max}$ and increase the volume of ablated bone. Moreover, if the treatment time increases, so does the tissue volume under ablation. However, not only bone but also muscle tissue reached ablation temperatures. After 5 min, the muscle volume ($V_{\_muscle}$) at ablation temperatures could be considered within the safety margin. Nevertheless, after 20 min, the volume of the heated muscle increased considerably, especially for those cases with *bt* = 20 mm and 25 mm, where $V_{\_muscle}$ = 13.55 cm^3 and 10.11 cm^3, respectively. Nevertheless, it will always depend on the tumor volume that is to be treated.

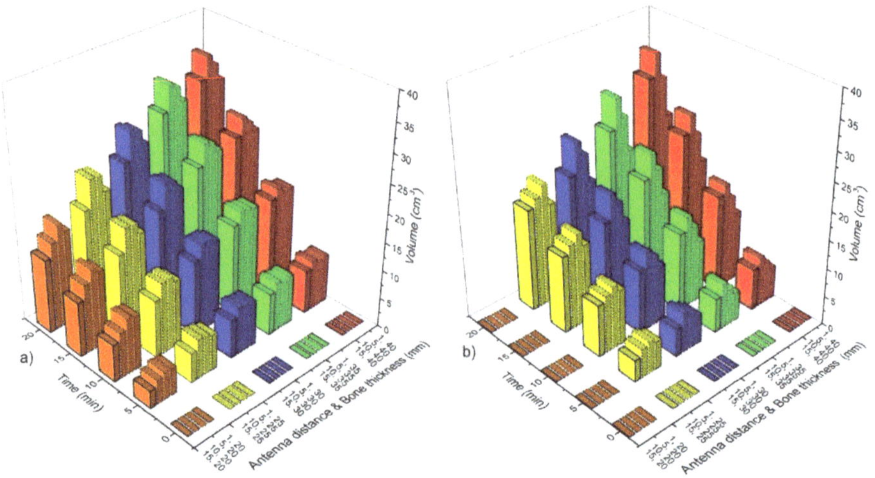

Figure 8. Bone tissue volume at ablation temperatures (T > 55 °C) as a function of time, antenna distance (*ad*), and bone thickness (*bt*). (**a**) Triangular array of DS antennas and (**b**) triangular array of MTM antennas.

Table 5. Triangular antenna array performance. Best-case scenarios were obtained for each analyzed bone thicknesses (*bt*) based on the SWR of the antennas. Maximum reached temperature and tissue volume at temperatures higher than 55 °C are presented.

Antenna Array	*ad* [mm]	*bt* [mm]	SWR			$T_{\_max}$ [°C]		$V_{\_bone}$ [cm^3]		$V_{\_muscle}$ [cm^3]	
			$A_{1'}$	A_2	A_3	5 min	20 min	5 min	20 min	5 min	20 min
3 double slot antennas (DS)	5	20	1.21	1.17	1.24	111.20	139.6	4.83	17.94	2.64	13.55
	10	25	1.30	1.30	1.10	92.05	121.3	6.87	22.92	0.71	10.11
	10	30	1.35	1.35	1.13	71.30	92.48	6.70	23.00	0	7.90
	10	35	1.35	1.35	1.12	70.25	92.62	7.30	28.47	0	2.56
	10	40	1.32	1.32	1.11	70.26	94.53	7.59	31.29	0	0.69
3 monopole antennas (MTM)	10	25	1.15	1.15	1.19	85.00	112.1	4.97	19.33	2.44	13.16
	15	30	1.56	1.56	1.52	69.05	91.70	4.92	20.30	0.32	9.52
	10	35	1.26	1.26	1.29	88.31	117.8	7.98	30.13	0	2.12
	10	40	1.17	1.17	1.21	90.20	120.9	8.75	34.91	0	0.30

Figure 9a–c show the performance of a triangular DS antenna array with *ad* = 10 mm and *bt* = 40 mm, at planes XZ, XY, and YZ, respectively, while Figure 9d–f show the performance of a triangular MTM antenna array with *ad* = 10 mm and *bt* = 40 mm at the same planes. As in the linear antenna array, the triangular configurations generated continuous ablation zones, even after 5 min of treatment time. In this case, the best-case scenarios had the same *ad* (10 mm) and *bt* (40 mm). Therefore, both configurations generated quite similar isothermal contours, with slight differences (See Table 6). By combining *ad* and *bt* dimensions adequately, the reached temperatures did not surpass the 100 °C in any of the analyzed planes (See Table 5).

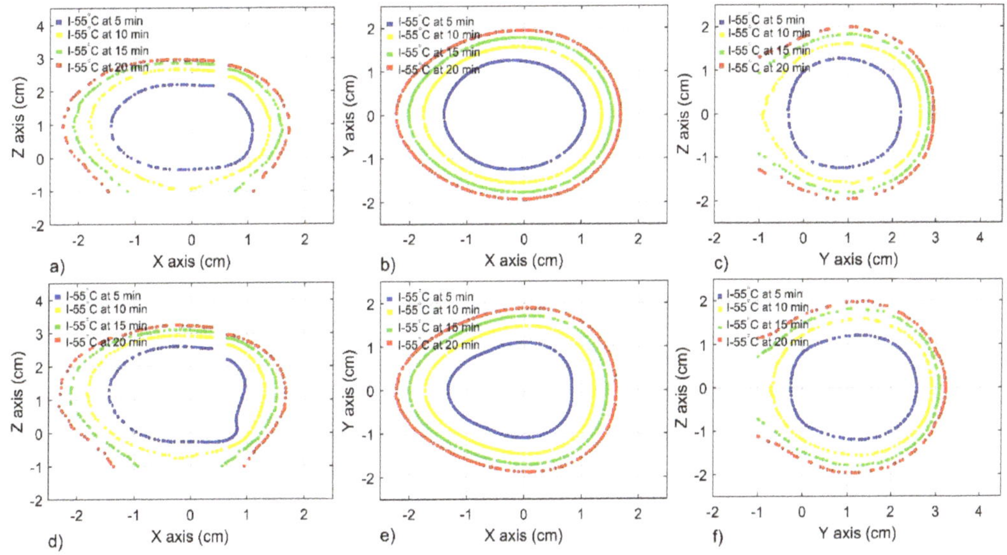

Figure 9. Isotherm contour at 55 °C generated by a triangular antenna array over different planes after 5 min, 10 min, 15 min, and 20 min of treatment time. (**a–c**) XZ, XY, and YZ planes for a DS antenna array with *ad* = 10 mm and *bt* = 40 mm, respectively (**d–f**) XZ, XY, and YZ planes for a MTM antenna array with *ad* = 10 mm and *bt* = 40 mm, respectively.

Table 6. Best-case scenarios of ablation zone dimensions for 5 min and 10 min (9 W) for the triangular configurations of DS and MTM antennas.

	DS Antenna Array		**MTM Antenna Array**	
Antenna distance (*ad*) (mm)	10		10	
Bone thickness (*bt*) (mm)	40		40	
Heating time	5 min	20 min	5 min	20 min
D_X (cm)	2.48	3.94	2.27	3.90
D_Y (cm)	2.53	3.94	2.84	4.21
D_Z (cm)	2.50	3.90	2.29	3.84
Sphericity index	0.96	0.98	0.64	0.84

Table 6 shows the ablation zone distances along the X, Y, and Z axis and the sphericity index for 5 and 20 min generated by the triangular configurations of DS and MTM antennas.

3.6. Square Antenna Array

Figure 10 shows the volume of bone tissue at ablation temperatures that were reached by the square configuration. Figure 10a shows the volumes that were generated by the DS antenna array. According to the SWR values (See Figure 4c), cases corresponding to *ad* = 1 mm and *bt* = 20 mm–40 mm had SWR values that were higher than 2, which means that their performance is not highly effective. Nevertheless, if ad increases, lower SWR values are achieved (See Table 7). Moreover, the tissue volume at ablation temperatures also increases. The volume of bone at ablation temperatures goes from approximately 7 cm^3 (5 min) to 44.5 cm^3 (20 min). Although the bone volume at ablation temperatures can be up to 44.5 cm^3, the temperature increase also affects muscle and fatty tissues. In the worst-case scenario, even muscle was more affected than bone tissue, i.e., the V_{-bone} = 19.5 cm^3, $V_{-muscle}$ = 25.33 cm^3, and V_{-fat} = 2.23 cm^3 for *ad* = 15 mm and *bt* = 20 mm. On the other hand, the MTM antenna array reached lower temperatures. Moreover, just cases where *ad* = 10 mm and 15 mm and *bt* = 25 mm–40 mm showed SWR values $\leq$2 (See Table 7).

Therefore, in these cases, the reached volumes of bone were from 7 cm^3 (5 min) to 41 cm^3 (20 min). In the worst-case scenario (*ad* = 15 mm and *bt* = 20 mm), $V_{\_bone}$ = 24.87 cm^3, $V_{\_muscle}$ = 19.5 cm^3, and $V_{\_fat}$ = 0.37 cm^3.

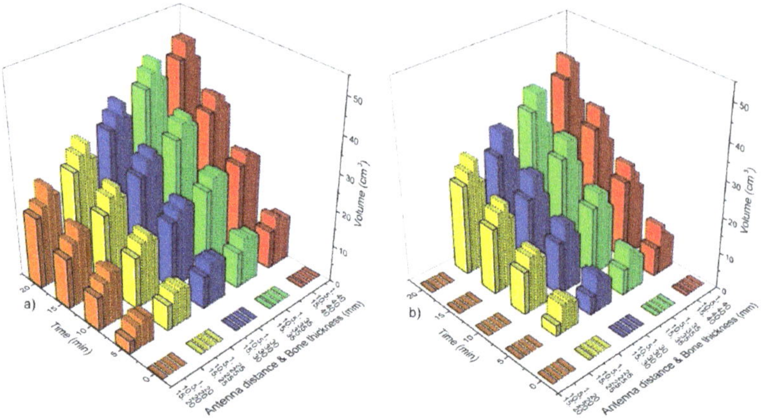

Figure 10. Bone tissue volume at ablation temperatures (T > 55 °C) as a function of time, antenna distance (*ad*), and bone thickness (*bt*). (**a**) Square array of DS antennas and (**b**) square array of MTM antennas.

Table 7. Square antenna array performance. Best-case scenarios were obtained for each analyzed bone thickness (*bt*) based on the SWR of the antennas. Maximum reached temperature and tissue volume at temperatures higher than 55 °C are presented.

Antenna Array	*ad* [mm]	*bt* [mm]	SWR				$T_{\_max}$ [°C]		$V_{\_bone}$ [cm^3]		$V_{\_muscle}$ [cm^3]	
			A_1	A_2	A_3	A_4	5 min	20 min	5 min	20 min	5 min	20 min
4 double slot antennas	5	20	1.21	1.21	1.20	1.21	132.3	139.9	7.15	26.22	4.30	20.79
	15	25	1.36	1.36	1.36	1.36	67.45	88.30	6.86	27.03	0.52	20.00
	15	30	1.32	1.35	1.36	1.35	67.83	91.44	9.04	33.63	0	14.36
	15	35	1.32	1.44	1.45	1.45	66.61	92.53	9.86	40.56	0	7.31
	15	40	1.25	1.43	1.44	1.44	67.03	93.7	10.46	44.53	0	3.86
4 monopole antennas	10	25	1.09	1.07	1.07	1.09	105.3	140	7.79	27.69	4.24312	17.51
	10	30	1.04	1.04	1.04	1.03	110.4	140	10.17	34.09	2.11448	13.21
	10	35	1.02	1.03	1.03	1.02	109.2	140	12.28	40.85	0.42405	7.75
	10	40	1.04	1.03	1.03	1.04	108.1	140	13.56	46.41	0	3.10

Table 7 shows the best-case scenarios for each analyzed *bt* with a square configuration. For a square DS antenna array with *ad* = 5 mm and *bt* = 20 mm, tissue overheating was observed, and maximum temperatures of 132.3 °C and 139.9 °C were reached after 5 min and 20 min, respectively. Moreover, after 20 min, volumes of bone and muscle at ablation temperatures were quite similar ($V_{\_bone}$ = 26.22 cm^3 vs. $V_{\_muscle}$ = 20 cm^3); therefore, the focalization of the EM energy is not predominant over bone tissue. Nevertheless, the DS antennas array had the best performance with a maximum distance between the antennas (*ad* = 15 mm) and bone thickness higher than 25 mm (*bt* = 25 mm–40 mm). In these cases, the SWR values were lower than 1.5, and the reached temperatures did not overpass the ablation range (55–100 °C) even after 20 min. Although muscle may still be affected, in order to reduce its damage, the treatment time can be reduced. On the other hand, for the square MTM antenna, the achieved SWR values were the lowest (approx. 1.1); therefore, a maximum energy transmission was obtained; consequently, an overheating of tissue was reached, even after 5 min, where temperatures between 105 °C and 108 °C and a maximum energy focus over bone tissue were presented. At 20 min of treatment time, a maximum temperature of 140 °C was reached, and muscle tissue was highly affected by the temperature increase.

Figure 11a–c show the performance of a square DS antenna array with *ad* = 15 mm and *bt* = 40 mm, at planes XZ, XY, and YZ, respectively, while Figure 11d–f show the performance of a square MTM antenna array with *ad* = 10 mm and *bt* = 25 mm at the same planes. After 5 min of treatment time, both configurations generated continuous ablation zones, which became more extensive as a function of treatment time. Both configurations generated different isothermal contours. Figure 10 shows how the isothermal contour can be modified in accordance with antenna type, antenna distance (*ad*), and bone thickness (*bt*). The fact that the total input power, in these cases, was 12 W must be addressed (3 W per antenna) because the reached temperatures were the highest from the study. Moreover, the MTM array generates maximum temperatures that are higher than 140 °C just after 5 min of treatment time. Therefore, in this case, just the isothermal contours at 5 min are shown in Figure 11.

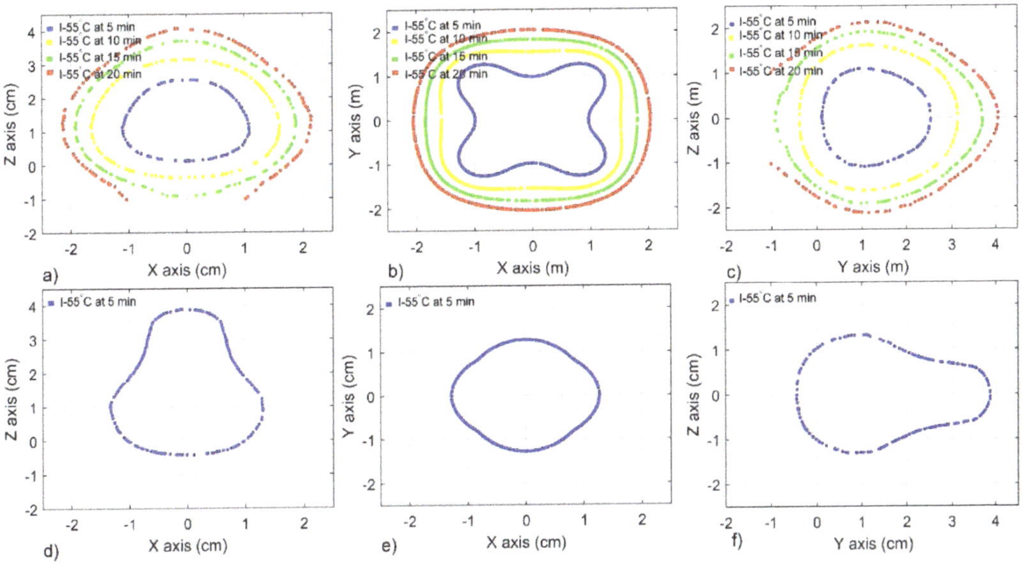

Figure 11. Isotherm contour at 55 °C that was generated by a square antenna array over different planes after 5 min, 10 min, 15 min, and 20 min of treatment time. (**a**–**c**) XZ, XY, and YZ planes for a DS antenna array with *ad* = 15 mm and *bt* = 40 mm, respectively; (**d**–**f**) XZ, XY, and YZ planes for a MTM antenna array with *ad* = 10 mm and *bt* = 25 mm, respectively.

Table 8 shows the ablation zone distances along the X, Y, and Z axis and the sphericity index for 5 and 20 min that was generated by the square configurations of DS and MTM antennas. For the MTM antenna, the sphericity index shows a reduction of the ablation zone uniformity; however, this configuration can still be used to treat different tumor shapes. The values for 20 min are not reported because the tissue is overheated (140 °C).

Table 8. Best-case scenarios of ablation zone dimensions for 5 min and 20 min (12 W) for the square configurations of DS and MTM antennas.

	DS Antenna Array		MTM Antenna Array	
Antenna distance (*ad*) (mm)	15		10	
Bone thickness (*bt*) (mm)	40		25	
Heating time	5 min	20 min	5 min	20 min
D_X (cm)	2.074	4.19	2.58	—
D_Y (cm)	2.68	5.06	4.14	—
D_Z (cm)	2.06	4.15	2.56	—
Sphericity index	0.59	0.67	1.5	

4. Discussion

Thermal ablation as bone tumors treatment has been poorly analyzed; just a few studies about it are reported in the literature. Moreover, in most of these cases, antennas that are designed to treat soft tissue have been used, making it necessary to use either a high input power or large treatment time. Recently, new micro-coaxial antennas specifically designed to treat bone tumors has been proposed by this research group. However, the first evaluations showed that to treat large bone tumors, multi-antenna arrays must be used. The main goal of this paper was to evaluate the performance of three array configurations (linear, triangular, and square) of antennas that were designed specially to treat bone tissue. The evaluation was based on SWR analysis, tissue volume at ablation temperatures, maximum reached temperatures, and isothermal contours. The double slot (DS) and the monopole (MTM) antennas were chosen to form the arrays, as they were previously designed and tested [17], i.e., their correct performance has been evaluated by experimentation in phantom and porcine ex vivo tissue. Previous experimental tests showed that both antennas could generate ablation temperatures at bone using 10 W of input power applied for durations between 5 and 10 min. Therefore, to avoid tissue overheating, the input power was reduced. In all the analyzed cases, each antenna was fed with 3 W; hence, the treatment time was up to 20 min to generate the largest coverage region. It was observed that the distance between the antennas (*ad*), bone thickness (*bt*), and treatment time play a key role in the antenna array performance.

The SWR evaluation showed that the DS antenna arrays had a better performance in all the analyzed configurations, while *ad* = 1 mm and *bt* = 25 mm generated the worse-case scenarios. With these dimensions, maximum SWR values of 1.36, 1.95, and 2.15 were found for the linear, triangular, and squared configurations, respectively. In general, the linear configuration shows no problems using antenna distances (*ad*) around 1 mm–15 mm and a bone thickness (*bt*) from 20 mm–40 mm. However, for triangular and square configurations, it was observed that *ad* = 1 mm and *bt* = 25 mm generated the highest SWR values (1.95 and 2.15, respectively), which will make it difficult to work under such conditions because either the patient or the MW equipment can be damaged. On the other hand, the MTM antenna arrays generated higher SWR values than those from the DS antenna arrays. In fact, to implement any configuration of MTM antennas, the bone thickness must be greater than 20 mm, to reduce the SWR values. For a linear configuration, the maximum SWR was 2.24 (*ad* = 1 and *bt* = 30 mm); however, in general, *ad* = 1 mm generated SWR values that were closer to 2. For triangular and squared configurations, the dimension *ad* = 1 mm and *ad* = 5 mm generated SWR between 2.0 and 3.6. Therefore, these cases could be implemented just by adding an impedance coupler to reduce the SWR as much as possible and avoid large power losses that could cause patient overheating as well as some damage to the MW equipment.

The analyzed antenna distance (*ad* = 1, 5, 10, and 15 mm) allows the generation of a continuous ablation zone even after just 1 min of heating by using a total input power of 6 W (linear configuration), 9 W (triangular configuration), and 12 W (square configuration). However, after 1 min of heating, the coverage region is narrow, focused in the area surrounding the slots and monopole; the treatment time must be increased to enhance the thermal ablation effect. After 5 min, the linear configuration of both antennas generated volumes of ablated bone similar to those that were reported by a single antenna under similar conditions [28]. A single DS antenna fed by 5 W applied per 5 min generated 2.4 cm^3 of ablated bone, while a linear DS antenna array fed by 6 W at the same time generated from 2.69 cm^3 to 4.65 cm^3 depending on antenna distances (*ad*) and bone thickness (*bt*). On the other hand, an MTM antenna fed by 5 W applied per 5 min generated an ablation volume of 2.09 cm^3, while a linear MTM antenna array fed by 6 W at the same time generated from 2.08 cm^3 to 3.24 cm^3, also depending on *ad* and *bt*. Moreover, for each configuration, antenna type, and bone thickness (*bt*), a recommended antenna distance (*ad*) was set (See Table 2, Table 4, and Table 6) based on the lowest SWR values, the highest volumes of bone under ablation, and the lowest thermal effect over muscle tissue. As expected, the longer the treatment time, the higher the reached temperatures and the volume of bone under ablation; however, muscle is also affected by the temperature increase. On the other hand, the volume of bone tissue under ablation can also be increased by using either a triangular or a square configuration of any antenna; however, the volume of muscle at ablation temperatures also increases. Therefore, tuning the input power and treatment times could be enough to reduce the thermal effects on muscle. Nevertheless, a cooling system can be implemented if we want to reduce the thermal effect over muscle without modifications on the reached temperatures and volume of ablated bone. Another essential fact to be considered is that the bone thickness is strongly related to the volume of muscle at ablation temperatures, i.e., the thicker the bone, the more negligible effect over the surrounding tissues will be generated. Figures 9 and 11 show the symmetry of the temperature distributions that were generated over the planes XZ and YZ for triangular and square configurations, respectively. Moreover, it is observed how the size of the isothermal contour is modified as a function of treatment time. The linear array does not show symmetry; therefore, Figure 7 shows how the temperature distributions tend to be different at each analyzed plane.

On the other hand, to our understanding, this study is the first one that was performed to evaluate the heating characteristics of arrays that are composed of micro-coaxial antennas that are specifically designed to treat bone. The DS and the MTM antennas were previously optimized using the finite element method; consequently, their design allows achieving a maximum energy transference. Hence, the required input power to generate thermal ablation can be reduced as much as possible. The evaluation tests that were performed to characterize both antennas showed that 10 W were enough to produce thermal ablation in bone tissue with treatment times around 5–10 min. Therefore, to avoid tissue overheating when antenna arrays are used, each antenna was fed with 3 W, i.e., a total of 6W, 9 W, and 12 W were used to feed the linear, triangular, and square configurations, respectively. These input power levels are far away from those that were reported by other authors. Karampatzakis et al. performed a similar study, implemented by using a triangular and square configuration of DS antennas [23]; they reported 50 W to generate continuous ablation zones with *ad* = 10 mm. Moreover, if the ad increases, for example, *ad* = 15 mm (triangular configuration), at least 75 W is required to generate a continuous ablation zone, while *ad* = 20 mm requires 100 W. Karampatzakis et al. reported some results for ex vivo tissue, they used a triangular array with *ad* = 15 mm and a total input power of 100 W; after 10 min of treatment time, the reported ablation zone dimensions are 5.2 cm × 5.2 cm × 5.0 cm. In the present study, a triangular configuration with 9 W and *ad* = 10 mm and *bt* = 40 mm, after 5 min, generates a $T_{\_max}$ = 70.26 °C, $V_{\_bone}$(T > 55 °C) = 7.59 cm^3, and a coverage region of 2.48 cm × 2.53 cm × 2.50 cm. After 20 min, the same configuration generates $T_{\_max}$ = 94 °C, $V_{\_bone}$ (T > 55 °C) = 31.29 cm^3, and a coverage region of 3.94 cm × 3.94 cm × 3.90 cm. In both cases, muscle is hardly affected. Although the coverage region that was reported by Karampatzakis et al. was larger than the ones that were reported in the present study, in our case, the level of input power that was used was about one-tenth of the reported values. In fact, the distance ad can be increased to increase the coverage region; therefore, the input power could also be increased. Unfortunately, most of the literature reports the evaluation of using antenna array configurations to treat soft tissues [20–22,29], making it impossible to compare our results in more detail. As it is reported in the literature, electromagnetic models are maturing rapidly; however, the accuracy of thermal models is still under development. The main problems to achieve accurate models are the uncertainties in tissue thermal properties. These properties are different among tissues, patients, etc. Moreover, these properties are temperature-dependent, i.e., they change while the temperature is changing due to the thermal ablation treatment. Therefore, to develop accurate models to predict temperature distributions is still a challenge. Not only because of the difficulty of modeling tissue properties, but also because of the high computational resources that are required to implement such models. Due to this, our research is a first approach about the performance of multi-antenna arrays to treat bone tumors; constant values of these properties were considered to reduce the complexity of the models and computational resources. However, one of the main goals of this research group is to improve the accuracy of thermal models. Therefore, our next step is to evaluate the performance of these antenna arrays to validate its performance by using phantoms, ex vivo, and in vivo tissue. The information from the experimentation in vivo will help to improve the accuracy of the thermal models. Moreover, the inclusion of a cooling system could help to reduce the thermal effect on muscle tissue. It is important to address that due to the lack of bone tumor properties that are reported in literature, just healthy bone properties were used to implement this study.

5. Conclusions

Our main scientific contribution is the evaluation of the thermal performance of different antenna arrays to know the possibility of treating large bone tumors. Moreover, this study is the first one investigating the feasibility of implementing linear, triangular, and square antenna array configurations to treat bone tumors. The linear configuration with DS antennas showed SWR $\leq$ 1.36 for ad = 1 mm–15 mm and bt = 20 mm–40 mm, while the same configuration with MTM antennas showed SWR $\leq$ 1.6 for ad = 10 mm–15 mm and bt = 25 mm–40 mm. The triangular configuration for DS and MTM antennas generated SWR $\leq$ 1.5 for ad = 5 mm–15 mm and bt = 20 mm–40 mm and SWR $\leq$ 1.5 for ad = 10 mm–15 mm and bt = 25 mm–40 mm, respectively. The square configuration with DS antennas generated SWR $\leq$ 1.5 for ad = 5 mm–20 mm and bt = 20 mm–40 mm. However, the square configuration with MTM antennas generated SWR $\leq$ 1.5 just for those cases where ad = 10 mm and bt = 25 mm–40 mm. Therefore, the analyzed antenna arrays could be used under these considerations to produce a larger ablation zone in bone tissue without damaging the surrounding muscle and fat tissue. All the other cases generated higher SWR values (>1.6), which means a lower energy transference from the MW system to the tissue. Moreover, to use the MTM in such configurations, the bone thickness (bt) must be wider than 20 mm. Bone thickness can be directly related to the tumor size where the antenna is inserted. In accordance with the treatment time, and antenna configuration, the T_max and the volume of ablated tissue could be modified, e.g., V_bone = 4.65 cm^3 and V_bone = 3.24 cm^3 were obtained with a linear DS and MTM antenna arrays that were fed with a total power of 6 W applied during 5 min, respectively. However, the triangular configuration (9 W) generated V_bone = 7.59 cm^3 and V_bone = 8.75 cm^3 with the DS and the MTM antenna arrays, respectively. Moreover, the square configuration (12 W) tends to overheat the tissue, i.e., temperatures higher than 100°C were reached. In the best-case scenarios, V_bone = 10.46 cm^3 and V_bone = 7.79 cm^3 were generated by the DS and MTM antenna arrays, respectively. To reduce the maximum temperature, the input power of each antenna can be reduced to less than 3 W. If treatment time increases (20 min), the volume of ablated bone increases; however, muscle tissue is also affected. Nevertheless, this could help to treat a larger region as a safe margin to avoid tumor recurrence. Micro-coaxial antenna arrays could be used to increase the volume of the treated region. Moreover, by using different antenna types and treatment times, different shapes of the ablation zones are generated. Our study provides a wider evaluation of several case scenarios that could happen in the clinic. Therefore, it could help as a guide to choose the antenna type, configuration, input power, treatment time, etc., in accordance with the tumor that is to be treated. To provide a stronger evaluation for future work, modeling including the thermal dependence of tissue properties and blood perfusion must be performed. Moreover, an experimental evaluation must be carried out, either in phantoms, ex, or in vivo tissues.

Author Contributions: Conceptualization, C.J.T.-R.; Data curation, J.D.M.; Formal analysis, C.J.T.-R. and G.R.-M.; Investigation, C.J.T.-R., J.D.M., T.J.R.-G. and E.S.-R.; Methodology, C.J.T.-R.; Resources, L.L.-S., A.V.-H. and J.G.-M.; Software, A.V.-H.; Supervision, C.J.T.-R., L.L.-S., G.R.-M., J.G.-M. and E.S.-R.; Validation, R.M.-V. and E.S.-R.; Visualization, C.J.T.-R. and J.D.M.; Writing–original draft, C.J.T.-R.; Writing–review & editing, T.J.R.-G., R.M.-V., J.J.A.F.-C. and E.S.-R. All authors have read and agreed to the published version of the manuscript.

Funding: This research received no external funding.

Institutional Review Board Statement: Not applicable.

Informed Consent Statement: Not applicable.

Data Availability Statement: Data available on request from the authors.

Conflicts of Interest: The authors declare no conflict of interest.

References

1. Radiation Therapy for Bone Cancer. Available online: https://www.cancer.org/cancer/bone-cancer/treating/radiation.html (accessed on 17 January 2022).
2. Chemotherapy for Bone Cancer. Available online: https://www.cancer.org/cancer/bone-cancer/treating/chemotherapy.html (accessed on 17 January 2022).
3. Riadh, W.Y.H.; Rajeev, B.; Daniel, K.; Hafid, T.A. Thermal therapy, Part III: Ablation techniques. *Crit. Rev. Biomed. Eng.* **2007**, *35*, 37–121.
4. Niu, X. Microwave Ablation for Bone Tumors. *Orthop. Muscular Syst.* **2014**, *3*, 3–6. [CrossRef]
5. Brace, C.L. Radiofrequency and Microwave Ablation of the Liver, Lung, Kidney, and Bone: What Are the Differences? *Curr. Probl. Diagn. Radiol.* **2009**, *38*, 135–143. [CrossRef] [PubMed]
6. Montademi, K.; Levine, B.D.; Bukata, S.V.; Genshaft, S. Percutaneous Image-Guided Musculoskeletal Tumor Treatments. *AJR Am. J. Roentgenol.* **2016**, *207*, 517–525. [CrossRef]
7. Filippiadis, D.K.; Tutton, S.; Kelekis, A. Percutaneous bone lesion ablation. *Radiol. Medica* **2014**, *119*, 462–469. [CrossRef] [PubMed]
8. Moser, T.; Buy, X.; Goyault, G.; Tok, C.H.; Irani, F.; Gangi, A. Image-guided ablation of bone tumors: Review of current techniques. *J. Radiol.* **2008**, *89*, 461–471. [CrossRef]
9. Knavel, E.; Brace, C. Tumor Ablation: Common Modalities and General Practices. *Tech. Vasc. Interv. Radiol.* **2013**, *16*, 192–200. [CrossRef]
10. Pusceddu, C.; Sotgia, B.; Fele, R.M.; Melis, L. Treatment of Bone Metastases with Microwave Thermal Ablation. *J. Vasc. Interv. Radiol.* **2012**, *24*, 229–233. [CrossRef] [PubMed]
11. Fan, Q.Y.; Zhou, Y.; Zhang, M.; Ma, B.; Yang, T.; Long, H.; Yu, Z.; Li, Z. Microwave ablation of malignant extremity bone tumors. *Springerplus* **2016**, *5*, 1373. [CrossRef] [PubMed]
12. Trujillo-Romero, C.J.; Rico-Martínez, G.; Leija-Salas, L.; Vera-Hernández, A.; Gutiérrez-Martínez, J. Microwave ablation to treat bone tumors by using a double slot antenna: A modelling study. *Pan Am. Health Care Exch.* **2017**, 66–69.
13. Lujan, F.; Pinilla, B.; Gutierrez-Martinez, J.; Vera-Hernandez, A.; Leija, L.; Trujillo-Romero, C.J. Theoretical model of MW antennas to treat bone tumors: One slot and one slot choked antennas. In Proceedings of the 2017 14th International Conference on Electrical Engineering, Computing Science and Automatic Control, CCE, Mexico City, Mexico, 20–22 September 2017.
14. Trujillo-Romero, C.J.; Rico-Martínez, G.; Gutiérrez-Martínez, J. Thermal ablation: An alternative to bone cancer. *Investig. En Discapac.* **2018**, *7*, 35–46.
15. Trujillo, C.J.; Rico, G.; Leija, L.; Vera, A.; Gutiérrez, J. Micro-Coaxial Slot Antenna to Treat Bone Tumors by Thermal Ablation: Theoretical and Experimental Evaluation. *IEEE Lat. Am. Trans.* **2018**, *16*, 2731–2737. [CrossRef]
16. Trujillo-Romero, C.J.; Leija-Salas, L.; Vera-Hernández, A.; Rico-Martínez, G.; Gutiérrez-Martínez, J. Double Slot Antenna for Microwave Thermal Ablation to Treat Bone Tumors: Modeling and Experimental Evaluation. *Electronics* **2021**, *10*, 761. [CrossRef]
17. Ramírez-Guzmán, T.J.; Trujillo-Romero, C.J.; Martínez-Valdez, R.; Leija-Salas, L.; Vera-Hernández, A.; Rico-Martínez, G.; Ortega-Palacios, R.; Gutiérrez-Martínez, J. Thermal Evaluation of a Micro-Coaxial Antenna Set to Treat Bone Tumors: Design, Parametric FEM Modeling and Evaluation in Multilayer Phantom and Ex Vivo Porcine Tissue. *Electronics* **2021**, *10*, 2289. [CrossRef]
18. Stages of Bone Cancer | American Cancer Society. Available online: https://www.cancer.org/cancer/bone-cancer/detection-diagnosis-staging/staging.html (accessed on 17 January 2022).

19. Brace, C.L.; Laeseke, P.F.; Sampson, L.A.; Frey, T.M.; Van Der Weide, D.W.; Lee, F.T. Microwave ablation with multiple simultaneously powered small-gauge triaxial antennas: Results from an in vivo swine liver model. *Radiology* **2007**, *244*, 151–156. [CrossRef] [PubMed]
20. Wright, A.S.; Lee, F.T.; Mahvi, D.M. Hepatic microwave ablation with multiple antennae results in synergistically larger zones of coagulation necrosis. *Ann. Surg. Oncol.* **2003**, *10*, 275–283. [CrossRef]
21. Phasukkit, P.; Tungjitkusolmun, S.; Sangworasil, M. Finite-element analysis and in vitro experiments of placement configurations using triple antennas in microwave hepatic ablation. *IEEE Trans. Biomed. Eng.* **2009**, *56*, 2564–2572. [CrossRef]
22. Pauff, S.M.; Miller, S.C. Multiple-Antenna Microwave Ablation: Spatially Distributing Power Improves Thermal Profiles and Reduces Invasiveness. *J. Interv. Oncol.* **2009**, *2*, 65–72.
23. Karampatzakis, A.; Kühn, S.; Tsanidis, G.; Neufeld, E.; Samaras, T.; Kuster, N. Heating characteristics of antenna arrays used in microwave ablation: A theoretical parametric study. *Comput. Biol. Med.* **2013**, *43*, 1321–1327. [CrossRef] [PubMed]
24. Jin, J.-M.; Riley, D.J. *Finite Element Analysis of Antennas and Arrays*; Jhon Wiley & Sons, Inc.: Hoboken, NJ, USA, 2009; ISBN 9780470401286.
25. Sysoev, S.; Kislitsy, A. Modeling of Microwave Heating and Oil Filtration in Stratum. *Numer. Simul. —Appl. Ex. Theory* **2011**. [CrossRef]
26. Hasgall, P.; Neufeld, E.; Gosselin, M.; Klingenbock, A.; Kuster, N. IT'IS Database for Thermal and Electromagnetic Parameters of Biological Tissues. Available online: http://www.itis.ethz.ch/itis-for-health/tissue-properties/overview/ (accessed on 6 September 2022).
27. Gebauer, B.; Tunn, P. Thermal Ablation in Bone Tumors. In *Recent Results in Cancer Research*; Springer-Verlag: Berlin/Heidelberg, Germany, 2006; Volume 167.
28. Ramírez-Guzmán, T.J. Estudio del uso de un Aplicador de Radiaciones Electromagnéticas y del Ultrasonido Focalizado Para su Posible uso en el Tratamiento de Tumores Óseos. Master's Thesis, Center for Research and Advanced Studies (CINVESTAV), Mexico city, Mexico, 2019.
29. Andreozzi, A.; Brunese, L.; Iasiello, M.; Tucci, C.; Vanoli, G.P. A novel local thermal non-equilibrium model for biological tissue applied to multiple-antennas configurations for thermal ablation. *Numer. Heat Transf. Part A Appl.* **2020**, *79*, 111–121. [CrossRef]

sensors

MDPI

Article

Microwave Ablation of Liver, Kidney and Lung Lesions: One-Month Response and Manufacturer's Charts' Reliability in Clinical Practice

Julien Frandon *, Philippe Akessoul, Tarek Kammoun, Djamel Dabli, Hélène de Forges, Jean-Paul Beregi and Joël Greffier

IMAGINE UR UM 103, Department of Medical Imaging, Nîmes University Hospital, Montpellier University, 30029 Nîmes, France; philippe.akessoul@chu-nimes.fr (P.A.); tarek.kammoun@chu-nimes.fr (T.K.); djamel.dabli@chu-nimes.fr (D.D.); helene.deforges@chu-nimes.fr (H.d.F.); jean.paul.beregi@chu-nimes.fr (J.-P.B.); joel.greffier@chu-nimes.fr (J.G.)
* Correspondence: jfrandon38@gmail.com

Abstract: Microwave ablation systems allow for performing tumoral destruction in oncology. The objective of this study was to assess the early response and reliability of the microwave ablation zone size at one month for liver, kidney and lung lesions, as compared to the manufacturer's charts. Patients who underwent microwave ablation with the Emprint^{TM} ablation system for liver, kidney and lung lesions between June 2016 and June 2018 were retrospectively reviewed. Local response and ablation zone size (major, L, and minor, l, axes) were evaluated on the one-month follow-up imaging. Results were compared to the manufacturers' charts using the Bland–Altman analysis. Fifty-five patients (mean age 68 ± 11 years; 95 lesions) were included. The one-month complete response was 94%. Liver ablations showed a good agreement with subtle, smaller ablation zones (L: −2 ± 5.7 mm; l: −5.2 ± 5.6 mm). Kidney ablations showed a moderate agreement with larger ablations for L (L: 8.69 ± 7.94 mm; l: 0.36 ± 4.77 mm). Lung ablations showed a moderate agreement, with smaller ablations for l (L: −5.45 ± 4.5 mm; l: −9.32 ± 4.72 mm). With 94% of early complete responses, the system showed reliable ablations for liver lesions, but larger ablations for kidney lesions, and smaller for lung lesions.

Keywords: interventional radiology; percutaneous ablation; tumour response; microwave; oncology

Citation: Frandon, J.; Akessoul, P.; Kammoun, T.; Dabli, D.; de Forges, H.; Beregi, J.-P.; Greffier, J. Microwave Ablation of Liver, Kidney and Lung Lesions: One-Month Response and Manufacturer's Charts' Reliability in Clinical Practice. *Sensors* **2022**, *22*, 3973. https://doi.org/10.3390/s22113973

Academic Editors: Hoi-Shun Antony Lui and Mikael Persson

Received: 21 April 2022
Accepted: 19 May 2022
Published: 24 May 2022

1. Introduction

Thermoablation is now part of the wide therapeutic arsenal in oncology. Several studies have shown the non-inferiority of ablation techniques compared with conventional surgery in the treatment of some liver [1], pulmonary [2] or renal tumours [3]. These techniques led to a lower complication rate, a shorter hospital stay and an overall cost reduction. They are preferable for patients with important comorbidities or those who refuse surgery.

Ablation techniques include radiofrequency, microwave, cryotherapy, high-intensity focused ultrasound (HIFU) or laser. Microwave ablation is emerging as a favoured thermal technique thanks to technological advances allowing for a faster treatment time, a larger ablation zone and its use in various tissues as compared with the other ablation techniques [4]. The result is an enlarged ablation zone and theoretically fewer heat sink effects, such as cooling related to the proximity of a blood vessel [5,6]. Another advantage of microwave is the possibility to modulate the size and shape of the ablation zone by modifying the power delivered and the heating duration. To do this, the manufacturer proposes ex or in vivo indicative chart predictions to allow adaptation of the treatment to the proposed ablation with a given equipment (same generator and same needle).

There are various microwave ablation systems available, with different frequencies and technologies, thus producing different sized and shaped ablation zones [7]. In all systems, a difference between the expected volume provided by the manufacturer's chart predictions and the effective ablation volumes is frequently reported [8]. The Emprint™ Ablation system proposes an implemented microwave system with the Thermosphere™ Technology, presented as more reliable and reproducible than others, and producing more spherical ablation zones [9].

The objective of the present study was to evaluate the early local response and reliability of the procedure in clinical practice, i.e., the size of the ablation at one month for kidney, liver and lung lesions compared with the chart provided by the manufacturer.

2. Patients and Methods

2.1. Patients

This monocentric study received approval from our Institutional review board for a retrospective review of consecutive patients who underwent microwave ablation for primary or secondary liver, kidney or lung tumours from June 2016 to June 2018. Patients with no reliable measurement of the ablation zone or with lesions treated with multiple overlapping ablations were not included.

2.2. Ablation Procedure

The ablations were conducted by two interventional radiologists with more than three years of experience in the technique. The microwave generator was the Emprint™ system with Thermosphere™ Technology from Medtronic® (Minneapolis, MN, USA). Both the power delivered as well as the heating duration were at the operator's discretion, depending on the charts provided by the manufacturer. In vivo charts were used for liver and lung lesions, and ex vivo charts for kidney lesions (Table 1). The choice of the imaging technique used during needle placement, ultrasound, conventional CT scan or cone beam CT depended on the tumour location and was left to the operator's discretion.

Table 1. Charts provided by the manufacturer for liver, kidney and lung ablations.

Organ	Power (Watt)/Time (Min) (Number of Ablations)	Major Axis Expected (mm)	Minor Axis Expected (mm)
Liver * (n = 63)	100 w/10 min (n = 23)	41	36
	100 w/7 min (n = 8)	40	35
	100 w/5 min (n = 1)	39	34
	100 w/4 min (n = 1)	38	33
	75 w/10 min (n = 7)	36	33
	75 w/7 min (n = 2)	35	32
	75 w/5 min (n = 5)	33	30
	75 w/4 min (n = 2)	32	29
	75 w/2.30 min (n = 8)	30	27
	45 w/5 min (n = 2)	27	27
	45 w/4 min (n = 2)	26	26
	45 w/2.30 min (n = 2)	24	23
Kidney ** (n = 14)	100 w/2.30 min (n = 2)	29	26
	75 w/7 min (n = 5)	32	31
	75 w/5 min (n = 2)	30	29
	75 w/4 min (n = 2)	28	27
	75 w/2.30 min (n = 2)	25	23
	45 w/5 min (n = 1)	25	25
Lung * (n = 18)	75 w/5 min (n = 1)	38	34
	75 w/4 min (n = 1)	38	33
	75 w/2.30 min (n = 3)	37	32
	45 w/10 min (n = 1)	34	30
	45 w/5 min (n = 4)	33	29
	45 w/2.30 min (n = 8)	32	27

*: in vivo chart. **: ex vivo chart.

2.3. Endpoints and Assessments

The primary endpoint was the local response on the first post-ablation CT scan or MR follow-up imaging scheduled at around one month for liver, kidney and lung lesions. Ballistic and size of the ablation zone were compared to the prior imaging to evaluate the complete tumour ablation. Secondary objectives were tumours' characteristics, the size of the ablation zone and the comparison with the manufacturer's chart. All measurements were performed by one observer (P.A.) on an axial acquisition at the portal time for the liver and kidney lesions, and with a parenchymal window for the lung lesions. The major (L) and minor (l) axes were measured for all ablation zones. A sphericity index (SI) was used [10,11], defined as the ratio between the volume of the ellipsoid and the volume of a sphere, whose diameter would be the largest axis of the ellipsoid. The ablation volume was calculated as the ellipsoid volume, as: $4\pi l^2 L/3$. Using the major axis, the volume of the sphere was calculated as: $4\pi L^3/3$.

Thus, the sphericity index was calculated as follows:

$$\mathrm{SI} = \frac{4\pi l^2 L/3}{4\pi L^3/3} = \frac{l^2}{L^2}.$$

A sphericity index of 1.0 corresponded to a perfect sphere, and a sphericity index approaching 0 to an extreme ellipsoid.

2.4. Statistical Analysis

Data were reported as mean values with standard deviations and ranges. The values were compared using the Student's t-test (parametric variables) or the Wilcoxon–Mann–Whitney test (nonparametric variables). Pearson correlation coefficients between the ablation zone measurements at one month (major and minor axes, sphericity index) and the manufacturer's charts were assessed. One-month measurements and manufacturer's measurements were compared using a Bland–Altman analysis, taking the manufacturer's charts as a reference. A p-value < 0.05 was considered statistically significant.

3. Results

3.1. Patients and Lesions Characteristics

During the study period, 77 patients with 113 lesions (liver n = 73, kidney n = 18, lung n = 21 lesions) underwent microwave thermoablations using the Emprint™ ablation system (Figure 1). Twelve (12/77, 16%) patients with eighteen lesions (18/113, 16%) were excluded due to multiple overlapping ablations for the same lesion (n = 15 lesions) or no reliable measurements (n = 3 lesions, one lost to follow-up, one bilioma, one patient with an ablation outside the range of the manufacturer's charts).

Finally, 55 patients with a mean age of 68 ± 11 years (range: 33–91) with 95 lesions were included: 63 liver lesions (mean lesion long axis: 19.5 ± 7.6 mm), 14 kidney lesions (24.6 ± 8.7 mm) and 18 lung lesions (9.9 ± 5.5 mm) (Figure 2, Table 2). The indications were primary (n = 29/55, 53%) or secondary malignant tumours (n = 26/55, 47%), mainly metastases from colorectal carcinoma (n = 24/26, 92%) (Table 2). Among them, 33/55 (60%) patients had a single ablation and 22/55 (40%) patients had 2 to 4 simultaneous ablations.

3.2. Early Local Response

One month after the procedure, 89 ablations (89/95, 94%) were complete. Five liver ablations were partial, due to non-optimal needle placement during the ultrasound-guided treatment. These lesions were not clearly identified on sonography despite MRI fusion. One kidney ablation was partial, due to a tumour size of 31 mm with no optimal margins. All these patients received a second ablation treatment with CT guidance and needle placement guided by the prior ablation zone. This second treatment was not included in the study due to overlapping ablation on the same lesion.

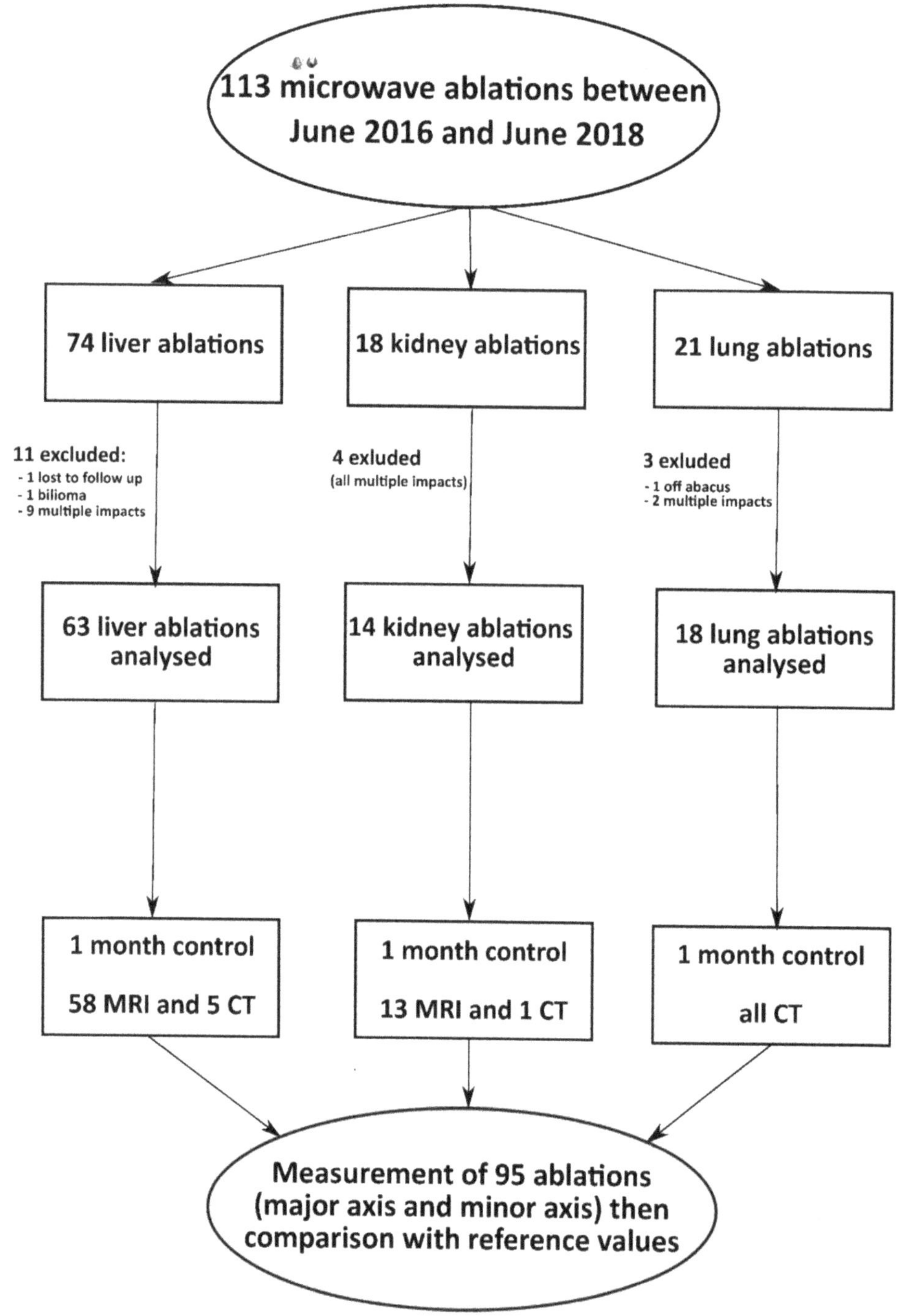

Figure 1. Flowchart of the study.

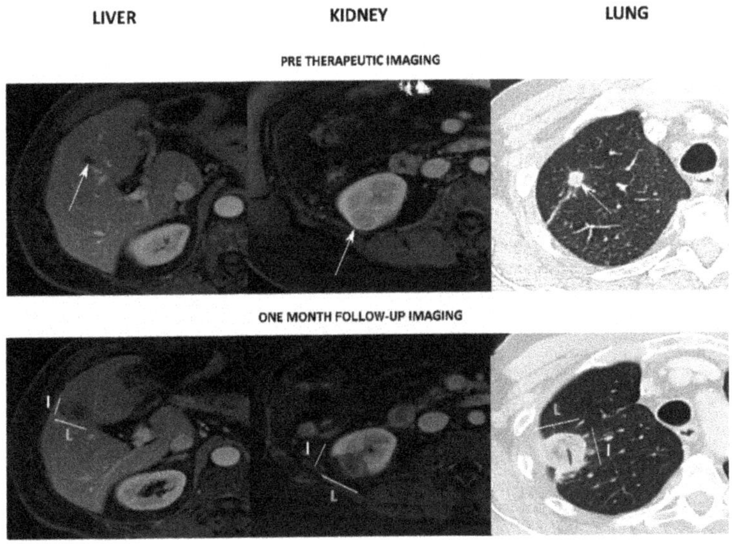

Figure 2. Examples of assessment of the ablation zones for liver (**left**), kidney (**middle**) and lung (**right**) lesions. **Top**: pre-treatment assessment of the target lesion (white arrows). **Bottom**: assessment on the one-month follow-up imaging, with the major (*L*) and minor (*l*) axes measurements. Note: air was found inside the ablation zone (tubular structure).

Table 2. Patients' characteristics.

Characteristics	Liver	Kidney	Lung
Patients, n (men/women)	31 (22/9)	13 (9/4)	11 (6/5)
Lesions, n	63	14	18
Mean age, years (SD)	68 (±10)	71 (±13)	65 (±9)
Tumour origin, n (%)			
Primitive	14/31 (45%)	12/13 (92%)	3/11 (27%)
Metastatic	17/31 (55%)	1/13 (8%)	8/11 (63%)
Metastatic origin, n (%)			
Colon	16/17 (94%)	1/1 (100%)	7/8 (87%)
Others	1/17 (6%)	0/1 (0%)	1/8 (23%)
Tumour size, mean (SD) [range], mm			
Long axis	19.5 (±7.6) [8;35]	23.7 (±6.5) [13;37]	9.9 (±5.5) [5;25]
Minor axis	15.5 (±6.2) [6;29]	19.4 (±6.6) [9;30]	7.5 (±4.8) [2;19]
Needle guidance (per lesion), n (%)			
CT	19/63 (30%)	12/14 (86%)	12/18 (67%)
CBCT	2/63 (3%)	2/14 (4%)	6/18 (33%)
US	42/63 (67%)	0/14 (0%)	0/18 (0%)
Follow-up imaging (per patient), n (%)			
MRI	28/31 (90%)	12/13 (92%)	0/11 (0%)
CT	3/31 (10%)	1/13 (8%)	11/11 (100%)
One-month response (per lesion), n (%)			
Complete	58/63 (92%)	13/14 (93%)	18/18 (100%)
Partial	5/63 (8%)	1/14 (7%)	0/18 (0%)

3.3. *Microwave Ablations' Reliability*

The ablation zones data are presented in Table 3, and 73% of the measurements were performed on MRI. The Bland–Altman analysis results for *L* and *l* are presented in Figure 3. Concerning liver lesions, 28 patients (28/31, 90%) with 58 ablations (58/63, 92%) underwent an MRI, and 3 patients (3/31, 10%) with 5 ablations (5/63, 8%) had a CT scan performed at a median time of 32 ± 7 days (range: 22–48) after treatment. The results of the Bland–Altman test showed a good agreement with a subtle, smaller, less spherical ablation zone than expected according to the manufacturer's chart: −2 ± 5.7 mm for L, −5.2 ± 5.6 mm for l, −0.15 ± 0.18 for the SI. Correlations were moderate for L (r = 0.69, $p < 0.001$) and l (r = 0.59, $p < 0.001$). There was no correlation for SI (r = 0, $p = 0.99$).

Table 3. Ablation zones sizes and sphericity index expected according to the manufacturer's charts and measured on the one-month follow-up.

	Charts (mm)	One-Month Follow-Up (mm)	*p*-Values
Liver			
Major axis, mean (SD) [range] (mm)	37.4 (±5.1) [24;44]	35.3 (±7.9) [22–46]	**0.006**
Minor axis, mean (SD) [range] (mm)	32.9 (±3.9) [23;36]	27.7 (±7.0) [12–38]	**<0.001**
Sphericity index, mean (SD) [range]	0.78 (±0.06) [0.7;1]	0.63 (±0.17) [0.32–0.9]	**<0.001**
Kidney			
Major axis, mean (SD) [range] (mm)	32.0 (±5.1) [24;42]	40.7 (±8.5) [29–58]	**0.003**
Minor axis, mean (SD) [range] (mm)	29.9 (±3.7) [23;36]	30.3 (±5.3) [20–38]	0.67
Sphericity index, mean (SD) [range]	0.89 (±0.09) [0.7;1]	0.60 (±0.23) [0.43–0.97]	**0.005**
Lung			
Major axis, mean (SD) [range] (mm)	33.7 (±3.3) [30;40]	28.2 (±6.4) [17–39]	**<0.001**
Minor axis, mean (SD) [range] (mm)	29.5 (±3.0) [27;36]	20.2 (±6.6) [10–33]	**<0.001**
Sphericity index, mean (SD) [range]	0.77 (±0.03) [0.71;0.81]	0.52 (±0.2) [0.25–0.93]	**<0.001**

Sizes according to the manufacturer's charts were elaborated in accordance with the treatments administered to the patients. Figures in bold indicate significant differences (<0.05).

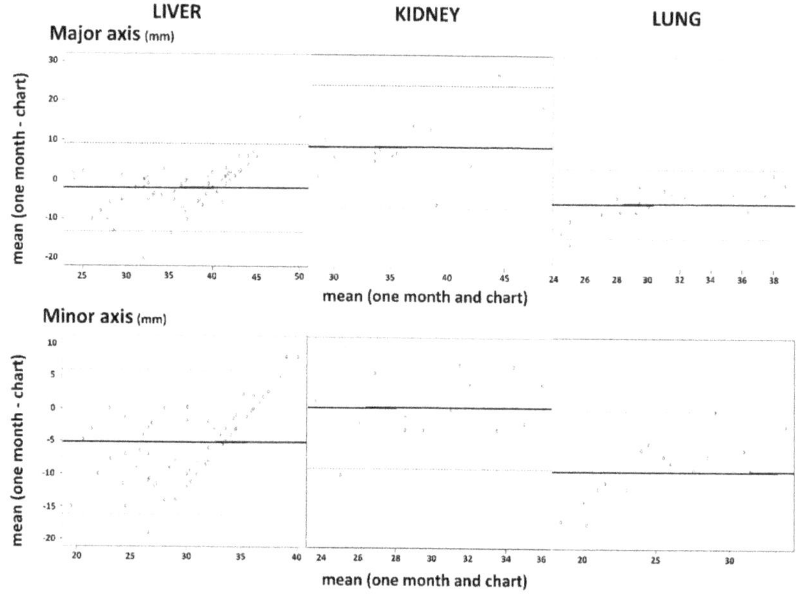

Figure 3. Bland–Altman plots showing agreement between the one-month evaluation and charts' data for the major (**top**) and minor (**bottom**) axes, for liver (**left**), kidney (**middle**) and lung (**right**) lesions. Charts' data were chosen as the reference. Note: Mean (one month–chart): mean difference between L and l on the charts and the ablation zone measured on the one-month follow-up patient imaging. Mean (one month and chart): mean of the sizes proposed by the charts and the ablation zone measured on the one-month follow-up patient image.

For kidney lesions, 12 patients (12/13, 92%) with 13 ablations (13/14, 93%) had an MRI and 1 patient (1/13, 10%) with 1 ablation (1/14, 7%) had a CT scan performed at a median time of 32 $\pm$ 8 days (range: 12–50) after treatment. The Bland–Altman test showed a moderate agreement with a bigger and less spherical ablation zone than expected: +8.69 $\pm$ 7.94 mm for *L*, +0.36 $\pm$ 4.77 mm for l, -0.28 ± 0.27 for the SI (Figure 2). There were no significant correlations for *L* (r = 0.41, p = 0.14), *l* (r = 0.48, p = 0.08) or SI (r = -0.36, p = 0.21).

For lung lesions, 11 patients (11/11, 100%) with 18 ablations (18/18, 100%) had a CT scan performed at a median of 32 $\pm$ 6 days (range: 15–47) after treatment. A moderate agreement with a smaller, less spherical ablation zone than expected was found using the Bland–Altman test: -5.45 ± 4.5 mm for *L*, -9.32 ± 4.72 mm for *l*, -0.24 ± 0.2 for the SI (Figure 2). Correlations were strong for *L* (r = 0.76, $p < 0.001$) and *l* (r = 0.75, $p < 0.001$). There was no correlation for SI (r = 0.24, p = 0.33).

4. Discussion

The microwave ablation system evaluated in this study showed a very good early response, with 94% of complete ablation on the one-month follow-up imaging. The size of the ablation zone showed a good agreement for liver and moderate agreement for lung and kidney lesions with the ablation zone announced in the manufacturer's chart. We reported smaller ablation zones for liver and lung lesions, and bigger ablation zones for kidney lesions. All ablations were less spherical than expected.

For hepatic lesions, the ablation area was significantly smaller than expected on the first follow-up imaging one month after the procedure, with only small differences for the major (2 mm) and minor axes (5 mm) but resulting in an ablation zone less spherical than expected. Although the differences were significant, the underestimation of 2 and 5 mm is acceptable in clinical practice. The early local response was very good, with 92% of complete ablations, concordant with that previously described in [10]. Smaller ablation zones at one month were expected because of tissue retraction and were different from previous studies that evaluated ablation areas on immediate postoperative imaging [11,12]. The follow-up was performed at one month according to the clinical practice in our centre. Thermosphere™ was shown to perform reproducible and expected ablation zones at 100 Watts, but it may not reflect overall clinical practice, which is more heterogeneous, with the possibility of using the 25, 50, 75 and 100 Watts charts. In our study, we have not restricted power use to 100 Watts, it was left to the operator's discretion as to reflect standard clinical practice. Although the sphericity index was lower than expected from the manufacturer's charts (0.63 vs. 0.78), the Covidien® material technology seems to produce more spherical ablation zones for liver lesions than other currently available devices such as Certus PR® and AMICA® materials, which have reported in vivo sphericity indices of 0.49 and 0.39, respectively [8].

For renal ablations, the major axis obtained on the first follow-up imaging was significantly longer than expected according to the manufacturer's charts, with a potentially clinically significant difference (8.69 $\pm$ 7.94 mm) in case of proximity with structures at risk, such as the pyelon or ureter. There was no correlation with the chart. This result might be explained by the specific peritumoral environment. Indeed, percutaneous renal ablations often concerned cortical lesions located at the interface between the kidney and retroperitoneal fat. The surrounding fat has dielectric properties, reflecting the electromagnetic energy that may impact on the ablation [13]. A previous study showed that depending on tissue limitations, the shape of the thermoablation zone may range from 7.5% to 23.4% without any effect on the minor axis [14]. Another explanation may be the lack of an in vivo chart for renal ablations, unlike for liver and lung. A study evaluating a high-frequency microwave on ex vivo bovine liver and in vivo pig liver tissue showed that whatever the power delivered, the ablation zones developed differently according to their in vivo or ex vivo environment [15]. These differences, with larger ablation zones than expected, should be taken into consideration in clinical practice.

For pulmonary ablations, the major and minor axes obtained, and thus the ablation zone, were significantly much smaller than expected according to the manufacturer's charts. Indeed, ablations performed were of 3 cm. For bigger lesions, the underestimation of the small axis could be a problem, with only partial ablation obtained. However, the correlation with the chart was strong, probably due to the use of in vivo references and to the homogeneous environment of lungs. Treated lesions were small (around 1 cm), with 100% of complete response. The ablations were less spherical than expected. This might, as suggested for liver lesions, be explained by the delay of evaluation, one month after the procedure. Kodama et al. showed, in a swine model, that the best temporal evaluation for microwave ablation was one week after the procedure [16]. Performing an earlier follow-up imaging, at one week, for example, may allow a better evaluation of the ablation zone.

The significant difference found on the ablation shape with a sphericity index lower than expected might be due to tissue retraction. Microwaves, with high temperatures generated, induce tissue shrinkage through dehydration and collapse. An ex vivo study showed that microwaves produced a more important tissue retraction (about 30%) than radiofrequency (15%) in the liver [17]. The authors showed that this phenomenon has a greater impact on the minor than on the major axis. In the same study, retraction was shown to be even more important in the lungs (about 50%), but with no difference between microwave and radiofrequency [17]. This was coherent with our results, with a smaller minor axis and a lower sphericity index for pulmonary ablations than for liver ablations (0.52 for lung lesions, 0.63 for liver lesions). The phenomenon of retraction was also demonstrated in ex vivo kidney tissue in another study [18]. Additionally, Lee et al. confirmed this tissue-retraction effect in vivo for liver lesions in 65 patients. In their study, the ablation zone was evaluated earlier than in our study, with MRI follow-up 24 h after the procedure. They showed a shrinkage of the ablation zone greater for microwave than for radiofrequency ablations (-2.45 ± 0.47 mm for microwaves vs. 0.94 ± 0.38 mm for radiofrequency) [19].

This study had several limitations, mainly due to its retrospective and monocentric design. Imaging follow-up was performed at one month, according to the standard clinical practice in our Institute, but it may have resulted in an underestimation of the ablation size due to tissue retraction. An immediate post-procedural imaging using contrast-enhanced ultrasound [20] or CT perfusion imaging [21,22] could have been performed to estimate the real ablation volume, with less retraction effect. Additionally, only axial imaging was used to evaluate the major and minor axes. Indeed, the great majority of follow-up imaging was performed with MRI with standard axial acquisitions, without 3D acquisitions. We thus preferred to use an axial acquisition for more reproducibility between different imaging modalities. Nevertheless, these preliminary results could be used as a basis for future prospective and multicentric studies.

5. Conclusions

The microwave ablation system evaluated in this study showed a very good early local response, with 94% of complete ablations on the one-month follow-up imaging. For liver lesions, in comparison with the manufacturer's charts, despite statistically significant differences, ablations were reliable. For kidney lesions, ablations were bigger than those expected in the charts, which should be taken into account by the operators. For lung lesions, the retraction effect was significant, and the ablation zone should be evaluated earlier than at one month.

Author Contributions: Conceptualization, J.F. and J.G.; methodology, J.F., J.-P.B. and J.G.; software, Not applicable; validation, J.F. and J.-P.B.; formal analysis, P.A.; investigation, J.F., P.A., T.K., D.D. and J.G.; resources, Not applicable; data curation, J.F. and P.A.; writing—original draft preparation, J.F. and H.d.F.; writing—review and editing, H.d.F.; visualization, J.F., J.-P.B. and J.G.; supervision, J.-P.B.; project administration, Not applicable; funding acquisition, Not applicable. All authors have read and agreed to the published version of the manuscript.

Funding: This research received no external funding.

Institutional Review Board Statement: The study was conducted in accordance with the Declaration of Helsinki and approved by the Institutional Review Board of the Hospital University of Nîmes (France) (IRB: 18.09.01, approved on 23 October 2018).

Informed Consent Statement: Patient consent was waived due to the retrospective design.

Data Availability Statement: The data presented in this study are available upon request from the corresponding author.

Conflicts of Interest: The authors declare no conflict of interest.

References

1. Eisele, R.M. Advances in local ablation of malignant liver lesions. *World J. Gastroenterol.* **2016**, *22*, 3885–3891. [CrossRef] [PubMed]
2. Wang, Y.; Liu, B.; Cao, P.; Wang, W.; Wang, W.; Chang, H.; Li, D.; Li, X.; Zhao, X.; Li, Y. Comparison between computed tomography-guided percutaneous microwave ablation and thoracoscopic lobectomy for stage I non-small cell lung cancer. *Thorac. Cancer* **2018**, *9*, 1376–1382. [CrossRef] [PubMed]
3. Campbell, S.; Uzzo, R.G.; Allaf, M.E.; Bass, E.B.; Cadeddu, J.A.; Chang, A.; Clark, P.E.; Davis, B.J.; Derweesh, I.H.; Giambarresi, L. Renal Mass and Localized Renal Cancer: AUA Guideline. *J. Urol.* **2017**, *198*, 520–529. [CrossRef]
4. Wright, A.S.; Sampson, L.A.; Warner, T.F.; Mahvi, D.M.; Lee, F.T. Radiofrequency versus microwave ablation in a hepatic porcine model. *Radiology* **2005**, *236*, 132–139. [CrossRef] [PubMed]
5. Schramm, W.; Yang, D.; Haemmerich, D. Contribution of direct heating, thermal conduction and perfusion during radiofrequency and microwave ablation. In Proceedings of the International Conference of the IEEE Engineering in Medicine and Biology Society, New York, NY, USA, 30 August–3 September 2006; pp. 5013–5016. [CrossRef]
6. Yu, N.C.; Raman, S.S.; Kim, Y.J.; Lassman, C.; Chang, X.; Lu, D.S.K. Microwave liver ablation: Influence of hepatic vein size on heat-sink effect in a porcine model. *J. Vasc. Interv. Radiol.* **2008**, *19*, 1087–1092. [CrossRef] [PubMed]
7. Hoffmann, R.; Rempp, H.; Erhard, L.; Blumenstock, G.; Pereira, P.L.; Claussen, C.D.; Clasen, S. Comparison of four microwave ablation devices: An experimental study in ex vivo bovine liver. *Radiology* **2013**, *268*, 89–97. [CrossRef]
8. Winokur, R.S.; Du, J.Y.; Pua, B.B.; Talenfeld, A.D.; Sista, A.K.; Schiffman, M.A.; Trost, D.W.; Madoff, D.C. Characterization of in vivo ablation zones following percutaneous microwave ablation of the liver with two commercially available devices: Are manufacturer published reference values useful? *J. Vasc. Interv. Radiol.* **2014**, *25*, 1939–1946. [CrossRef]
9. Alonzo, M.; Bos, A.; Bennett, S.; Ferral, H. The Emprint^{TM} Ablation System with Thermosphere^{TM} Technology: One of the Newer Next-Generation Microwave Ablation Technologies. *Semin. Interv. Radiol.* **2015**, *32*, 335–338. [CrossRef]
10. De Cobelli, F.; Marra, P.; Ratti, F.; Ambrosi, A.; Colombo, M.; Damascelli, A.; Sallemi, C.; Gusmini, S.; Salvioni, M.; Diana, P.; et al. Microwave ablation of liver malignancies: Comparison of effects and early outcomes of percutaneous and intraoperative approaches with different liver conditions: New advances in interventional oncology: State of the art. *Med. Oncol.* **2017**, *34*, 49. [CrossRef]
11. Zaidi, N.; Okoh, A.; Yigitbas, H.; Yazici, P.; Ali, N.; Berber, E. Laparoscopic microwave thermosphere ablation of malignant liver tumors: An analysis of 53 cases. *J. Surg. Oncol.* **2016**, *113*, 130–134. [CrossRef]
12. Ierardi, A.M.; Mangano, A.; Floridi, C.; Dionigi, G.; Biondi, A.; Duka, E.; Lucchina, N.; Lianos, G.D.; Carrafiello, G. A new system of microwave ablation at 2450 MHz: Preliminary experience. *Updates Surg.* **2015**, *67*, 39–45. [CrossRef]
13. Bottiglieri, A.; Ruvio, G.; O'Halloran, M.; Farina, L. Exploiting Tissue Dielectric Properties to Shape Microwave Thermal Ablation Zones. *Sensors* **2020**, *20*, 3960. [CrossRef] [PubMed]
14. Cavagnaro, M.; Amabile, C.; Cassarino, S.; Tosoratti, N.; Pinto, R.; Lopresto, V. Influence of the target tissue size on the shape of ex vivo microwave ablation zones. *Int. J. Hyperthermia.* **2015**, *31*, 48–57. [CrossRef] [PubMed]
15. Hines-Peralta, A.U.; Pirani, N.; Clegg, P.; Cronin, N.; Ryan, T.P.; Liu, Z.; Goldberg, S.N. Microwave ablation: Results with a 2.45-GHz applicator in ex vivo bovine and in vivo porcine liver. *Radiology* **2006**, *239*, 94–102. [CrossRef] [PubMed]
16. Kodama, H.; Ueshima, E.; Howk, K.; Lee, S.W.; Erinjeri, J.P.; Solomon, S.B.; Srimathveeravalli, G. Temporal evaluation of the microwave ablation zone and comparison of CT and gross sizes during the first month post-ablation in swine lung. *Diagn. Interv. Imaging* **2019**, *100*, 279–285. [CrossRef] [PubMed]
17. Brace, C.L.; Diaz, T.A.; Hinshaw, J.L.; Lee, F.T. Tissue contraction caused by radiofrequency and microwave ablation: A laboratory study in liver and lung. *J. Vasc. Interv. Radiol.* **2010**, *21*, 1280–1286. [CrossRef]
18. Sommer, C.M.; Sommer, S.A.; Mokry, T.; Gockner, T.; Gnutzmann, D.; Bellemann, N.; Schmitz, A.; Radeleff, B.A.; Kauczor, H.U.; Stampfl, U.; et al. Quantification of tissue shrinkage and dehydration caused by microwave ablation: Experimental study in kidneys for the estimation of effective coagulation volume. *J. Vasc. Interv. Radiol.* **2013**, *24*, 1241–1248. [CrossRef]
19. Lee, J.K.; Siripongsakun, S.; Bahrami, S.; Raman, S.S.; Sayre, J.; Lu, D.S. Microwave ablation of liver tumors: Degree of tissue contraction as compared to RF ablation. *Abdom. Radiol.* **2016**, *41*, 659–666. [CrossRef]
20. Meloni, M.F.; Smolock, A.; Cantisani, V.; Bezzi, M.; D'Ambrosio, F.; Proiti, M.; Lee, F.; Aiani, L.; Calliada, F.; Ferraioli, G. Contrast enhanced ultrasound in the evaluation and percutaneous treatment of hepatic and renal tumors. *Eur. J. Radiol.* **2015**, *84*, 1666–1674. [CrossRef]

21. Lv, Y.; Jin, Y.; Yan, Q.; Yuan, D.; Wang, Y.; Li, X.; Shen, Y. The value of 64-slice spiral CT perfusion imaging in the treatment of liver cancer with argon-helium cryoablation. *Oncol. Lett.* **2016**, *12*, 4584–4588. [CrossRef]
22. Joo, I.; Morrow, K.W.; Raman, S.S.; McWilliams, J.P.; Sayre, J.W.; Lu, D.S. CT-monitored minimal ablative margin control in single-session microwave ablation of liver tumors: An effective strategy for local tumor control. *Eur. Radiol.* **2022**, *1*, 1–9. [CrossRef]

sensors

MDPI

Article

Walking Step Monitoring with a Millimeter-Wave Radar in Real-Life Environment for Disease and Fall Prevention for the Elderly

Xuezhi Zeng *, Halldór Stefán Laxdal Báruson and Alexander Sundvall

Department of Electrical Engineering, Chalmers University of Technology, SE412-96 Gothenburg, Sweden
* Correspondence: xuezhi@chalmers.se

Abstract: We studied the use of a millimeter-wave frequency-modulated continuous wave radar for gait analysis in a real-life environment, with a focus on the measurement of the step time. A method was developed for the successful extraction of gait patterns for different test cases. The quantitative investigation carried out in a lab corridor showed the excellent reliability of the proposed method for the step time measurement, with an average accuracy of 96%. In addition, a comparison test between the millimeter-wave radar and a continuous-wave radar working at 2.45 GHz was performed, and the results suggest that the millimeter-wave radar is more capable of capturing instantaneous gait features, which enables the timely detection of small gait changes appearing at the early stage of cognitive disorders.

Keywords: radar; gait analysis; millimeter wave; micro-Doppler; FMCW; CW; fall prevention; illness prediction

Citation: Zeng, X.; Báruson, H.S.L.; Sundvall, A. Walking Step Monitoring with a Millimeter Wave Radar in Real-Life Environment towards Disease and Fall Prevention for the Elderly. *Sensors* **2022**, *22*, 9901. https://doi.org/10.3390/s22249901

Academic Editor: Herve Aubert

Received: 30 October 2022
Accepted: 9 December 2022
Published: 16 December 2022

1. Introduction

Improvements in public health have led to a significant increase in life expectancy, with the consequence of an increasingly aging population. According to WHO, the proportion of the world's population over 60 years will double from approximately 11% to 22% between 2000 and 2050. The absolute number of people aged 60 years and over is expected to increase from 605 million to 2 billion over the same period [1].

The normal aging process entails declines in both cognitive and physical functions [2] that largely affect the quality of life for the elderly. It has long been known that there is a direct relationship between cognitive impairment severity and increased gait abnormalities [3]. Early motor dysfunction co-exists with or even precedes the onset of cognitive decline in older adults [4]. For example, gait patterns tend to differ from their normal behavior at the early onset of some neurodegenerative diseases, such as Alzheimer's and Parkinson's. A person in the primary phase of Parkinson's tends to make small and shuffled steps and may also experience difficulties in performing key walking events, such as starting, stopping, and turning [5]. Short shuffling steps with difficulty lifting the feet off the ground were reported to be associated with an increased risk of developing dementia [6].

Gait impairments are also associated with fall incidents [7], which are considered to be a major risk for the elderly living independently, as falls often result in serious physical and psychological consequences, or even death. The rapid detection of fall incidents can reduce the mortality rate and raise the chance of surviving the event, but predicting the fall risk and preventing fall occurrence is of the uttermost importance. Several studies have identified gait abnormalities as predictors of fall risk [8–10]. However, the gait changes that appear at the early development stage of neurodegenerative diseases or are associated with fall risk are usually too subtle and discrete to be detected by clinical observation alone. Objective, quantitative, and continuous measurements and assessments of gaits are needed in order to detect these clinically relevant gait changes, enabling the timely introduction of individually tailored interventions.

Rapid progress in new technologies has given rise to devices and techniques that allow for an objective measurement of different gait parameters, resulting in a more efficient measurement and providing specialists with a large amount of reliable information on patients' gaits. These technologies can be broadly divided into wearable and non-wearable methods. The wearable methods [11] require the person to wear sensors in specific locations on their body, which can be incorrectly applied or forgotten completely, especially by the elderly. In addition, the sensors may obstruct natural movement and affect the gait. For these reasons, wearable methods are not applicable for long-term monitoring purposes. Non-wearable gait analysis methods usually involve the use of motion capture cameras or floor sensors [12]. They are usually laboratory-based and the systems are very costly. In addition, the motion capture cameras can be affected by poor lighting conditions and often involve the use of a number of markers placed on the body, which is not practical for daily use.

Radar technology has appeared as the most suitable candidate for continuous gait monitoring at home due to its safety, simplicity, low cost, lack of contact, and unobtrusiveness while preserving privacy. Over the past decade, indoor gait measurement and analysis with different types of radars have been investigated and have showed promising results [13]. Most of the studies focused on the measurement of walking speed [14–16], while a few also attempted to measure instantaneous gait. Work [17] presented a study on the use of a 5.8 GHz pulse Doppler radar for gait speed and step time measurement. The feasibility of using radars to track different limb joints was first reported in [18] by using a continuous-wave (CW) radar working at 2.45 GHz, but no quantitative measure of gait parameters was presented. The most promising work on using radar for gait parameters extraction was reported in [19], where eleven biomechanical parameters were acquired using two 24 GHz CW radars. However, this work was carried out in a well-controlled environment, with the subjects walking on a treadmill.

In this work, we explored the use of millimeter waves for in-home gait analysis, and the intention was to continuously measure the gait parameters of clinical significance for the prediction and prevention of cognitive diseases and falls in the elderly. Several studies have reported that step (or stride) time variability (SVT) is a key gait feature in persons with neurodegenerative disorders, such as Parkinson's disease and Alzheimer's disease [20,21]. In addition, it has also been found that an increased STV was associated with fall risk. A one-year prospective study on fifty-two older adults suggested that stride time variability was significantly increased in those who subsequently fell compared with those who did not fall. It was also pointed out that although stride time variability correlated significantly with gait speed, the latter did not discriminate future fallers from nonfallers [22]. The same findings were verified by a study performed on persons with multiple sclerosis, and it was concluded that SVT may be a more sensitive marker of fall risk than the average walking speed [23]. SVT is usually expressed as a coefficient of variation, which is defined as the ratio of the standard deviation to the mean of the step (or stride) time [24]. Therefore, a reliable risk assessment relies on the accurate measurement of the step (or stride) time.

The aim of the study was to investigate the reliability of using a millimeter-wave frequency-modulated continuous wave (FMCW) radar for step time measurement in a real-life environment. There have been a few studies employing a millimeter-wave radar sensor for human recognition based on gait analysis [25–28], but, to the best knowledge of the authors, none of these studies have presented any quantitative measure of gait parameters.

2. Method

In this section, we describe the developed method for instantaneous gait analysis, including waveform design, measurement setup, data collection, and data analysis.

2.1. Hardware and Waveform Design

The millimeter-wave radar sensor used in this work was the AWR1642BOOST module from Texas Instruments [29]. The sensor operates from 77 GHz and supports a bandwidth of

4 GHz. The module includes two onboard-etched transmitting antennas and four receiving antennas. A data capture board DCA1000EVM [30] was used along with the radar sensor in order to capture the raw data.

As aforementioned, we were interested in capturing instantaneous gait features. Therefore, both good spatial resolution and time resolution are important. The achievable spatial resolution of the FMCW radar is determined by the chirp's bandwidth, B, according to the following equation [31]:

$$\delta_D = \frac{c}{2B} = \frac{c}{2T_c \cdot S} \tag{1}$$

Here, c stands for the speed of light, T_c is the chirp duration, and S is the chirp slope rate.

In the test, the bandwidth was chosen heuristically to be 3.6 GHz, which yields a 4.16 cm range resolution, giving a good possibility of tracking different limb joints. The chirp-to-chirp interval was set at 0.5 milliseconds, which allowed for a measurement of a maximum velocity of approximately 2 m/s according to the following relationship [31]:

$$v_{max} = \frac{\lambda}{4T_s} \tag{2}$$

Here, λ is the wavelength and T_s is the chirp-to-chirp interval. We considered this velocity as high enough as our work is mainly intended for elderly care, where people usually walk very slowly.

Each frame was configured as one chirp and, in total, 30,000 frames were transmitted, which corresponds to a recording time of 15 s. The sampling rate needs to be high enough to resolve the frequency of the received signal, which is related to the distance of the subject according to the following equation [31]:

$$f_r = \frac{2S \cdot D}{c} \tag{3}$$

where D is the distance of the subject. We set the sampling rate at 6.25 MSa/s and the resulting maximum detection distance was approximately 5.86 m, which is a reasonable size for a room or a corridor in home environment.

The key radar parameters used in the work are given in Table 1.

Table 1. Key radar parameters used in the work.

Parameters	**Value (unit)**
Chirp slope rate	80 (MHz/μs)
Chirp duration	45 (μs)
Sampling rate	6250 (kSa/s)
Start frequency	77 (GHz)
No. chirps per frame	1
Frame-to-frame interval	0.5 (ms)
No. frames	30000

2.2. Data Collection

The data collection was performed in two different environments as shown in Figure 1. One was a large and open gym hall that was mostly free of clutter, and the other was a lab corridor, which has a smaller free space and is considered to be a more challenging environment.

(a) (b)

Figure 1. The two measurement environments for data collection: (**a**) a gym hall and (**b**) a lab corridor.

The measurements performed in the gym hall were mainly for finding an optimal measurement setup and developing a data analysis method. Different sensor heights and orientations were investigated in order to determine a suitable operating position, and, in the end, the sensor was placed at a height of 8 cm above the floor in order to focus the energy on the lower body parts, i.e., legs and feet, which are of the most interest for step time measurement. The subject was tasked with walking at a self-regulated pace along a 4 m long (from 5 m to 1 m away from the radar sensor) gym track with different types of gait, including away from or towards the radar sensor with a normal gait at different speeds, as well as imitated limp gaits. One of the limp gaits involved one leg swinging normally whereas the other sought support quickly after lift-off, and the other case was very similar but at a slower pace. During the measurements, video recordings were made by using a smartphone camera with the consent of the measured subject in order to provide the ground truth of some basic information, such as distance, number of steps, start and end time, etc. The track was marked at half-meter intervals for observational convenience, which made it convenient for the subject to step exactly at those intervals. This would result in exactly 8 steps, which gives a good reference for us to compare the radar measurement and video recordings.

A quantitative investigation on the step time measurement was performed in the lab corridor. Three healthy subjects (one female and two males) in the age range of 20–40 years were measured and each subject walked from approximately 6 m away towards the radar with a slow and self-regulated pace in 15 s. The same type of measurement was repeated ten times for each subject, resulting in a total measurement time of approximately 2.5 min each. During the measurements, the subjects wore two commercial motion tracking sensors (Xsens DOT) at the left and right ankle positions, respectively. The Xsens DOT sensor provides 3D angular velocity and acceleration using a gyroscope and an accelerometer [32]. The two motion sensors were synchronized during the measurement and the sampling rate of the motion sensor was 60 Hz. Best efforts were made to start the radar and motion sensor data collection at the same time.

The collected radar data were stored in a data matrix, as shown in Figure 2, corresponding to the transmitted frames. Each row represents the captured signal corresponding to each transmitted frame and is the "fast-time" data, and each column reflects the data change over frames and is the "slow-time" data.

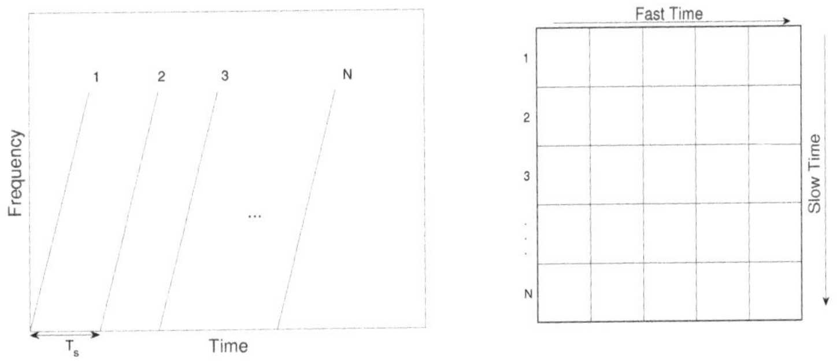

(a) (b)

Figure 2. Recorded data corresponding to transmitted signals: (**a**) the transmitted frames and (**b**) the data matrix for storing the collected data.

2.3. Data Analysis

Figure 3a is the flow chart of the developed method for processing the collected data to obtain temporal gait parameters such as cadence and step time. Firstly, a fast Fourier transform (FFT) was applied to each row of the data matrix, as shown in Figure 2b, to generate a so-called "range profile", which presents the locations of strongly reflected objects. By subtracting the range profile obtained from the first frame from others, peaks that correspond to static objects were eliminated and the remaining highest peaks were considered to be the measured subject. These peaks were then combined in time to form a range–time plot, which indicates the location of the measured subject over time.

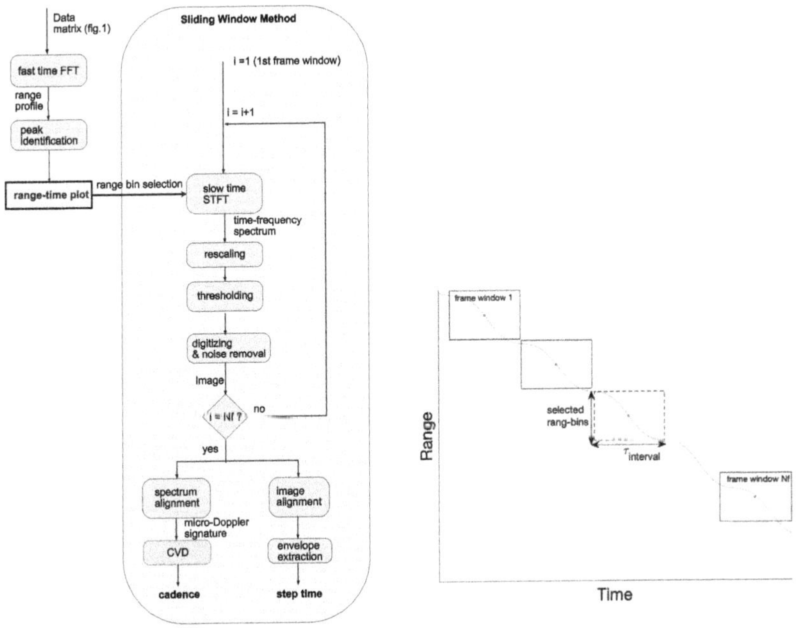

(a) (b)

Figure 3. The data analysis method: (**a**) flow chart and (**b**) the illustration of the main idea of the sliding window method.

A sliding window method (SWM) was then used to generate the gait pattern of the measured subject, and the main idea is illustrated in Figure 3b. With this method, the complete recording window was divided into many small frame windows (e.g., window 1...Nf) and, for each frame window, only a few range bins (one range bin corresponds to one column of the data matrix in Figure 2b) were selected for generating the gait pattern by referring to the range–time plot. The first step was to apply a short-time Fourier transform (STFT) to each selected range bin according to the following equation [33]:

$$S(n,k) = |\sum_{m=0}^{M-1} s(n+m)w(m)e^{-j2\pi mk/K}| \quad (4)$$

Here, S is the time–frequency spectrum, which is a two-dimensional representation of energy versus time and frequency. s is the slow-time signal for the selected range bin, which is the data along one column after the aforementioned FFT processing, and w is the window function. $n = 0, 1, \dots, N-1$ is the sample index of the signal, $k = 0, 1, \dots, K-1$ is the frequency index, and $m = 0, 1, \dots, M-1$ is the sample index of the window.

The time–frequency spectra generated for each range bin were added up and the resulting spectrum was rescaled to have a maximum value of one. This was carried out in order to diminish the effect of distance propagation loss. The rescaled spectrum was then thresholded to eliminate the background noise and the threshold value was determined by the following equation:

$$Threshold = \frac{\sum_{i=1,j=1}^{I,J} S_b(i,j)}{\sum_{i=1,j=1}^{I,J} S_m(i,j)} \quad (5)$$

Here, S_b and S_m are the time–frequency spectra obtained from measurements, where there is no subject and one subject walking, respectively. I and J define the size of the spectrum in the time and frequency dimensions.

After the thresholding, the spectrum was digitized to "zeros" and "ones", resulting in a binary image. Connected components within a size of 30,000 pixels were treated as noise and thus taken away. The same process was applied to all of the frame windows and, at the end, the time–frequency spectra obtained for each frame window were aligned in time, resulting in a micro-Doppler signature for the entire recording window. The generated binary images for each frame window were also aligned, forming a complete gait pattern image.

From the micro-Doppler signature, we can calculate the cadence velocity diagram (CVD), which represents the repetition frequency of certain Doppler shifts:

$$\mathrm{CVD}(l,k) = |\sum_{n=0}^{N-1} S_{doppler}(n,k)e^{-j2\pi nl/L}| \quad (6)$$

Here, $l = 0, 1, \dots, L-1$ is the index of the Doppler repetition frequency. CVD enables a better analysis of the periodic patterns that are inherent to a human gait, such as the cadence, which is the number of steps per second.

The step time was estimated from the gait pattern image by extracting the upper envelope, which gives a good representation of the foot velocity over time.

This proposed method largely saved computational resources and time as it only needs to handle a small portion of the recorded data. Another advantage of this method is that it can give a high signal-to-noise ratio and robust handling of unknown measurement scenarios as it only deals with the location of interest under a specific time.

3. Results

This section includes important results obtained from the tests performed both in the gym hall and the lab corridor. Both qualitative and quantitative results are presented. Results from simultaneous measurements by using the millimeter-wave radar and a CW radar are also presented.

3.1. Micro-Doppler Signature and Cadence

Figure 4a,b are two measurement examples carried out in the gym hall, where the subject walked toward the radar sensor at a relatively fast and slow speed, respectively. Figure 4c,d are two similar measurements, but the subject was walking away from the radar sensor. The top plots are range–time plots, showing the distance between the subject and the radar sensor over time, and the middle and lower plots are the micro-Doppler signatures and the extracted envelope obtained by using the sliding window method shown in Figure 3.

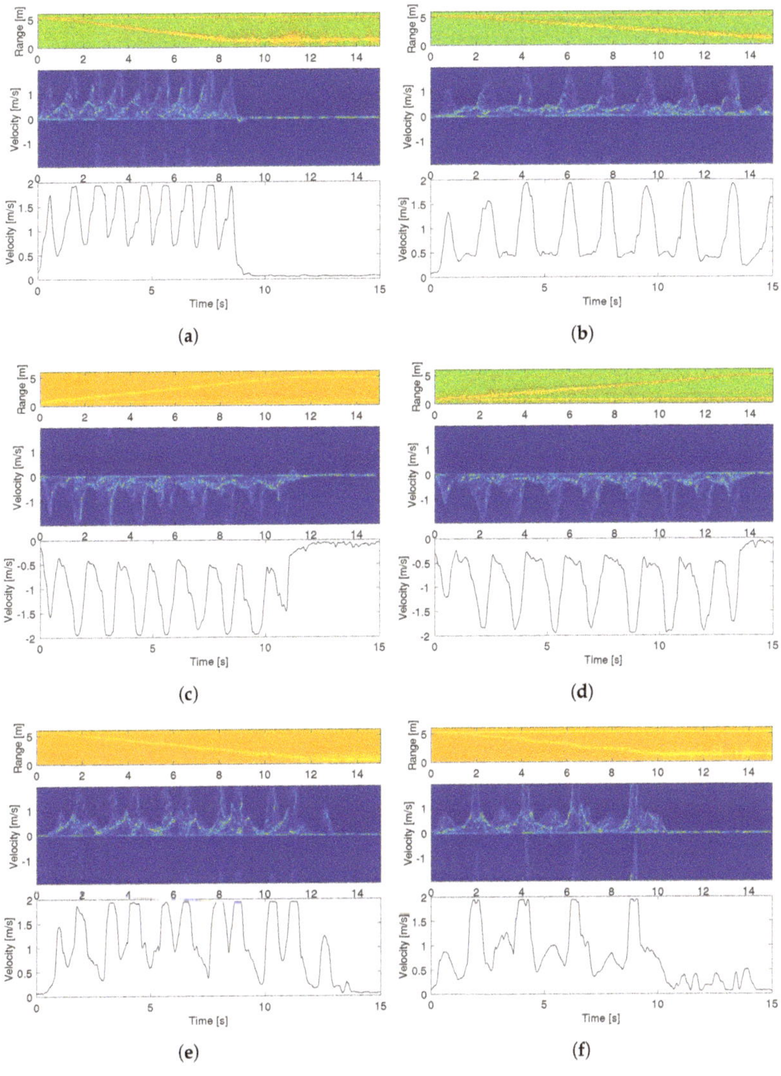

Figure 4. The range–time plot micro-Doppler signature, and extracted envelope for different measurement cases in the gym hall: (**a**,**b**) are two tests where the subject walked toward the radar sensor at different speeds; (**c**,**d**) are two tests where the subject walked away from the radar sensor at different speeds; (**e**,**f**) are two tests where the subject tried to imitate a limp with different intensities.

The average walking speeds calculated from the range–time plots for the four measurement examples are approximately 0.48 m/s, 0.28 m/s, 0.37 m/s, and 0.30 m/s, respectively. These values are very close to those obtained from video recordings, which are 0.49 m/s, 0.29 m/s, 0.39 m/s, and 0.31 m/s.

Figure 4e,f shows the obtained micro-Doppler signature and the extracted envelope for the two test cases when the subject was asked to alter their gait in order to replicate a gait similar to a limp.

The cadence velocity diagram obtained according to Equation (6) and the mean cadence spectrum (mCS), which is computed as the average energy of each Doppler repetition frequency in the CVD, are shown in Figure 5 for the six measurement examples described above. The peaks in the mCS correspond to the harmonic components of the gait, where the peak close to DC corresponds to the oscillating movement of the torso whereas the second highest peak in the mCS tends to correspond to the oscillating motion of the legs in the case of an unassisted gait.

As the radar sensor's radiation energy is mainly directed to the lower limb joints, the peaks corresponding to the leg/foot movement are the most prominent and are referred to as cadence. According to the mCS, the cadence for the first four test cases is 60 steps/min, 34 steps/min, 45 steps/min, and 35 steps/min, respectively. These values are in good agreement with the extracted envelope given in Figure 4 and the video recordings. However, the agreement does not hold for the limping cases. The cadence according to the mCS is 25 steps/min for both cases, which is significantly lower than the actual number of steps.

3.2. *Quantitative Measure of Step Time*

Figure 6a shows the range–time plot, micro-Doppler signature, and the extracted envelope of one test case performed in the lab corridor. The subject was out of the measurement zone at the beginning of the data recording and became "visible" at approximately 3.5 s. The differential of the extracted foot velocity in comparison with the acceleration data obtained with the Xsens DOT sensor is shown in Figure 6b. To provide a good illustration, the radar acceleration data were normalized and the Xsens sensor data were scaled and offset along the vertical axis. It can clearly be seen that every second peak of the radar acceleration data align well with the Xsens acceleration data recorded at the left ankle and right ankle, respectively. The time instants corresponding to these acceleration peaks were then used to calculate the step times.

The step times obtained from the radar data versus those obtained from the Xsens sensor data for all of the measurements are presented in Figure 7a. The calculated intra-class correlation coefficient (ICC) is 0.93. Figure 7b shows the relative error for each measurement subject, which is defined as the following equation:

$$\Delta = \frac{|ST_{radar} - ST_{Xsens}|}{ST_{Xsens}} \times 100\% \tag{7}$$

Here, ST_{radar} and ST_{Xsens} are the step time obtained from radar sensor and Xsens sensors, respectively.

The bottom whisker of each box indicates the lowest error and the topmost whisker indicates the highest one. The top and bottom edges of the blue rectangle indicate the 75th and 25th percentiles of the error, respectively. The red mark within the rectangle indicates the median of the error for each subject. Table 2 is a comparison of the step time measured by the radar and the Xsens sensors.

Table 2. Comparison of step time measured by the radar and the Xsens sensors.

Subject	ST_{Xsens} (mean)	ST_{radar} (mean)	ST_{Xsens} (std)	ST_{radar} (std)	Δ (mean)	Δ (median)
A	1.1548	1.1484	0.1010	0.1112	0.0517	0.0443
B	1.4317	1.4249	0.1593	0.1583	0.0407	0.0331
C	1.3459	1.3384	0.1626	0.1640	0.0361	0.0296
A+B+C					0.0428	0.0362

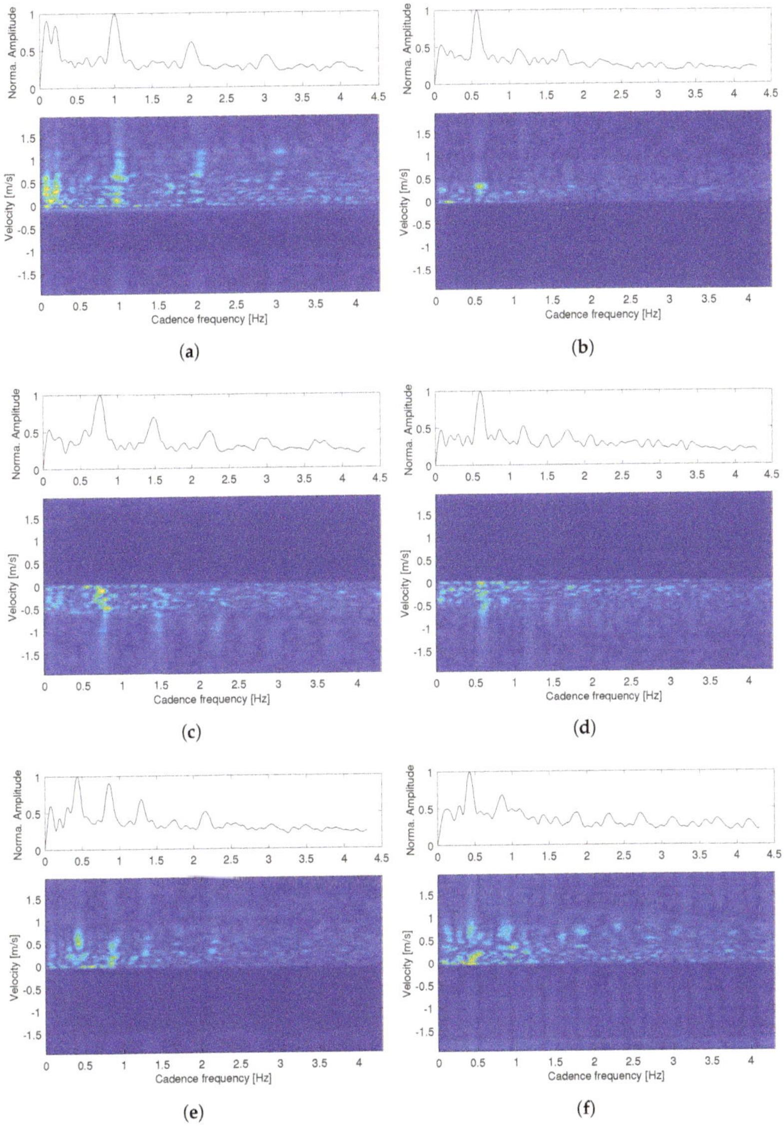

Figure 5. The cadence velocity diagram (lower plots) and mean cadence spectrum (upper plots) for the test cases (**a**–**f**) shown in Figure 4.

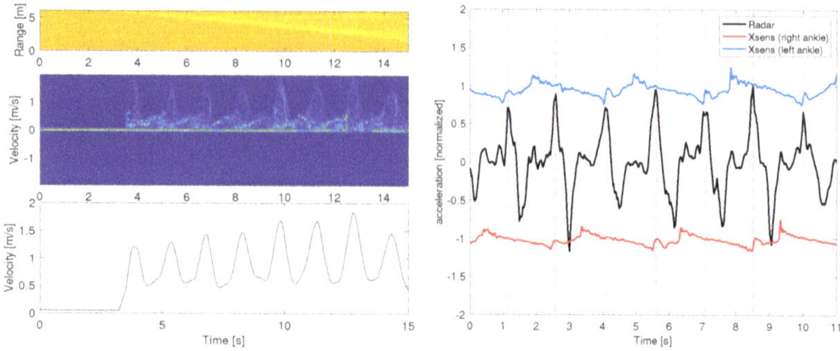

(**a**) (**b**)

Figure 6. One measurement example for illustrating the calculation of the step time: (**a**) the range–time plot, micro-Doppler signature, and extracted envelope for one measurement example in the lab corridor; (**b**) comparison between acceleration data obtained with the radar and the Xsens sensors.

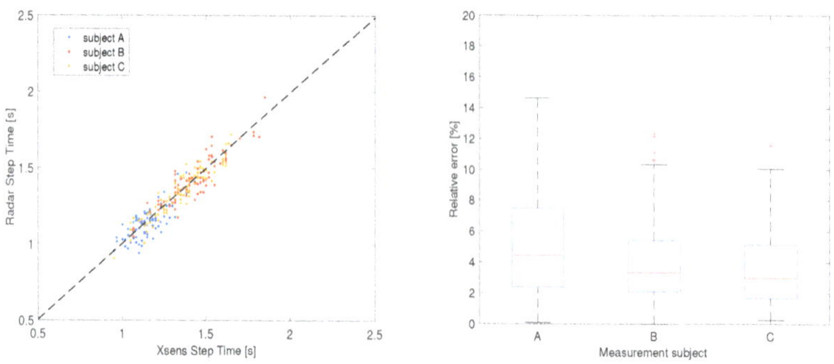

(**a**) (**b**)

Figure 7. The measurement of step time by using the millimeter wave FMCW radar: (**a**) the plot of the step times obtained with the radar versus those obtained by using the Xsens sensor; (**b**) the relative error of the measured step time for each subject.

3.3. Comparison between the Millimeter-Wave FMCW Radar and a Microwave CW Radar

We conducted several simultaneous tests in the gym hall using the millimeter-wave radar and a microwave radar sensor. Figure 8a shows the measurement setup for the simultaneous measurement. The CW radar system is a software-defined ratio board (USRP2901 from National Instruments) operating from 70 MHz to 6 GHz [34]. A pair of wide-band bow tie antennas that provide conical coverage were used for transmitting and receiving signals [35]. The operating frequency was set at 2.45 GHz, which is the same as in the work [18]. The micro-Doppler signatures from two measurement examples are shown in Figure 8b–e. In the first case, the subject walked slowly along the defined track away from the sensors at a certain pace and, in the second case, the subject walked toward the sensors from five meters away with a corner reflector attached to one of the subject's knees in order to enhance the corresponding echoes.

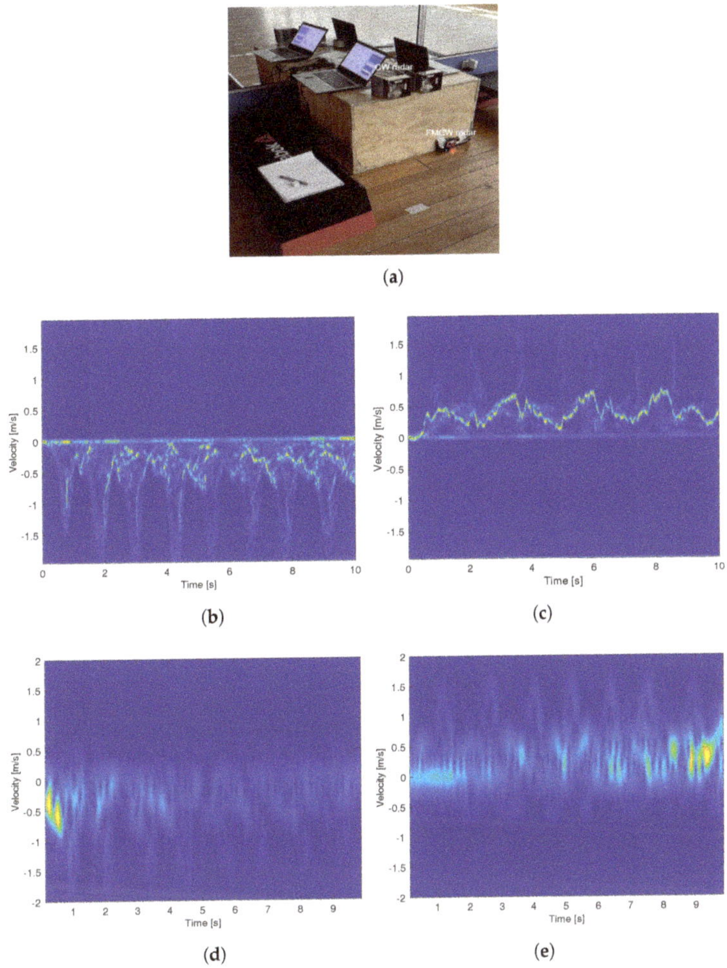

Figure 8. The comparison test between the millimeter-wave radar and a 2.45 GHz CW radar: (**a**) measurement setup; (**b**,**c**) are micro-Doppler signatures obtained by using the millimeter-wave radar for test case 1 and case 2, respectively; (**d**,**e**) are corresponding micro-Doppler signatures obtained with the CW radar.

4. Discussion

In this section, we provide an explanation and interpretation of the presented results and compare our study with other works, as well as discuss the limitations and suggest future work.

4.1. Comments on the Results

For all of the measurement examples presented in Figure 4, the range–time plots are in good agreement with the video recordings in terms of the walking distance and walking time. The micro-Doppler signatures show clear patterns of each step, which facilitates envelope extraction. The extracted upper envelope shows the foot velocity as the subject walked, and we can clearly distinguish where each step ends and another begins. In general, we see a relatively lower foot top velocity when the subject was farthest away from the radar sensor, and this is highly attributed to the weaker reflections.

A big variation in step time is clearly seen in Figure 4e,f, where the subject was imitating a limp. The extracted envelope in Figure 4f is capable of capturing the limp near-perfectly as the stiff leg is presented with a much lower top velocity. These results demonstrate the good robustness of the developed method for detecting different types of gaits.

Whereas the cadence of the normal gait cases were correctly measured, we see an inaccurate measurement of the cadence for the altered gait cases. This suggests that cadence is a good measure of the pace of normal gaits, but not effective for abnormal gait cases.

Although the range–time plot shown in Figure 6a is more noisy than those shown in Figure 4, the quality of the obtained micro-Doppler signature is equally as high as those carried out in the gym hall. This indicates that the developed method is capable of dealing with a more challenging measurement environment, such as the lab corridor. Figure 7b shows that the measurement accuracy of the step time for the two males (subject B and C) is slightly better than that for the female (subject A), which may be attributed to the weaker reflections due to a smaller radar cross-section area of the female's feet. We noticed that, in a few measurement tests for subject B, the acceleration peaks in the Xsens sensor data are not always prominent, which makes it challenging to identify the right peaks. This may be the reason for several outliers in the relative error plot. Overall, the median accuracy for the three subjects are all over 95%. The ICC of 0.93 indicates the excellent reliability of the proposed method for step time measurement.

The comparison test between the millimeter-wave radar and the 2.45 GHz CW radar clearly demonstrated the benefit of using millimeter waves for gait analysis. Especially for the second measurement example, where the subject wore the reflector on the knee while walking, the velocity pattern of the knee is largely enhanced and clearly seen in the micro-Doppler signatures obtained with the FMCW radar while the knee is hardly distinguishable from other body parts in CW measurements. This indicates that, with sufficiently strong radiation in a certain direction, we are able to track different limb joints using the millimeter-wave FMCW radar sensor. However, this is difficult to achieve by using the microwave CW sensor due to the insufficient spatial resolution.

The obtained results suggest that the millimeter-wave FMCW radar sensor is highly capable of capturing instantaneous gait features thanks to its inherent high spatial resolution. High accurate measurements of the step time were achieved with the developed method. The micro-Doppler signatures obtained with the millimeter-wave radar reveal much greater details of the gait pattern than those by using the microwave CW radar, which suggests a good potential for identifying different phases of a gait cycle and, as a consequence, giving a reliable measurement of more gait parameters.

4.2. Comparison with Other Works

As the proposed method is dedicated to in-home gait monitoring, where the use of wearable sensors is not preferable, the comparison to other works is limited to non-wearable methods. Paper [36] presented an electrostatic-sensing-based method where temporal gait parameters were estimated by sensing and analyzing the electrostatic field generated from human foot stepping. The reported average accuracy in the gait cycle measurement was 97% in the range of 3 m. Our method achieved almost the same measurement accuracy (96% in mean) in a range that was twice as long.

Work [17] reported an excellent reliability in the step time measurement in a lab environment by using a 5.8 GHz pulse Doppler radar with an ICC of 0.97 between the radar and a motion capture system. The drawback of the method is the relatively large size of the radar sensor and the use of a large metal shield (60 cm × 60 cm) at the back of the radar, which is unfavorable for integrating the system at home. In addition, two types of calibration need to be performed prior to the data collection.

Our work presents a simple method that needs neither calibration nor empirical values. Besides the available high spatial resolution, millimeter-wave radar has several other unique features that make it especially suitable for in-home gait analysis. For example, at the millimeter-wave range, the antenna size is very small, which allows for the deployment of an antenna array, resulting in a finer beam width. With effective beam-forming, most of the radiated energy can be directed to specific body parts, which consequently enhances the echoes of interest and reduces interference. Moreover, the millimeter-wave radar sensor is very compact and cheap, and can be easily integrated into furnitures and walls in a home environment.

4.3. Limitation of the Work

The presented work has several limitations. Firstly, the accuracy assessment of the step time measurement is subject to some errors. The sampling rate of the Xsens sensor is 60 Hz, providing a time resolution of 0.0167 s. In some of the measurements, the calculated ground truth may be off by one or two time instants compared to reality due to the difficulties in identifying the right peaks in the Xsens acceleration data, which correspond to a potential offset of ± 0.0167 s to ± 0.0333 s for each step.

Secondly, the data collection was limited to a small number of subjects. In order to make the collected data more representative, we included both male and female subjects in the study and mainly focused on a slow speed/walking pace. The step time of the collected data spans from approximately 0.9 s to 1.8 s, which represents a wide variation range. The next step is to perform a large-scale study among the target group (i.e., old adults) to further verify the developed method.

Thirdly, the developed method is highly dependent on the accurate localization of the measured subject, and this work demonstrated the effective tracking of a single subject in real-life environment with a single sensor. For the reliable tracking of multiple subjects and (or) a single subject in a more complex environment, e.g., including many pieces of furniture, the use of multiple sensors is preferred. The inherent tracking function of the employed FMCW radar makes it preferable for in-home monitoring in comparison to a CW radar, as it is less vulnerable to surrounding interference.

Lastly, although the FMCW radar sensor is configured with several antennas, only one antenna pair was used in this work for the sake of simplicity. It would be interesting to explore the use of multiple antenna pairs for beamforming to enhance echoes from the body parts of interest. As the focus of the work is to measure the step time, a low sensor elevation was chosen to focus the radiation energy on the foot in consideration of the antenna radiation pattern. In order to effectively capture the echoes from upper body parts, e.g., the torso, the deployment of a few sensors at different elevations is suggested.

5. Conclusions

The presented work demonstrated the reliable measurement of temporal gait parameters, and, more specifically, the step time, in real-life environments by using a millimeter-wave FMCW radar. These promising results suggest that this type of radar has good potential for the timely detection of discrete and subtle gait changes that appear at the early stage of cognitive disorders at home, enabling the prediction and prevention of cognitive diseases and fall accidents for the elderly.

Author Contributions: Conceptualization, X.Z.; methodology, X.Z., H.S.L.B. and A.S.; software, H.S.L.B. and A.S.; validation, X.Z., H.S.L.B. and A.S.; formal analysis, X.Z., H.S.L.B. and A.S.; investigation, H.S.L.B. and A.S.; data curation, H.S.L.B. and A.S.; writing—original draft preparation, X.Z.; writing—review and editing, X.Z.; supervision, X.Z.; project administration, X.Z. All authors have read and agreed to the published version of the manuscript.

Funding: This research received no external funding.

Institutional Review Board Statement: Ethical review and approval were not needed for this study, as this is a non-invasive experiment with very low power which is not harmful to humans.

Informed Consent Statement: Informed consent was obtained from all subjects involved in the study.

Data Availability Statement: Data available on request from the authors.

Conflicts of Interest: The authors declare no conflict of interest.

Abbreviations

The following abbreviations are used in this manuscript:

FMCW	Frequency modulated continuous wave
CW	Continuous wave
SWM	Sliding window method
STFT	Short-time Fourier transform
CVD	Cadence velocity diagram
mCS	Mean cadence spectrum
STV	Step time variability
SDR	Software defined radio

References

1. World Health Organization. Multisectoral action for a life course approach to healthy ageing: Draft global strategy and plan of action on ageing and health. In Proceedings of the 69th World Health Assembly, Geneva, Switzerland, 22 April 2016.
2. Camicioli, R.; Wang, Y.; Powell, C.; Mitnitski, A.; Rockwood, K. Gait and posture impairment, parkinsonism and cognitive decline in older people. *J. Neural Transm.* **2007**, *114*, 1355–1361. [CrossRef] [PubMed]
3. Parihar, R.; Mahoney, J.R.; Verghese, J. Relationship of gait and cognition in the elderly. *Curr. Transl. Geriatr. Exp. Gerontol. Rep.* **2013**, *2*, 167–173. [CrossRef] [PubMed]
4. Verghese, J.; Lipton, R.B.; Hall, C.B.; Kuslansky, G.; Katz, M.J.; Buschke, H. Abnormality of gait as a predictor of non-Alzheimer's dementia. *N. Engl. J. Med.* **2002**, *347*, 1761–1768. [CrossRef] [PubMed]
5. Raccagni, C.; Nonnekes, J.; Bloem, B.R.; Peball, M.; Boehme, C.; Seppi, K.; Wenning, G.K. Gait and postural disorders in parkinsonism: A clinical approach. *J. Neurol.* **2020**, *267*, 3169–3176. [CrossRef] [PubMed]
6. Scherder, E.; Eggermont, L.; Swaab, D.; van Heuvelen, M.; Kamsma, Y.; de Greef, M.; Mulder, T. Gait in ageing and associated dementias; its relationship with cognition. *Neurosci. Biobehav. Rev.* **2007**, *31*, 485–497. [CrossRef]
7. Tinetti, M.E.; Speechley, M.; Ginter, S.F. Risk factors for falls among elderly persons living in the community. *N. Engl. J. Med.* **1988**, *319*, 1701–1707. [CrossRef]
8. Verghese, J.; Ambrose, A.F.; Lipton, R.B.; Wang, C. Neurological gait abnormalities and risk of falls in older adults. *J. Neurol.* **2010**, *257*, 392–398. [CrossRef]
9. Maki, B.E. Gait changes in older adults: Predictors of falls or indicators of fear. *J. Am. Geriatr. Soc.* **1997**, *45*, 313–320. [CrossRef]
10. Pavol, M.J.; Owings, T.M.; Foley, K.T.; Grabiner, M.D. Gait Characteristics as Risk Factors for Falling From Trips Induced in Older Adults. *J. Gerontol. Ser. A* **1999**, *54*, 583–590. [CrossRef]
11. Chen, S.; Lach, J.; Lo, B.; Yang, G.Z. Toward pervasive gait analysis with wearable sensors: A systematic review. *IEEE J. Biomed. Health Informat.* **2016**, *20*, 1521–1537. [CrossRef]
12. Muro-De-La-Herran, A.; Garcia-Zapirain, B.; Mendez-Zorrilla, A. Gait analysis methods: An overview of wearable and non-wearable systems, highlighting clinical applications. *Sensors* **2014**, *14*, 3362–3394. [CrossRef]
13. Argañarás, J.G.; Wong, Y.T.; Begg, R.; Karmakar, N.C. State-of-the-Art Wearable Sensors and Possibilities for Radar in Fall Prevention. *Sensors* **2021**, *21*, 6836. [CrossRef]
14. Boroom, A.; Shaker, G.; Morita, P.P.; Wong, A.; Boger, J. Autonomous gait speed estimation using 24GHz FMCW radar technology. In Proceedings of the 2018 IEEE EMBS International Conference on Biomedical and Health Informatics (BHI), Las Vegas, NV, USA, 4–7 March 2018; pp. 66–69.
15. Saho, K.; Uemura, K.; Sugano, K.; Matsumoto, M. Using micro- Doppler radar to measure gait features associated with cognitive function in elderly adults. *IEEE Access* **2019**, *7*, 24122–24131. [CrossRef]
16. Morita, P.P.; Rocha, A.S.; Shaker, G.; Lee, D.; Wei, J.; Fong, B.; Boger, J. Comparative Analysis of Gait Speed Estimation Using Wideband and Narrowband Radars, Thermal Camera, and Motion Tracking Suit Technologies. *J. Healthc. Inform. Res.* **2020**, *4*, 215–237. [CrossRef]
17. Wang, F.; Skubic, M.; Rantz, M.; Cuddihy, P.E. Quantitative gait measurement with pulse-Doppler radar for passive in-home gait assessment. *IEEE Trans. Biomed. Eng.* **2014**, *61*, 2434–2443. [CrossRef]
18. Quaiyum, F.; Tran, N.; Piou, J.E.; Kilic, O.; Fathy, A.E. Noncontact Human Gait Analysis and Limb Joint Tracking Using Doppler Radar. *IEEE J. Electromagn. Microwaves Med. Biol.* **2019**, *3*, 61–70. [CrossRef]
19. Seifert, A.K.; Grimmer, M.; Zoubir, A.M. Doppler radar for the extraction of biomechanical parameters in gait analysis. *IEEE J. Biomed. Health Inform.* **2021**, *25*, 547–558. [CrossRef]
20. Hausdorff, J.M.; Cudkowicz, M.E.; Firtion, R.; Wei, J.Y.; Goldberger, A.L. Gait variability and basal ganglia disorders: Stride-to stride variations of gait cycle timing in Parkinson's disease and Huntington's disease. *Mov. Disord.* **1998**, *13*, 428–437. [CrossRef]
21. Webster, K.E.; Merory, J.R.; Wittwer, J.E. Gait variability in community dwelling adults with Alzheimer Disease. *Alzheimer Dis. Assoc. Disord.* **2006**, *20*, 37–40. [CrossRef]

22. Hausdorff, J.M.; Rios, D.A.; Edelberg, H.K. Gait Variability and Fall Risk in Community-Living Older Adults: A 1-Year Prospective Study. *Arch. Phys. Med. Rehabil.* **2001**, *82*, 1050–1056. [CrossRef]
23. Moon, Y.; Wajda, D.A.; Motl, R.W.; Sosnoff, J.J. Stride-Time Variability and Fall Risk in Persons with Multiple Sclerosis. *Mult. Scler. Int.* **2015**, 964790. [CrossRef] [PubMed]
24. Beauchet, O.; Annweiler, C.; Lecordroch, Y.; Allali, G.; Dubost, V.; Herrmann, F.R.; Kressig, R.W. Walking speed-related changes in stride time variability: Effects of decreased speed. *J. Neuroeng. Rehabil.* **2009**, *6*, 32. [CrossRef] [PubMed]
25. Hajar, A. Use of Millimeter Wave FMCW Radar to Capture Gait Parameters. *Am. J. Biomed. Sci. Res.* **2019**, *6*, 122–123. [CrossRef]
26. Jiang, X.; Zhang, Y.; Yang, Q.; Deng, B.; Wang, H. Millimeter-Wave Array Radar-Based Human Gait Recognition Using Multi-Channel Three-Dimensional Convolutional Neural Network. *Sensors* **2020**, *20*, 5466. [CrossRef]
27. Alanazi, M.A.; Alhazmi, A.K.; Alsattam, O.; Gnau, K.; Brown, M.; Thiel, S.; Chodavarapu, V.P. Towards a Low-Cost Solution for Gait Analysis Using Millimeter Wave Sensor and Machine Learning. *Sensors* **2022**, *22*, 5470. [CrossRef]
28. Ozturk, M.Z.; Wu, C.; Wang, B.; Liu, K.J.R. GaitCube: Deep Data Cube Learning for Human Recognition With Millimeter-Wave Radio. *Internet Things J.* **2022**, *9*, 546–557. [CrossRef]
29. Texas Instruments. AWR1642BOOST Evaluation board | TI.com. [Online]. Available online: https://www.ti.com/tool/AWR1642BOOST-overview (accessed on 28 January 2021).
30. Texas Instruments. DCA1000EVM Evaluation board | TI.com. [Online]. Available online: https://www.ti.com/tool/DCA1000EVM (accessed on 28 January 2021).
31. The Fundamentals of Millimeter Wave Radar Sensors (Rev.A) [Online]. Available online: https://www.ti.com/lit/wp/spyy005a/spyy005a.pdf?ts=1670061381545 (accessed on 28 November 2022).
32. Available online: https://www.xsens.com/xsens-dot (accessed on 1 January 2022).
33. Devasahayam, S.R. *Signals and Systems in Biomedical Engineering: Physiological Systems Modeling and Signal Processing*; Springer: New York, NY, USA, 2000; Chapter 5.3, ISBN 9781461453314.
34. National Instruments. USRP-2901 USRP Software Defined Radio Device. Available online: https://www.ni.com/sv-se/support/model.usrp-2901.html (accessed on 28 July 2022).
35. Moghaddam, S.M.; Kildal, P.S.; Glazunov, A.A.; Yang, J.; Gustafsson, M. A self-grounded dual-polarized wideband bowtie with improved mimo performance in random-los. In Proceedings of the 2016 IEEE International Symposium on Antennas and Propagation (APSURSI), Fajardo, PR, USA, 26 June–1 July 2016.
36. Li, M.; Li, P.; Tian, S.; Tang, K.; Chen, X. Estimation of Temporal Gait Parameters Using a Human Body Electrostatic Sensing-Based Method. *Sensors* **2018**, *28*, 1737. [CrossRef]

sensors

MDPI

Article

Wearable Sensor Based on Flexible Sinusoidal Antenna for Strain Sensing Applications

Mehran Ahadi [1,2], Mourad Roudjane [3], Marc-André Dugas [4], Amine Miled [2] and Younès Messaddeq [3,*]

1 Center for Optics, Photonics and Lasers (COPL), Department of Electrical and Computer Engineering, Université Laval, Quebec City, QC G1V 0A6, Canada; mehran.ahadi.1@ulaval.ca
2 LABioTRON Bioengineering Research Laboratory, Department of Electrical and Computer Engineering, and Research Centre for Advanced Materials (CERMA), Université Laval, Quebec City, QC G1V 0A6, Canada; amine.miled@gel.ulaval.ca
3 Center for Optics, Photonics and Lasers (COPL), Department of Physics, Université Laval, Quebec City, QC G1V 0A6, Canada; mourad.roudjane.1@ulaval.ca
4 Département de Pédiatrie, Faculté de Médecine, Centre Mére-Enfant Soleil du CHU de Québec, Université Laval, and Centre de Recherche du CHU de Québec, Quebec City, QC G1V 4G2, Canada; marc-andre.dugas.med@ssss.gouv.qc.ca
* Correspondence: younes.messaddeq@copl.ulaval.ca

Abstract: A flexible sinusoidal-shaped antenna sensor is introduced in this work, which is a modified half-wave dipole that can be used for strain sensing applications. The presented antenna is an improved extension of the previously introduced antenna sensor for respiration monitoring. The electrical and radiative characteristics of the sinusoidal antenna and the effects of the geometrical factors are studied. An approach is provided for designing the antenna, and equations are introduced to estimate the geometrical parameters based on desired electrical specifications. It is shown that the antenna sensor can be designed to have up to 5.5 times more sensitivity compared to the last generation of the antenna sensor previously introduced for respiration monitoring. The conductive polymer material used to fabricate the new antenna makes it more flexible and durable compared to the previous generation of antenna sensors made of glass-based material. Finally, a reference antenna made of copper and an antenna sensor made of the conductive polymer are fabricated, and their electrical characteristics are analyzed in free space and over the body.

Keywords: dipole antenna; miniaturized antenna; sinusoidal antenna; strain sensor; tunable antenna; conductive polymer; antenna sensor

Citation: Ahadi, M.; Roudjane, M.; Dugas, M.-A.; Miled, A.; Messaddeq, Y. Wearable Sensor Based on Flexible Sinusoidal Antenna for Strain Sensing Applications. *Sensors* **2022**, 22, 4069. https://doi.org/10.3390/s22114069

Academic Editors: Hoi-Shun Antony Lui and Mikael Persson

Received: 16 April 2022
Accepted: 25 May 2022
Published: 27 May 2022

1. Introduction

The electrical and radiative characteristics of antennas are functions of their geometrical structure and the material specifications of the conductors and dielectrics in the antenna's vicinity [1]. Consequently, antennas can be exploited for sensing applications, where the geometrical deformations or material changes can be detected by monitoring the antenna's radiative and electrical characteristics. Applications of antenna sensors can be in body movement capturing for computer animation or robot controlling, monitoring structural deformations, such as tracking cracks and displacements in buildings, monuments, and similar structures, and most importantly, monitoring vital signals for diagnosis and rehabilitation [2–6]. A Serpentine meshed patch antenna is reported for stretch strain sensing fabricated using laser-cut conductive textiles on Ecoflex substrate [7]. Recently, an RFID-incorporated meandered line dipole antenna in Ecoflex has also been reported to detect stretching strain [8].

In addition, some recently published works are focused on detecting bending strain. For example, Graphene-based patch antennas are introduced in recent works for detecting bending strain with applications in identifying human posture and joint movements [9,10].

An aluminum tape patch over a cellulose substrate is also reported in another work for bending strain detection. The use of cellulose makes the antenna recyclable and suitable to employ in disposable electromechanical sensors [11]. Some other works are focused on structural health monitoring (SHM) applications. Recent works in this area are in the form of rectangular [12], circular [13], and folded patch antennas [14]. Fractal-shaped patch antennas are also studied by Herbko and Lopato for a more miniaturized SHM antenna sensor [15]. More recently, a novel metamaterial-based SHM antenna sensor was also reported by the same team using a double split-ring resonator (dSRR) structure to achieve even more miniaturization while increasing the strain sensitivity [16].

Antenna sensors can also be embedded in wearables for vital signal monitoring applications. Although many sensing technologies have been developed for monitoring vital signals [17,18], applying on-body antenna sensors for this purpose is a relatively new field of study. A spiral-shaped flexible dipole antenna was reported for respiration detection by analyzing the received signal strength indicator (RSSI) of a Bluetooth connection [2]. Recently, a low-profile fully textile patch antenna was proposed for respiration monitoring applications [19]. A new antenna sensor in the form of a fully embroidered meander line dipole was also proposed in a recent work for real-time respiration monitoring [20].

This work presents a flexible sinusoidal-shaped half-wave dipole antenna sensor that can be used in strain sensing and vital signal monitoring applications. The proposed sinusoidal antenna sensor is the new generation of a previously introduced antenna sensor for respiration monitoring [2]. Using flexible conductors as antenna material, the changes in the antenna's impedance due to the mechanical compressions or stretchings can be picked up by a measurement device as an indicator of the strain applied to the antenna [4]. It is shown that the antenna sensor introduced in this paper could be up to 5.5 times more sensitive than the previous generation [2].

The sinusoidal antenna introduced in this paper is a modified version of the half-wave dipole antenna. Modified dipoles are reported and studied in the literature for the sake of miniaturization and impedance control, such as meandered, zigzag [21–24], and monopole sinusoidal geometries [25,26]. They are also employed in Log Periodic Dipole Array (LPDA) antennas [27,28] and Radio frequency identification (RFID) tags [29,30] due to their short axial length. Similarly, the sinusoidal antenna introduced here has a resonant impedance lower than the traditional straight dipole antenna and an axial length shorter than $\lambda/2$. For example, a sinusoidal antenna designed for 50 Ω is 20% axially shorter than a traditional straight half-wave dipole. The miniature size of the sinusoidal antenna makes it suitable for wearable applications.

Our implemented antenna sensor for vital signal monitoring is designed to be placed over the front of the chest area and embedded in a T-shirt [4]. This method of vital signal monitoring is different from non-contact systems, where both antenna and the measurement and detection system are located remotely from the subject [17]. The changes in the circumference of the upper body may lead to a geometrical deformation of the wearable antenna sensor, which changes its radiative and electrical characteristics, which will be detected by a measurement system. Sensitivity to strain, stretchability, flexibility, and durability are crucial factors for achieving a viable vital signal sensing system, as well as the Specific Absorption Rate (SAR) since these antenna sensors are placed over the body.

In the light of these requirements, this paper paves the way for realizing a vital signal monitoring system with a more sensitive, flexible, durable, and miniaturized antenna sensor compared to the previous generation [2–4]. A detailed study of the sinusoidal antenna's radiative and electrical specifications for various configurations is provided, its sensitivity to deformations is studied, and a design guide is provided for the antenna sensor. Finally, a prototype antenna is fabricated and measured in free space and over the body, and its durability and SAR compliance are studied. An upcoming paper will cover the antenna's application in a vital signal monitoring system and provide measurement data for the antenna sensor.

The sinusoidal antenna is introduced and studied in detail in the second and third sections of this paper. The antenna is simulated using CST Studio Suite® 2020 software [31], and the effects of the geometrical parameters are analyzed on its radiation characteristics and strain sensitivity. A design guide is provided in the fourth section using two methods, and equations are introduced for estimating the geometrical parameters based on desired characteristics. In the fifth section, a reference copper antenna and a flexible polymer antenna sensor are fabricated, their electrical parameters are measured, and their environmental durability is analyzed through an experiment. Discussions are made in the sixth section about the antenna's SAR, its behavior under bending and twisting, and its application in strain sensing. Additionally, a summary of the state-of-the-art is provided, and it is shown that higher sensitivity to strain is achievable using this antenna sensor compared to the traditional design used in our previous work, known as a half-turn Archimedean spiral antenna [2].

2. Antenna Geometry

The design of the antenna sensor, shown in Figure 1, is based on the traditional straight half-wave dipole. The antenna wires are bent n times to form a sinusoidal shape in the domain of zero to $n\pi$. Equation (1) can be considered for plotting the shape of a single pole of the antenna in a cartesian coordinate system where parameters W_A and L_A define the width and the length of the antenna, respectively. The n factor indicates the number of extrema in the structure of a single antenna pole.

$$y = W_A \sin\left(\frac{n\pi}{L_A}z\right) \quad z = (0, L_A) \tag{1}$$

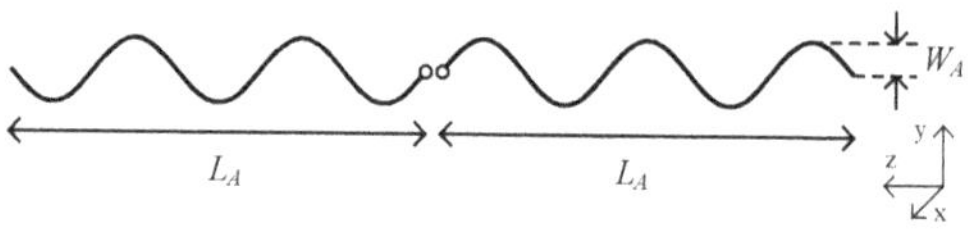

Figure 1. Antenna Geometry with $n = 5$. Small circles in the middle indicate the feeding point. The antenna is placed along Z-axis, and the peaks and dips are along the Y-axis.

3. Specifications and Intrinsic Parameters

A straight half-wave dipole antenna has a total wire length of $2L_W = \frac{\lambda}{2}$ relative to its wavelength of operation, and ideally has an inductive impedance of $Z_W = 73.1 + 43j$ on the respective frequency [32]. For the modified half-wave dipole antennas, the Shortening Ratio (SR) is defined as the ratio between the reduction in its axial length and its total wire length, which is shown as [21,25,26]:

$$SR = \frac{\frac{\lambda}{2} - 2L_A}{\frac{\lambda}{2}} = 1 - \frac{L_A}{L_W} \tag{2}$$

The antenna introduced here is simulated using CST Studio Suite® 2020 full-wave electromagnetic simulation software [31]. The antenna is modeled by very thin wires made of Perfect Electric Conductor (PEC) and with a diameter d of less than $\lambda \times 10^{-4}$ as an approximation of an infinitesimally thin antenna [1]. A feeding point gap of $L_g = 1.25 \times 10^{-5}\lambda$ is considered to keep it as small as possible. The model details mentioned here are considered for all of the simulations presented in this work.

A set of calculations are made on the introduced antenna geometry for $n = 1, \ldots, 9$, in which the SR is increased in fine steps while keeping wire length (L_W) constant, as shown in Figure 2. The antenna's width has to increase in each step to ensure the constancy of the wire length. The simulation results are presented in Figure 3. The antenna's resonance frequency is normalized to the resonance frequency of the straight half-wave dipole (f_{D1}). It is evident that the more the antenna becomes compressed, the lower the radiation resistance on resonance, but the higher the resonance frequency.

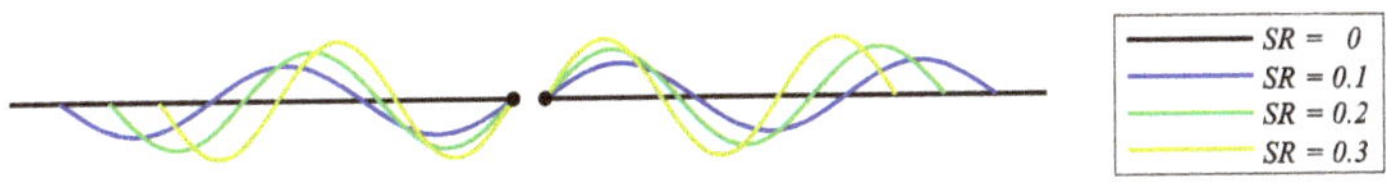

Figure 2. Sample design of an antenna with $n = 3$ for different values of SR. It is evident that the more the SR increases, the higher the width of the antenna.

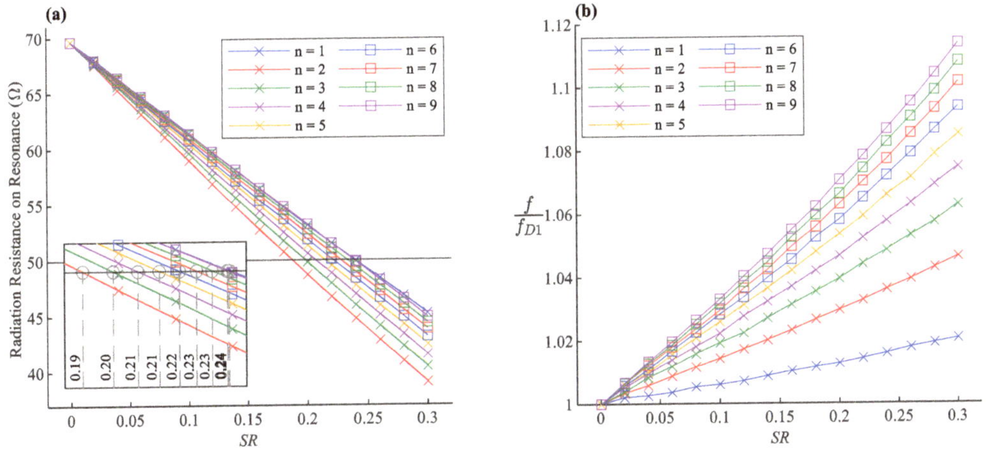

Figure 3. (**a**) Radiation Resistance of the antenna on resonance frequency. Inset: zoomed-in detail of the crossing around the 50 Ω line. (**b**) The resonance frequency of the antenna normalized to the resonance frequency of the straight half-wave dipole (f_{D1}).

3.1. Radiation Resistance

The decrease of radiation resistance due to the increase of SR seen in Figure 3a is expected behavior. To analyze the radiation resistance, we need to observe the antenna from a far-field point of view, with a distance of r from the antenna, where $r \gg \lambda$. With the assumption of $W_A \ll \lambda$, the oscillations of the sinusoidal shape can be ignored from a far-field standpoint. Therefore, the antenna can be approximated as a straight dipole with a physical length of $2L_A$ which is less than half of the operation wavelength. The antenna seen from the far-field is electrically shorter than a half-wave dipole. The real part of its impedance, indicating the radiation resistance, will be less than $\Re e\,\{Z_w\}$ which is expected to become even smaller as it becomes a shorter dipole [1,21].

3.2. Resonance Frequency

The normalized resonance frequency of the antenna is shown in Figure 3b as a function of SR for the different number of bents (n parameter). The point $SR = 0$ is equivalent to a straight half-wave dipole $L_A = L_W$, and therefore the simulation results show a resonance at around $R_{D1} \approx 70\ \Omega$ and a normalized frequency of unity. While the wire length is kept constant, the resonance frequency increases as the SR rises, which means that the rise of peaks and dips in antenna geometry causes an extra capacitive effect on the antenna [21].

3.3. Effects of the n Factor

It can be concluded from Figure 3a that the higher the n factor, the shorter the axial length of the antenna for specific radiation resistance, making it more miniaturized. Additionally, the antenna's sensitivity to the deformations becomes more significant by choosing higher n values.

In the case of $n = 1$, the antenna becomes so wide that it violates the assumption of $W_A \ll \lambda$ and cannot be categorized as a linear dipole antenna from a far-field point of view. For example, the required designs to achieve 50 Ω using $n = 1$, 5, and 9 are shown in

Figure 4. The width of the antenna $n = 1$ is noticeably large and around $\approx 0.15\lambda$, which is violating $W_A \ll \lambda$. Consequently, by choosing $n = 1$, the antenna cannot be approximated with a linear equivalent antenna from the far-field point of view anymore. The antenna would virtually become a superposition of two perpendicular equivalent dipoles with specifications out of this work's context.

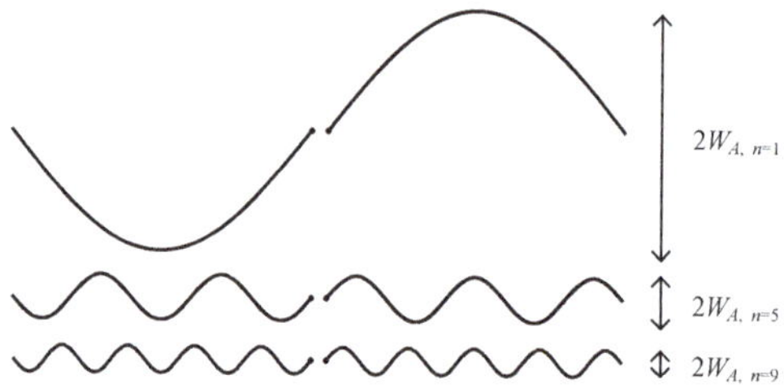

Figure 4. Antennas designed for radiation resistance of 50 Ω on a specific frequency using values of 1, 5, and 9 for the n factor. The higher the n factor, the less the antenna width for the same resonance frequency and radiation resistance, resulting in a more linear structure.

3.4. Radiation Pattern and Maximum Gain

The radiation patterns of antennas designed for 50 Ω are illustrated in Figure 5. The antennas designed with the constraints of $n > 1$ have a radiation pattern similar to a straight half-wave dipole. The maximum gain and Half-power beamwidth (HPBW) are presented in Table 1 for a straight half-wave dipole antenna ($n = 0$) and sinusoidal antennas $R_R = 50\ \Omega$ and $n = 1, 3, \ldots, 9$. It can be concluded that a larger n makes the antenna more similar to the straight half-wave dipole antenna in terms of HPBW and far-field pattern. The HPBW is slightly wider than the straight dipole in lower n values and becomes narrower as n rises, resulting in more directivity (D) and maximum gain (G), as $G \propto D$ [1]. Following the discussion above about the effects of the n factor, it can be seen that the unusual radiation pattern for the case of an antenna $n = 1$ resembles a superposition of two dipoles along the Z- and Y-axis due to its noticeably large width of $W_A \approx 0.15\lambda$.

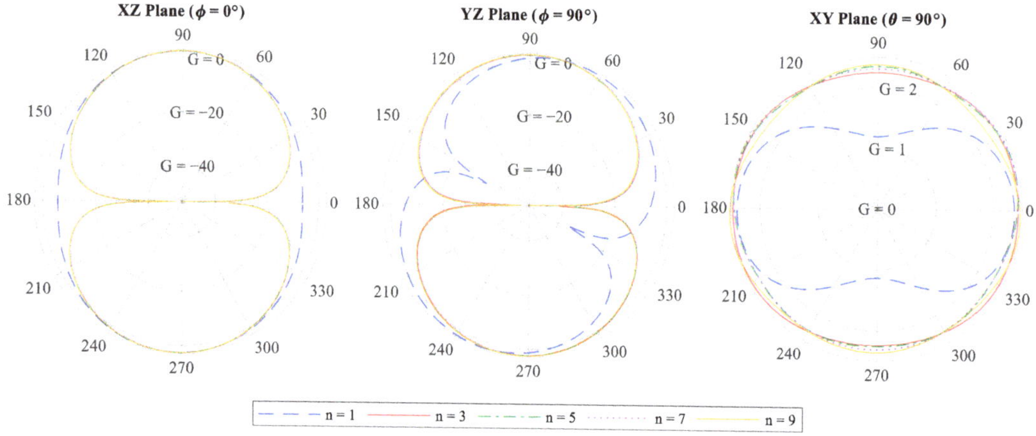

Figure 5. Far-field radiation gain (G) pattern of the 50 Ω sinusoidal dipole antenna for $n = 1, 3, \ldots, 9$. The antenna is placed along Z-axis, and the sinusoidal peaks and dips are spread along Y-axis.

Table 1. The Maximum Gain and HPBW of the straight half-wave dipole and 50 Ω sinusoidal dipoles for different n values.

n	Max Gain (dBi/dBd)	HPBW XZ Plane (ϕ=0°)	HPBW YZ Plane (ϕ=90°)
0 *	2.14/0	78°	78°
1	2.419/0.269	89.6°	82.6°
3	2.451/0.301	79.2°	80.6°
5	2.467/0.317	78.5°	79.7°
7	2.474/0.324	78.3°	80.1°

* Indicates traditional straight half-wave dipole.

4. Design Methods

Here a set of curve fittings are made of the simulation data to provide equations based on geometrical parameters for estimating the impedance on resonance and the resonance frequency of the sinusoidal antenna, which can provide a starting point for fine-tuning the antenna parameters. Two methods are presented, based on two constraints of fixed wire length or fixed axial length, and the pros and cons of each are described. The curve fittings are made through a Nonlinear Least Squares (NLS) method based on the Trust Region algorithm [33].

4.1. Method 1: Designing Based on L_A for a Known L_W

4.1.1. Curve Fittings Based on SR

In the data presented in Figure 3, the radiation characteristics are expressed based on SR, which is the antenna length L_A relative to the fixed total wire length L_W. According to the curve fittings, the resonance frequency f increases with the rise of SR, and the slope is proportional to the square root of n. It can be written in the following form:

$$f = f_{D1}\left(1 + \frac{\sqrt{n}}{k_{11}} \cdot SR\right) \tag{3}$$

where f_{D1} is the resonance frequency of a straight half-wave dipole with a length of L_W. The impedance on resonance R_R drops as SR increases, and the drop rate is approximately proportional to the 8th root of n. Therefore, it can be fitted on the following form:

$$R_R = R_{D1}\left(1 - \frac{k_{12}}{\sqrt[8]{n}} \cdot SR\right) \tag{4}$$

By choosing $k_{11} = 8.265$ in Equation (3), and $R_{D1} = 69.54$, $k_{12} = 1.587$ in Equation (4), an R^2 of 99.55% and 99.85% is achieved for each Equation, respectively, as a measure of goodness-of-fit [34]. The curve fitting is made of the data in the domain of $n = 3, \ldots, 9$ and $SR = 0.05, \ldots, 0.3$. The precision of the curve fittings is shown in Figure A1 in Appendix A. It is also possible to choose a R_R or f of choice and solve the introduced equations for SR. It should be noted that n factor can only take integer values and should be chosen according to the fabrication capabilities.

4.1.2. The Design Steps Using Method 1

1. Choosing a wire length L_W and n
2. Calculating R_R for different SR values, or calculate SR for a given R_R
3. Calculating f for the SR chosen in step 2
4. Readjusting L_W (and subsequently updating f_{D1}) while keeping SR fixed to reach the desired resonance frequency
5. Calculating W_A based on the finalized L_A and L_W using the integral Equation introduced in the following.
6. Verify the design by simulating the antenna model based on Equation (1)
7. Finish if the desired frequency is acquired; otherwise, repeat from Step 4.

It is worth mentioning that the designer has to redo all the steps if they decide to choose another n value.

4.1.3. Calculating Antenna width W_A

With L_W and L_A as known variables, calculating the width of the antenna (W_A) requires solving an integral equation. A small arc dL can be fit on the hypotenuse of a right triangle. According to the Pythagorean theorem, its length can be written as $dL = \sqrt{dy^2 + dz^2}$. By integrating dL over the curve, the total curve length can be calculated as follows:

$$L = \int_a^b \sqrt{1 + \left(\frac{dy}{dz}\right)^2} dz. \tag{5}$$

By combining (1) and (5), the wire length can be calculated as the following:

$$L_W = \int_0^{L_A} \sqrt{1 + \left(W_A \frac{n\pi}{L_A} \cos\left(\frac{n\pi}{L_A} z\right)\right)^2} dz\,. \tag{6}$$

4.1.4. Disadvantages of Method 1 Based on SR

The integral in Equation (6) does not have an elementary antiderivative and is an elliptic integral of the second kind. Even though numerical methods and software packages such as MATLAB can be used to solve the integral Equation for W_A effortlessly [35,36], it would not be a convenient method in the antenna design synthesis process, especially if the design needs to be made based on antenna width W_A parameter.

Although the definition of SR could help to understand the behavior of the antenna, it is not a decent choice for providing a design method since its dependency on constant wire length L_W requires solving Equation (6) for W_A before each iteration of the simulation to obtain the full geometrical parameters of the antenna. Additionally, the designer has to redo all the design steps in the case they decide to go with another value of n. Moreover, the estimation of R_R using Equation (4) based on SR cannot differentiate well between adjacent n values since the data lines are very close.

4.2. *Method 2: Designing Based on W_A for a Known L_A*

4.2.1. Widening Ratio

Widening Ratio (WR) is presented in Equation (7) for studying the antenna characteristics directly based on the geometric parameters of W_A and L_A and alleviate the need for solving the integral equations during the antenna design process.

$$WR = \frac{W_A}{L_A} \times 100. \tag{7}$$

A new set of simulations were performed on antennas with different WR values while keeping L_A constant and ignoring the assumption of fixed total wire length L_W. This definition is beneficial while modeling the antenna based on L_A and W_A in electronic design automation (EDA) software and electromagnetic simulators. Figure 6 shows an example representation of the simulated model configurations for $n = 3$. This set of simulations are repeated for different n values, and the results are presented in Figure 7.

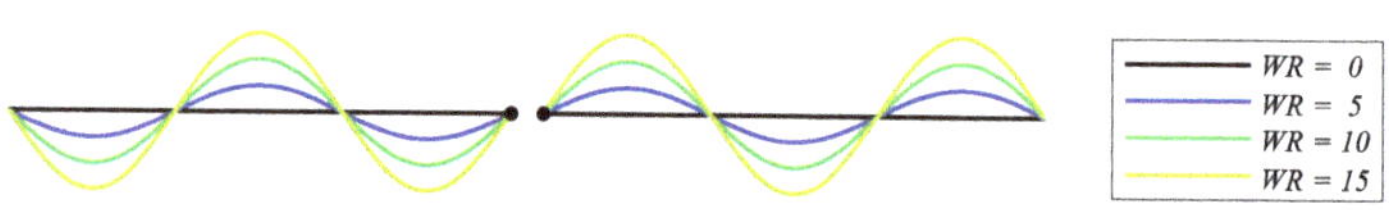

Figure 6. Representation of increasing WR of an example antenna with $n = 3$, while keeping L_A as constant and ignoring the fixed wire length L_W constraint.

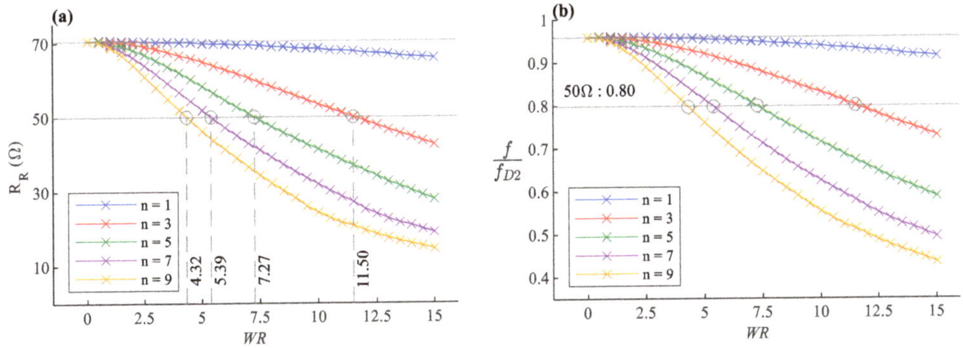

Figure 7. Antenna characteristics for different n values expressed versus WR while the axial length L_A is kept constant (**a**) Radiation Resistance of the antenna on resonance frequency. The required WR values to design a 50 Ω antenna are marked for $n = 3, \ldots, 9$ (**b**) Resonance frequency normalized to f_{D2}.

4.2.1.1. Curve Fittings Based on WR

According to the data presented in Figure 7, the decrease in f and R_R is approximately proportional to n and WR, and Equations (8) and (9) are provided based on this observation. These equations provide approximations for a given n and WR, as a starting point for fine-tuning. In this Equation f_{D2} is the resonance frequency of a straight half-wave dipole with a length of L_A, and by setting $k_{21} = 182.3$ in Equation (8) and $R_{D2} = 72.78$, $k_{22} = 120.94$ in Equation (9), the equations fit approximately on the data points with an R^2 of 98.41% and 99.07%, respectively. The precision of the fitting is illustrated in Figure A2a,b in Appendix A.

$$f = f_{D2}\left(1 - \frac{n}{k_{21}} \cdot WR\right) \tag{8}$$

$$R_R = R_{D2}\left(1 - \frac{n}{k_{22}} \cdot WR\right) \tag{9}$$

The surface fitting is made with the data in the domain of $n = 3, \ldots, 9$, $WR = 1, \ldots, 15$ and the range of $R_R = 30, \ldots, 65$ and $f/f_{D2} = 0.6, \ldots, 1$. Similarly, these equations can also be solved for WR considering a f or R_R of choice. By combining Equations (8) and (9), we reach the following Equation (10), which defines f solely based on R_R and does not depend on n, as shown in Figure A2c in Appendix A.

$$f = f_{D2}\left(1 - k_{31}(R_{D3} - R_R)\right) \tag{10}$$

where:

$$k_{31} = \frac{k_{22}}{k_{21}}, \; R_{D3} = \frac{k_{22}}{k_{21}} R_{D2} \tag{11}$$

4.2.1.2. The Design Steps Using Method 2

1. Choosing a wire length L_A and n
2. Calculating R_R for different WR values, or calculate WR for a given R_R
3. Calculating f for the WR chosen in step 2
4. Readjusting L_A (and subsequently updating f_{D2}) while keeping WR fixed to reach the desired resonance frequency
5. Verify the design by simulating the antenna model based on Equation (1)
6. Finish if the desired frequency is acquired; otherwise, repeat from Step 4.

4.2.1.3. Advantages of Method 2 Based on WR

This design method has three advantages compared to the previous method, based on SR. First, the design is made directly based on L_A and W_A values and no integrals need to be solved to calculate W_A for each iteration of the design process. Second, the estimation of R_R has a better separation for adjacent n values compared to the previous method. Third, if the designer finishes the design process and then decides to go with another n factor, they will not need to start over. By only repeating the second step, a new WR can be calculated for the previously chosen resistance, and then W_A can be readjusted. As shown in Equation (10), the resonance frequency of the antenna will not change as long as the designer keeps the previously chosen radiation resistance for the design.

4.3. Tuning Considerations

The factors affecting classic straight dipole antenna characteristics also apply to the sinusoidal dipoles, such as feeding point gap width, wire conductivity, and wire thickness [32]. All simulations were achieved using PEC as the material of the antenna wires. For convenience, the designer might consider extending the feeding point gap of $L_g = 1.25 \times 10^{-5}\lambda$ to a larger value for high-frequency antennas where λ is shorter than a kilometer. In this case, the WR (or SR) factor needs to be adjusted to a slightly lower value for compensating the inductive effect caused by the extra gap widening.

All the data presented from the simulation runs in this work were prepared with the assumption of a very thin wire with a diameter d of less than $\lambda \times 10^{-4}$. For an antenna made of a thicker wire, the WR (or SR) parameter needs to be adjusted to a slightly higher value to achieve the desired radiation resistance on resonance.

5. Fabrication and Measurement

5.1. Fabrication Process

Two sample high-frequency antennas with $n = 5$ are fabricated as a proof-of-concept. Table 2 shows the geometrical parameters used for the fabrication of both antennas. The antenna is designed and simulated for 800 MHz and 50 Ω impedance. A copper-made antenna is fabricated as the reference, and a second antenna is also made using a conductive flexible polymer suitable for wearable sensor applications.

Table 2. Geometrical Parameters of the antennas.

Parameter	Axial Length (L_A)	Width (W_A)	n	Wire Thickness
Value	74.54 mm	5.65 mm	5	1.4 mm

Compared to the previously introduced traditional antenna sensor based on silica hollow-core fibers, the newly developed polymer fiber is enduring, flexible, and sustains its electrical characteristics better than silica hollow-core fibers [37]. The conductive polymer is biocompatible, highly flexible, and resistant to water and other perturbations. It can be easily sewn on textiles and bending, twisting, or stretching does not break it. The measured resistance of the material is around $\approx 8\ \Omega\cdot\text{cm}^{-1}$ and is observed to have a good performance in high frequency.

The composition of the conductive polymer fiber is a combination of poly (ethylene-co-vinyl acetate) (PEVA) polymer (Sigma-Aldrich, St. Louis, MO, USA) and multi-walled carbon nanotubes (MWCNTs) (commercially available at Cheaptubes, Grafton, VT, USA, with a carbon purity of 95 wt%) with a composition of 41 wt% mass of MWCNT and 59 wt% mass of PEVA and without any purifications.

The fabrication steps of the conductive polymer are shown in Figure 8a. For an hour, the MWCNT nanoparticles are sonicated in 10 mL of tetrahydrofuran (THF) (Fisher Scientific International, Waltham, MA, USA). Afterward, the PEVA polymer and the MWCNTs solution are mixed by mechanical stirring for one hour at 1400 rpm. The mixture is then sonicated for an additional 180 min for better dispersion. Finally, the colloidal solution is placed in the oven at 100 °C for 15 min to obtain a high-viscosity composite.

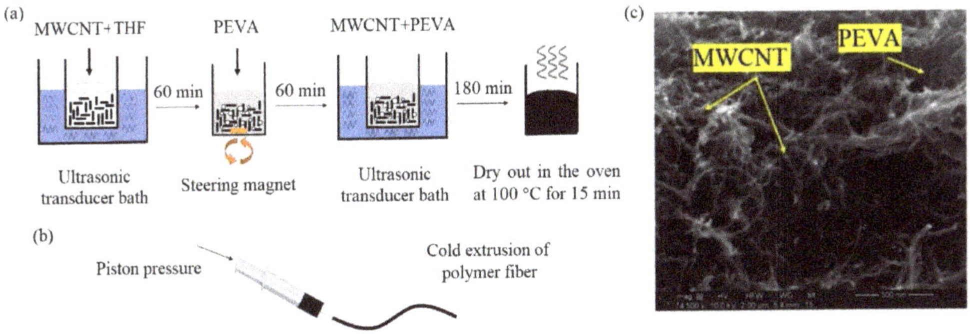

Figure 8. (**a**) Fabrication process of the MWCNT-PEVA conductive polymer (**b**) the extrusion process of the polymer wire (**c**) SEM image of the cross-section of the MWCNT-PEVA polymer wire.

The composite of the conductive fiber is extruded [38] using a commercially available syringe, as shown in Figure 8b, and is left to dry out. The initial thickness of conductive fiber is 1.6 mm, which reduces to 1.4 mm after the drying process. The scanning electron microscopy (SEM) image of the cross-section of the polymer wire is presented in Figure 8c.

5.2. Measurements

The fabricated antennas are shown in Figure 9a,b and are fed using the commercially available 1:1 balun TC1-1-13MA+ from Mini-Circuits [39]. The measurements are made using a calibrated VNA system, with effects of the transmission line de-embedded from the final scattering parameters (S-Parameters) readout [40]. Table 3 shows the measured specifications of the fabricated antennas. The return loss of the antennas is also presented in Figure 9c. Each measurement is repeated eight times, and the average values are reported. The measurements show a good agreement between the antennas and the simulation. The differences are due to the error in fabrication, the material specifications, and non-rigid nature of the polymer wire.

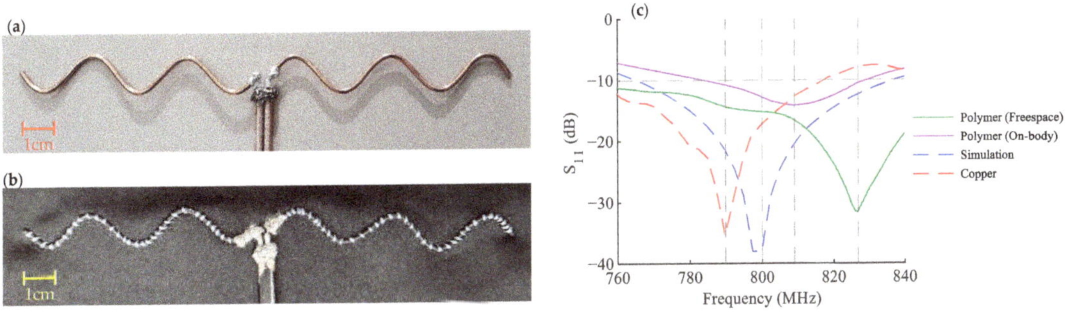

Figure 9. (**a**) The Copper antenna (**b**) The Polymer antenna, sewn on a T-shirt (**c**) Return loss of the antenna in simulation, the Copper antenna, and the Polymer antenna, both in free space and over the body.

Table 3. Measured Antenna Specifications.

Antenna	Operation Frequency	Impedance on Frequency
Copper	790 MHz	52 + 0.2 i Ω
Conductive Polymer (Free space)	827 MHz	50.4 + 2.5 i Ω
Conductive Polymer (Over the Body)	808 MHz	49.2 + 19.9 i Ω

It can be seen that the resonance frequency of the polymer antenna is changed when it is placed over the body. There are two factors contributing to this frequency shift. The first one is the changes in the antenna's surrounding material in its reactive near-field region, which makes a change in the impedance of the antenna seen from the feeding circuit, resulting in an impedance mismatch and therefore affecting the resonance frequency and the radiation resistance of the antenna [41].

The other factor causing this shift is the deviation of the antenna's dimensions due to its initial stretching when the patient wears the smart textile, as shown in Figure 10. Therefore, it is recommended that the T-shirt selected for the antenna integration be a right fit for the patient's body form and not too tight. Otherwise, the initial state of the antenna sensor will be considerably stretched, which would potentially limit the dynamic range of the antenna sensor.

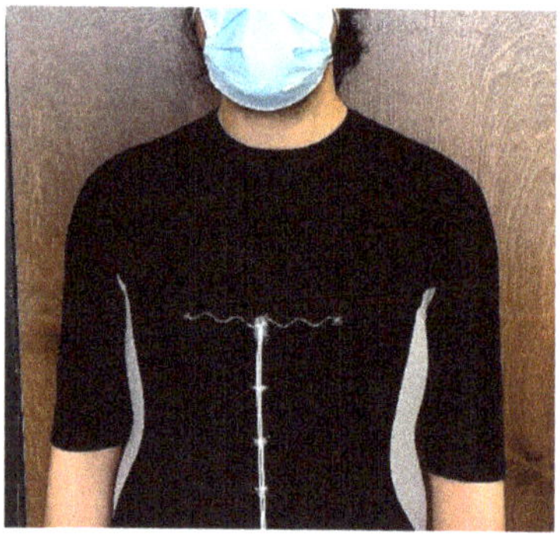

Figure 10. A 50 Ω antenna sensor $n = 5$, embedded on a smart T-shirt for vital signal monitoring applications.

5.3. The Durability of the Antenna Sensor

An experiment is performed in order to demonstrate the durability of the conductive polymer material for wearable smart textile applications intended for everyday use. A 50 Ω antenna sensor is fabricated and sewn on a piece of fabric, and its electrical specifications are measured. The fabric and the antenna sensor are washed for 20 cycles, and the measurements are performed again after each cycle.

During each step, the fabric is submerged in a container filled with tap water and detergent and is stirred vigorously to simulate a washing procedure. The fabric is taken out after 5 min, and then it is rinsed using tap water. Next, a piece of a napkin is used to remove the excessive wetness of the fabric. Finally, a heat gun is used for 10 to 15 min to completely dry out the fabric and antenna sensor. The specifications of the antenna sensor are remeasured and recorded after the complete dry out.

The container water and the detergent were refreshed every five cycles. The SMA connectors were held outside the water during the washing process, as shown in Figure 11. The heat gun is placed at least 15 cm away from the fabric during the drying process to prevent accidental burning due to its high temperature and is manually swung over the fabric to ensure complete dryness.

The measurements after each cycle are shown in Figure 12. It can be seen that there is a slight shift in the antenna's operation frequency throughout the cycles, which could be due to the antenna deformations or fabric shrinkage caused by the heat during the drying process. The reflection loss of the antenna is still ideally below −10 dB, and despite the slight frequency shift, the antenna's performance is not significantly affected after 20 wash cycles.

Figure 11. The fabric is completely submerged in water and detergent. The SMA connectors are held outside.

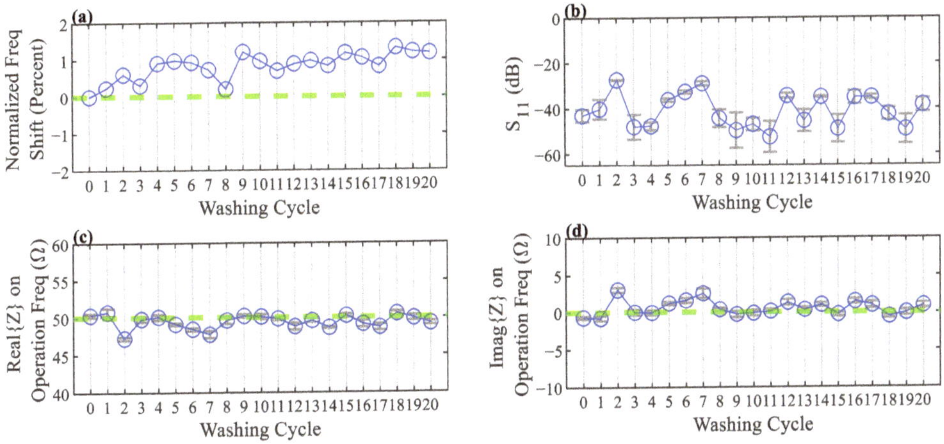

Figure 12. Antenna electrical characteristics are measured after each washing cycle. Each measurement is made four times, and the average is reported. Error bars show the standard deviation of each measurement. (**a**) Normalized frequency shift of the antenna. Green dashed line indicates zero shift. (**b**) Return Loss of the antenna on resonance frequency. (**c**,**d**) Real and Imaginary part of the antenna's impedance on operation frequency, respectively. Green dashed line indicates the ideal values for a 50 Ω impedance matching.

6. Discussion

6.1. Strain Sensitivity

The introduced antenna design is notably valuable in strain sensing applications. It was previously shown in Figure 3 that the impedance and the resonance frequency of the antenna shift as SR changes when the sinusoidal dipole becomes stretched or compressed along its axis. One can exploit this behavior and make a sinusoidal antenna out of flexible conductors and record the S-parameters of the antenna over time as an indicator of the strain applied to the antenna [4]. The strain detection can be achieved by tracking the resonance frequency or measuring the reflection coefficient on a fixed frequency.

The traditional antenna sensor employed in previous works on respiration monitoring [2–4] is essentially a sinusoidal half-wave dipole $n = 1$. Higher n values can increase the sensitivity of the antenna sensor. For comparison, by choosing $n = 2$, the resonance frequency sensitivity of the antenna versus SR will be ≈ 2.2 times more than the sensitivity demonstrated by the traditional antenna. It increases to ≈ 4.1 and ≈ 5.5 times more for the antennas $n = 5$ and $n = 9$, respectively, which is a significant improvement. Figure 13 shows the trend of sensitivity improvement for different n values.

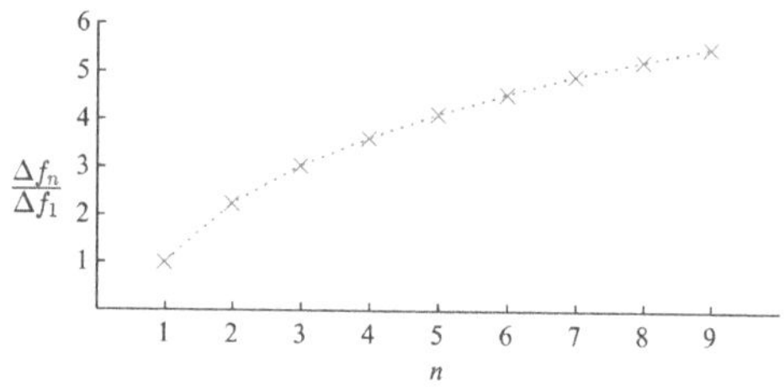

Figure 13. Sensitivity of the resonance frequency of the sinusoidal antenna sensor to the applied strain, expressed relative to the sensitivity of the traditional antenna sensor with $n = 1$, for antennas $n > 1$.

Although a higher n value can provide better sensitivity, the advantage is reduced as n become larger and larger. For instance, raising n from 7 to 9 only improves the sensitivity by 12%, while changing n from 2 to 4 will boost the sensitivity by a significant amount of 83%. Moreover, an antenna sensor designed with a very high n value could be challenging to fabricate if the wire is relatively thick, and it will not be easy to integrate the antenna into wearable applications.

Table 4 summarizes the characteristics of this work compared to other recently published works on flexible antennas for strain sensing. Stretching strain is defined as $\epsilon = \Delta L / L_0$ where L_0 is the initial antenna sensor length, and stretchability is $\epsilon_{max} \times 100\%$ which is the maximum amount of the possible strain ϵ that can be applied to the sensor, expressed in percentage [7]. Bending strain is defined as $\epsilon = h/2r$ where h is the antenna sensor thickness and r is the bending radius. The maximum bending is defined as the angle at which the sensor cannot be bent any further [11]. Exceeding the limits of the reported stretchability (or maximum bending) is either destructive for the antenna sensor or yields unreliable sensor readings [7,11]. The sensitivity to strain is also defined as $S = (\Delta f / f_0)/\epsilon$ which is the normalized frequency shift $\Delta f / f_0$ for an applied strain of ϵ [7,11]. Table 5 compares recent works on another category of antenna strain sensors primarily used in structural health monitoring to detect surface strains and cracks in the structures.

Table 4. Comparison of recent works on stretchable antennas for strain sensing.

Description	Strain Type	Stretchability/Max. Bending	Sensitivity to Strain	Year	Ref.
Sinusoidal dipole antenna *	Stretching	30%	0.40	2022	This work
Serpentine meshed patch over ground plane	Stretching	40%	0.20	2021	[7]
Serpentine meshed in patch and ground planes	Stretching	100%	0.25	2021	[7]
RFID Meandered half-wave dipole in Ecoflex	Stretching	Not provided	0.141 **	2019	Based on [8]
Flexible planar dipole antenna over Kepton tape	Stretching	Not provided	0.066 **	2012	Based on [42]
Liquid metal loop antenna	Stretching	40%	0.18	2009	[43]
Graphene patch antenna over copper tape	Bending	Not provided	1.4	2021	[9]
Flexible multi-layer graphene film	Bending	Not provided	5.39	2018	[10]
Aluminum tape patch over cellulose substrate	Bending	160°	3.49	2016	[11]

* With the assumption of $n = 9$ and the initial $SR = 0.3$. In the case of using adequately thin wires, a higher initial SR and therefore higher stretchability could be achieved. ** The original author does not provide the sensitivity directly. The presented value is calculated from the reported data.

Table 5. Comparison of recent works on antenna sensors for structural health monitoring.

Description	Resonance Freq	Sensitivity to Strain (kHz/με) *	Year	Ref.
Double split-ring resonator (dSRR) antenna	2.725 GHz	−1.548	2022	[16]
Rectangular microstrip antenna	2.725 GHz	−2.379	2022	[16]
Rectangular microstrip antenna	2.469 GHz	−2.847	2021	[12]
Sierpinski fractal microstrip patch	2.725 GHz	−1.18	2019	[15]
Circular patch antenna	2.5 GHz	−2.05	2018	[13]
RFID folded patch antenna	911.6 MHz	−0.76	2015	[14]

* The sensitivity of this category of antenna sensors is usually reported in absolute frequency.

A crucial factor for antenna sensor comparison is the magnitude of force needed to achieve a specific strain. This factor becomes especially important in applications with very small stretching forces. To the best of our knowledge, such a parameter is not reported in any of the works summarized in Table 4. However, the materials used in the fabrication of each antenna sensor are well described in the other works and this paper, which might indirectly address this issue. Nonetheless, a study on the magnitude of force required to achieve a specific strain on the antenna introduced here is undoubtedly an interesting point that could be experimentally measured and included in a forthcoming paper.

6.2. Effects of Bending and Twisting

Although the antenna sensor introduced here is ideally designed for applications where the deformations are mainly along the Z-axis, the effects of other forms of deformations are also investigated to understand the antenna's behavior better. A sample 50 Ω sinusoidal antenna with the geometrical parameters introduced in Table 2 is simulated in twisted and bent conditions, as illustrated in Figure 14. The twisting is performed around the Z-axis up to 90°, and the cylindrical bending is applied along the X-axis up to 180°.

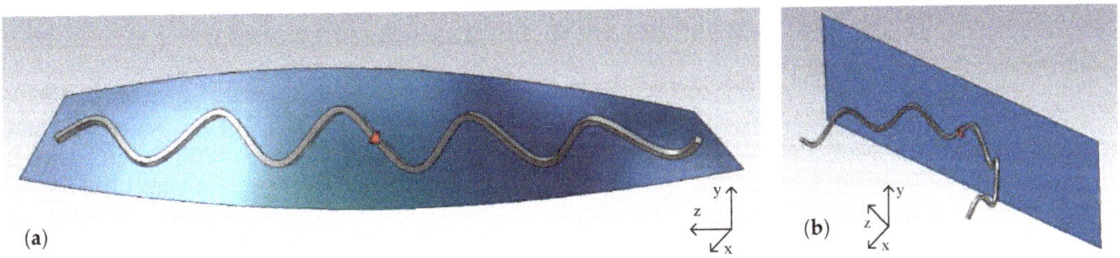

Figure 14. Illustration of (**a**) the twisting and (**b**) the bending applied to the modeled antenna in simulation software. The blue metallic-colored plane, the thick wire, and the lighting effects are added for a better presentation of the 3D model.

Figure 15 presents the antenna simulation results for different bend and twist angles. There is a significant change in the antenna's resistance on the resonance frequency under bending deformation. It is shown that the more the antenna becomes bent, the lower becomes the resistance on the resonance frequency. Bending can also shift the resonance frequency to slightly higher, which is negligible in low bending angles and will be less than 2% for 180°. In comparison, twisting does not significantly affect the resistance on resonance and shows a slightly decreasing trend. It also has a similar effect on the resonance frequency, making it drop by as much as 2.5% at 90° of twisting according to the simulation.

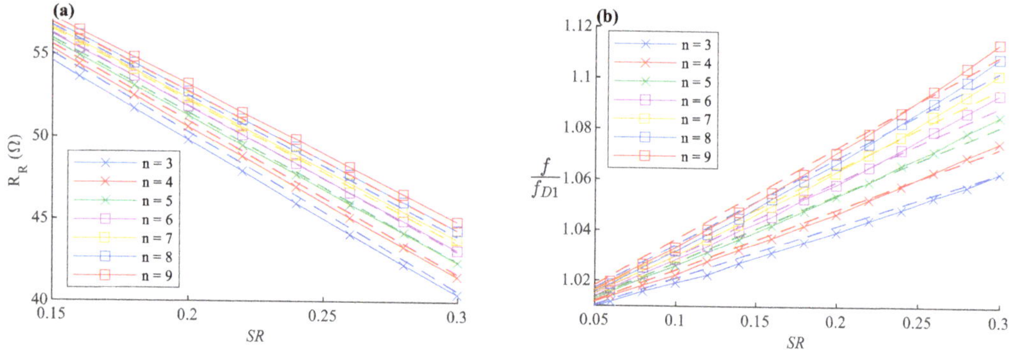

Figure A1. Correlation of the data and the equations achieved via curve fitting based on SR for (**a**) radiation resistance on resonance frequency (zoomed in) and (**b**) resonance frequency normalized to f_{D1}. Solid lines represent the data, and dashed lines represent the fitted function. It is clear that the fitted function on R_R is ambiguous for adjacent n values.

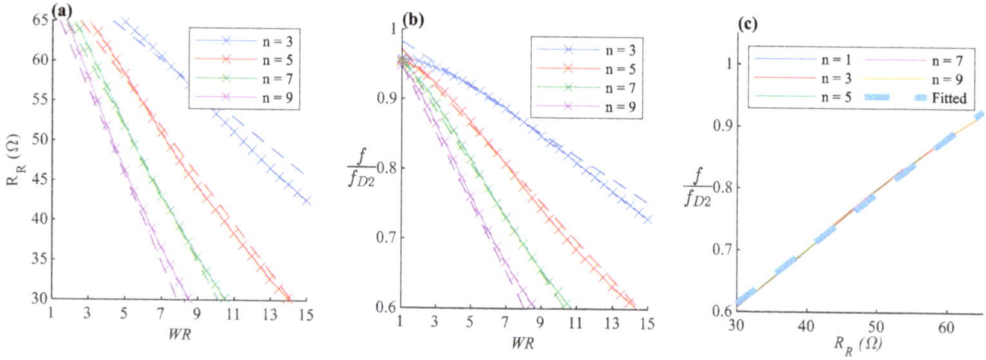

Figure A2. Correlation of the data and the equations achieved via curve fitting based on WR for (**a**) radiation resistance on resonance frequency and (**b**) resonance frequency normalized to f_{D2}. Solid lines represent the data, and dashed lines represent the fitted function. (**c**) Correlation of the data and Equation (10), it is evident that the data are almost independent of n factor. The dashed line shows the fitted Equation.

References

1. Kraus, J.D. *Antennas*, 2nd ed.; McGraw-Hill Series in Electrical Engineering; McGraw-Hill: New York, NY, USA, 1988; ISBN 978-0-07-035422-7.
2. Roudjane, M.; Bellemare-Rousseau, S.; Khalil, M.; Gorgutsa, S.; Miled, A.; Messaddeq, Y. A Portable Wireless Communication Platform Based on a Multi-Material Fiber Sensor for Real-Time Breath Detection. *Sensors* **2018**, *18*, 973. [CrossRef] [PubMed]
3. Roudjane, M.; Bellemare-Rousseau, S.; Drouin, E.; Belanger-Huot, B.; Dugas, M.-A.; Miled, A.; Messaddeq, Y. Smart T-Shirt Based on Wireless Communication Spiral Fiber Sensor Array for Real-Time Breath Monitoring: Validation of the Technology. *IEEE Sens. J.* **2020**, *20*, 10841–10850. [CrossRef]
4. Guay, P.; Gorgutsa, S.; LaRochelle, S.; Messaddeq, Y. Wearable Contactless Respiration Sensor Based on Multi-Material Fibers Integrated into Textile. *Sensors* **2017**, *17*, 1050. [CrossRef] [PubMed]
5. Mulholland, K.; Virkki, J.; Raumonen, P.; Merilampi, S. Wearable RFID Perspiration Sensor Tags for Well-Being Applications—From Laboratory to Field Use. In *EMBEC & NBC 2017*; Eskola, H., Väisänen, O., Viik, J., Hyttinen, J., Eds.; IFMBE Proceedings; Springer: Singapore, 2018; Volume 65, pp. 1012–1015, ISBN 978-981-10-5121-0.
6. Panunzio, N.; Bianco, G.M.; Occhiuzzi, C.; Marrocco, G. RFID Sensors for the Monitoring of Body Temperature and Respiratory Function: A Pandemic Prospect. In Proceedings of the 2021 6th International Conference on Smart and Sustainable Technologies (SpliTech), Bol and Split, Croatia, 8–11 September 2021; pp. 1–5.
7. Nikbakhtnasrabadi, F.; El Matbouly, H.; Ntagios, M.; Dahiya, R. Textile-Based Stretchable Microstrip Antenna with Intrinsic Strain Sensing. *ACS Appl. Electron. Mater.* **2021**, *3*, 2233–2246. [CrossRef] [PubMed]

8. Teng, L.; Pan, K.; Nemitz, M.P.; Song, R.; Hu, Z.; Stokes, A.A. Soft Radio-Frequency Identification Sensors: Wireless Long-Range Strain Sensors Using Radio-Frequency Identification. *Soft Robot.* **2019**, *6*, 82–94. [CrossRef] [PubMed]
9. Sindhu, B.; Kothuru, A.; Sahatiya, P.; Goel, S.; Nandi, S. Laser-Induced Graphene Printed Wearable Flexible Antenna-Based Strain Sensor for Wireless Human Motion Monitoring. *IEEE Trans. Electron Devices* **2021**, *68*, 3189–3194. [CrossRef]
10. Tang, D.; Wang, Q.; Wang, Z.; Liu, Q.; Zhang, B.; He, D.; Wu, Z.; Mu, S. Highly Sensitive Wearable Sensor Based on a Flexible Multi-Layer Graphene Film Antenna. *Sci. Bull.* **2018**, *63*, 574–579. [CrossRef]
11. Kanaparthi, S.; Sekhar, V.R.; Badhulika, S. Flexible, Eco-Friendly and Highly Sensitive Paper Antenna Based Electromechanical Sensor for Wireless Human Motion Detection and Structural Health Monitoring. *Extreme Mech. Lett.* **2016**, *9*, 324–330. [CrossRef]
12. Ossa-Molina, O.; Duque-Giraldo, J.; Reyes-Vera, E. Strain Sensor Based on Rectangular Microstrip Antenna: Numerical Methodologies and Experimental Validation. *IEEE Sens. J.* **2021**, *21*, 22908–22917. [CrossRef]
13. Lopato, P.; Herbko, M. A Circular Microstrip Antenna Sensor for Direction Sensitive Strain Evaluation. *Sensors* **2018**, *18*, 310. [CrossRef]
14. Yi, X.; Wu, T.; Wang, Y.; Tentzeris, M.M. Sensitivity Modeling of an RFID-Based Strain-Sensing Antenna With Dielectric Constant Change. *IEEE Sens. J.* **2015**, *15*, 6147–6155. [CrossRef]
15. Herbko, M.; Lopato, P. Microstrip Patch Strain Sensor Miniaturization Using Sierpinski Curve Fractal Geometry. *Sensors* **2019**, *19*, 3989. [CrossRef] [PubMed]
16. Herbko, M.; Lopato, P. Application of a Single Cell Electric-SRR Metamaterial for Strain Evaluation. *Materials* **2021**, *15*, 291. [CrossRef] [PubMed]
17. Gouveia, C.; Loss, C.; Pinho, P.; Vieira, J. Different Antenna Designs for Non-Contact Vital Signs Measurement: A Review. *Electronics* **2019**, *8*, 1294. [CrossRef]
18. De Fazio, R.; Stabile, M.; De Vittorio, M.; Velázquez, R.; Visconti, P. An Overview of Wearable Piezoresistive and Inertial Sensors for Respiration Rate Monitoring. *Electronics* **2021**, *10*, 2178. [CrossRef]
19. Wagih, M.; Malik, O.; Weddell, A.S.; Beeby, S. E-Textile Breathing Sensor Using Fully Textile Wearable Antennas. *Eng. Proc.* **2022**, *15*, 9. [CrossRef]
20. El Gharbi, M.; Fernández-García, R.; Gil, I. Embroidered Wearable Antenna-Based Sensor for Real-Time Breath Monitoring. *Measurement* **2022**, *195*, 111080. [CrossRef]
21. Nakano, H.; Tagami, H.; Yoshizawa, A.; Yamauchi, J. Shortening Ratios of Modified Dipole Antennas. *IEEE Trans. Antennas Propag.* **1984**, *32*, 385–386. [CrossRef]
22. Rashed, J.; Tai, C.-T. A New Class of Resonant Antennas. *IEEE Trans. Antennas Propag.* **1991**, *39*, 1428–1430. [CrossRef]
23. Olaode, O.O.; Palmer, W.D.; Joines, W.T. Effects of Meandering on Dipole Antenna Resonant Frequency. *IEEE Antennas Wirel. Propag. Lett.* **2012**, *11*, 122–125. [CrossRef]
24. Endo, T.; Sunahara, Y.; Satoh, S.; Katagi, T. Resonant Frequency and Radiation Efficiency of Meander Line Antennas. *Electron. Commun. Jpn. Pt. II* **2000**, *83*, 52–58. [CrossRef]
25. Ali, M.; Stuchly, S.S. Short Sinusoidal Antennas for Wireless Communications. In Proceedings of the IEEE Pacific Rim Conference on Communications, Computers, and Signal Processing, Victoria, BC, Canada, 17–19 May 1995; pp. 542–545.
26. Kakoyiannis, C.G.; Constantinou, P. Radiation Properties and Ground-Dependent Response of Compact Printed Sinusoidal Antennas and Arrays. *IET Microw. Antennas Propag.* **2010**, *4*, 629–642. [CrossRef]
27. Chang, L.; He, S.; Zhang, J.Q.; Li, D. A Compact Dielectric-Loaded Log-Periodic Dipole Array (LPDA) Antenna. *IEEE Antennas Wirel. Propag. Lett.* **2017**, *16*, 2759–2762. [CrossRef]
28. Trinh-Van, S.; Kwon, O.H.; Jung, E.; Park, J.; Yu, B.; Kim, K.; Seo, J.; Hwang, K.C. A Low-Profile High-Gain and Wideband Log-Periodic Meandered Dipole Array Antenna with a Cascaded Multi-Section Artificial Magnetic Conductor Structure. *Sensors* **2019**, *19*, 4404. [CrossRef]
29. Marrocco, G. Gain-Optimized Self-Resonant Meander Line Antennas for RFID Applications. *IEEE Antennas Wirel. Propag. Lett.* **2003**, *2*, 302–305. [CrossRef]
30. Rao, K.V.S.; Nikitin, P.V.; Lam, S.F. Antenna Design for UHF RFID Tags: A Review and a Practical Application. *IEEE Trans. Antennas Propag.* **2005**, *53*, 3870–3876. [CrossRef]
31. CST Studio Suite 3D EM Simulation and Analysis Software. Available online: https://www.3ds.com/products-services/simulia/products/cst-studio-suite/ (accessed on 3 May 2022).
32. Furse, C.M.; Gandhi, O.P.; Lazzi, G. Wire Elements: Dipoles, Monopoles, and Loops. In *Modern Antenna Handbook*; John Wiley & Sons, Ltd.: Hoboken, NJ, USA, 2008; pp. 57–95, ISBN 978-0-470-29415-4.
33. Coleman, T.F.; Li, Y. An Interior Trust Region Approach for Nonlinear Minimization Subject to Bounds. *SIAM J. Optim.* **1996**, *6*, 418–445. [CrossRef]
34. Ritter, A.; Muñoz-Carpena, R. Performance Evaluation of Hydrological Models: Statistical Significance for Reducing Subjectivity in Goodness-of-Fit Assessments. *J. Hydrol.* **2013**, *480*, 33–45. [CrossRef]
35. Carlson, B.C. Numerical Computation of Real or Complex Elliptic Integrals. *Numer. Algorithms* **1995**, *10*, 13–26. [CrossRef]
36. MathWorks—Makers of MATLAB and Simulink. Available online: https://www.mathworks.com/ (accessed on 30 April 2021).

37. Gauthier, N.; Roudjane, M.; Frasie, A.; Loukili, M.; Saad, A.B.; Pagé, I.; Messaddeq, Y.; Bouyer, L.J.; Gosselin, B. Multimodal Electrophysiological Signal Measurement Using a New Flexible and Conductive Polymer Fiber-Electrode. In Proceedings of the 2020 42nd Annual International Conference of the IEEE Engineering in Medicine Biology Society (EMBC), Montreal, QC, Canada, 20–24 July 2020; pp. 4373–4376.
38. Buckley, A.; Long, H.A. The Extrusion of Polymers below Their Melting Temperatures by the Application of High Pressures. *Polym. Eng. Sci.* **1969**, *9*, 115–120. [CrossRef]
39. TC1-1-13MA+ on Mini-Circuits. Available online: https://www.minicircuits.com/WebStore/dashboard.html?model=TC1-1-13MA%2B (accessed on 5 August 2021).
40. Dambrine, G. Millimeter-Wave Characterization of Silicon Devices under Small-Signal Regime: Instruments and Measurement Methodologies. In *Microwave De-Embedding;* Elsevier Science: Amsterdam, The Netherlands, 2013; pp. 47–96. ISBN 978-0-12-806856-4.
41. Nikolova, N.K.; Ravan, M.; Amineh, R.K. Substrate-Integrated Antennas on Silicon. In *Advances in Imaging and Electron Physics;* Elsevier: Amsterdam, The Netherlands, 2012; Volume 174, pp. 391–458, ISBN 978-0-12-394298-2.
42. Jang, S.-D.; Kim, J. Passive Wireless Structural Health Monitoring Sensor Made with a Flexible Planar Dipole Antenna. *Smart Mater. Struct.* **2012**, *21*, 027001. [CrossRef]
43. Cheng, S.; Rydberg, A.; Hjort, K.; Wu, Z. Liquid Metal Stretchable Unbalanced Loop Antenna. *Appl. Phys. Lett.* **2009**, *94*, 144103. [CrossRef]
44. *C95.1-1991;* IEEE Standard for Safety Levels with Respect to Human Exposure to Radio Frequency Electromagnetic Fields, 3 KHz to 300 GHz. IEEE: Piscataway, NJ, USA, 1992. [CrossRef]
45. Specific Absorption Rate (SAR) for Cellular Telephones | Federal Communications Commission. Available online: https://www.fcc.gov/general/specific-absorption-rate-sar-cellular-telephones (accessed on 5 May 2022).

sensors

MDPI

Article

Brain Implantable End-Fire Antenna with Enhanced Gain and Bandwidth

Lisa Sapari [1], Samnang Hout [2] and Jae-Young Chung [1,*]

[1] Department of Electrical & Information Engineering, SeoulTech, Seoul 01811, Korea; lisasapari@yahoo.com
[2] Department of Integrated IT Engineering, SeoulTech, Seoul 01811, Korea; hout.samnang22@gmail.com
* Correspondence: jychung@seoultech.ac.kr; Tel.: +82-2-970-6445

Abstract: An end-fire radiating implantable antenna with a small footprint and broadband operation at the frequency range of 3–5 GHz is proposed for high-data-rate wireless communication in a brain–machine interface. The proposed Vivaldi antenna was implanted vertically along the height of the skull to avoid deformation in the radiation pattern and to compensate for a gain–loss caused by surrounding lossy brain tissues. It was shown that the vertically implanted end-fire antenna had a 3 dB higher antenna gain than a horizontally implanted broadside radiating antenna discussed in recent literature. Additionally, comb-shaped slot arrays imprinted on the Vivaldi antenna lowered the resonant frequency by approximately 2 GHz and improved the antenna gain by more than 2 dB compared to an ordinary Vivaldi antenna. An antenna prototype was fabricated and then tested for verification inside a seven-layered semi-solid brain phantom where each layer had similar electromagnetic material properties as actual brain tissues. The measured data showed that the antenna radiated toward the end-fire direction with an average gain of −15.7 dBi under the frequency of interest, 3–5 GHz. A link budget analysis shows that reliable wireless communication can be achieved over a distance of 10.8 cm despite the electromagnetically harsh environment.

Keywords: brain–machine interface; implantable antenna; link budget analysis; specific absorption rate; tissue-emulating phantom; ultra-wideband antenna; Vivaldi antenna

Citation: Sapari, L.; Hout, S.; Chung, J.-Y. Brain Implantable End-Fire Antenna with Enhanced Gain and Bandwidth. *Sensors* **2022**, *22*, 4328. https://doi.org/10.3390/s22124328

Academic Editors: Hoi-Shun Antony Lui and Mikael Persson

Received: 29 April 2022
Accepted: 6 June 2022
Published: 7 June 2022

1. Introduction

Brain signal monitoring has gained considerable attention not only from brain scientists but also from electronics engineers. Real-time neural data extracted by a brain–machine interface (BMI) or brain–computer interface (BCI) can be used for various applications, such as restoring sensory functions and controlling robotic prostheses [1]. A review of the basic concept of BCI, its applications, and challenges were extensively discussed in [2]. A conventional technique such as electroencephalography (EEG) requires a wired electrode to be attached on the scalp to monitor brain signals [3]. However, several studies have demonstrated the need for implanting a wireless BMI deep into the brain to monitor both the electroencephalogram (EEFG) and electrocorticography (ECoG) for cognitive and speech control [4–9]. Neuralink [10], a neurotechnology company, has recently presented a pioneering deep BMI with wireless communication and power-charging functions.

A wireless BMI consists of electrodes, an analog integrated circuit, a digital signal processing unit, a radio frequency (RF) front-end, and an antenna. They are packed into a biocompatible housing whose footprint typically ranges from 10 × 10 mm^2 to 20 × 20 mm^2 [5–13].

The slightly large size of a brain implant is primarily due to the antenna size. For instance, the size of a half-wavelength patch antenna at the 2.4 GHz industrial-scientific-medical (ISM) frequency band in free space is approximately 60 × 60 mm^2. The antenna size can be reduced to fit into the housing by considering the high dielectric constants of brain tissues (e.g., cortical bone or dura) and by applying antenna miniaturization techniques (e.g., meandering, folding, and shorting). However, most of the reported works suffer from a low antenna gain (<−20 dBi) that is due to the high dielectric loss of brain tissues. The study showed that the antenna gain reduced by 10.7 dB after implanting it in the brain [5].

Typically, a brain-implanted antenna is located under the skull, immersed horizontally in the dura or cerebrospinal fluid (CSF), as shown in Figure 1a. This circumstance lowers the antenna gain because the skull is thick (~7 mm at the bregma) and lossy (loss tangent, tanδ, ~0.3) [14,15]. A full-wave electromagnetic simulation study indicated a reduction of at least 2 dB in antenna gain because of the thick skull. Deformation of the antenna radiation pattern is another issue. A broadside antenna horizontally placed under the skull is expected to radiate toward the zenith. However, unexpected large back lobes and side lobes are often seen after implanting an antenna in such a complex brain environment [16], i.e., the broadside radiation is not guaranteed because of the impact of the thick skull layer, high permittivity brain tissues, and small antenna ground plane.

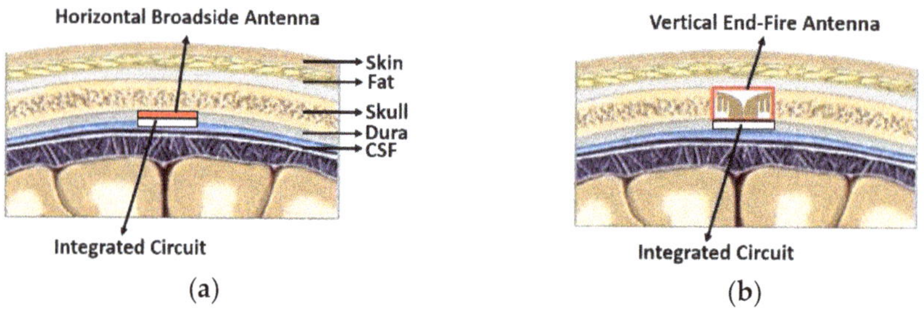

Figure 1. Conceptual illustrations of the brain-implanted antenna placement: (**a**) conventional horizontal placement and (**b**) proposed vertical placement.

This paper presents an end-fire radiating antenna implanted vertically in the skull. Figure 1b shows the conceptual illustration of the vertical placement. The antenna was placed along the thickness of the skull and then connected upright to the integrated circuit (IC). Hence, the antenna had more design freedom as long as the height conformed to the thickness of the skull. More importantly, the antenna gain can be significantly improved throughout the bandwidth of interest. The proposed antenna was designed for 3–5 GHz impulse radio ultra-wideband (IR-UWB), which could transfer the data at a high rate with a low power consumption because of its wider operation bandwidth [17,18]. A tapered slot antenna, the so-called Vivaldi antenna, was employed to cater to this wide bandwidth. The Vivaldi antenna is a well-known end-fire radiating antenna that provides broadband impedance matching and radiation performance owing to its gradual tapered structure [19]. However, we found that an abrupt tapering profile was required because the end-fire length was limited to the skull thickness. This abrupt profile limited the end-fire gain and bandwidth. Therefore, a slot array was implemented in the proposed design to resolve the issue. The slot array improved the gain and reduced the antenna resonant frequency, implying the size miniaturization. As a result, the antenna gain is enhanced approximately 2 dB and 3 dB by introducing the new Vivaldi antenna and by implanting the antenna vertically in the skull.

The rest of the paper is organized as follows. Section 2 describes the antenna design. Furthermore, it provides details of the brain environment and slot array structure. Section 3 presents the antenna prototype fabrication process and measurement results. Section 4 discusses the specific absorption rate (SAR) simulation and measurement results along with the link budget analysis to estimate the performance of the communication system equipped with the proposed antenna. Section 5 concludes the paper.

2. Antenna Design

Figure 2 provides an overview of the proposed skull-embedded Vivaldi antenna. It was vertically installed against the dura matter below the skull. The antenna was sandwiched inside a Taconic RF-35, a biocompatible insulator with relative permittivity (ε_r) and loss tangent (tanδ) of 3.5 and 0.002, respectively. Its low tanδ value at the antenna design frequency (i.e., 3–5 GHz) is beneficial for improving the antenna gain [11]. In addition, the RF-35 is mechanically durable (tensile strength of 27,000 psi and dimensional stability of 0.00004 mm/mm) and has a low moisture absorption of 0.02%. The height of the insulator was fixed to 7 mm, corresponding to a typical height of an adult human skull. The thickness and width of the insulator were 0.5 mm and 12 mm, respectively (see Figure 2). The width of 12 mm matched half of the guided wavelength (λ_g) at the center frequency (4 GHz). The geometry of the insulated Vivaldi antenna was optimized using full-wave electromagnetic simulation software (Ansys HFSS). The goal was to achieve a good impedance matching condition (reflection coefficient, $S_{11} < -10$ dB) and high end-fire gain (>−15 dB) over a wide bandwidth (3–5 GHz) even in the lossy brain environment. It consisted of seven different layers of brain tissues; their material properties and thicknesses assigned in the simulation model are listed in Table 1 [20]. The material properties of each layer are presented in the center frequency 4 GHz of the target bandwidth (3–5 GHz).

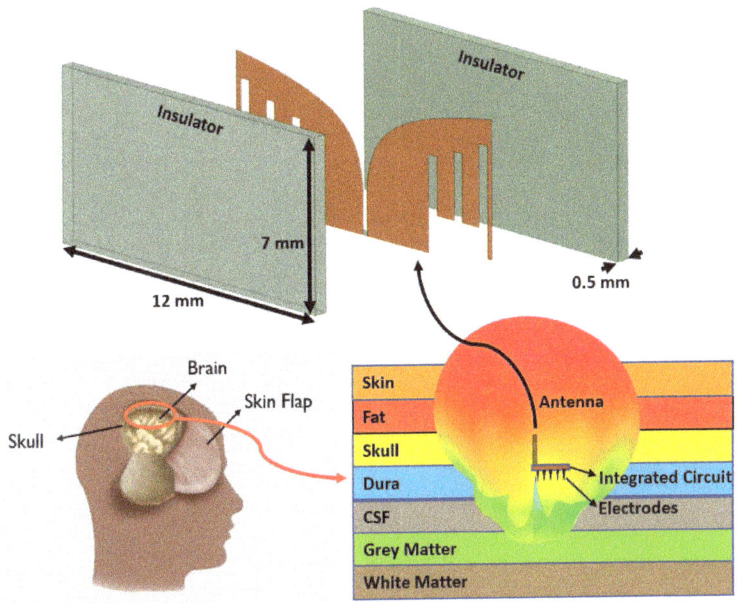

Figure 2. The proposed Vivaldi antenna surrounded by insulators and embedded in the skull.

Table 1. Material properties of brain tissues at 4 GHz.

Layer	Relative Permittivity (ε_r)	Loss Tangent (tanδ)	Thickness (mm)
Skin	40.84	0.297	1
Fat	5.12	0.160	2
Skull	10.53	0.310	7
Dura	40.10	0.308	1.5
CSF	63.73	0.366	2

The geometry of the Vivaldi antenna is depicted in Figure 3. The tapered slot at the middle gradually opened up to support a smooth impedance transition and to generate end-fire radiations over a broad bandwidth. Simulation results showed that an ordinary Vivaldi antenna modeled in the given area of 7×12 mm^2 resonated around 6 GHz, which is higher than the desirable 4 GHz (i.e., the center frequency of 3–5 GHz). Therefore, an antenna miniaturization technique was required to reduce the antenna footprint. One way to miniaturize a Vivaldi antenna is to add horizontal slots along the side edges [21–23]. The horizontal slots act as a choke to lessen undesirable currents flowing at the side edges, which can improve the impedance-matching condition. However, this method accompanies the decrease of end-fire gain. The substrate size along the longitudinal direction was extended [24] and driving elements between the tapered slots were added to recover the end-fire gain [22].

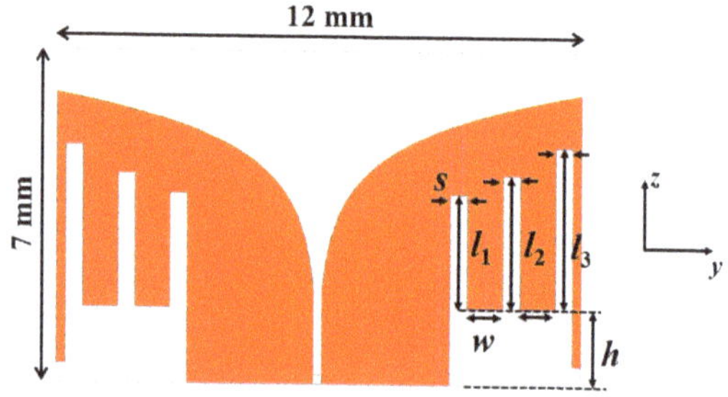

Figure 3. Geometry of the proposed Vivaldi antenna with vertical slots.

Instead of horizontal slots, the proposed Vivaldi implemented comb-shaped vertical slots to miniaturize the Vivaldi antenna. We found that the method effectively improved the end-fire gain by concentrating more currents along the tapered slot in the middle. Figure 4 shows the surface current densities at 3, 4, and 5 GHz for the conventional Vivaldi without slots and proposed Vivaldi with slots. The conventional design exhibited excessive currents at the bottom edge where the antenna feed was located. Stronger currents were observed at the lower frequency of 3 GHz, which has a longer wavelength. However, the proposed design gradually distributed these currents to the center tapered slot and three vertical slots, making the electrical length longer (miniaturization) and main radiating source stronger (improved gain). The similarity in current distributions at 3, 4, and 5 GHz imply that a stable radiation characteristic can be maintained over a broad bandwidth.

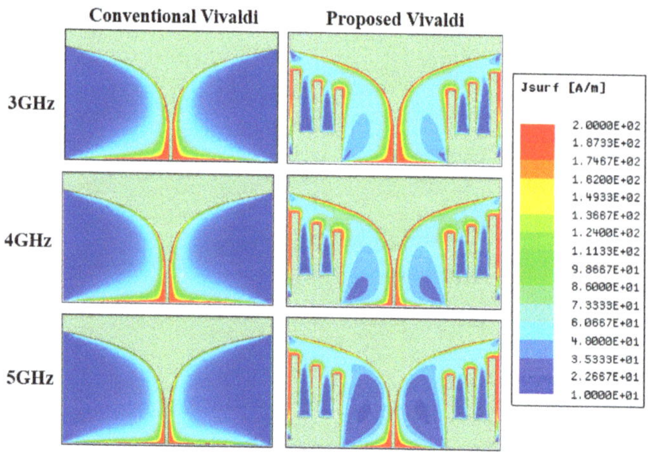

Figure 4. Comparisons of surface current densities of conventional and proposed Vivaldi antennas.

Figure 5a,b show the simulation results of S_{11} and realized gain while embedding the antenna in the seven-layer brain phantom. We compared S_{11} and the realized gain of the proposed Vivaldi antenna to that of the conventional Vivaldi antenna. The resonant frequency was shifted down from 6 GHz to 4 GHz by introducing the vertical slots. Moreover, the realized gain plot showed an improvement of 1–3 dB at the target frequency range,

3–5 GHz; an average of −13 dBi realized gain can be achieved. It is worth noting that the realized gain of a conventional Vivaldi is low, about 6 GHz, despite the S_{11} being low, implying its antenna impedance matching and radiation performances have a discrepancy. In contrast, the proposed Vivaldi's resonant frequency and the frequency exhibiting high realized gain are matched. Altogether, the vertical installation of the end-fire antenna and optimization of its geometry improved the realized gain by approximately 3 dB and 2 dB (total of 5 dB) relative to horizontally installed broadside antennas, respectively.

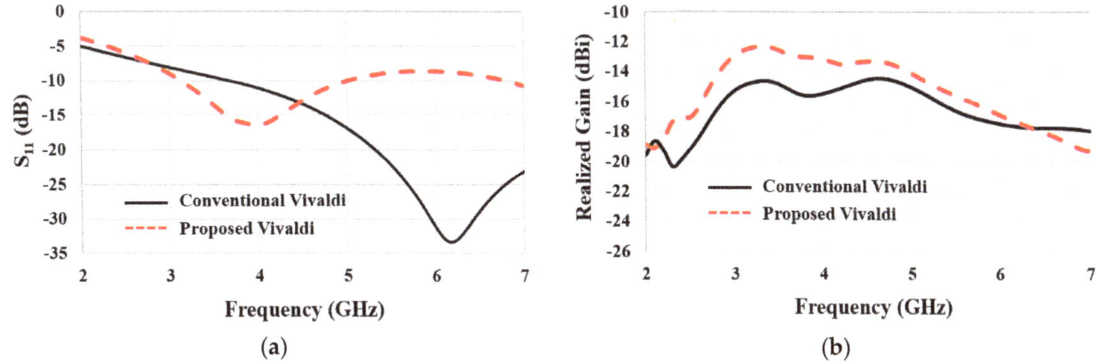

Figure 5. Comparisons of (**a**) S_{11} and (**b**) realized gain of conventional and proposed Vivaldi antennas.

Figure 6 shows parametric studies of S_{11} by altering the slot's geometry. The width of slot (s) can be used to tune the antenna's resonant frequency (see Figure 6a). Here, s between each slot is set to be the same to make the optimization process concise. The wider s shifted the resonant frequency toward the lower end, resulting in antenna miniaturization by introducing more slot inductance than capacitance. Slot length (l_1) was another parameter for adjusting the resonant frequency (see Figure 6b). The longer l_1 provided more inductance without altering the capacitance. Therefore, the resonant frequency shifted left with increasing l_1. We note that l_1 is the length of the first slot. The second and third slots were longer. Their lengths were determined by the Vivaldi's exponential curvature profile at the middle. In particular, l_1 = 2.4 mm, l_2 = 2.8 mm, and l_3 = 3.4 mm. Table 2 lists the final antenna's geometrical parameters. These values were obtained for the target frequency range, 3–5 GHz, with the given antenna space, 12 mm × 7 mm; however, the s and l parametric optimizations can be applied for any frequency band and antenna size.

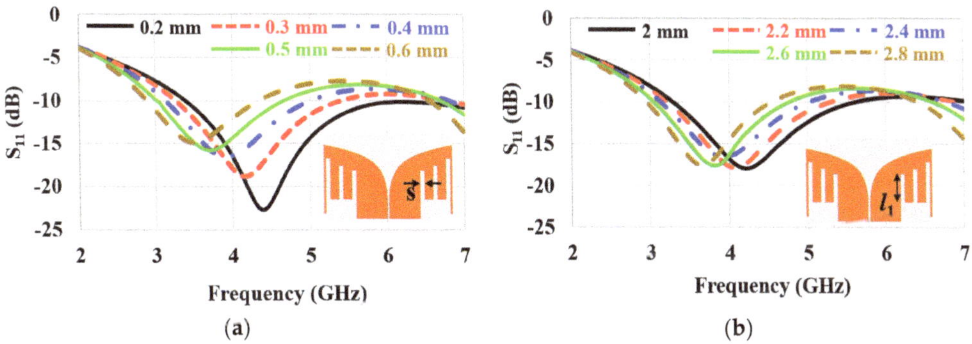

Figure 6. Parametric studies of S_{11} by varying (**a**) slot width s and (**b**) slot length l_1.

Table 2. Optimized antenna parameters.

Parameter	Length (mm)
s	0.4
w	0.8
h	1.6
l_1	2.4
l_2	2.8
l_3	3.4

3. Antenna Prototype Fabrication and Measurement

Having obtained promising broadband and high gain simulation results, an antenna prototype was fabricated and then tested for experimental validation. The measured antenna parameters were S_{11}, radiation patterns, and realized gain. They were measured by inserting the antenna prototype into an in-house fabricated seven-layer brain phantom.

3.1. Fabrication of Brain-Tissue-Emulating Phantom

The radiation performance of an implantable antenna is highly affected by its surrounding environment. Hence, it is important to test the antenna inside a human tissue-mimicking phantom exhibiting similar electromagnetic material properties (i.e., ε_r and tanδ) of the actual environment—the brain for this study. A liquid phantom is often used to test implantable antennas [25,26]. However, such a homogeneous phantom is insufficient to represent the complex brain environment consisting of multiple layers with different material properties. We fabricated seven different semi-solid tissue-emulating layers following recipes provided in [12]. Figure 7 shows the fabricated seven layers and their stack-up. The material properties of each layer were measured by an open-ended coaxial probe [27] and compared to the known values listed in Table 1 for validation. The size of the stack-up was 10 cm × 10 cm × 7.2 cm.

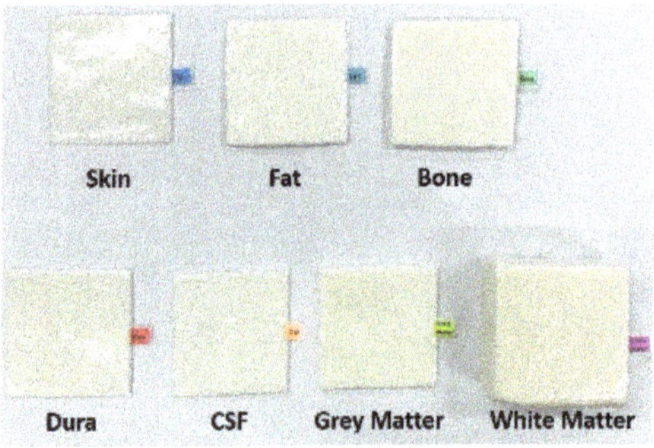

(a)

(b)

Figure 7. Fabricated brain-tissue-emulating materials: (**a**) pictures of each layer and (**b**) stack-up.

3.2. Fabrication of Antenna Prototype

Figure 8 shows the fabricated antenna prototype. The optimized Vivaldi geometry, including the vertical slot array, was implemented on a 0.5 mm thick Taconic RF-35 substrate. A conventional printed circuit board (PCB) fabrication process was used to etch the antenna footprint on the substrate. Figure 8a shows the fabricated antenna itself, while Figure 8b shows a combination of the antenna and coaxial cable. As can be seen, the antenna was directly fed by a coaxial cable instead of a bulky RF connector (e.g., SMA connector). The outer conductor of the cable was directly soldered to one Vivaldi arm to feed the balanced Vivaldi antenna with the unbalanced coaxial cable; the inner conductor was routed through a hole punctured at the substrate and then soldered to the other arm. After that, the antenna was covered by another piece of 0.5 mm Taconic RF-35 as an insulator (i.e., superstrate) as depicted in Figure 8c.

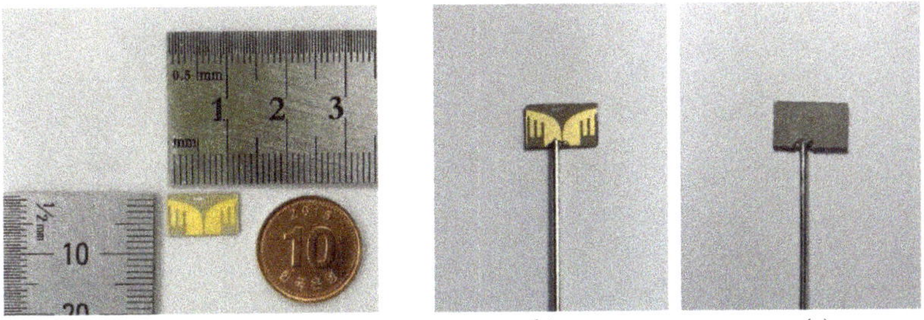

(a) (b) (c)

Figure 8. Fabricated antenna prototype: (**a**) antenna printed on a substrate, (**b**) antenna connected to a coaxial cable, and (**c**) antenna covered by a superstrate.

3.3. Measurement of S_{11}

The fabricated antenna was placed into the seven-layer phantom for measurements. More specifically, the antenna was vertically inserted in the skull layer; hence, the top and bottom of the antenna were touching the fat and dura layer, respectively (see Figure 2). Figure 9 shows the test setup for S_{11} measurement. The phantom (with the antenna inside) was placed on a mount made with low permittivity and low loss Rohacell® foam. The coaxial cable sticking out from the phantom was connected to a vector network analyzer (Anritsu MS2038C). Figure 10 compares the measured and simulated S_{11} of the proposed and conventional Vivaldi antennas. The latter is an ordinary Vivaldi that does not have the vertical slot array, as depicted in the inset of Figure 10. The red and black lines correspond to S_{11} responses of the proposed and conventional Vivaldi, respectively. The measured S_{11} data indicated that the resonant frequency of the proposed Vivaldi was 2 GHz lower than the conventional Vivaldi (4.3 GHz versus 6.3 GHz), which confirms the antenna miniaturization effect caused by the vertical slot array. The simulation results of S_{11} are drawn with solid lines. They agree well with the measurements. The measured resonant frequencies were higher than those from simulations by approximately 300 MHz and 150 MHz for the proposed and conventional antennas, respectively, possibly because of slight discrepancies in the phantom's material properties. We note that the phantom's ε_r and tanδ are highly affected by the amount of water evaporation with time. It is hard to avoid the water evaporation in spite of precautions when handling the semi-solid phantoms. Solutions to prevent this difficulty can include wrapping each tissue phantom with a thin layer of low permittivity material or using 3D-printed biomaterials with a low moisture content.

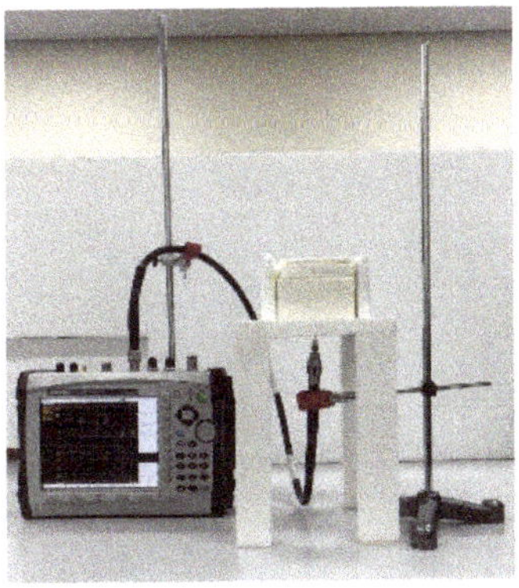

Figure 9. Test setup for S_{11} measurement.

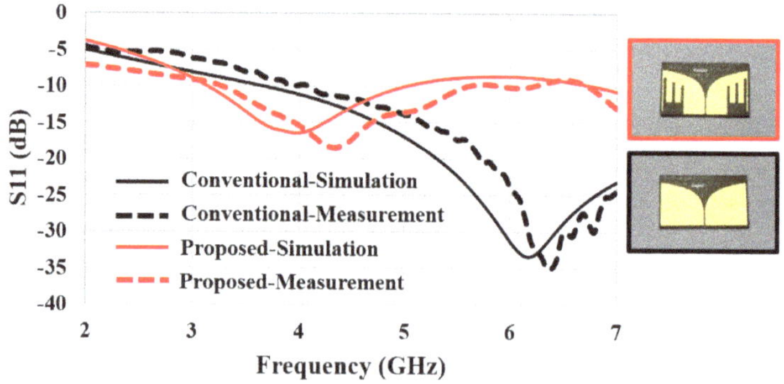

Figure 10. Comparisons of measured and simulated S_{11} of conventional and proposed Vivaldi antennas.

3.4. Measurement of Radiation Pattern

The far-field radiation patterns of the proposed antenna were measured in an accredited antenna chamber [28]. Figure 11 shows the seven-layer phantom (with the antenna inside) mounted on a positioner. The latter was capable of 3D rotation (180° in elevation and 360° in azimuth). The z-direction shown in the figure corresponds to the end-fire direction where the aperture of the antenna points is. Figure 12a shows the measured 3D radiation pattern at the center frequency, 4 GHz. It shows that most radiation is pointed toward the zenith (z-direction) with a high front-to-back ratio (FBR) of 16 dB. Furthermore, Figure 12b,c present the measured 2D E-plane and H-plane patterns. They were normalized by the peak gain value and then compared with the simulated radiation patterns. Good agreements can be observed, implying the prototype fabrication and measurement procedures were valid. Figure 13 shows the measured realized gain in the z-direction at the frequency range of 2 to 6 GHz. We compared the measured realized gain of the conventional Vivaldi (see Figure 10 b) with that of the proposed Vivaldi (see Figure 10). The measured realized gain data was not steady in the bandwidth of interest, and it was approximately 2 dB lower than the simulation data (see Figure 5b); however, the gain improvement of the proposed design compared to the conventional Vivaldi was clearly observed. A gain improvement is observed because of the added vertical slots, which redirect more currents along the tapered slot as described in the simulation study, Figure 4. The average improvement was 2.68 dB throughout 3–5 GHz, which is similar to the improvement demonstrated in Figure 5b. Table 3 compares previously reported brain-implanted antennas and the proposed Vivaldi in terms of their operation frequency, size, and gain. It also includes the conventional Vivaldi's gain to highlight the gain improvement of the proposed Vivaldi.

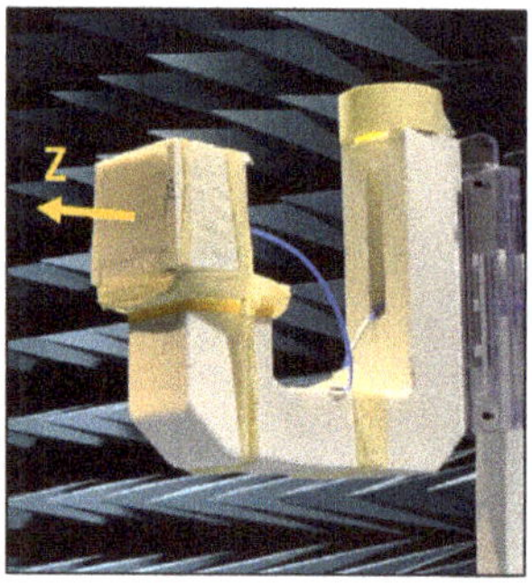

Figure 11. The seven-layer phantom containing the antenna prototype is mounted on the positioner inside the anechoic chamber.

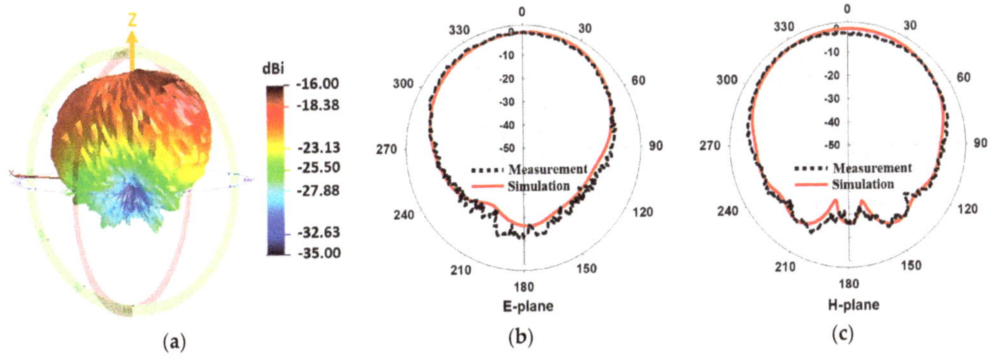

Figure 12. Radiation patterns of the antenna prototype inside the phantom at 4 GHz: (**a**) measured 3D radiation pattern, (**b**) measured and simulated 2D E-plane radiation pattern (normalized by the peak), and (**c**) H-plane radiation pattern (normalized by the peak).

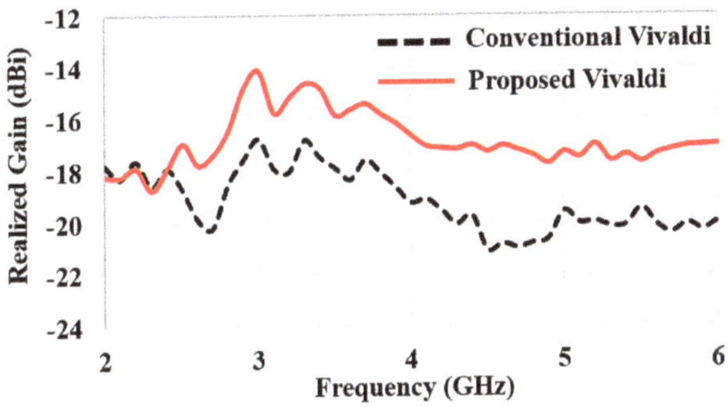

Figure 13. A comparison of measured realized gain of the conventional and proposed Vivaldi antennas.

Table 3. Comparison of brain-implanted antennas.

Antenna	Frequency (GHz)	Size (mm^3)	Gain (dBi)
[11]	2.40–2.48	39.9	−20.75
[12]	2.42–2.50	50	−25
[14]	2.40–2.48	101.6	−17.3
Conventional Vivaldi	3–5	42	−18.3
Proposed Vivaldi	3–5	42	−15.7

4. Specific Absorption Rate and Link Budget Analysis

4.1. Specific Absorption Rate

It is required to examine the specific absorption rate (SAR)—the amount of non-ionizing radiated power absorbed by the surrounding biological tissues—for an implantable wireless device. SAR standards differ by countries or regulatory agencies; however, two SAR standards are mainly considered: IEEE C95.1-1999 [29] and IEEE C95.1-2005 [30]. The maximum allowable SAR values are 1.6 W/kg averaged over 1 g of tissue and 2 W/kg over 10 g of tissue for IEEE C95.1-1999 and IEEE C95.1-2005, respectively.

SAR values were computed and analyzed using the same simulation setup as the antenna performance analysis (see Section 2). Figure 14a,b show the simulated SAR-1g and SAR-10g for various frequencies after supplying an input power of 1 W to the antenna embedded in the bone layer. The SAR-1g in Figure 14a continuously increased with increasing frequency, while the SAR-10g in Figure 14b shows a peak and null at 3.6 GHz and 5.1 GHz, respectively. The SAR values were very high because of the high input power of 1 W, e.g., 240 W/kg and 59.4 W/kg at 4 GHz for SAR-1g and SAR-10g, respectively.

However, the actual SAR is expected to have a much lower value because the power consumed by the RF-front-end of implantable devices generally lies within 100 μW to a few mW [31]. Hence, we calculated the maximum allowable input power to the antenna that satisfied the SAR-1g (1.6 W/kg) and SAR-10g (2 W/kg) criteria. They are marked by the red dashed lines. The SAR-1g criterion can be fulfilled as long as the input power is less than 5.9 mW for the frequency range of 3–5 GHz as in Figure 14a. The maximum allowable input power for the SAR-10g was 33.6 mW as in Figure 14b, which is less stringent than SAR-1g.

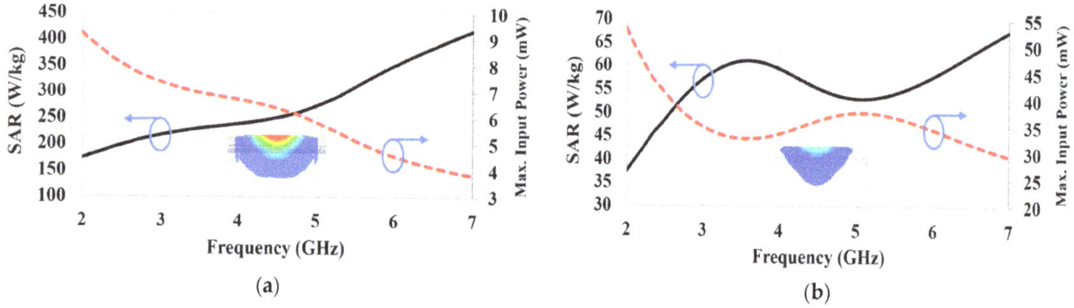

Figure 14. The simulated SAR and maximum allowable input power of the proposed antenna inside the seven-layer phantom: (**a**) SAR-1g and (**b**) SAR-10g. The insets show simulated SAR value distributions around the antenna.

We measured SAR using a SAR robot in an accredited test facility [32]. Figure 15a shows the SAR robot and probe and Figure 15b shows the actual test set-up with the phantom and signal generator as the source. Figure 15c provides a zoomed-in view of the phantom placements. The seven-layer phantom with the antenna inside was attached at the bottom of a SAR flat phantom. A SAR probe was scanned by the robot arm at the opposite side of the empty flat phantom, and the E-field magnitudes radiated from the antenna were collected. The antenna was fed by a coaxial cable connected to a signal generator. The SAR values at a wireless local area network (WLAN) of 2.45 GHz and 5.8 GHz were measured because of the lack of SAR measurement procedure for 3–5 GHz IR-UWB. The output power from the signal generator was set to 1 mW. Figure 16 shows the measured SAR distribution. The total scan area was 150 × 150 mm^2. The zoomed scan volume after identifying the hot spot was 40 × 40 × 35 mm^3. The hot spot locations for 2.45 GHz and 5.8 GHz were comparable. The higher frequency (5.8 GHz) showed a higher averaged SAR-1g value of 0.42 W/kg than that of the lower frequency (2.45 GHz) (i.e., 0.11 W/kg). Both of them were much lower than the 1.6 W/kg limit. These measurement trials provide a reasonable postulation that SAR is not a problematic issue despite that the measured frequencies were not exactly matched to the target frequencies.

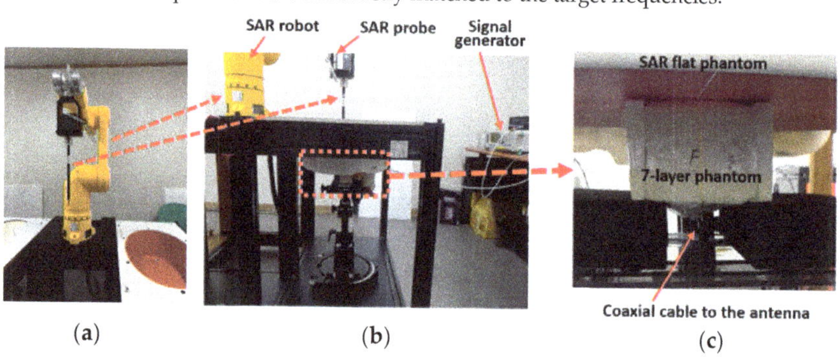

Figure 15. SAR measurement setup with DASY 5 SAR robot: (**a**) SAR robot with the probe, (**b**) whole measurement setup, and (**c**) antenna placement.

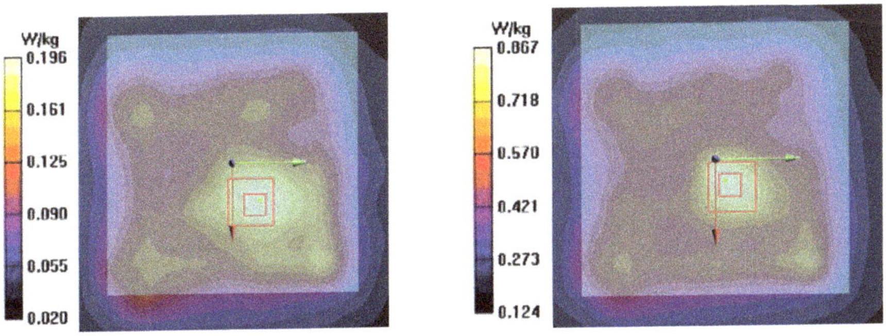

(a) (b)

Figure 16. Measured SAR distribution: (**a**) 2.45 GHz and (**b**) 5.8 GHz. Red boxes indicate the hot spot.

4.2. Link Budget Analysis

A link budget analysis [33,34] was conducted to estimate the approximate performance of an implantable wireless communication system equipped with the proposed Vivaldi antenna. We assumed a point-to-point wireless communication system whose transmitting antenna was the proposed Vivaldi implanted in the brain and the receiving antenna was a broadband testing antenna [35] situated outside of the head. Table 4 summarizes the parameters for the link budget analysis. The link margin (LM) is a power margin at the receiver, allowing a satisfying wireless communication quality. More specifically:

$$LM(dB) = P_{\mathrm{r}} - P_{\mathrm{r}(min)} \tag{1}$$

where P_{r} corresponds to the received power and $P_{\mathrm{r}(min)}$ denotes the minimum required power for the receiver. LM typically spans from 3 to 20 dB. We set it to 20 dB, the most demanding requirement, to reflect the harsh wireless communication environment. The assigned transmit power (P_{t}) was −25 dBm, which is a typical output power of a transmitter for implantable devices [31]. The realized gain of the transmitting (Tx) antenna (i.e., implanted antenna) was given by −16.67 dB based on the measurement in the data presented in Section 3. Furthermore, the receiving (Rx) antenna's realized gain was set to 6.65 dB, which corresponds to the antenna gain at 4 GHz of a broadband tapered slot antenna [35]. The required signal-to-noise ratio (SNR) per bit, or the energy per bit to noise power spectral density ratio (E_{b}/N_0), was set to 9.6 dB by assuming an ideal phase-shift keying (PSK) performance. The bit rate was set to 256 Mbps, which is reasonably high for brain-signal monitoring [34]. Finally, the path loss (L_0) was calculated for the free-space attenuation. In the equation, $\lambda_{4\mathrm{GHz}}$ denotes the free-space wavelength of 4 GHz (i.e., 75 mm) and D denotes the distance between the Tx and Rx. In fact, D is the parameter of interest for this link budget analysis. According to the Friis transmission formula [33]:

$$P_{\mathrm{r}}(dB) = P_{\mathrm{t}} + RG_{\mathrm{t}} + RG_{\mathrm{r}} - L_0 \tag{2}$$

$$P_{\mathrm{r}(min)}(dB) = \frac{E_{\mathrm{b}}}{N_0} + KT_0 + B \tag{3}$$

Plugging (2) and (3) into (1) and then applying the parameters from Table 4 provided D = 108.1 mm, i.e., the transmitted brain signal can be reliably received with LM of 20 dB at the receiver located at 108.1 mm above the head. We note that this distance was reduced to 80.4 mm if the conventional Vivaldi with a realized gain of −19.24 dB was used instead of using the proposed Vivaldi.

Table 4. Parameters for link budget analysis.

Parameters	Values at 4 GHz
Link margin (LM)	20 dB
Transmit power (P_t)	−25 dBm
Tx Ant. realized gain (RG_t)	−16.67 dB
Rx Ant. realized gain (RG_r)	6.65 dB
SNR per bit (E_b/N_0)	9.6 dB
Boltzmann's constant (K)	1.38×10^{-23}
Temperature (T_0)	298 K
Bit rate (B)	256 Mbps
Path Loss (L_0)	$20 \log\left(\frac{4\pi D}{\lambda_{4GHz}}\right)$ dB

5. Conclusions

The full-wave electromagnetic simulations showed that the end-fire antenna vertically embedded in the skull exhibited two times (3 dB) higher antenna gain than an ordinary case—a broadside antenna horizontally embedded below the skull. The proposed end-fire Vivaldi antenna was measured to have a small footprint of 12×7 mm^2 because of the novel comb-shaped slot arrays behind the main aperture. These slot arrays not only promote the antenna miniaturization but also enhance the gain and bandwidth. The geometry of the antenna was carefully optimized by full-wave simulations to operate in the 3–5 GHz IR-UWB frequency range. An antenna prototype was fabricated and a series of measurements were performed by embedding the antenna in an in-house-made seven-layer brain-tissue-emulating phantom to verify the antenna performance. The measurement results of the proposed Vivaldi showed that the resonant frequency was 2 GHz lower, and the gain was 2.6 dB higher than the conventional Vivaldi without slot arrays. Furthermore, the proposed Vivaldi can be a promising candidate for brain-to-outside wireless communication based on the link budget and SAR analyses. Based on our findings, it could be worthwhile for surgeons and medical professionals to identify pathways for implanting antennas in the skull during a brain surgery (e.g., craniotomy).

Author Contributions: Conceptualization, J.-Y.C.; methodology, L.S., S.H. and J.-Y.C.; validation, L.S. and S.H.; formal analysis, L.S. and J.-Y.C.; investigation, L.S. and J.-Y.C.; resources, S.H. and J.-Y.C.; data curation, L.S. and S.H.; writing—original draft preparation, L.S. and S.H.; writing—review and editing, J.-Y.C.; visualization, L.S.; supervision, J.-Y.C.; project administration, J.-Y.C.; funding acquisition, J.-Y.C. All authors have read and agreed to the published version of the manuscript.

Funding: This study was supported by the Research Program funded by SeoulTech (Seoul National University of Science and Technology).

Institutional Review Board Statement: Not applicable.

Informed Consent Statement: Not applicable.

Data Availability Statement: The data presented in this study are available on request from the corresponding authors.

Conflicts of Interest: The authors declare no conflict of interest.

References

1. Becedas, J. Brain–Machine Interfaces: Basis and Advances. *IEEE Trans. Syst. Man Cybern. Part C (Appl. Rev.)* **2012**, *42*, 825–836. [CrossRef]
2. Mudgal, S.; Sharma, S.; Chaturvedi, J.; Sharma, A. Brain computer interface advancement in neurosciences: Applications and issues. *Interdiscip. Neurosurg.* **2020**, *20*, 100694. [CrossRef]
3. Butt, A.; Alsaffar, H.; Alshareef, M.; Qureshi, K. AI Prediction of Brain Signals for Human Gait Using BCI Device and FBG Based Sensorial Platform for Plantar Pressure Measurements. *Sensors* **2022**, *22*, 3085. [CrossRef]
4. Schalk, G.; Leuthardt, E.C. Brain-Computer Interfaces Using Electrocorticographic Signals. *IEEE Rev. Biomed. Eng.* **2011**, *4*, 140–154. [CrossRef]

5. Ma, S.; Björninen, T.; Sydänheimo, L.; Voutilainen, M.H.; Ukkonen, L. Double Split Rings as Extremely Small and Tuneable Antennas for Brain Implantable Wireless Medical Microsystems. *IEEE Trans. Antennas Propag.* **2021**, *69*, 760–768. [CrossRef]
6. Chen, W.-C.; Lee, C.W.L.; Kiourti, A.; Volakis, J.L. A Multi-Channel Passive Brain Implant for Wireless Neuropotential Monitoring. *IEEE J. Electromagn. RF Microw. Med. Biol.* **2018**, *2*, 262–269. [CrossRef]
7. Lee, C.W.L.; Kiourti, A.; Chae, J.; Volakis, J.L. A High-Sensitivity Fully Passive Neurosensing System for Wireless Brain Signal Monitoring. *IEEE Trans. Microw. Theory Tech.* **2015**, *63*, 2060–2068. [CrossRef]
8. Song, L.; Rahmat-Samii, Y. An End-to-End Implanted Brain–Machine Interface Antenna System Performance Characterizations and Development. *IEEE Trans. Antennas Propag.* **2017**, *65*, 3399–3408. [CrossRef]
9. Blauert, J.; Kang, Y.-S.; Kiourti, A. In Vivo Testing of a Miniature 2.4/4.8 GHz Implantable Antenna in Postmortem Human Subject. *IEEE Antennas Wirel. Propag. Lett.* **2018**, *17*, 2334–2338. [CrossRef]
10. Neuralink approach interfacing with the brain, Neuralink. 2021. Available online: https://neuralink.com (accessed on 1 January 2022).
11. Hout, S.; Chung, J.-Y. Design and Characterization of a Miniaturized Implantable Antenna in a Seven-Layer Brain Phantom. *IEEE Access* **2019**, *7*, 162062–162069. [CrossRef]
12. Biswarup, R.; Shim, J.-Y.; Chung, J.-Y. An Implantable Antenna With Broadside Radiation for a Brain–Machine Interface. *IEEE Sens. J.* **2019**, *19*, 9200–9205.
13. Lee, C.W.L.; Kiourti, A.; Volakis, J.L. Miniaturized Fully Passive Brain Implant for Wireless Neuropotential Acquisition. *IEEE Antennas Wirel. Propag. Lett.* **2016**, *16*, 645–648. [CrossRef]
14. Yang, Z.-J.; Zhu, L.; Xiao, S. An Implantable Wideband Microstrip Patch Antenna Based on High-Loss Property of Human Tissue. *IEEE Access* **2020**, *8*, 93048–930572020. [CrossRef]
15. Liapatis, O.; Nikita, K.S. Development of a biocompatible patch antenna for retinal prosthesis: Comparison of biocompatible coatings. In Proceedings of the IEEE 20th International Conference on Bioinformatics and Bioengineering (BIBE), Cincinnati, OH, USA, 26–28 October 2020; pp. 819–825.
16. Bahrami, H.; Mirbozorgi, S.A.; Nguyen, A.T.; Gosselin, B.; Rusch, L.A. System-Level Design of a Full-Duplex Wireless Transceiver for Brain–Machine Interfaces. *IEEE Trans. Microw. Theory Tech.* **2016**, *64*, 3332–3341. [CrossRef]
17. Lim, H.; Lee, D.-H.; Kim, J.; Hong, S. Spectroscopic Sensing Method of Liquid Permittivity with On-Chip Capacitor. *J. Electromagn. Eng. Sci.* **2022**, *22*, 28–33. [CrossRef]
18. Mahmood, H.U.; Utomo, D.R.; Kim, J.; Lee, S.-G. A 27 dB Sidelobe Suppression, 1.12 GHz BW−10dB UWB Pulse Generator With Process Compensation. *IEEE Trans. Circuits Syst. II Express Briefs* **2021**, *68*, 2805–2809. [CrossRef]
19. Schaubert, D.; Kollberg, E.; Korzeniowski, T.; Thungren, T.; Johansson, J.; Yngvesson, K. Endfire tapered slot antennas on dielectric substrates. *IEEE Trans. Antennas Propag.* **1985**, *33*, 1392–1400. [CrossRef]
20. Gabriel, S.; Lau, R.; Gabriel, C. The dielectric properties of biological tissues: II. Measurements in the frequency range 10 Hz to 20 GHz. *Phys. Med. Biol.* **1996**, *41*, 2251–2269. [CrossRef]
21. Fei, P.; Jiao, Y.-C.; Hu, W.; Zhang, F.-S. A Miniaturized Antipodal Vivaldi Antenna With Improved Radiation Characteristics. *IEEE Antennas Wirel. Propag. Lett.* **2011**, *10*, 127–130.
22. Teni, G.; Zhang, N.; Qiu, J.; Zhang, P. Research on a Novel Miniaturized Antipodal Vivaldi Antenna With Improved Radiation. *IEEE Antennas Wirel. Propag. Lett.* **2013**, *12*, 417–420. [CrossRef]
23. Kim, J. Configuration of a Monopulse Antenna Assembly for Small Diameter Flight Vehicle Applications. *J. Electromagn. Eng. Sci.* **2021**, *21*, 246–248. [CrossRef]
24. Nassar, I.T.; Weller, T.M. A Novel Method for Improving Antipodal Vivaldi Antenna Performance. *IEEE Trans. Antennas Propag.* **2015**, *63*, 3321–3324. [CrossRef]
25. YEl-Saboni; Magil, M.K.; Conway, G.A.; Cotton, S.L.; Scanlon, W.G. Measurement of Deep Tissue Implanted Antenna Efficiency Using a Reverberation Chamber. *IEEE J. Electromagn. RF Microw. Med. Biol.* **2017**, *1*, 90–97. [CrossRef]
26. Felício, J.M.; Fernandes, C.A.; Costa, J.R. Wideband Implantable Antenna for Body-Area High Data Rate Impulse Radio Communication. *IEEE Trans. Antennas Propag.* **2016**, *64*, 1932–1940. [CrossRef]
27. Shim, J.-Y.; Chung, J.-Y. Complex Permittivity Measurement of Artificial Tissue Emulating Material Using Open-Ended Coaxial Probe. *IEEE Sens. J.* **2020**, *20*, 4688–4693. [CrossRef]
28. Electromagnetic Wave Technology Institute. Available online: https://emti.or.kr (accessed on 1 January 2022).
29. *IEEE Std C95.1, 1999 Edition*; IEEE Standard for Safety Levels with Respect to Human Exposure to Radio Frequency Electromagnetic Fields, 3 kHz to 300 GHz. IEEE: New York, NY, USA, 1999; pp. 1–83.
30. *IEEE Std C95.1-2005*; IEEE Standard for Safety Levels with Respect to Human Exposure to Radio Frequency Electromagnetic Fields, 3 kHz to 300 GHz. Revision of IEEE Std C95.1-1991; IEEE: New York, NY, USA, 2006; pp. 1–238.
31. Duan, Z.; Guo, Y.-X.; Je, M.; Kwong, D.-L. Design and in Vitro Test of a Differentially Fed Dual-Band Implantable Antenna Operating at MICS and ISM Bands. *IEEE Trans. Antennas Propag.* **2014**, *62*, 2430–2439. [CrossRef]
32. KES Co., Ltd. Available online: http://www.kes.co.kr/ (accessed on 1 January 2022).
33. Pozar, D.M. Introduction to Microwave Systems. In *Microwave Engineering, 4th Ed*; John Wiley & Sons: Hoboken, NJ, USA, 2011; Chapter 4; pp. 671–676.

34. Bahrami, H.; Mirbozorgi, S.A.; Rusch, L.A.; Gosselin, B. Biological Channel Modeling and Implantable UWB Antenna Design for Neural Recording Systems. *IEEE Trans. Biomed. Eng.* **2015**, *62*, 88–98. [CrossRef]
35. Jeon, G.-H.; Dzagbletey, P.A.; Chung, Y.J. A Cross-Joint Vivaldi Antenna Pair for Dual-Pol and Broadband Testing Capabilities. *J. Electromagn. Eng. Sci.* **2021**, *21*, 201–209. [CrossRef]

sensors

MDPI

Review

Digital Pulmonology Practice with Phonopulmography Leveraging Artificial Intelligence: Future Perspectives Using Dual Microwave Acoustic Sensing and Imaging

Arshia K. Sethi [1], Pratyusha Muddaloor [1], Priyanka Anvekar [2], Joshika Agarwal [3], Anmol Mohan [1], Mansunderbir Singh [4], Keerthy Gopalakrishnan [1,5], Ashima Yadav [6], Aakriti Adhikari [1], Devanshi Damani [6,7], Kanchan Kulkarni [8,9], Christopher A. Aakre [2], Alexander J. Ryu [2], Vivek N. Iyer [3] and Shivaram P. Arunachalam [1,2,4,5,*]

1 GIH Artificial Intelligence Laboratory (GAIL), Division of Gastroenterology and Hepatology, Department of Medicine, Mayo Clinic, Rochester, MN 55905, USA; sethi.arshia@mayo.edu (A.K.S.); anmolmohanvan@gmail.com (A.M.); gopalakrishnan.keerthy@mayo.edu (K.G.); aakritiadhikari11@gmail.com (A.A.)
2 Department of Medicine, Mayo Clinic, Rochester, MN 55905, USA; aakre.christopher@mayo.edu (C.A.A.); ryu.alexander@mayo.edu (A.J.R.)
3 Division of Pulmonary and Critical Care Medicine, Department of Medicine, Mayo Clinic, Rochester, MN 55905, USA; iyer.vivek@mayo.edu (V.N.I.)
4 Department of Radiology, Mayo Clinic, Rochester, MN 55905, USA
5 Microwave Engineering and Imaging Laboratory (MEIL), Division of Gastroenterology & Hepatology, Department of Medicine, Mayo Clinic, Rochester, MN 55905, USA
6 Department of Cardiovascular Medicine, Mayo Clinic, Rochester, MN 55905, USA; yadav.ashima@mayo.edu (A.Y.); damani.devanshi@mayo.edu (D.D.)
7 Department of Internal Medicine, Texas Tech University Health Science Center, El Paso, TX 79995, USA
8 INSERM, Centre de Recherche Cardio-Thoracique de Bordeaux, University of Bordeaux, U1045, F-33000 Bordeaux, France; kanchan.kulkarni@ihu-liryc.fr
9 IHU Liryc, Heart Rhythm Disease Institute, Fondation Bordeaux Université, F-33600 Pessac, France
* Correspondence: poigaiarunachalam.shivaram@mayo.edu

Citation: Sethi, A.K.; Muddaloor, P.; Anvekar, P.; Agarwal, J.; Mohan, A.; Singh, M.; Gopalakrishnan, K.; Yadav, A.; Adhikari, A.; Damani, D.; et al. Digital Pulmonology Practice with Phonopulmography Leveraging Artificial Intelligence: Future Perspectives Using Dual Microwave Acoustic Sensing and Imaging. *Sensors* **2023**, *23*, 5514. https://doi.org/10.3390/s23125514

Academic Editors: Mikael Persson and Hoi-Shun Antony Lui

Received: 31 March 2023
Revised: 1 June 2023
Accepted: 5 June 2023
Published: 12 June 2023

Abstract: Respiratory disorders, being one of the leading causes of disability worldwide, account for constant evolution in management technologies, resulting in the incorporation of artificial intelligence (AI) in the recording and analysis of lung sounds to aid diagnosis in clinical pulmonology practice. Although lung sound auscultation is a common clinical practice, its use in diagnosis is limited due to its high variability and subjectivity. We review the origin of lung sounds, various auscultation and processing methods over the years and their clinical applications to understand the potential for a lung sound auscultation and analysis device. Respiratory sounds result from the intra-pulmonary collision of molecules contained in the air, leading to turbulent flow and subsequent sound production. These sounds have been recorded via an electronic stethoscope and analyzed using back-propagation neural networks, wavelet transform models, Gaussian mixture models and recently with machine learning and deep learning models with possible use in asthma, COVID-19, asbestosis and interstitial lung disease. The purpose of this review was to summarize lung sound physiology, recording technologies and diagnostics methods using AI for digital pulmonology practice. Future research and development in recording and analyzing respiratory sounds in real time could revolutionize clinical practice for both the patients and the healthcare personnel.

Keywords: respiratory disorders; lung sounds; AI; phonopulmogram; auscultation; electronic stethoscope; machine learning; deep learning

1. Introduction

Respiratory diseases are a major public health concern and a leading cause of mortality globally. According to the World Health Organization, respiratory disorders were among the top 10 global causes of death in 2019 and account for more than 8 million fatalities each year. The burden of these diseases is particularly high in low- and middle-income nations where access to healthcare is limited and air quality is suboptimal [1]. Chronic obstructive pulmonary disease (COPD) is the third-most common cause of death globally, causing 3.2 million deaths annually, while over 250 million individuals worldwide suffer from asthma [2–4]. Infections such as tuberculosis (TB) are also a significant contributor to the disease burden, with more than 10 million new cases and 1.4 million deaths annually [4–6]. Even in affluent nations, lung cancer remains one of the deadliest types of cancer, with a 5-year survival rate of just 10–20% [7]. The epidemiology of respiratory diseases highlights the need for increased efforts to prevent and manage these conditions.

Auscultation is a critical technique that is frequently used in conjunction with clinical and laboratory methods to diagnose respiratory illnesses. Auscultation is the process of using a stethoscope to listen to the chest to hear respiratory sounds and evaluate breathing patterns. This quick and easy technique offers crucial information for diagnosis [8]. In order to detect respiratory disorders, chest imaging and pulmonary function tests (PFTs) are also frequently performed. Chest X-rays (CXRs) or computed tomography (CT) visualize the chest, and PFTs assess lung capacity and function [9–11]. Bronchoscopy and biopsy entail inserting a scope into the airways in order to visually inspect the lung tissue up close and collect tissue samples for further examination. These techniques have helped to improve patient outcomes by supplementing correct diagnosis and treatment of respiratory disorders [12,13]. The field of pulmonary diagnostics is undergoing a significant transition as a result of the integration of artificial intelligence (AI) in healthcare, with AI algorithms assisting in the interpretation of imaging investigations, real-time analysis and clinical decision making [14].

Although successful, current techniques using traditional stethoscopes for identifying respiratory illnesses have some drawbacks, one of them being its subjective nature and dependence on the knowledge and expertise of the healthcare provider [15]. The intra-operator variability and subjectivity associated with auscultation leads to a lack in uniformity, which can make it challenging to evaluate and understand results over time or between various practitioners. The capacity of CXRs to identify several respiratory disorders, particularly in the early stages of disease, is also limited [16]. There are dangers associated with invasive diagnostic procedures such as bronchoscopy and biopsy, including infection and bleeding [17,18]. Additionally, patients in rural areas struggle to receive correct and timely diagnosis and treatment due to a lack of resources [19].

Lung sounds (LSs), or auscultation as they are commonly known, can be used to supplement diagnosis in several lung diseases, including pneumonia, bronchitis and asthma [8]. The variations in lung sounds can provide valuable information for both the diagnosis and treatment of respiratory diseases. Lung sounds can also be used to check on the success of respiratory disorder treatments [8]. Conventional stethoscopes, although non-invasive, quick and inexpensive, frequently provide weak sounds, making it challenging to recognize and identify some sounds, such as mild cardiac murmurs or pulmonary wheezes [20,21]. Since their normal frequency range is constrained, they frequently miss out on some high- or low-frequency sounds that can be crucial for diagnosis [22].

The need to increase the efficacy and accuracy of auscultation gave rise to the evolution of AI-based analysis. With previous definitions of pathological LSs in place, computer algorithms and programs have been developed to detect them automatically using the electrical recordings (done using electronic stethoscopes) of LSs known as phonopulmograms (PPGs). AI has the capacity for self-improvement as it learns from new data and cases and can be trained to perform better than traditional processing methods [23,24]. In recent years, AI algorithms have been used for the processing and recognition of LSs, among which the most frequently used algorithms include artificial neural networks, Gaussian mixture models and support vector machines [25]. Utilization of a digital stethoscope to record and store LSs of high quality and integration with AI enables the classification of LSs into normal or abnormal in real-time and serves as an essential screening step for physicians [21]. Asthma, COPD and pneumonia are among the respiratory illnesses that AI-based smart stethoscopes and machine learning algorithms are being utilized to identify; the stethoscopes can also analyze LSs and provide real-time feedback for more precise diagnosis [24,26]. AI-based systems can also be useful as a diagnostic tool to triage patients and identify those in need of serious care and referral to a specialist [24,26].

Over the years, there has been an evolution of technologies which have been able to pick up subtle clues to aid in diagnosis of respiratory sounds. While existing literature highlights the need for this technology, it fails to provide a clear understanding of the mechanism of LS production and its clinical usability. The purpose of this review was to study the physiology of LS origin, factors affecting its frequency, AI-assisted clinical applications and recording technologies in existing literature. Additionally, this review reflects on the prospects of using AI-assisted microwave-based dual sensing systems for PPG acoustics and lung tissue imaging and their impact on transforming pulmonology practice for improving patient care.

2. Physiology of Lung Sounds

LSs, believed to be the result of a structure–function continuum, are primarily produced by the airflow along the tracheobronchial tree. Ideally, the air should flow laminarly as it passes through the respiratory tract. However, laminar flow only occurs at small terminal components such as bronchioles. Usually when a large volume/tidal volume of air passes through the respiratory tract, it encounters branching and irregular-walled airways such as the trachea or bronchi, which causes a turbulent and haphazard airflow producing sound from the collision of air molecules with each other or with the airway walls [27]. Another mechanism for breath sound generation is the development of whirlpools between the 5th and the 13th generations of the bronchial tree [28]. The whirlpools or vortices are produced when air flows from a narrower circular circumferential opening into a wider one at the origin of these sounds inside the chest wall, ranging over a frequency of 50 Hz to 2500 Hz and possibly reaching up to 4000 Hz at the trachea [29]. However, as the sound traverses the lung parenchyma, pleura and chest wall, it becomes dampened over higher frequencies and the auscultated sounds over the chest wall are thus limited to a frequency range of 100–200 Hz [28].

LSs originate within the lungs, which differentiates them from the transmitted voice sounds originating from the larynx. LSs comprise normal breath sounds (Table 1) and adventitious/abnormal sounds (Table 2) as auscultated over the chest wall. The normal sounds can be further distinguished as normal tracheal sounds, normal or vesicular breath sounds or bronchial breath sounds, based on their characteristics and location of auscultation as shown in Figure 1. The various LSs are described in Tables 1 and 2 [8].

Table 1. Normal Breath Sounds.

S. No.	Location	Mechanism of Production	Characteristics	Acoustics	Associated Pathological Conditions
1. Tracheal Sounds	Over trachea	Passage of large volume of air at high flow rate	• Biphasic (inspiratory, expiratory) • Harsh, high-pitched • Expiratory phase > inspiratory phase	100–5000 Hz	

Table 1. *Cont.*

S. No.	Location	Mechanism of Production	Characteristics	Acoustics	Associated Pathological Conditions
2. Bronchial Sounds	Manubrium (between 2nd and 3rd intercostal spaces)	Passage of air through progressively smaller airways	• Hollow, high-pitched • Biphasic (inspiratory, expiratory) • Expiratory phase > inspiratory phase (I: E: 1:2) • a/w Whispering pectoriloquy	Highly variable depending on site of auscultation and underlying pathology.	• Consolidation • Pleural effusion • Alveolar collapse • Mediastinal tumor
3. Vesicular Sounds	All over chest	Passage of air through bronchi and bronchioles	• Soft, low-pitched • Biphasic (inspiratory, expiratory) • I: E: 2:1 • Intensity of inspiratory phase> expiratory phase	Auscultation: 100–200 Hz Sensitive microphone: up to 800 Hz	

Table 2. Abnormal Lung sounds.

S. No.	Location	Mechanism of Production	Characteristics	Acoustics	Associated Pathological Conditions
1. Stridor [31]	Proximal/upper airway	Airway obstruction/narrowing	• High-pitched • Inspiratory (supraglottic narrowing/obstruction) • Biphasic (glottis/subglottis/ cervical trachea) • Expiratory (thoracic trachea/bronchi)	>500 Hz	• Adenoid hypertrophy, craniofacial abnormalities, choanal atresia, etc. (inspiratory) • Laryngomalacia, vocal cord palsy, laryngeal mass, etc. (biphasic) • Tracheal stenosis, foreign body, vascular compression, etc. (expiratory)
2. Wheeze [32]	Anterior/ posterior chest wall	Airway narrowing (spasm/mass/ mucus plugs/ foreign body/ parasite infestation)	• High-pitched • Shrill, coarse whistling/ rustling • Intensity on expiration > inspiration	100–5000 Hz	• Asthma • COPD • Endobronchial mass • Mucus plugging • Foreign body
3. Rhonchus	Anterior/ posterior chest wall	Passage of air through lower respiratory tract secretions	• Low-pitched, squeaky • Intensity on expiration > inspiration • Character affected by coughing	~150 Hz	• Pneumonia • Chronic bronchitis • Bronchiectasis

Table 2. *Cont.*

S. No.	Location	Mechanism of Production	Characteristics	Acoustics	Associated Pathological Conditions
4. Coarse crackles [33]	Anterior/ posterior chest wall	Passage and opening of airways clogged by secretions and fluids	• Low-pitched • Biphasic beginning at early inspiration	~350 Hz	• Pulmonary edema • Pneumonia • Bronchiectasis
5. Fine crackles [33]	Anterior/ posterior chest wall	Opening of collapsed terminal airways	• High-pitched	~650 Hz	• Interstitial lung diseases • Congestive heart failure • Pneumonia

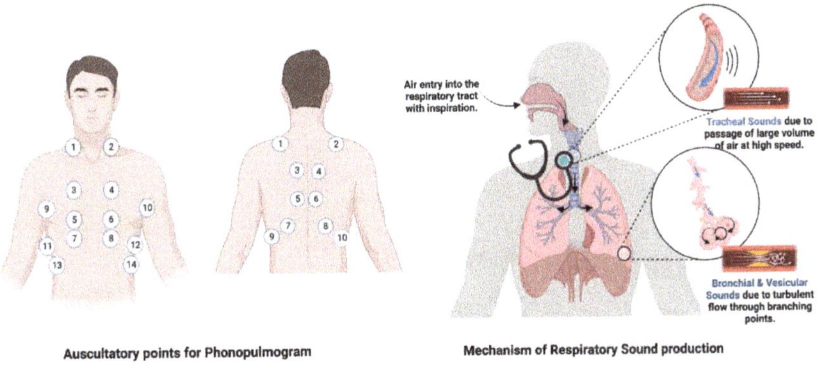

Figure 1. Physiological origin of lung sounds and primary sites of auscultation [30]. Numbers in the figure represent the points of auscultation.

3. Recording Technologies

Conventional stethoscopes, constrained by the subjectivity and expertise of the clinician, have found limited use in pulmonology practice [21,34]. Another drawback is their lack of use in telemedicine, remote care and care for COVID-19 patients because of personal protective equipment [35]. Stethoscope auscultation in busy clinic settings often results in poor signal transmission due to noise, tubular resonance effects and greater attenuation of higher-frequency sounds ranging from 50 Hz to 2500 Hz [34].

To overcome the shortcomings of a conventional pulmonary auscultation device, deep learning-based models through convolutional neural networks (CNNs) have been developed to enable electronic auscultation of LSs with digital stethoscopes for increased diagnostic accuracy and precision. In their comparative study of the effectiveness of doctor auscultation and machine learning-based analysis based on neural networks, Grzywalski et al. suggested that automatic analysis could increase efficiency [26]. A study revealed that AI algorithms were superior to physicians in detecting adventitious LSs [25].

Though machine learning has wide applications in analyzing LSs, the analysis is nonetheless constrained by the fact that it performs less accurately when the noises from the stethoscope itself and the surrounding environment are mixed into the recorded sounds or when two or more breathing sounds are present at the same time [21,36]. In addition, deep learning algorithms' black box-type algorithmic aspect results in a certain lack of interpretability of the analyzed comprehensive information. Interpretability being a crucial component of the analysis, it also closely relates to technological challenges and data dependencies, hence the need for standardization and a clear definition [37]. Table 3 shows the various technological modalities and their shortcomings to gauge a better understanding.

Table 3. Summary of studies on technology applying AI in lung sound auscultation through phonopulmography to aid in disease detection.

Year, Author	Study	Technique	Results & Limitations
1989, Pasterkamp [38].	Assessing lung sound amplitudes, frequencies and timing using digital respirosonography.	Piezoelectric accelerometers → four-channel FM tape recorder → filtered and played through an analog-to-digital converter → IBM sensitive personal computer.	Sonograms of tracheal and vesicular sounds with sound intensities displayed on a color scale identified phases of respiration in normal and asthmatic patients.
1995, Forkheim et al. [39].	Testing of various neural networks to identify wheezes from different lung segments.	Raw data and Fourier transform data used to train and test back-propagation neural network (BPNN).	Fourier transform data provided a better classification rate than the raw signal using the BPNN with accuracy of 91%. Large training set is required to yield better results.
1997, Kahya et al [40].	Classification of lung sounds into obstructive, restrictive and healthy.	Autoregressive models applied to overlapping lung sounds were used to retrieve feature parameters using k-NN-voting and k-NN-multinominal classifiers. Leave-one-out method was used to classify.	The multinominal classifier showed higher performance in both expiration and combined inspiration and expiration cycle vs. the voting classifier.
1999, Rietveld [41].	Comparison of neural networks (NNs) and human examiners in classifying normal and asthmatic lung sounds.	Samples digitized and related to PEFR → Fourier spectrum was calculated from selected breath cycle → spectral vectors obtained were classified using NN.	Self-classifying networks were better (identified 96% of the spectrograms) at discriminating the classes of breath sounds than human examiners.
2000, Waitman et al. [42].	Representing and classifying breath sounds in an intensive setting.	Breath sounds represented by power spectral density → feature vectors → individual breath sounds → inspiratory and expiratory segments → number of inputs featured, hidden units and hidden layers calculated using BPNN.	The training tapes were better classified (91%) with a higher sensitivity (87%) and specificity (95%) vs. the ICU breath sounds (73%, 62% and 85%).
2000, Oud et al. [43].	Analysis of breath sounds produced by asthmatics and corelating them with degree of obstruction.	Air-coupled electret microphone attached to trachea → wireless tape-recorder → high-pass filtering → discrete Fourier transform (DFT) and Welch method → K-NN-based classifier.	Welch spectra are comparatively more convenient; 60–90% of the sound data classified according to their FEV1 value.

Table 3. *Cont.*

Year, Author	Study	Technique	Results & Limitations
2002, Alsmadi et al. [44].	Digital signal processor (DSP) used for classification of lung sounds into healthy and pathological.	Microphone attached to the chest → breath sounds split into inspiration and expiration → segmented and modeled by an auto-regressive model of order 6 BY Levinson–Durbin algorithm → classified using k-NN and minimum distance classifier.	Encouraging results obtained for classifying sounds into two classes.
2003, Baydar et al. [45].	Automatic classification of respiratory sounds using signal coherence method.	Recorded breath sounds were amplified and digitized → signal coherence was calculated using the feature vectors.	Performance was unsatisfactory but could have promising application in wheeze analysis due to their sinusoidal structure.
2003, Bahoura et al. [46].	Classification of respiratory sounds using cepstral analysis.	Segmented sound characterized by fewer cepstral coefficients → classified using Vector Quantization (V) method.	Higher classification results vs. Autoregressive representation and the wavelet transform method of feature.
2004, Folland et al. [47].	Comparing constructive probabilistic neural network (CPNN) with multilayer perceptron (MLP) and radial-basis function network (RBFN) in classifying tracheal–bronchial breath sounds.	Data were presented as signal-estimation models of the tracheal–bronchial frequency spectra.	The classification by CPNN, MLP and RBFN was 97.8,77.8 and 96.2% accurate, respectively.
2004, Kandaswamy et al. [48].	Lung sound analysis using wavelet transform method.	Decomposed lung sounds into frequency sub-bands using wavelet transform → features extraction → classified using an artificial neural network (ANN)-based system.	Lung sounds classified into normal, wheeze, crackle, squawk, stridor or rhonchus.
2004, Gnitecki et al. [49].	Analysis of amplitude and patterns of lung sounds (LSs) in children before and after methacholine challenge test.	From root mean square (RMS) of LS and breath hold (BH) signals, signal-to-noise ratio (SNR) was determined, and 2 fractal-dimension (FD) algorithms based on signal variance and morphology were applied.	RMS-SNR and morphology-based FD values better classified bronchoconstriction with LSs.
2004, Bahoura et al. [50].	Classification of respiratory sounds into normal and wheeze using Gaussian mixture models (GMM).	Cepstral or wavelet transform used to characterize the sound signal divided into overlapping segments. This method compared with vector quantization (VQ) and multi-layer perceptron NN.	
2007, Chien et al. [51].	Classification of normal lung and wheezing sounds using cepstral analyses in Gaussian mixture models (GMM).	Lung sound recorded using electro-condenser microphone, amplified, filtered and analyzed using MFCC and Fourier transform-based model.	Accuracy of 90% at Gaussian mix 16 and increase in performance with longer length of time for training sound.

Table 3. *Cont.*

Year, Author	Study	Technique	Results & Limitations
2008, Alsmadi et al. [52].	Using k-NN and minimum-distance classifiers to design an instrument to acquire, parametrize and classify LSs.	Sound signal from chest microphone and flow signal from pneumotachograph → feature extracted using LPC → classified based on 12 reference libraries	Clinical testing had a 96% accuracy.
2008, Lu et al. [53].	Automated crackle detection and classification.	Crackle separation, detection and classification using fractal dimension, wavelet packet filter (WPST) and GMM.	Separation using WPST 98%, detection sensitivity of 92.9% and a classification performance of 91.5%.
2009, Riella et al. [54].	Automatic wheeze detection in digitally recorded LSs.	Pre-processing of respiratory cycle → computing the spectrogram → stored as an array → multi-layer perceptron ANN.	84.82%, 92.86% accuracy for identification of wheeze in isolated and groups of respiratory cycle respectively.
2009, Bahoura et al. [55].	Comparing feature extraction by Fourier transform, linear predictive coding, wavelet transform and MFCC and classification using vector quantization, GMM and ANN.	Recorded sound split and extracted features used to train and test the model for classification.	Results achieved best by a combination of MFCC and GMM with $p < 0.05$ compared to other methods.
2009, Matsunaga et al. [56].	Segregation of normal and abnormal lung sounds based on maximum likelihood approach using hidden Markov models.	Two acoustic modeling methods were used: one for classifying abnormal sounds and the other for normal lung sounds.	Both models showed increase in recall rate for identifying abnormal and normal lung sounds. Noises hindered the improvement of recall rates.
2010, Mayorga et al. [57].	Evaluation and definition of lung sounds to assess relationship with respiratory diseases.	Electronic stethoscope to record lung sounds → analysis through GMM models to determine frequency of wheezing and crackles to predict disease state.	52.5% accuracy in cross-validation evaluation, 98.75% accuracy in reference recognition. This method could be used in <5-year-olds or to aid physicians with sensorial restrictions. Inability to process unwanted sounds and small sample size.
2010, Azarbarzin et al. [58].	Unsupervised snore classification algorithm of patients during their sleep.	LSs during sleep were recorded via polysomnography (PSG) by two tracheal and ambient microphones → detected with vertical box algorithm → K-means clustering algorithm to label as snore or no-snore.	Accuracy was 98.2% for tracheal recordings and 95.5% for ambient recordings. No requirement of prior training; robust and fast model.
2010, Flietstra et al. [59].	Automated analysis of crackles in interstitial pulmonary fibrosis (IPF) and ability to differentiate from crackles due to congestive heart failure (CHF) and pneumonia (PN).	Lung sounds from patients with IPF, CHF and PN were examined using a 16-channel lung sound analyzer and classified using neural networks and support vector machines (SVM)	IPF crackles were distinguished from PN crackles with a 0.82 sensitivity, 0.88 specificity, 0.86 accuracy. IPF crackles were separated from CHF crackles with 0.77 sensitivity, 0.85 specificity, 0.82 accuracy.

Table 3. *Cont.*

Year, Author	Study	Technique	Results & Limitations
2011, Serbes et al. [60].	Novel method for crackle identification to aid in diagnosis of pulmonary disorders.	LSs with and without crackles → dual tree complex wavelet transforms (DTCWT) time-frequency (TF) and timescale analysis → feature subsets → SVMs	Usage of DTCWT enhances crackle detection ability of the model. Inability to use model in real time.
2011, Jin et al. [61].	Novel identification and extraction method of adventitious LSs based on instantaneous frequency (IF) analysis using temporal–spectral dominance-based features.	Electret condenser microphone to record LSs from healthy subjects and subjects with varying degrees of airway obstruction a TF decomposition method.	Accuracy of 92.4 ± 2.9%. Validity of results is required from more test subjects as well as pathological confirmation. Exploration of crackle LSs is required.
2011, Charleston-Villalobos et al. [62].	Assessment of parametric representation of LSs to classify them as normal or abnormal (ILD).	LSs → conventional power spectral density, eigenvalues of the covariance matrix and univariate autoregressive (UAR) and multivariate autoregressive models (MAR) → feature vectors→ supervised neural network.	The UAR model showed effectiveness with accuracy of 75% in healthy people and 93% in patients with ILD in LS parameterization.
2011, Yamashita et al. [63].	Distinction between healthy subjects and pulmonary emphysema patients based on LSs.	LSs → two-step classification process → hidden Markov models and bigram models → label acoustic segments as "confident abnormal respiration".	Classification rate of 88.7% between diseased and healthy patients. Need for a refined threshold to finetune and improve performance.
2012, Xie et al. [64].	LS extraction using a multi-scale analysis system to aid in LS classification.	Healthy and pathological subjects with airway obstruction → multi-scale principal component analysis → enhance and extract signal → empirical classification.	Accuracy of 98.34%
2017, Gronnesby et al. [65].	Machine learning-based detection of crackles in lung sounds	Microphone with a recorder → reference database training sets with crackle and normal windows → preprocessing a classification and server implementation	5-dimensional vector and SVM with a radial-basis function kernel performed best with a precision of 0.86 and recall of 0.84.
2021, Karimizadeh et al. [66].	Multichannel LS analysis in determining severity of pulmonary disease in cystic fibrosis (CF) patients.	30-channel acquisition system → expiration-to-inspiration LS power ratio features calculated → support vector machine, ANN, decision tree and naïve Bayesian classifiers.	Upper and peripheral airways features were more effective in distinguishing between mild (91.1%) and moderate-to-severe (92.8%). The NN classifier had the best accuracy, of 89.05%.
2021, Chung et al. [67].	Artificial intelligence (AI)-based pneumonia diagnostic algorithm.	Loudness and energy ratio were used to represent the level of cough sounds and spectral variations.	90.0% sensitivity, 78.6% specificity and 84.9% accuracy.
2021, Nguyen et al. [68]	Transfer learning to tackle the mismatch of recording setup.	Pre-trained network used to build a multi-input CNN model.	F-score of 9.84% on the target domain.

Table 3. *Cont.*

Year, Author	Study	Technique	Results & Limitations
2021, Ulukaya et al. [69].	Resonance-based decomposition to isolate crackles and wheezes.	Crackle and/or wheeze signals decomposed using tunable Q-factor wavelet transform and morphological component analysis	Significant superiority over its competitors in terms of crackle localization and signal reconstruction ability.
2021, Kim et al. [70].	Automated classification of breath sounds.	Deep-learning CNN to categorize LSs (normal, crackles, wheezes, rhonchi) → LS classification combining pretrained image feature extractor.	Accuracy of 85.7% and a mean AUC of 0.92 for classification of lung sounds.
2021, Ullah et al. [71].	LS classification.	LSs of varying duration → pre-processed segmented mel-frequency cepstral coefficients (MFCCs) and short-time Fourier transform (STFT) analysis → features used to train (70%) and validate (30%) models including ANN, SVM, K-nearest neighbor (KNN), decision tree (DT) and random forest (RF).	The best results were obtained with STFT + MFCC-ANN combination with an accuracy of 98.61%, 98% F1 score, 98% recall and 99% precision.
2021, Srivastava et al. [72].	CNN-based deep learning method for COPD detection.	Machine learning library features such as MFCC, mel-spectrogram, chroma and chroma CENS.	Classification accuracy score of 93%.
2021, Rani et al. [73].	Machine learning-based classification of pulmonary diseases from LSs.	LSs → Four machine-learning classifiers (SVM, KNN, naïve Bayes and ANN).	Low time complexity, robust and non-invasive.
2022, Nguyen et al. [74].	Classification of adventitious lung sounds and respiratory diseases.	Pre-trained ResNet model → vanilla finetuning, co-tuning, stochastic normalization and the combination of the three → data augmentation in both time domain and time frequency domain.	58.29 ± 0.24% and 64.74 ± 0.05% average score for the 4- and 2-class adventitious LS task and 92.72 ± 1.30% and 93.77 ± 1.41% average score for the 3- and 2-class respiratory disease classification tasks, respectively.
2022, Pancaldi et al. [75].	Automatic detection of pathological LSs in patients with COVID-19 pneumonia.	LSs of patients in the ER processed using software VECTOR, suitably devised for ILD.	Diagnostic accuracy of 75%.
2022, Wu et al. [76].	Overcoming subjectivity of conventional stethoscopes and filtering cardiopulmonary sounds.	An electronic stethoscope and an AI-based classifier recorded cardiopulmonary sounds which were then analyzed using fast FT.	Accuracy of 73.3%, sensitivity of 66.7%, specificity of 80% and F1 score of 71.5%.

Table 3. *Cont.*

Year, Author	Study	Technique	Results & Limitations
2022, Neili et al. [77].	Evaluation and comparison of time frequency techniques such as spectrogram, scalogram, mel spectrogram and gammatone gram representations in lung sound classification.	LS signals obtained from the ICBHI 2017 respiratory sound database → converted into images of spectrogram, scalogram, mel spectrogram and gammatone gram TF → fed into VGG16, ResNet-50 and Alex Net deep learning architectures → network performances were analyzed.	Gammatone gram and scalogram TF images coupled with ResNet-50 achieved maximum classification accuracy.
2022, Vidhya et al. [78].	Diagnosis of pneumonia from lung sounds using gradient-boosting algorithm.	Electronic stethoscope → audacity software→ separates the required sound from unwanted noises.	Good identification properties with 97% accuracy.
2022, Dori et al. [79].	Full-spectrum auscultation device using machine learning analysis to detect COVID-19 pneumonia.	COVID, non-COVID patients, healthy LSs → full-spectrum stethoscope → machine learning classifier.	Sensitivity 97% and specificity 93%.
2022, Alqudah et al. [80].	Evaluation of different deep learning models in diagnosing respiratory pathologies.	Augmented datasets → three different deep learning models → generate four different sub-datasets.	Highest accuracy of CNN–LSTM model using non-augmentation was 99.6%, 99.8%, 82.4% and 99.4% for datasets 1, 2, 3 and 4.
2022, Kim et al. [21].	Diagnosing respiratory sounds using deep learning-based LS analysis algorithm		Overcoming the subjectivity of a conventional stethoscope.
2022, Kwon et [81]	Shifted δ-cepstral coefficients in lower-subspace (SDC-L) as a novel feature of lung sound classification	Performance of SDC-L evaluated with 3 machine learning techniques (SVM, k-NN, RF), two deep learning algorithms (MLP and CNN) and one hybrid deep learning algorithm combining CNN with long short-term memory (LSTM).	SVM, MLP and a hybrid deep learning algorithm (CNN plus LSTM) outperformed SDC-L, and the other classifiers achieved equivalent results with all features.

Implications and Limitations

Various AI models have been used in detecting and analyzing lung sounds [38–81]. These methods have been tested in and proposed to be used in a multitude of clinical settings. From classification of lung sounds using different models [40–42,44–46,48] to corelating lung sounds with degree of obstruction in asthmatics, AI shows promising capability. Along with its use in the diagnosis and management of various pulmonary disorders including pneumonia, COPD, asthma and IPF, its ability to filter cardiovascular sounds makes it superior to conventional stethoscopes [76]. Despite extensive research in the field, the lack of substantial sample sizes and the inability of current models to filter environmental noise have hindered AI's development and use in everyday clinical practice [56]. Furthermore, since clinical decision making is feasible with interpretable AI, current reviews of AI models are mostly black box-type models without clarity regarding the exploitability of the features that relate to underlying pathophysiology in order to guide practice. AI researchers in this field should apply physiologically consistent signal processing and AI approaches with interpretable models that can augment physicians' clinical decision making to diagnose and treat various lung diseases using phonopulmograms.

4. Clinical Applications of Lung Sounds

4.1. Infectious Respiratory Disorders

4.1.1. Pulmonary Tuberculosis

In 2018, 10 million persons had incident TB and 1.5 people died of TB [82]. The sound properties of infected lungs differ from those of healthy lungs [83]. As a result, it is expected that infected lungs will exhibit adventitious LSs, which frequently signifies an abnormality in the lungs, such as obstruction in the airway passages or pulmonary disease. The lung damage brought on by active TB results in displaced lung tissue, which obstructs the airways and may cause wheezing. Crackles could be a sign of fibrosis brought on by the healing of the lungs [83]. In a study performed on healthy volunteers and patients with pulmonary TB, a large database of respiratory sounds was created and studied using multiple approaches, such as time domain, frequency domain and accidental wheezing and crackling analysis. The subjects in this study had their respiratory sounds recorded at 14 different sites on their posterior and anterior chest walls. The statistical overlap factor (SOF) was used to identify the most important signal characteristics in the temporal and frequency domains connected to the presence of TB. The auscultation recordings were then automatically classified into their respective groups for healthy or TB-origin using a neural network that was trained using these features. This study illustrates the potential of computer-aided auscultation in the detection and management of TB. Although the diagnostic accuracy of the neural network was 73% with automated noise filtering, more data training and potentially other signal processing techniques, the outcomes of future models can be enhanced. Such analyses will also enable follow-up with TB patients and gather more data as they receive treatment and recover to ascertain whether there is potential for complete recovery [84]. More in-depth research on electronic recording and digital analysis needs to be done on the peculiarities of respiratory sounds related to TB [84].

4.1.2. Pneumonia

Every year, about 450 million people worldwide are affected by pneumonia, and delayed diagnosis results in about 4 million deaths. Respiratory sounds can be recorded with computerized stethoscopes and AI can be used to diagnose pneumonia with the gradient-boosting model, a machine learning model with an accuracy of 97%. This eliminates the need to perform CXRs, blood tests and pulse oximetry tests for diagnosing pneumonia, ensuring early diagnosis and management [80].

Signal processing and machine learning models are also used to classify normal, COPD and pneumonia patients with an accuracy of 99.7% according to a study conducted by Naqvi et al. [85]. Among children aged 1–59 months, hospitalized with WHO-defined clinical pneumonia without WHO danger signs (e.g., chest in-drawing, stridor, labored breathing, fast breathing), recorded LS analysis using machine learning and digital stethoscopes showed the presence of wheezing (without crackles) was correlated with lower odds of radiographic pneumonia and lower mortality as compared to children with normal recordings [86].

4.1.3. COVID-19

CNN models have helped classify normal and abnormal lung sounds in COVID-19 patients and categorize them into normal, moderate, severe and critical cases with high accuracy and precision. Limitations existed in the study due to background noises interrupting lung sound analysis with CNN models. However, this method can provide clinicians with useful early prognostic information to facilitate pre-treatment risk stratification and guide medical staff to conduct more intensive surveillance and treatment of patients at high risk of severe illness to reduce mortality [35,79].

4.2. Non-Infectious Respiratory Disorders

4.2.1. Restrictive Lung Disease

Interstitial Pulmonary Fibrosis

Patients with interstitial pulmonary fibrosis (IPF) frequently present with crackles similar to those of patients with pneumonia or congestive heart failure (CHF), leading to difficulty in diagnosis and potentially errors in management. Crackle pitch is one of the characteristics that notably differs between these diseases, which supports the widely held belief that IPF crackles are produced in smaller airways than those of CHF and pneumonia. Smither referred to the crackles of lung fibrosis brought on by asbestos as "characteristic in their sound and distribution," and Wood and Gloyne described them as a major hallmark of this industrial disease as early as 1930 [87,88]. Using a 16-channel lung sound analyzer, 39 individuals with IPF, 95 with CHF and 123 with pneumonia were studied and machine learning techniques such as neural networks and support vector machines were used to assess crackle properties. With a sensitivity of 0.82, specificity of 0.88 and accuracy of 0.86, the IPF crackles could be distinguished from those in patients with pneumonia due to their distinctive features and with a sensitivity of 0.77, specificity of 0.85 and accuracy of 0.82, they were distinguished from those of CHF patients [61]. Fine crackles produced from a number of abnormally closed small airways increase in a lung with advanced fibrosis, which can be quantified by the machine learning-based analyzing algorithm. They were associated with the progression of lung fibrosis seen on high-resolution CT images in IPF patients, and the AI analysis had higher sensitivity than CXR findings of IPF [89]. Clinicians can make use of bedside computer analysis of crackles to diagnose IPF quickly and reduce medication errors [90]. In another study, patients with rheumatoid arthritis had their lung sounds recorded using an electronic stethoscope and analyzed using a Velcro sound detector (VECTOR) which showed a 93.2% sensitivity and hence proved to be a significant potential screening technique for rheumatoid arthritis patients with interstitial lung disease [90].

Asbestos-Related Lung Injury

Frequency distribution of lung sounds using computerized lung sound analyzer is significantly associated with interstitial lung fibrosis on high-resolution computed tomography (HRCT) scoring in patients with asbestos-related lung injury. The inspiratory crackles and high sound frequencies are associated with fibrotic changes to the lung while low sound frequencies were associated with emphysematous components of the asbestos-injured lung [91].

Pulmonary Edema

For many years, diagnosing pulmonary edema and tracking treatment response relied heavily on roentgenography and chest auscultation. Rales, which are now more commonly referred to as "crackles" in medical terminology, are still the primary auscultation feature used to diagnose pulmonary edema. Pulmonary edema can be cardiogenic and non-cardiogenic. One study described a multimodal sensing system that tracks changes in cardiopulmonary health by collecting data from bioimpedance spectroscopy, multi-channel lung sounds from four contact microphones, multi-frequency impedance pneumography, temperature and kinematics. The authors carried out a feasibility study on HF patients ($n = 14$) in clinical settings after initially validating the system on healthy people ($n = 10$). The ratio of resistance, from 5 kHz to 150 kHz (K), to respiratory timings (e.g., respiratory rate) were derived from three measurements conducted over the course of the hospitalization, and the researchers discovered an increase in K that was statistically significant ($p < 0.05$) from admission to discharge, as well as respiratory timings that were within physiologically reasonable limits. It was possible to identify Cheyne–Stokes breathing patterns and inspiratory crackles from patient recordings using integrated power (IP)-derived respiratory signals and lung sounds, respectively. This showed that the suggested system can record precise respiratory signals and lung sounds in a clinical scenario, as well as identify changes in pulmonary fluid status [92].

4.2.2. Obstructive Lung Diseases

Chronic Obstructive Lung Disease

COPD causes the narrowing of air passages, making breathing difficult. The conventional methods of COPD diagnosis, via pulmonary function test, CXRs or AI-based analysis of CXRs or chest CT, are time-consuming, expensive and complex. Automated detection of LSs to diagnose COPD early can be timesaving for both the patient and the doctor. The physician can record and relay LSs to a pre-processing module, where it is augmented and passed to a convolutional neural network and classified into either COPD or non-COPD [72]. In addition, analyzing recordings from different auscultation points using multichannel lung sounds could help assess the whole lung rather than a specific region [93]. Machine learning models can also be used to predict acute exacerbation of COPD symptoms by telemonitoring computerized respiratory sounds, proving the significance of telehealth care systems for COPD management [72,94].

Computerized respiratory sounds are sensitive to short- and mid-term effects of pulmonary rehabilitation (PR) in patients with COPD. A study showed a decrease in inspiratory and expiratory median frequency of computerized respiratory sound related to improving the lung function of patients with COPD after PR in the band range of 100–300 Hz. Positive relationships between inspiratory median frequency and subjects' symptoms (e.g., rest dyspnea, self-reported sputum) and health-related quality of life were found at the high-frequency band (300–600 Hz) [95].

Asthma

Lung wheezes can be detected by analyzing respiratory sounds' frequency in asthma patients. High-pitched wheezing is associated with frequencies higher than 500 Hz. Frequency spectra in asthmatic patients can be categorized into three groups: asthma during an exacerbation, asthma in remission and normal state [41]. Several studies showed strong correlations between lung function parameter (FEV1) and median frequency of respiration sound power spectra computed from expiratory tracheal sounds, which can be established by computational techniques such as artificial neural networks [41,43]. A study by Islam et al. distinguished normal and asthmatic people using their posterior lung sound signals to reduce the inference of heart sounds, with the uniqueness of wheezing not being a necessary requirement for asthma detection [96].

Recently, studies have also identified asthma severity levels (mild, moderate and severe) by extracting integrated power features from respiratory sound signals, i.e., the energy of breath sounds in different sub-bands, which are not affected by airflow rate. In another study, the expiration/inspiration lung sound power ratio in a low-frequency band was used as a sign of airway obstruction and inflammation in bronchial asthma patients [66].

Cystic Fibrosis

The severity of lung disease can be monitored in cystic fibrosis (CF) patients using an artificial neural network with 89.05% average accuracy. Although conventional spirometry and a drop in FEV1% are commonly used tests to indicate the severity of lung disease in patients with CF, they require significant patient cooperation, especially in the pediatric population [66]. In a study by Karimizadeh et al., multichannel lung sounds were recorded from various regions of the lungs (large airways, upper airways and peripheral airways), expiration-to-inspiration lung sound power ratio features in different frequency bands (E/I F) were extracted and compared between the groups of different severity levels of lung disease using support vector machine, artificial neural network, decision tree and naïve Bayesian classifiers by the leave-one-sample-out method. Results showed that more severe lung disease occurred in the upper lobes compared to the lower lobes, hence discriminating between severity levels of CF lung disease [66].

Smoking and AI

Significant differences between digitally recorded respiratory sounds of healthy smokers and non-smokers have been noticed and can be used as the earliest indicator for detecting smoking-related respiratory diseases such as COPD, lung cancer, etc. [97].

4.2.3. Lung Cancer

In one study, researchers showed how artificial neural networks were used to classify normal and crackle noises collected from 20 healthy subjects and 23 lung cancer patients, respectively. First, using a discrete wavelet transform (DWT) based on the Daubechies 7 (db7) and Haar mother wavelets, the sound data were divided into seven distinct frequency bands. Second, for five frequency bands (D3, D4, D5, D6 and D7), the detail coefficients' mean, standard deviation and maximum PSD were computed as features. The ANN classifier took fifteen features as input. The classification results demonstrate that, when utilizing 15 nodes at the hidden layer, db7-based wavelets outperformed Haar wavelets with flawless 100% sensitivity, specificity and accuracy during the testing and validation phases. When utilizing 10 nodes at the hidden layer, Haar's testing stage is the only one that demonstrated 100% sensitivity, specificity and accuracy [98]. However, we are looking for more literature regarding lung sounds in lung cancer to draw a definite conclusion.

5. Discussion

The pulmonary system is the site of the top 10 causes of mortality in 2019, with many fatal respiratory pathologies such as COPD, ILD and asthma and infectious diseases such as pneumonia, TB and most recently COVID-19. Rapid and easy screening has never been more essential [1–5,7]. While radiological investigations are an important confirmatory diagnostic method, initial pulmonary examinations by auscultation can help detect respiratory abnormalities [8,9,23]. Improvement and augmentation of the initial auscultation step could result in better screening of lung diseases as shown in Figure 2.

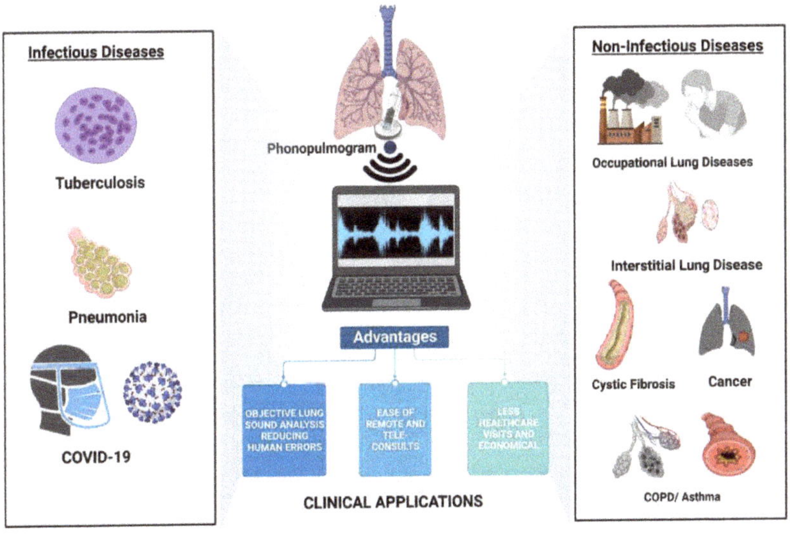

Figure 2. Pictorial representation of various AI-assisted clinical applications of phonopulmograms [30].

LSs, generated by the flow of air through the respiratory tract, can be altered by disruption of laminar flow [25]. Different types of LSs, both normal and abnormal, have been identified and studied which can help both guide diagnosis and monitor the progress of treatment. Utilizing these modulations of respiratory sounds, it has been possible to screen individuals with a respiratory pathology with the help of auscultation. However, the commonly used conventional stethoscopes are subject to inter-observer variability and produce weak sounds or sounds superimposed with background noise, posing a risk of missing out on certain sound frequencies essential for narrowing the diagnosis [21–23]. With the advent of digital stethoscopes, superior quality sound recording is possible and integration with artificial intelligence through neural networks, automated processing and analyses of sound recordings can offer a promising alternative [22–24]. Employing lung sound amplitudes, frequencies and timing as an input, an output of automatic breath sound identification is the goal of AI-integrated respiratory sound analysis [35].

Over the years, multiple technologies incorporating neural networks have been used to analyze LSs. In the 1990s and early 2000s, self-classifying networks and lung sound classification using back-propagation neural networks and wavelet transform methods showed high accuracy. Gaussian mixture models (GMM) were used to increase efficacy, with a hybrid of mel-frequency cepstral co-efficient and GMM showing higher reference recognition. This has been recently followed by using deep learning and machine learning-based classification of lung sounds and of pulmonary diseases ranging from pneumonia to COVID-19.

A phonopulmogram using machine learning methods could potentially transfigure respiratory clinical practice. There is a growing need for research with larger sample sizes and a standardized database of normal and pathological lung sounds, which could be used to diagnose patients quickly and efficiently. Such a system would also help patients who are in remote areas and unable to travel with the early diagnosis of disabling conditions such as interstitial lung disease and tuberculosis, thus significantly reducing both expenditure and strain on the healthcare system.

As illustrated in Figure 1, the 24 auscultatory sites could offer significant assistance in the simultaneous acquisition and analysis of phonopulmogram signals. Novel innovations in phonopulmogram acoustic sensor designs and implementation strategies are required to optimize effective acquisition across all auscultatory sites to obtain high-fidelity data for various lung diseases. AI-assisted sensor deployment will revolutionize the design and use of these sensors for specific lung diseases. Additionally, the data obtained from these acquisitions can further improve analysis of the phonopulmogram for effective detection, diagnosis and prognostication of various lung diseases as well as for treatment-monitoring applications. Standardized recording technologies and a dataset of various characteristic lung sounds will subsequently lead to the development of reliable AI-based models for automated lung sound analysis. These advancements will lead to an effective clinical decision support system that will impact digital pulmonology practice and reduce health care costs. The following section describes the author's perspectives on the dual application of microwave systems for acoustic sensing of phonopulmograms as well as microwave imaging of the lung tissues for dielectric property measurement for a combined real-time digital assessment for improved patient care in pulmonology.

AI-Assisted Microwave Based Dual Sensor System for Digital Pulmonology-Future Perspectives

Electrical impedance distribution in the human body is different as conductivity in each tissue is different. Conductivity also changes with pathology [99]. This principle has been used in electrical impedance tomography (EIT) imaging systems to diagnose various diseases. EIT is a new technology with clinical applications in specific lung pathology diagnosis, tumor detection and real time monitoring of lung volume changes [99]. Frerichs et al. conducted a study with EIT and reported that specific lung volumes related to spontaneous and mechanical ventilation could be separated, which helps optimize the ventilatory pattern for patients who are on artificial ventilation and therapy management for those patients [100]. Another study suggested that EIT can be used to identify imbalances in regional lung ventilation during mechanical ventilation [101]. EIT has also been used in diagnosing certain lung diseases. EIT reconstructs a cross-sectional image of lung conductivity, which correlates with regional ventilation. A study showed that EIT had

for practicing digital pulmonology using a dual sensing approach with microwave-based phonopulmography system.

6. Conclusions

Auscultation of lung sounds has been known to be a clinically useful technique for assisting with diagnosis of various lung diseases. Various studies have demonstrated the promising potential of digital lung sounds towards impacting pulmonology practice, though more research is warranted. While reasonable knowledge on the origin of normal lung sounds is well documented, further research is needed in better understanding the pathophysiology of abnormal lung sounds is needed to effectively translate acoustic features into clinical practice. The recording and analysis of lung sounds shows tremendous potential for the design and development of a patient friendly sensing device that can provide real-time analytics on the lung status. Microwave-based dual sensing approach for PPG sensing and microwave imaging for digital phonopulmography offers a huge opportunity to impact pulmonology practice as well as patient care. Technological advancements on the design of novel AI-assisted microwave acoustic and dielectric sensors with effective telemetry system designs will lead to an enhanced digital pulmonology practice in the future.

Author Contributions: A.K.S. and S.P.A. defined the review scope, context and purpose of the study. C.A.A., A.J.R. and V.N.I. provided clinical perspectives and expertise for the study. A.K.S., P.M., P.A., J.A., A.M., M.S., K.G., A.Y. and A.A. conducted the literature review and drafted the manuscript. S.P.A., A.K.S. and P.A. conceived and crafted the illustrative figures. D.D., K.K., C.A.A., A.J.R., V.N.I. and S.P.A. provided consulting and performed a critical review of the manuscript. A.K.S., P.M. and S.P.A. performed the proofreading and organization of the manuscript. S.P.A. provided conceptualization, supervision and project administration. All authors have read and agreed to the published version of the manuscript.

Funding: This research received no external funding.

Institutional Review Board Statement: Not applicable.

Informed Consent Statement: Not applicable.

Data Availability Statement: The review was based on publicly available academic literature databases.

Acknowledgments: This work was supported by the Advanced Analytics and Practice Innovation Unit for Artificial Intelligence and Informatics Research within the Department of Medicine, Mayo Clinic, Rochester, MN, USA. This work was also supported by the GIH Division for the GIH Artificial Intelligence Laboratory (GAIL) and Microwave Engineering and Imaging Laboratory (MEIL), Department of Medicine, Mayo Clinic, Rochester, MN, USA.

Conflicts of Interest: The authors declare no conflict of interest.

References

1. The Top 10 Causes of Death. Who. Int. Available online: https://www.who.int/news-room/fact-sheets/detail/the-top-10-causes-of-death (accessed on 14 January 2023).
2. Meghji, J.; Mortimer, K.; Agusti, A.; Allwood, B.W.; Asher, I.; Bateman, E.D.; Bissell, K.; E Bolton, C.; Bush, A.; Celli, B.; et al. Improving lung health in low- and middle-income countries: From challenges to solutions. *Lancet* **2021**, *397*, 928–940. [CrossRef]
3. GBD Chronic Respiratory Disease Collaborators. Prevalence and attributable health burden of chronic respiratory diseases, 1990–2017: A systematic analysis for the Global Burden of Disease Study 2017. *Lancet Respir. Med.* **2020**, *8*, 585–596. [CrossRef]
4. Chronic Respiratory Diseases. Who. Int. Available online: https://www.who.int/health-topics/chronic-respiratory-diseases (accessed on 14 January 2023).
5. Pneumonia: The Forgotten Killer of Children. Who. Int. Available online: https://fctc.who.int/publications/i/item/pneumonia-the-forgotten-killer-of-children (accessed on 14 January 2023).
6. World Health Organization. *Global Tuberculosis Program. Global Tuberculosis Report 2020*; World Health Organization: Geneva, Switzerland, 2020.

7. Sung, H.; Ferlay, J.; Siegel, R.L.; Laversanne, M.; Soerjomataram, I.; Jemal, A.; Bray, F. Global cancer statistics 2020: GLOBOCAN estimates of incidence and mortality worldwide for 36 cancers in 185 countries. *CA Cancer J. Clin.* **2021**, *71*, 209–249. [CrossRef]
8. Sarkar, M.; Madabhavi, I.; Niranjan, N.; Dogra, M. Auscultation of the respiratory system. *Ann. Thorac. Med.* **2015**, *10*, 158–168. [CrossRef]
9. Kelly, B. The chest radiograph. *Ulster Med. J.* **2012**, *81*, 143–148. [PubMed]
10. Ponce, M.C.; Sankari, A.; Sharma, S. *Pulmonary Function Tests*; StatPearls Publishing: Treasure Island, FL, USA, 2022.
11. Patel, P.R.; De Jesus, O. *CT Scan*; StatPearls Publishing: Treasure Island, FL, USA, 2022.
12. Valentini, I.; Lazzari, L.; Michieletto, L.; Innocenti, M.; Savoia, F.; Del Prato, B.; Mancino, L.; Maddau, C.; Romano, A.; Puorto, A.; et al. Competence in flexible bronchoscopy and basic biopsy technique. *Panminerva Med.* **2019**, *61*, 232–248. Available online: https://pubmed.ncbi.nlm.nih.gov/30394711/ (accessed on 15 January 2023). [CrossRef]
13. Modi, P.; Uppe, A. *Lung Biopsy Techniques and Clinical Significance*; StatPearls Publishing: Treasure Island, FL, USA, 2022.
14. Estépar, R.S.J. Artificial intelligence in functional imaging of the lung. *Br. J. Radiol.* **2022**, *95*, 20210527. [CrossRef]
15. Hafke-Dys, H.; Bręborowicz, A.; Kleka, P.; Kociński, J.; Biniakowski, A. The accuracy of lung auscultation in the practice of physicians and medical students. *PLoS ONE* **2019**, *14*, e0220606. [CrossRef] [PubMed]
16. Del Ciello, A.; Franchi, P.; Contegiacomo, A.; Cicchetti, G.; Bonomo, L.; Larici, A.R. Missed lung cancer: When, where, and why? *Diagn. Interv. Radiol.* **2017**, *23*, 118–126. [CrossRef] [PubMed]
17. Bronchoscopy. Mayoclinic.org. 2019. Available online: https://www.mayoclinic.org/tests-procedures/bronchoscopy/about/pac-20384746 (accessed on 4 February 2023).
18. Wu, C.C.; Maher, M.M.; Shepard, J.A. Complications of CT-guided percutaneous needle biopsy of the chest: Prevention and management. *AJR Am. J. Roentgenol.* **2011**, *196*, W678–W682. [CrossRef]
19. Yadav, H.; Shah, D.; Sayed, S.; Horton, S.; Schroeder, L.F. Availability of essential diagnostics in ten low-income and middle-income countries: Results from national health facility surveys. *Lancet Glob. Health* **2021**, *9*, e1553–e1560. Available online: https://www.thelancet.com/journals/langlo/article/PIIS2214-109X(21)00442-3/fulltext (accessed on 15 January 2023). [CrossRef]
20. Vasudevan, R.S.; Horiuchi, Y.; Torriani, F.J.; Cotter, B.; Maisel, S.M.; Dadwal, S.S.; Gaynes, R.; Maisel, A.S. Persistent value of the stethoscope in the age of COVID-19. *Am. J. Med.* **2020**, *133*, 1143–1150. [CrossRef]
21. Kim, Y.; Hyon, Y.; Lee, S.; Woo, S.-D.; Ha, T.; Chung, C. The coming era of a new auscultation system for analyzing respiratory sounds. *BMC Pulm. Med.* **2022**, *22*, 119. [CrossRef]
22. Nowak, L.J.; Nowak, K.M. Sound differences between electronic and acoustic stethoscopes. *Biomed Eng. Online* **2018**, *17*, 104. [CrossRef]
23. van der Wall, E.E. The stethoscope: Celebration or cremation after 200 years? *Neth. Heart J.* **2016**, *24*, 303–305. [CrossRef]
24. Kevat, A.; Kalirajah, A.; Roseby, R. Artificial intelligence accuracy in detecting pathological breath sounds in children using digital stethoscopes. *Respir. Res.* **2020**, *21*, 253. [CrossRef]
25. Zhang, J.; Wang, H.S.; Zhou, H.Y.; Dong, B.; Zhang, L.; Zhang, F.; Liu, S.J.; Wu, Y.F.; Yuan, S.H.; Tang, M.Y.; et al. Real-World Verification of Artificial Intelligence Algorithm-Assisted Auscultation of Breath Sounds in Children. *Front. Pediatr.* **2021**, *9*, 627337. [CrossRef]
26. Grzywalski, T.; Piecuch, M.; Szajek, M.; Bręborowicz, A.; Hafke-Dys, H.; Kociński, J.; Pastusiak, A.; Belluzzo, R. Practical implementation of artificial intelligence algorithms in pulmonary auscultation examination. *Eur. J. Pediatr.* **2019**, *178*, 883–890. [CrossRef] [PubMed]
27. Forgacs, P. Lung sounds. *Br. J. Dis. Chest* **1969**, *63*, 1–12. [CrossRef] [PubMed]
28. Hardin, J.C.; Patterson, J.L., Jr. Monitoring the state of the human airways by analysis of respiratory sound. *Acta Astronaut.* **1979**, *6*, 1137–1151. [CrossRef] [PubMed]
29. Reichert, S.; Gass, R.; Brandt, C.; Andrès, E. Analysis of respiratory sounds: State of the art. *Clin. Med. Circ. Respirat. Pulm. Med.* **2008**, *2*, 45–58. [CrossRef]
30. BioRender.com. BioRender. Available online: https://biorender.com/ (accessed on 1 December 2022).
31. Sicari, V.; Zabbo, C.P. Stridor. In *StatPearls*; StatPearls Publishing: Treasure Island, FL, USA, 2022.
32. Patel, P.H.; Mirabile, V.S.; Sharma, S. Wheezing. In *StatPearls*; StatPearls Publishing: Treasure Island, FL, USA, 2022.
33. Piirilä, P.; Sovijärvi, A.R. Crackles: Recording, analysis and clinical significance. *Eur. Respir. J.* **1995**, *8*, 2139–2148. [CrossRef]
34. Gurung, A.; Scrafford, C.G.; Tielsch, J.M.; Levine, O.S.; Checkley, W. Computerized lung sound analysis as diagnostic aid for the detection of abnormal lung sounds: A systematic review and meta-analysis. *Respir. Med.* **2011**, *105*, 1396–1403. [CrossRef] [PubMed]
35. Zhu, H.; Lai, J.; Liu, B.; Wen, Z.; Xiong, Y.; Li, H.; Zhou, Y.; Fu, Q.; Yu, G.; Yan, X.; et al. Automatic pulmonary auscultation grading diagnosis of Coronavirus Disease 2019 in China with artificial intelligence algorithms: A cohort study. *Comput. Methods Programs Biomed.* **2022**, *213*, 106500. [CrossRef]
36. Emmanouilidou, D.; McCollum, E.D.; Park, D.E.; Elhilali, M. Computerized lung sound screening for pediatric auscultation in noisy field environments. *IEEE Trans. Biomed. Eng.* **2018**, *65*, 1564–1574. [CrossRef] [PubMed]
37. Goodfellow, I.; Bengio, Y.; Courville, A.J.C. *Deep Learning*; Adaptive Computation and Machine Learning Series; MIT Press: Cambridge, MA, USA, 2017; pp. 321–339.
38. Pasterkamp, H.; Carson, C.; Daten, D.; Oh, Y. Digital respirosonography. *Chest* **1989**, *96*, 1405–1412. [CrossRef] [PubMed]

39. Forkheim, K.E.; Scuse, D.; Pasterkamp, H. A comparison of neural network models for wheeze detection. In Proceedings of the IEEE WESCANEX 95. Communications, Power, and Computing. Conference Proceedings, Winnipeg, MB, Canada, 15–16 May 1995; Volume 1, pp. 214–219. [CrossRef]
40. Kahya, Y.P.; Guler, E.C.; Sahin, S. Respiratory disease diagnosis using lung sounds. In Proceedings of the 19th Annual International Conference of the IEEE Engineering in Medicine and Biology Society. 'Magnificent Milestones and Emerging Opportunities in Medical Engineering' (Cat. No.97CH36136), Chicago, IL, USA, 30 October–2 November 1997; Volume 5, pp. 2051–2053. [CrossRef]
41. Rietveld, S.; Oud, M.; Dooijes, E.H. Classification of asthmatic breath sounds: Preliminary results of the classifying capacity of human examiners versus artificial neural networks. *Comput. Biomed. Res.* **1999**, *32*, 440–448. [CrossRef] [PubMed]
42. Waitman, L.R.; Clarkson, K.P.; Barwise, J.A.; King, P.H. Representation and classification of breath sounds recorded in an intensive care setting using neural networks. *J. Clin. Monit. Comput.* **2000**, *16*, 95–105. [CrossRef]
43. Oud, M.; Dooijes, E.H.; van der Zee, J.S. Asthmatic airways obstruction assessment based on detailed analysis of respiratory sound spectra. *IEEE Trans. Biomed. Eng.* **2000**, *47*, 1450–1455. [CrossRef] [PubMed]
44. Alsmadi, S.S.; Kahya, Y.P. Online classification of lung sounds using DSP. In Proceedings of the Second Joint 24th Annual Conference and the Annual Fall Meeting of the Biomedical Engineering Society, Engineering in Medicine and Biology, Houston, TX, USA, 23–26 October 2002; Volume 2, pp. 1771–1772. [CrossRef]
45. Baydar, K.S.; Ertuzun, A.; Kahya, Y.P. Analysis and classification of respiratory sounds by signal coherence method. In Proceedings of the 25th Annual International Conference of the IEEE Engineering in Medicine and Biology Society (IEEE Cat. No.03CH37439), Cancun, Mexico, 17–21 September 2003; Volume 3, pp. 2950–2953. [CrossRef]
46. Bahoura, M.; Pelletier, C. New parameters for respiratory sound classification. In Proceedings of the CCECE 2003—Canadian Conference on Electrical and Computer Engineering. Toward a Caring and Humane Technology (Cat. No.03CH37436), Montreal, QC, Canada, 4–7 May 2003; Volume 3, pp. 1457–1460. [CrossRef]
47. Folland, R.; Hines, E.; Dutta, R.; Boilot, P.; Morgan, D. Comparison of neural network predictors in the classification of tracheal-bronchial breath sounds by respiratory auscultation. *Artif. Intell. Med.* **2004**, *31*, 211–220. [CrossRef] [PubMed]
48. Kandaswamy, A.; Kumar, C.S.; Ramanathan, R.P.; Jayaraman, S.; Malmurugan, N. Neural classification of lung sounds using wavelet coefficients. *Comput. Biol. Med.* **2004**, *34*, 523–537. [CrossRef]
49. Gnitecki, J.; Moussavi, Z.; Pasterkamp, H. Classification of lung sounds during bronchial provocation using waveform fractal dimensions. *Conf. Proc. IEEE Eng. Med. Biol. Soc.* **2004**, *2004*, 3844–3847. [CrossRef]
50. Bahoura, M.; Pelletier, C. Respiratory sounds classification using Gaussian mixture models. In Proceedings of the Canadian Conference on Electrical and Computer Engineering 2004 (IEEE Cat. No.04CH37513), Niagara Falls, ON, Canada, 2–5 May 2004; Volume 3, pp. 1309–1312. [CrossRef]
51. Chien, J.C.; Wu, H.D.; Chong, F.C.; Li, C.I. Wheeze detection using cepstral analysis in Gaussian Mixture Models. *Annu. Int. Conf. IEEE Eng. Med. Biol. Soc.* **2007**, *2007*, 3168–3171. [CrossRef] [PubMed]
52. Alsmadi, S.; Kahya, Y.P. Design of a DSP-based instrument for real-time classification of pulmonary sounds. *Comput. Biol. Med.* **2008**, *38*, 53–61. [CrossRef] [PubMed]
53. Lu, X.; Bahoura, M. An integrated automated system for crackles extraction and classification. *Biomed. Signal Process. Control.* **2008**, *3*, 244–254. [CrossRef]
54. Riella, R.J.; Nohama, P.; Maia, J.M. Method for automatic detection of wheezing in lung sounds. *Braz. J. Med Biol. Res.* **2009**, *42*, 674–684. [CrossRef] [PubMed]
55. Bahoura, M. Pattern recognition methods applied to respiratory sounds classification into normal and wheeze classes. *Comput. Biol. Med.* **2009**, *39*, 824–843. [CrossRef]
56. Matsunaga, S.; Yamauchi, K.; Yamashita, M.; Miyahara, S. Classification between normal and abnormal respiratory sounds based on maximum likelihood approach. In Proceedings of the 2009 IEEE International Conference on Acoustics, Speech and Signal Processing, Taipei, Taiwan, 19–24 April 2009; pp. 517–520. [CrossRef]
57. Mayorga, P.; Druzgalski, C.; Morelos, R.L.; González, O.H.; Vidales, J. Acoustics based assessment of respiratory diseases using GMM classification. *Annu. Int. Conf. IEEE Eng. Med. Biol. Soc.* **2010**, *2010*, 6312–6316. [CrossRef]
58. Azarbarzin, A.; Moussavi, Z. Unsupervised classification of respiratory sound signal into snore/no-snore classes. *Annu. Int. Conf. IEEE Eng. Med. Biol. Soc.* **2010**, *2010*, 3666–3669. [CrossRef]
59. Flietstra, B.; Markuzon, N.; Vyshedskiy, A.; Murphy, R. Automated analysis of crackles in patients with interstitial pulmonary fibrosis. *Pulm. Med.* **2011**, *2011*, 590506. [CrossRef]
60. Serbes, G.; Sakar, C.O.; Kahya, Y.P.; Aydin, N. Feature extraction using time-frequency/scale analysis and ensemble of feature sets for crackle detection. In Proceedings of the 2011 Annual International Conference of the IEEE Engineering in Medicine and Biology Society, Boston, MA, USA, 30 August–3 September 2011; pp. 3314–3317. [CrossRef]
61. Jin, F.; Krishnan, S.S.; Sattar, F. Adventitious sounds identification and extraction using temporal-spectral dominance-based features. *IEEE Trans. Biomed. Eng.* **2011**, *58*, 3078–3087. [CrossRef] [PubMed]
62. Charleston-Villalobos, S.; Martinez-Hernandez, G.; Gonzalez-Camarena, R.; Chi-Lem, G.; Carrillo, J.G.; Aljama-Corrales, T. Assessment of multichannel lung sounds parameterization for two-class classification in interstitial lung disease patients. *Comput. Biol. Med.* **2011**, *41*, 473–482. [CrossRef] [PubMed]

63. Yamashita, M.; Matsunaga, S.; Miyahara, S. Discrimination between healthy subjects and patients with pulmonary emphysema by detection of abnormal respiration. In Proceedings of the 2011 IEEE International Conference on Acoustics, Speech and Signal Processing (ICASSP), Prague, Czech Republic, 22–27 May 2011; pp. 693–696. [CrossRef]
64. Xie, S.; Jin, F.; Krishnan, S.; Sattar, F. Signal feature extraction by multi-scale PCA and its application to respiratory sound classification. *Med. Biol. Eng. Comput.* **2012**, *50*, 759–768. [CrossRef] [PubMed]
65. Grønnesby, M.; Solis, J.C.A.; Holsbø, E.; Melbye, H.; Bongo, L.A. Feature extraction for machine learning based crackle detection in lung sounds from a health survey. *arXiv* **2017**, arXiv:1706.00005.
66. Karimizadeh, A.; Vali, M.; Modaresi, M. Multichannel lung sound analysis to detect severity of lung disease in cystic fibrosis. *Biomed. Signal Process. Control.* **2021**, *64*, 1746–8094. [CrossRef]
67. Chung, Y.; Jin, J.; Jo, H.; Lee, H.I.; Kim, A.; Chung, S.J.; Yoon, H.J.; Park, J.; Jeon, J.Y. Diagnosis of Pneumonia by Cough Sounds Analyzed with Statistical Features and AI. *Sensors* **2021**, *21*, 7036. [CrossRef]
68. Nguyen, T.; Pernkopf, F. Crackle Detection In Lung Sounds Using Transfer Learning And Multi-Input Convolutional Neural Networks. In Proceedings of the 2021 43rd Annual International Conference of the IEEE Engineering in Medicine & Biology Society (EMBC), Guadalajara, Mexico, 1–5 November 2021; pp. 80–83. [CrossRef]
69. Ulukaya, S.; Serbes, G.; Kahya, Y.P. Resonance based separation and energy based classification of lung sounds using tunable wavelet transform. *Comput. Biol. Med.* **2021**, *131*, 104288. [CrossRef]
70. Kim, Y.; Hyon, Y.; Jung, S.S.; Lee, S.; Yoo, G.; Chung, C.; Ha, T. Respiratory sound classification for crackles, wheezes, and rhonchi in the clinical field using deep learning. *Sci. Rep.* **2021**, *11*, 17186. [CrossRef]
71. Ullah, A.; Khan, M.S.; Khan, M.U.; Mujahid, F. Automatic Classification of Lung Sounds Using Machine Learning Algorithms. In Proceedings of the 2021 International Conference on Frontiers of Information Technology (FIT), Islamabad, Pakistan, 13–14 December 2021; pp. 131–136. [CrossRef]
72. Srivastava, A.; Jain, S.; Miranda, R.; Patil, S.; Pandya, S.; Kotecha, K. Deep learning based respiratory sound analysis for detection of chronic obstructive pulmonary disease. *PeerJ Comput. Sci.* **2021**, *7*, e369. [CrossRef]
73. Rani, S.; Chaurasia, A.; Dutta, M.K.; Myska, V.; Burget, R. Machine learning approach for automatic lungs sound diagnosis from pulmonary signals. In Proceedings of the 2021 44th International Conference on Telecommunications and Signal Processing (TSP), Brno, Czech Republic, 26–28 July 2021; pp. 366–371. [CrossRef]
74. Nguyen, T.; Pernkopf, F. Lung Sound Classification Using Co-tuning and Stochastic Normalization. *IEEE Trans. Biomed. Eng.* **2022**, *69*, 2872–2882. [CrossRef]
75. Pancaldi, F.; Pezzuto, G.S.; Cassone, G.; Morelli, M.; Manfredi, A.; D'Arienzo, M.; Vacchi, C.; Savorani, F.; Vinci, G.; Barsotti, F.; et al. VECTOR: An algorithm for the detection of COVID-19 pneumonia from velcro-like lung sounds. *Comput. Biol. Med.* **2022**, *142*, 105220. [CrossRef] [PubMed]
76. Wu, Y.C.; Han, C.C.; Chang, C.S.; Chang, F.L.; Chen, S.F.; Shieh, T.Y.; Chen, H.M.; Lin, J.Y. Development of an Electronic Stethoscope and a Classification Algorithm for Cardiopulmonary Sounds. *Sensors* **2022**, *22*, 4263. [CrossRef] [PubMed]
77. Neili, Z.; Sundaraj, K. A comparative study of the spectrogram, scalogram, melspectrogram and gammatonegram time-frequency representations for the classification of lung sounds using the ICBHI database based on CNNs. *Biomed. Tech.* **2022**, *67*, 367–390. [CrossRef] [PubMed]
78. Vidhya, B.; Madhav, M.N.; Kumar, M.S.; Kalanandini, S. AI Based Diagnosis of Pneumonia. *Wirel. Pers. Commun.* **2022**, *126*, 3677–3692. [CrossRef] [PubMed]
79. Dori, G.; Bachner-Hinenzon, N.; Kasim, N.; Zaidani, H.; Perl, S.H.; Maayan, S.; Shneifi, A.; Kian, Y.; Tiosano, T.; Adler, D.; et al. A novel infrasound and audible machine-learning approach to the diagnosis of COVID-19. *ERJ Open Res.* **2022**, *8*, 00152-2022. [CrossRef] [PubMed]
80. Alqudah, A.M.; Qazan, S.; Obeidat, Y.M. Deep learning models for detecting respiratory pathologies from raw lung auscultation sounds. *Soft Comput.* **2022**, *26*, 13405–13429. [CrossRef]
81. Kwon, A.M.; Kang, K. A temporal dependency feature in lower dimension for lung sound signal classification. *Sci. Rep.* **2022**, *12*, 7889. [CrossRef]
82. MacNeil, A.; Glaziou, P.; Sismanidis, C.; Date, A.; Maloney, S.; Floyd, K. Global Epidemiology of Tuberculosis and Progress Toward Meeting Global Targets—Worldwide, 2018. *MMWR Morb. Mortal. Wkly. Rep.* **2020**, *20*, 281–285. [CrossRef]
83. Majumder, A.K.; Chowdhury, S.K. Recording and preliminary analysis of respiratory sounds from tuberculosis patients. *Med. Biol. Eng. Comput.* **1981**, *19*, 561–564. [CrossRef]
84. Becker, K.W.; Scheffer, C.; Blanckenberg, M.M.; Diacon, A.H. Analysis of adventitious lung sounds originating from pulmonary tuberculosis. *Annu. Int. Conf. IEEE Eng. Med. Biol. Soc.* **2013**, *2013*, 4334–4337. [CrossRef]
85. Naqvi, S.Z.H.; Choudhry, M.A. An Automated System for Classification of Chronic Obstructive Pulmonary Disease and Pneumonia Patients Using Lung Sound Analysis. *Sensors* **2020**, *20*, 6512. [CrossRef]
86. McCollum, E.D.; Park, D.E.; Watson, N.L.; Fancourt, N.S.S.; Focht, C.; Baggett, H.C.; Brooks, W.A.; Howie, S.R.C.; Kotloff, K.L.; Levine, O.S.; et al. Digital auscultation in PERCH: Associations with chest radiography and pneumonia mortality in children. *Pediatr. Pulmonol.* **2020**, *55*, 3197–3208. [CrossRef] [PubMed]
87. Wood, W.B.; Gloyne, S.R. Pulmonary asbestosis complicated by pulmonary tuberculosis. *Lancet* **1931**, *218*, 954–956. [CrossRef]
88. Smither, W.J. Secular changes in asbestosis in an asbestos factory. *Ann. N. Y. Acad. Sci.* **1965**, *132*, 166–181. [CrossRef] [PubMed]

89. Horimasu, Y.; Ohshimo, S.; Yamaguchi, K.; Sakamoto, S.; Masuda, T.; Nakashima, T.; Miyamoto, S.; Iwamoto, H.; Fujitaka, K.; Hamada, H.; et al. A machine-learning based approach to quantify fine crackles in the diagnosis of interstitial pneumonia: A proof-of-concept study. *Medicine* **2021**, *100*, e24738. [CrossRef] [PubMed]
90. Manfredi, A.; Cassone, G.; Cerri, S.; Venerito, V.; Fedele, A.L.; Trevisani, M.; Furini, F.; Addimanda, O.; Pancaldi, F.; Della, C.G.; et al. Diagnostic accuracy of a velcro sound detector (VECTOR) for interstitial lung disease in rheumatoid arthritis patients: The InSPIRAtE validation study (INterStitial pneumonia in rheumatoid ArThritis with an electronic device). *BMC Pulm. Med.* **2019**, *19*, 111. [CrossRef] [PubMed]
91. Piirilä, P.; Lehtola, H.; Zitting, A.; Kivisaari, L.; Koskinen, H.; Luukkonen, R.; Salo, S.P.; Vehmas, T.; Nordman, H.; Sovijärvi, A.R. Lung sounds in asbestos induced pulmonary disorders. *Eur. Respir. J.* **2000**, *16*, 901–908. [CrossRef]
92. Sanchez-Perez, J.A.; Berkebile, J.A.; Nevius, B.N.; Ozmen, G.C.; Nichols, C.J.; Ganti, V.G.; Mabrouk, S.A.; Clifford, G.D.; Kamaleswaran, R.; Wright, D.W.; et al. A Wearable Multimodal Sensing System for Tracking Changes in Pulmonary Fluid Status, Lung Sounds, and Respiratory Markers. *Sensors* **2022**, *22*, 1130. [CrossRef]
93. Altan, G.; Kutlu, Y.; Allahverdi, N. Deep Learning on Computerized Analysis of Chronic Obstructive Pulmonary Disease. *IEEE IEEE J. Biomed. Heal. Inform.* **2019**, *24*, 1344–1350. [CrossRef]
94. Fernandez-Granero, M.A.; Sanchez-Morillo, D.; Leon-Jimenez, A. Computerised Analysis of Telemonitored Respiratory Sounds for Predicting Acute Exacerbations of COPD. *Sensors* **2015**, *15*, 26978–26996. [CrossRef]
95. Jácome, C.; Marques, A. Computerized Respiratory Sounds: Novel Outcomes for Pulmonary Rehabilitation in COPD. *Respir. Care* **2017**, *62*, 199–208. [CrossRef]
96. Islam, M.A.; Bandyopadhyaya, I.; Bhattacharyya, P.; Saha, G. Multichannel lung sound analysis for asthma detection. *Comput Methods Programs Biomed.* **2018**, *159*, 111–123. [CrossRef]
97. Oliveira, A.; Sen, I.; Kahya, Y.P.; Afreixo, V.; Marques, A. Computerised respiratory sounds can differentiate smokers and non-smokers. *J. Clin. Monit. Comput.* **2016**, *31*, 571–580. [CrossRef]
98. Malik, N.A.; Idris, W.; Gunawan, T.S.; Olanrewaju, R.F.; Ibrahim, S.N. Classification of Normal and Crackles Respiratory Sounds into Healthy and Lung Cancer Groups. *Int. J. Electr. Comput. Eng.* **2018**, *8*, 1530–1538. [CrossRef]
99. Shi, Y.; Yang, Z.; Xie, F.; Ren, S.; Xu, S. The Research Progress of Electrical Impedance Tomography for Lung Monitoring. *Front. Bioeng. Biotechnol.* **2021**, *9*, 726652. [CrossRef] [PubMed]
100. Frerichs, I.; Hahn, G.; Schiffmann, H.; Berger, C.; Hellige, G. Monitoring Regional Lung Ventilation by Functional Electrical Impedance Tomography during Assisted Ventilation. *Ann. N. Y. Acad. Sci.* **1999**, *873*, 493–505. [CrossRef] [PubMed]
101. Victorino, J.A.; Borges, J.B.; Okamoto, V.N.; Matos, G.F.; Tucci, M.R.; Caramez, M.P.; Tanaka, H.; Sipmann, F.S.; Santos, D.C.; Barbas, C.S.; et al. Imbalances in regional lung ventilation: A validation study on electrical impedance tomography. *Am. J. Respir. Crit. Care Med.* **2004**, *169*, 791–800. [CrossRef]
102. Costa, E.L.V.; Chaves, C.N.; Gomes, S.; Beraldo, M.A.; Volpe, M.S.; Tucci, M.R.; Schettino, I.A.L.; Bohm, S.H.; Carvalho, C.R.; Tanaka, H.; et al. Real-time detection of pneumothorax using electrical impedance tomography. *Crit. Care Med.* **2008**, *36*, 1230–1238. [CrossRef]
103. Yang, D.; Gu, C.; Gu, Y.; Zhang, X.; Ge, D.; Zhang, Y.; Wang, N.; Zheng, X.; Wang, H.; Yang, L.; et al. Electrical Impedance Analysis for Lung Cancer: A Prospective, Multicenter, Blind Validation Study. *Front. Oncol.* **2022**, *12*, 900110. [CrossRef] [PubMed]
104. Moloney, B.M.; McAnena, P.F.; Abd Elwahab, S.M.; Fasoula, A.; Duchesne, L.; Gil Cano, J.D.; Glynn, C.; O'Connell, A.; Ennis, R.; Lowery, A.J.; et al. Microwave imaging in breast cancer–results from the first-in-human clinical investigation of the wavelia system. *Acad. Radiol.* **2022**, *29*, S211–S222. [CrossRef]
105. Töpfer, F.; Oberhammer, J. Microwave Cancer Diagnosis. In *Principles and Applications of RF/Microwave in Healthcare and Biosensing*; Academic Press: Cambridge, MA, USA, 2017; pp. 103–149.
106. Gopalakrishnan, K.; Adhikari, A.; Pallipamu, N.; Singh, M.; Nusrat, T.; Gaddam, S.; Samaddar, P.; Rajagopal, A.; Cherukuri, A.S.S.; Yadav, A.; et al. Applications of Microwaves in Medicine Leveraging Artificial Intelligence: Future Perspectives. *Electronics* **2023**, *12*, 1101. [CrossRef]
107. Lin, X.; Gong, Z.; Ding, Y.; Chen, Y.; Sosa, P.A.V.; Sosa, M.J.V. Feasibility Study of Detection of Coronavirus Disease 2019 with Microwave Medical Imaging. In Proceedings of the 2021 15th European Conference on Antennas and Propagation (EuCAP), Dusseldorf, Germany, 22–26 March 2021; pp. 1–4. [CrossRef]
108. Khalesi, B.; Khalid, B.; Ghavami, N.; Raspa, G.; Ghavami, M.; Dudley-McEvoy, S.; Tiberi, G. A Microwave Imaging Procedure for Lung Lesion Detection: Preliminary Results on Multilayer Phantoms. *Electronics* **2022**, *11*, 2105. [CrossRef]
109. Ertek, D.; Gökhan, K.; Egemen, B. A Microwave Imaging Scheme for Detection of Pulmonary Edema and Hemorrhage. In Proceedings of the 2022 30th Signal Processing and Communications Applications Conference (SIU), Safranbolu, Turkey, 15–18 May 2022; pp. 1–4.
110. Babarinde, O.J.; Jamlos, M.F.; Soh, P.J.; Schreurs, D.M.M.-P.; Beyer, A. Microwave imaging technique for lung tumour detection. In Proceedings of the 2016 German Microwave Conference (GeMiC), Bochum, Germany, 14–16 March 2016; pp. 100–103. [CrossRef]
111. Zhang, J.; Zhang, X.; Wei, X.; Xue, Y.; Wan, H.; Wang, P. Recent advances in acoustic wave biosensors for the detection of disease-related biomarkers: A review. *Anal. Chim. Acta* **2021**, *1164*, 338321. [CrossRef] [PubMed]
112. Maskay, A.; Da Cunha, M.P. High-Temperature Microwave Acoustic Vibration Sensor. In Proceedings of the 2018 IEEE International Ultrasonics Symposium (IUS), Kobe, Japan, 22–25 October 2018; pp. 1–3. [CrossRef]

113. Hui, X.; Sharma, P.; Kan, E.C. Microwave Stethoscope for Heart Sound by Near-Field Coherent Sensing. In Proceedings of the 2019 IEEE MTT-S International Microwave Symposium (IMS), Boston, MA, USA, 2–7 June 2019; pp. 365–368. [CrossRef]
114. Kumar, R. Remote Acoustic Detection System Using Microwave Signals. 2006. Available online: https://www.researchgate.net/publication/230807188_Remote_Acoustic_Detection_System_using_Microwave_Signals (accessed on 31 December 2022).

sensors

Review

Practicing Digital Gastroenterology through Phonoenterography Leveraging Artificial Intelligence: Future Perspectives Using Microwave Systems

Renisha Redij [1], Avneet Kaur [2], Pratyusha Muddaloor [3], Arshia K. Sethi [3], Keirthana Aedma [3], Anjali Rajagopal [4], Keerthy Gopalakrishnan [1,2], Ashima Yadav [4], Devanshi N. Damani [5,6], Victor G. Chedid [3], Xiao Jing Wang [3], Christopher A. Aakre [4], Alexander J. Ryu [4] and Shivaram P. Arunachalam [1,2,3,4,7,*]

1 GIH Artificial Intelligence Laboratory (GAIL), Division of Gastroenterology and Hepatology, Department of Medicine, Mayo Clinic, Rochester, MN 55905, USA
2 Microwave Engineering and Imaging Laboratory (MEIL), Division of Gastroenterology and Hepatology, Department of Medicine, Mayo Clinic, Rochester, MN 55905, USA
3 Division of Gastroenterology and Hepatology, Mayo Clinic, Rochester, MN 55905, USA
4 Department of Medicine, Mayo Clinic, Rochester, MN 55905, USA
5 Department of Cardiovascular Medicine, Mayo Clinic, Rochester, MN 55905, USA
6 Department of Internal Medicine, Texas Tech University Health Science Center, El Paso, TX 79995, USA
7 Department of Radiology, Mayo Clinic, Rochester, MN 55905, USA
* Correspondence: poigaiarunachalam.shivaram@mayo.edu

Abstract: Production of bowel sounds, established in the 1900s, has limited application in existing patient-care regimes and diagnostic modalities. We review the physiology of bowel sound production, the developments in recording technologies and the clinical application in various scenarios, to understand the potential of a bowel sound recording and analysis device—the phonoenterogram in future gastroenterological practice. Bowel sound production depends on but is not entirely limited to the type of food consumed, amount of air ingested and the type of intestinal contractions. Recording technologies for extraction and analysis of these include the wavelet-based filtering, autoregressive moving average model, multivariate empirical mode decompression, radial basis function network, two-dimensional positional mapping, neural network model and acoustic biosensor technique. Prior studies evaluate the application of bowel sounds in conditions such as intestinal obstruction, acute appendicitis, large bowel disorders such as inflammatory bowel disease and bowel polyps, ascites, post-operative ileus, sepsis, irritable bowel syndrome, diabetes mellitus, neurodegenerative disorders such as Parkinson's disease and neonatal conditions such as hypertrophic pyloric stenosis. Recording and analysis of bowel sounds using artificial intelligence is crucial for creating an accessible, inexpensive and safe device with a broad range of clinical applications. Microwave-based digital phonoenterography has huge potential for impacting GI practice and patient care.

Keywords: phonoenterogram; PEG; computer-aided auscultation; bowel sounds; artificial intelligence; microwave telemetry; microwave acoustic sensors; gastroenterology; digital health

Citation: Redij, R.; Kaur, A.; Muddaloor, P.; Sethi, A.K.; Aedma, K.; Rajagopal, A.; Gopalakrishnan, K.; Yadav, A.; Damani, D.N.; Chedid, V.G.; et al. Practicing Digital Gastroenterology through Phonoenterography Leveraging Artificial Intelligence: Future Perspectives Using Microwave Systems. *Sensors* **2023**, *23*, 2302. https://doi.org/10.3390/s23042302

Academic Editor: Christian Baumgartner

Received: 1 January 2023
Revised: 10 February 2023
Accepted: 16 February 2023
Published: 18 February 2023

1. Introduction

Gastrointestinal diseases have significant implications on morbidity, mortality and quality of life in affected individuals. For instance, functional gastrointestinal diseases that produce symptoms, without any structural or visible pathological lesions, affect more than 40% people worldwide, according to a large multinational survey [1]. Irritable bowel syndrome (IBS) is a chronic functional disorder [2] that is diagnosed after excluding other medical conditions and fulfilling a clinical criterion. The lack of a definite test for IBS makes it a challenge for both physicians and patients, with the latter often undergoing extensive testing to rule out medical conditions, leading to higher expenditures and lower quality of life [3,4].

Similarly, managerial gaps exist in conditions such as post-operative ileus (POI) and intestinal obstruction. POI refers to disruption of normal bowel motility following surgery, leading to obstipation and intolerance to oral intake [5]. Physicians typically rely on clinical signs such as passage of flatus and intestinal auscultation to decide on the time to start oral feeds [6]. However, this method may not be reliable indicator as it is difficult to determine in unconscious patients and patients with prolonged POI and depends on subjective interpretation of clinical signs and clinical experience [7]. Imaging modalities can be used in these cases, but they increase radiation exposure and have limitations subject to availability. In emergent conditions such as intestinal obstruction, guidelines suggest plain X-ray or an abdominal CT scan for diagnostic confirmation [8]. While this is a reliable method, it presents time constrains for patients with unstable vitals who are often taken directly into surgery without any preliminary testing.

Furthermore, in chronic conditions such as ulcerative colitis (UC) and Crohn's disease (CD), frequent longitudinal monitoring with endoscopy is required to track severity and guide management protocols [9]. With the number of endoscopies increasing every year and countries such as the United States reporting 22.2 million endoscopies in 2021 [10], there is an increased burden on the healthcare system. Invasive procedures such as endoscopies increase the risk of infection and perforation in individuals [11]. In addition, they are costly, require substantial healthcare personnel, and are not a feasible option in resource limited settings. Therefore, there is an urgent need for alternative diagnostic modalities that relieve pressure on the healthcare system, reduce the number of invasive procedures on patients requiring frequent monitoring, are safe, cost-effective, and easily accessible and available, which can help in timely diagnosis and guide management.

In the search for a solution to the existing problems, there has been increasing research in the recent past to utilize bowel sounds (BS) as a new diagnostic tool. However, intestinal auscultation, which once drew considerable interest [12–14], is sparsely used in clinical practice today due to a lack of standardized recording technologies, interpersonal variations in interpretations, and poor understanding of the underlying physiology and clinical applications [15]. The term 'phonoenterography' was coined by Watson and Knox [16] in 1967 to describe the recording and analysis of BS. In the recent past, significant improvements have been made in developing a recording device that accurately detects and defines BS while differentiating it from other acoustic signals from the body. Moreover, there has been significant research in developing computer aided auscultation (CAA) [17,18] to reduce the interpersonal variability and subjective bias. Several review papers [19,20] have summarized the advancements in recording technologies with the latest studies using wireless devices [21,22] to record and transmit data. Analysis of BS can be used for diagnosis and or management of common gastrointestinal conditions such as intestinal obstruction [23], acute appendicitis [24], inflammatory bowel disease [25], diverticular disease [25], bowel polyps [25], ascites [26], post-operative complications and critical care [27] and irritable bowel syndrome [17]. It has also used in management of diabetes mellitus [28,29], neurodegenerative disorders [30] and the diagnosis of infantile hypertrophic pyloric stenosis [31].

While existing literature highlights the need for this technology, it fails to provide a clear understanding of the mechanism of BS production, its clinical usability, and the future of using a digital BS detector using a microwave-based sensor for recording phonoenterogram (PEG). The purpose of this review was to study the physiology of BS origin, factors affecting its frequency, clinical applications and recording technologies in existing literature. Additionally, this review reflects on the prospects of using microwave-based systems for PEG and its impact on transforming gastroenterological practice for improving patient care.

2. Physiology

The physiology of bowel sounds dates back to early 1900s where a detained explanation was given by Cannon [12], Plessis [13] and Milton [14]. Currently, we do not have an exact mechanism for the production of bowel sounds, but a majority suggest that intestinal motility is the primary origin [12–14]. Gut motility, contents of the gastrointestinal lumen and the presence of gas have been hypothesized as the major contributing factors [32–35]. Air that is consumed with food reaches the lumen of the gut, where gut motility leads to constant formation and resolution of gas bubbles [33] that generate sound in various portions of the gastrointestinal tract [36] (Figure 1) [37].

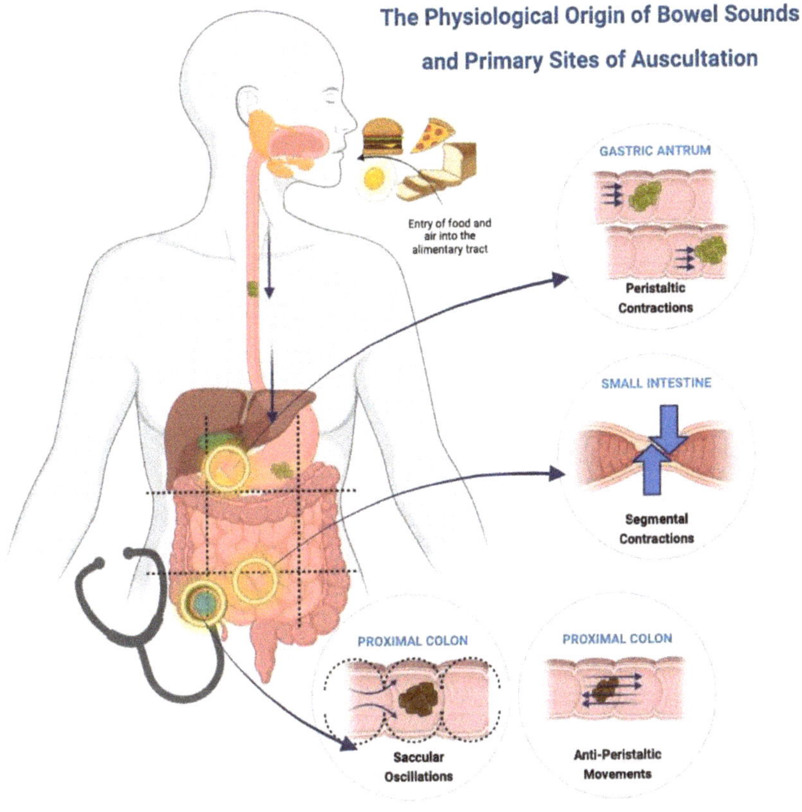

Figure 1. Physiological origin of bowel sounds and primary sites of auscultation.

2.1. Gastric and Pyloroduodenal Region

Food reaches the stomach and is pushed forward via peristaltic movements towards the pylorus [1]. The frequency of gastric peristalsis and pyloric sphincter relaxation do not coincide, leading to food hitting against the closed sphincter, which produces a loud, explosive sound described as 'bursting of bubbles' [12]. Peristaltic waves occur around 3 times per minute or every 20 s as cited by Plessis [13] and confirmed by Moritz's experiment on himself [12]. These propulsive movements are normally painless but can produce pain with an exaggerated sound in intestinal obstruction [13].

2.2. Small Intestine

The bolus of food in the small intestine is broken down into smaller fragments by segmental contractions of the circular muscles that occur about seven to twelve times a minute [13]. These contractions push the food forward and backward to allow mixing of the food with the intestinal secretions. Thus, a large number of contractions are required in the small intestine to propel the food forward. Additionally, intestinal motility is affected by bowel tone [12], creating a pressure gradient with higher tone in the upper gut as compared to the lower, aiding in downward movement of the food. Bowel sounds arising from the small intestinal have three distinctive features, namely [12]: (i) Pattern—slowly rising and gradually subsiding, or slowly rising with a peak and sudden drop, or sharply rising and gradually dropping; (ii) Rhythm—each bowel sound lasts for two to three seconds with multiple sounds occurring in same location for several minutes; and (iii) Intensity—loud sounds due to the presence of *valvulae conniventes* that alter the luminal diameter and contribute to pressure changes.

2.3. Ileocecal Region and Colon

Movements in the proximal colon are explained by two theories, namely anti-peristalsis and saccular oscillations. The food moving from the ileum to the caecum acts as a stimulus causing the caecum to contract and form a blind pouch which temporarily prevents the progression of food, creating a high-pressure zone. Food is pushed back towards the caecum due to this pressure gradient, and it strikes the ileocecal valve, thus producing a sound. This phenomenon is called anti-peristalsis [12,14]. The colon has numerous sacculae which produce oscillatory movements with the intestinal contents and contract to push the contents into the next sacculi. This phenomenon allows churning of the food and produces a sound described as a continuous popping and gurgling noise. Some researchers [12,38] believe the saccular oscillations contribute more to the bowel sound production than antiperistalsis. The right lower quadrant is a point of auscultation due to more activity in the ileocecal and proximal colon, as compared to the distal colon. Contractions from the distal colon push the contents forward and produce crackling noises followed by an urge to pass flatus [12].

Although bowel sound production and intestinal motility have been closely linked, there are studies that contradict this theory as bowel sounds have been recorded in abdominal quadrants independent of peristalsis, indicating they may not be a combined event [39]. Tomomasa et al. [40] suggested bowel sounds are a result of the transfer of energy between the contents of the lumen rather than propulsion. This phenomenon occurs during the second phase of migrating motor complex (MMC) in a fasting state. MMC refers to the motor activity of the intestine with three phases, namely quiescent motor, irregular and regular pattern of contractions [41]. Another study [42] suggested myoelectrical slow wave and spike burst activity of the intestine as the etiology leading to bowel sound production. Dual peaks of bowel sounds are heard after consumption of food [32,43,44]. The first occurs immediately after the meal and is hypothesized to be due to swallowed air forming intraluminal gas. The second occurs an hour later, which coincides with gastric emptying. The stomach is the most active site of bowel sound production, followed by the colon and then the small bowel [34]. Short frequency high amplitude sounds are produced in the colon whereas higher frequency sounds originate from the stomach. Sometimes a loud rumble [45] can be heard from the abdomen, which can be due to a pathological cause such as gut hypertrophy or due to physiological nervous air swallowing.

3. Effect of Modifiable and Non-Modifiable Factors on Bowel Sounds

Studies have researched the effect of various modifiable and non-modifiable factors on bowel sounds. Knowledge pertaining to these factors can help propagate further research in the following scenarios:

3.1. Serum 5-Hydroxytryptamine

Serum 5-Hydroxytryptamine (5-HT) is produced by the intestine in response to pressure changes and intestinal epithelium deformation. Increased bowel motility leads to increased release of 5-HT into the blood, producing intestinal symptoms in carcinoid syndrome [46]. 5-HT thus acts as a local hormone causing excessive loud bowel sounds known as borborygmi [46].

3.2. Medications

Tomomasa et al. [40] studied the relationship between gastrointestinal sounds and small intestinal motility. Their results concluded that the sum of sound index (SI) coincides with the gastric phase of migrating motor complex, with a lower SI seen in somatostatin [31,40] and scopolamine (due to decreased antral contraction and delayed gastric time respectively). A higher SI is seen with erythromycin and metoclopramide (due to increased antral contraction and shorter transit time, respectively). Gut stimulants such as carbachol and magnesium sulphate lead to an increased production of bowel sounds [46]. Furthermore, Martin et al. [47] studied the effect of anti-spasmodic drugs, oxybutynin and dicyclomine on gastrointestinal activity using a microphone with a panasonic recorder embedded in a polystyrene cotton-padded box. A decrease in bowel sounds following drug administration was noted. Another study by Emoto et al. [48], using autoregressive moving average (ARMA) spectrum to study the effect of mosapride, found a decreased sound to sound interval with increasing plasma concentrations of mosapride and peak gut activity. They concluded that this technique was highly sensitive and specific to detect bowel sounds.

3.3. Morphine

The post-operative course of a patient is determined by the status of bowel function and tolerability of feeds. Morphine and meperidine, used for postoperative pain control, decrease gut motility by inhibiting myoelectric complexes in the small intestine and colon [49]. A positive correlation [50] between the quantity of morphine used and the time of the return of bowel sounds, first flatus, and first bowel movement was found. However, there was no correlation between incision length and bowel motility. Limited use of morphine is recommended to attain early return of bowel function [50].

3.4. Coffee and Soda

Recreational drinks such as coffee and soda can be used for the treatment of constipation [51]. Coffee produces gastrin hormone in the pyloric antrum, whereas the carbon dioxide in the soda produces intraluminal gas that creates pressure in the gastrointestinal tract leading to increased gut motility [51,52]. Additionally, soda excites the trigeminal neurons in the tongue that stimulates the dorsal vagus nucleus in the brainstem, further activating the visceral sensory neurons to promote gut motility [53].

3.5. Stress

Holtmann and Enck noted that physical and physiological stressors lead to increased non-propulsive contractions of the esophagus, decreased antral motility of the stomach, decreased migrating motor complexes in the small intestine and an increased motor spike activity in the colon [54].

3.6. Age and Gender

Gastrointestinal motility is affected by non-modmodifiable factors such as age and gender. Safronov et al. [18] used computerised phonoenterography(CPEG) to study various sound indices (amplitude, frequency and duration) in different age groups and recorded the peristaltic sounds as gastric images. High fasting CPEG indices were seen in those between 6–9 years, whereas weak post-meal bowel motility and low motor evacuation was seen in ages 6–15 years. However, no significant difference between gender was seen.

4. Clinical Application of Bowel Sounds

Recording and analysis of bowel sounds using a phonoenterogram can function as a diagnostic modality and aid in the management of various clinical conditions (Figure 2) [37]. Some clinical scenarios for application of bowel sounds are described below:

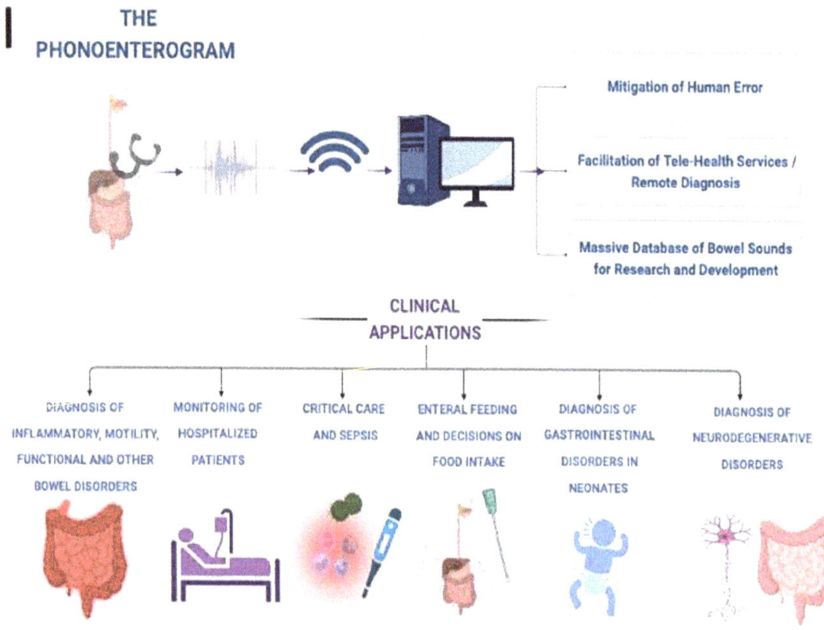

Figure 2. Potential clinical applications of digital phonoenterography.

4.1. Acute Appendicitis

Local inflammation around the appendix influences peristalsis, resulting in changes of bowel sound character [59,60]. The literature suggests that one-fourth of the patients undergoing appendicectomy have a normal appendix at operation [24]. Abdominal auscultation to analyze bowel sound features can aid in diagnosis to prevent unnecessary abdominal surgeries in such patients. Arnbjörnsson et al. [24] recorded bowel sounds pre and post appendicectomy in clinically diagnosed patients and found patients with gangrenous appendix to have a significant difference in pre- and post-operative median height of spike frequency, whereas patients with normal appendix had no significant difference in the two groups. Furthermore, this study stressed the importance of repeated recordings to avoid variations produced by abdominal movements such as breathing or muscle contractions which tend to affect the amplitude and frequency of bowel sound recording.

4.2. Large Bowel Disorders

Bowel sound features have been studied in pathologies of the large intestine such as Crohn's disease, ulcerative colitis, diverticular disease, and bowel polyps [61]. Hadjileontiadis et al. [61] studied scatter plots of higher order crossings, and found an overlap between post-polypectomy patients and healthy subjects, suggesting bowel sounds as a potential scale to determine the efficacy of the surgical procedure. Inflammatory bowel disease (IBD) is a chronic condition requiring repeated testing using colonoscopies [9], thus the need for a non-invasive modality for long-term monitoring of the disorder should be stressed. A case-control study by Craine et al. [25] using EnteroTach analysis found the sound-to-sound interval (SSI) to be shortest in irritable bowel syndrome (IBS), followed by Crohn's disease and largest in healthy controls. However, this study lacked specificity as patients with Crohn's disease having concurrent IBS symptoms were not considered. A study [62] comparing 2-min bowel sound recording in patients with IBD and drug-induced motility with mosapride and senna using EnteroTach analysis found no significant different in the sound-to-sound interval of both groups. The study concluded that the method fails to diagnose hyper-motility conditions and requires a longer recording interval.

Therefore, further research is required to establish the diagnostic yield of bowel sounds in this scenario.

4.3. Ascites

Ascites [43,44] refers to the collection of fluid in the abdominal cavity that is a sequel to decompensated liver cirrhosis. The third spacing of the fluid causes hypovolemia and alters the hemodynamic status, warranting swift diagnosis. Moderate to severe ascites is diagnosed with a bedside examination, but smaller volumes require imaging modalities. The abdominal ultrasound [63] can study fluid volume greater than 100 mL, but its results are affected by obesity, abdominal mass or distension. Computed tomography scans are an effective diagnostic modality but are not cost-effective. Liatsos et al. [26] studied bowel sound analysis for non-invasive diagnosis of small volume ascites using scatter plots of higher order crossings, which resulted in a significant difference in the bowel sound pattern amongst cases versus healthy controls. However, the small study sample could not determine the sensitivity and specificity of the technique.

4.4. Post-Operative Complications and Critical Care

Abdominal surgery increases the risk of complications such as post-operative ileus (POI), and infection and sepsis [27,64]. Post-operative ileus is the decreased intestinal activity due to surgery and anesthesia on bowel motility [13,27]. After surgery, bowel motility is characterized by initial segmental sounds, followed by gradual progression to propulsive sounds that mark the return to normal [13]. Anesthesia used during surgery affects bowel motility [64] and causes an immediate decrease in bowel sounds after surgery with a return to the normal state 3 h later. Kaneshiro et al. [27] used abdominal vibrations and acoustic signals to calculate intestinal rate in patients with post-operative ileus versus normal bowel recovery and found a significantly low intestinal rate in POI cases. Bowel sound analysis can be used for assessing gut activity to guide timely initiation of enteral feeds [65] and administration of purgatives and enema [13] to allow faster recovery from surgery. Additionally, bowel sounds can also be used to measure of severity of post-operative sepsis and guide management strategies. A study [66] noted that gastrointestinal motility decreases with increasing severity of sepsis that was gauged by the level of interleukin-6. Management with oral steroids increased the gastrointestinal motility and proved the treatment to be effective.

Auscultation of bowel sounds in critically ill patients is a valuable tool but has a subjective nature with technical limitations [67]. Although physicians can diagnose ileus by the auscultation of bowel sounds [6], the conventional stethoscope has been unreliable in promptly detecting ileus, with poor sensitivity with low positive predictive value [7,27,65]. Additionally, a noisy environment in the intensive care unit (ICU) makes it even more difficult to auscultate effectively [7]. Bowel sounds may not be a true measure [68] of gastrointestinal function in patients on mechanical ventilation and neuromuscular blocking agents as they swallow little air leading to a decreased intraluminal gas production. A study [69] found bowel sounds to have no association between flatus, bowel activity or tolerance to oral feeds in patients who underwent abdominal surgery and concluded the method was unreliable for determining time to start oral feeds and resolution of postoperative ileus. Similarly, Massey [70] found no association between bowel sounds and return of bowel activity after postoperative ileus, thus doubting the application of this science. Another study also observed some ICU patients with ileus showing the presence of bowel sounds instead of absence [71]. Thus, the discrepancies in literature and technical difficulties encourage the need for further research on pathophysiology and recording technologies [72].

4.5. Irritable Bowel Syndrome

Irritable bowel syndrome (IBS) is a chronic functional gastrointestinal disorder [2] characterized by abdominal pain associated with change in stool consistency and frequency, with no structural pathology on endoscopy. IBS is a clinical diagnosis based on patient's symptoms. Most patients commonly undergo invasive testing with colonoscopies to rule out other disorders before being diagnosed with IBS [9]. The lack of definite testing negatively impacts the affected population causing mental and financial strain [3,73]. Bowel sounds can be used for non-invasive monitoring of gastrointestinal activity in patients with severe diarrhea by recording the vibrations on the surface of the abdomen and processing the signals from the system with a computer [74]. Several studies have tested analysis of bowel sounds to be a potential diagnostic modality for IBS [4,17,25,48,61,73,75]. Craine et al. [17] in a case-control study noted a decreased fasting sound to sound interval (SSI) in IBS cases that was comparable to the decreased post-meal SSI in healthy controls. However, a similar average intensity and frequency of bowel sounds was noted in both groups. Bowel sounds have been extensively studied in IBS patients using computerized auscultation, two-dimensional positional mapping and enterotachogram analysis [25,61,75]. Patients with IBS had a short SSI as compared to healthy volunteers and IBD cases [25]. A significant increase in low frequency sounds was seen in healthy volunteers as compared to functional bowel disorders [75]. Studies [48,73] have found an increased post-meal bowel sounds with a higher density noted in healthy subjects when compared to IBS cases. Upon two-dimensional mapping, the right lower quadrant and mid-upper abdomen were the most active areas of bowel sound production. Further research is needed to identify specific bowel sound characteristics in IBS to formulate a diagnostic modality.

4.6. *Diabetes Mellitus*

Optimal blood glucose regulation is important for normal function of the vital organs [76]. Patients with diabetes mellitus must balance their caloric intake to avoid fluctuations in blood glucose that are affected by physiological factors such as time of food intake, the type of food, exercise, sleep, stress and digestion [29]. Bowel sounds can be studied to understand the post-meal gastrointestinal motility [77] in diabetics and healthy subjects. In diabetic patients, both the sound index (SI) and motility index (MI) decreases, while healthy subjects have an increased SI and MI observed in the gastroduodenal region compared to intestinal region.

An artificial pancreas system [28] is a device comprising a measuring unit that continuously monitors blood glucose to determine the appropriate time and amount of insulin bolus needed. Currently this device fails to measure the effect of dynamic physiological factors on blood glucose [78–80]. Mamun and Khandaker et al. [28,29] integrated a bowel sound measuring device within this system to record the digestive state and aid in insulin control. The device detects acoustic vibrations from the bowel for real-time monitoring of food ingestion and intestinal motility, and offers a meal notification feature within the insulin pump to notify the patients of their blood glucose levels [28].

4.7. *Neurodegenerative Disorders*

The dorsal motor nucleus of the vagus nerve [81] forms the parasympathetic nerve supply to the upper gastrointestinal tract mainly the stomach. Neurodegenerative conditions such as Parkinson's disease, multiple system atrophy and progressive supranuclear palsy damage this nucleus leading to gastroparesis. The slow forward movement of food significantly decreases the bowel sounds in such cases as compared to healthy controls [30]. Assessing bowel motility in these patients allows for timely intervention and prevents further complications.

4.8. *Neonates*

Premature or low birth-weight infants have an immature digestive system and are prone to various gastrointestinal abnormalities [82] such as necrotizing enterocolitis (NEC), vomiting, gastroesophageal reflux, pulmonary aspiration of gastric contents, electrolyte abnormalities, allergies, birth defects, enzyme deficiencies, systemic illnesses, infection, abnormal vascular supply and obstruction. Radiological techniques, although highly specific, delay the time of diagnosis and cannot be used for gastrointestinal monitoring. Hill et al. [82,83] recorded bowel sounds to continuously monitor and relay information to the physician for timely prevention of complications and diagnosis, as well as to determine the appropriate time for enteral nutrition as the premature gut is prone to rejection. A study [84] showed bowel sounds to have high accuracy in diagnosing early stages of NEC development. Tele-diagnostic ability for recording infantile bowel sounds at home using a smartphone and relaying these smartphone data to the clinician is yet another leveraging factor. Pyloric stenosis, an obstructive condition characterized by a hypertrophic gastric outlet has an excellent prognosis when detected early. It is surgically treated by pyloromyotomy, the effectiveness of which can be monitored by recording bowel sounds [31]. Fewer bowel sounds are heard prior to the procedure, due to the obstructive nature of the disease and delayed gastric emptying. The gut sounds reach their normal frequency 48–72 h post-operation. Hence, bowel sounds can be easily used as a reflection of severity of illness, aid in monitoring the post-operative status and help determine time to commence post-operative feeding.

5. Auscultation and Recording Technologies

Although auscultation forms an integral part of bedside clinical examination, the use of a stethoscope for listening to the abdominal sounds has limited use. This can be attributed to the poor quality of the recording device and interference by surrounding noise [85,86]. A suction microphone with a crystal inset and phonocardiogram amplifier [16] was used in the 1960s to determine peristalsis in order to diagnose motility disorders. However, the need for simultaneous recording of sound and motility limited the use of this device. Various changes in the structure of stethoscope have been made since the 20th century to improve the quality of auscultation. The primitive stethoscopes with a microphone-based sensor [87–89] relied on power supply and was highly sensitive to airborne noise. Using a similar device, real-time monitoring [90] of intestinal motility was obtained from single or multiple bursts pattern of bowel sounds. Soon, non-contact microphones [91,92] were used, but required longer duration of recording making it uncomfortable for the patient. Other modifications that followed were skin adhering stethoscopes [93] and stethoscopes with a diaphragm replaced by a piezoelectric transducer [74]. Bray et al. [94] studied the workings of the transducer device during fasting and post-meals. He noted 500 to 700 Hz epigastric sounds during fasting, a low gastric activity in the inter-digestive state and an increase in the gastric and intestinal sounds post-meals.

Electronic stethoscopes can be used to study conditions of acute abdomen [95] as well as to differentiate patients [96] with small bowel obstruction and postoperative ileus. However, the technique was ineffective due to variability in auditory characteristics across clinicians and surgeons. Although studies [58] show inter-physician agreement in categorizing auscultated bowel sounds into normal and pathological, it cannot be applied clinically due to physician inconvenience. Eventually, all the conventional recording technologies were proved insignificant [97] due to dependence on the operator's knowledge, interruptions by the surrounding air, need for longer supervision, and poor detection of low amplitude bowel sounds. Bowel sound auscultation was digitally revolutionized with the development of computerized bowel sound detectors coupled to microphone-based sensors. These devices were able to adequately detect subtypes of bowel sounds with accurate start and end points [98]. Single burst (SB), multiple bursts (MB), continuous random sound (CRS) and harmonic sound (HS) patterns were recognized that were previously not detected by any device [98].

The drawbacks of auscultation include a lack of specific guidelines for the area and duration of auscultation. Some scientists state no specific site for bowel sound auscultation [99–101] as sounds generated from any location could radiate to the entire abdomen, whereas some [102,103] proposed specific auscultating regions. The advised auscultation duration varies from 30 s to 7 min [102,104,105], preferably prior to palpation [106,107] as it may stimulate peristalsis [99]. However, a recent study [108] found no difference in bowel sounds before and after palpation. An attempt [109] to localize the source of bowel sounds using absorbent and non-absorbent sound propagation models found majority of the sounds [110] in mid-lower and the right lower abdomen. A similar association with the right lower quadrant was revealed by Wang et al. [98] while studying effect of food intake on bowel sounds. They noticed increased number of sounds from this region and explained it by the movement of the ileo-caecal valve upon food consumption [98].

Bowel sound auscultation has transformed multiple folds over the past century, but some studies [96] show its unworthiness to detect bowel pathologies. There is a need of a standardized procedure for auscultation and development of novel technologies that can record and analyze bowel sounds efficiently. Incorporating digital processing of the auscultated sounds could minimize human error and prevent excess recruitment of skilled health care staff. Recent studies [21,22] have developed recording technologies to create a wearable device that is Bluetooth enabled for wireless transmission of data, thus allowing remote and telemedicine healthcare practices. A study by Kutsumi et al. [111] recorded BS using a prototype application on a smartphone and successfully recognized BS using a CNN model. Hence, BS auscultation has a future potential to form a non-invasive diagnosis of various gastrointestinal disorders.

The studies between 1967 and 2022 on this data set have been summarized in Table 1 [21,22,28,42,61,65,83,87–89,91,111–133].

Table 1. Studies with bowel sounds recording technologies and analytical methods.

Year, Author	Study	Technique	Results & Limitations
1967, Georgoulis [112]	Intestinal sounds classification in post-operative patients.	Capsule microphone → tape recorder → B filter → paper record.	Simple and compound sounds showing interpersonal variation. Requires 48-h long recording.
1988, Radnitz [113]	Biofeedback with bowel sounds for irritable bowel syndrome patients.	Audio-visual bowel sound recording for training patient's bowel activity.	Reduced mean daily diarrhea reporting, maintained up to 1 year, affected by stress.
1998, Hadjileontiadis [114]	Symmetrical alpha-stable distribution for lung sounds and bowel sounds analysis.	15 to 30 s signal → converter (sampling rate of 2.5 KHz for lung, and 5 KHz for bowel) → WTST-NST and inverse filter.	Contaminated signal- alpha is ~1.5. Denoised signal- alpha decreased significantly.
1994, Sugrue [115]	Computer aided sound analysis system (C.A.S.A.S) in acute abdomen cases vs. healthy controls.	Microphone → analog to digital converter (ADC) → computerized analysis for bowel sounds features	Increased mean sound length and amplitude, and reduced frequency in cases. Patients need to remain still during recording.
1999, Hadjileontiadis [61]	Higher order crossings (HOC) in large bowel disorders vs. healthy controls.	Audioscope → WTST-NST filter → Number of axis crossings (equally spaced points of time) counted → HOC pattern plotted.	Post-polypectomy HOC comparable to control, proving efficacy of the procedure.
2000, Hadjileontiadis [116]	Wavelet based stationary and non-stationary filter (WTST-NST).	Signal divided with wavelet transform (WT) → decomposed into multiple scales with applied power and threshold → filtered with WT coefficient → denoised signal.	Efficiently removed interfering noises and enhanced signal quality.
2001, Ranta [117]	Bowel sound processing (denoising, segmentation and characterization) based on wavelet-based algorithm (39)	Multiple microphones to localize bowel sounds → wavelet coefficients vector with feature extraction for segmentation	Correct interpretation and decontamination of recorded data needed.

Table 1. Cont.

Year, Author	Study	Technique	Results & Limitations
2003, Hadjileontiadis [118]	Bowel sound enhancement with reduction of background noise.	Kurtosis-based detector → time domain of explosive bowel sounds → separated from background noise.	Reliable detector for extracting bowel sound peaks.
2003, 2005, Hadjileontiadis [119,120]	To detect explosive lung and bowel sounds in patients with pulmonary and gastrointestinal pathology respectively.	Fractal Dimension (FD) based detector in wavelet transform (WT) domain → detects FD variation and WT coefficients related to lung or bowel sounds.	Low noise susceptibility proved with noise stress test.
2008, Dimoulas [121]	Autonomous intestinal motility analysis for long-term bowel sound monitoring.	Time-frequency features and wavelet parameters in combination with multi-layer perceptron.	Recognition accuracy of 94.84% and 2.19% error in separating interfering noises
2008, Hill [76]	Efficacy of a novel device in NICU patients before and after feeding.	Electronic stethoscope → amplifier → acquisition card → computer → picked up hyperactive bowel sound	Significant background noise not accounted for.
2011, Kim [88]	Modified iterative kurtosis-based detector and estimation algorithms based on regression model of jitter and shimmer.	Piezo-polymer microphone → filtered, digitized, segmented, modified (kurtosis-based algorithm) and characterized (absolute jitter and shimmer method)	Longer colon transit time in delayed bowel motility cases. Small sample size. Lack of technical specifications of the device.
2011, Kim [89]	Back propagation neural network (BPNN) and Artificial neural network (ANN)	Signal modified (kurtosis-based algorithm) and characterized (absolute jitter and shimmer)→ analyzed using BPNN and ANN model.	Longer colon transit time in delayed gastric emptying and spinal cord injury cases. Short sample size and duration of recordings.
2011, Tsai [42]	LabVIEW technique for real-time monitoring of bowel sounds.	Electric condenser microphone attached to a stethoscope → data acquisition interface.	Proved the effectiveness of the digital infinite impulse responses (IIR) filter.
2013, Lin [122]	Higher order statistics based radial basis function network.	A three-layer network with input, hidden and output layers to augment and enhance sound.	Enhancement of bowel sounds during both stationary and non-stationary conditions.
2013, Sakata [87]	Fasting and post meals bowel sounds in healthy volunteers.	Recording device with sensors and built-in amplifiers → computer with WTST-NST filter	Unsynchronized recording of stethoscope and device with conditions not indicative of normal digestive activities.
2014, Spiegel [65]	Bowel sounds in patients with post-operative ileus (POI) vs. those tolerating oral feed.	Real time monitoring using a surveillance biosensor.	Intestinal rate of healthy controls → patients tolerating oral feeds → POI. Failed to isolate coordinated bowel activity.
2015, Mamun [123]	Low power integrated bowel sound measurement system.	Piezoelectric film used as a sensor, amplified, filtered and characterized.	Detected regularly sustained bowel sounds from surrounding noises.
2015, Longfu [124]	Spectral entropy for bowel sound signal identification.	Dynamic weighing threshold and spectral subtraction for detecting and increasing signal to noise ratio (SNR)	Accurate detection of endpoint of bowel sounds in low SNR condition.
2014, Sheu [125]	Higher order crossings-based fractal dimension method in noisy conditions	Recorded bowel sounds → analyzed using higher order crossings.	Superior performance to conventional fractal dimension algorithms.

Table 1. *Cont.*

Year, Author	Study	Technique	Results & Limitations
2015, Yin [126]	Artificial neural network to recognize digestive state.	Extracted bowel sounds → adaptive filtering using 2 reference signals → least mean square algorithm for denoising → threshold detection block	Detected the ongoing digestive state in 3 volunteers.
2016, Mamun [28]	Ultra-low power real time bowel sound detector to measure meal instances in artificial pancreas device.	Piezoelectric sensor → transduced into voltage signal by front end processor → feature extractor identifies bowel sound segment.	Consumes 53microW power from 1V supply in 0.96 mm^2 area. Suitable for portable devices with 85% accuracy and low false positive rates.
2018, Sato [91]	Non-contact bowel sound analysis after consumption of carbonated water.	Bowel sound segment detection → extraction→ classification → evaluation to detect signal to noise ratio (SNR)	Number of bowel sound segments inversely related to SNR. Accuracy inversely related to post-meals SNR. Small sample size & low sound pressure in stethoscope.
2018, Liu [127]	Mel Frequency Cepstrum Coefficient Feature (MFCC) and Long Short-Term Memory (LSTM) neural network.	Compressed 1 min voice recording→ screened by two doctors for presence or absence of sound signals → further processing and extraction.	Effective results in same environment; decreased sensitivity with noisy signals.
2019, Kolle [128]	Filtering of bowel sounds using multivariate empirical mode decomposition.	Model increases the non-linear components of signals and separates them from other signals.	False events identified and filtered out with easy identification of relevant events. Contamination by artefacts.
2020, Kodani [129]	Long-term bowel sound measurement with elimination of movement-related cloth rubbing noises.	Portable sensor, with the notch, wavelet and low-pass filters → increase focus on bowel sounds and cloth-rubbing noise → separated based on the number of peaks at specific frequency signals.	Effective in differentiating bowel sounds from noise. Difficulty in separating when both overlap.
2020, Zhao [130]	Long-term bowel sound monitoring with Convolutional Neural Network (CNN).	Wearable bowel sound system used for monitoring and CNNs used for segment recognition.	High sensitivity and moderate accuracy for bowel sound monitoring. Time consuming. Noisy-labels present.
2020, Zheng [131]	Convolutional Recurrent Neural Network (CRNN) system-based sound detection.	Gastrointestinal sound set with collection instrument, dataset annotation and distribution, to detect bowel sounds, speech, snoring, cough, rub and groan.	Effective in identifying snore and cough. Weak performance due to low frequency of bowel sound.
2021, Namikawa [132]	Real time bowel sound analysis system for peri-operative monitoring in gastric surgery patients.	Recording equipment and acoustic sensors used to record frequency of bowel sounds.	Frequency of bowel sound was higher in post-gastrectomy cases, with inverse relation to operation time. Small sample size & large-sized equipment.
2021, Ficek [133]	Hybrid convolutional, recursive neural network for bowel sound analysis.	Intestinal sound contact microphone → analyzed using deep neural network.	Efficiently analyzed bowel sound sequences. Lacks wireless technology.

Table 1. *Cont.*

Year, Author	Study	Technique	Results & Limitations
2022, Sitaula [84]	Convolutional Neural Network (CNN) to classify neonatal bowel sounds.	Digital stethoscope recording → computer analysis based on CNN system → refined with Laplace hidden semi-Markov model	Classified bowel sounds into peristaltic and non-peristaltic. Imbalanced data without noise cancellation.
2022, Zhao [22]	Binarized CNN-based BS recognition algorithm with time-domain histogram features for wearable device.	Wearable BS recorder → Gateway via Bluetooth → relayed to cloud servers (wired or wireless)	Algorithm reached 99.92% classification accuracy and very low false alarm rate. Validated by hardware implementation and computation overhead reduction ratio of 58.28 for overall operation.
2022, Wang [21]	Flexible dual-channel digital auscultation patch with active noise reduction for long-term BS monitoring.	Digital auscultation patch (two channels for BS and one channel for ambient noise) → transmitted via Bluetooth → computer processing with adaptive filtering for active noise reduction, feature extraction and source localization → BS analysis created with intelligent systems.	Flexible, soft, light patch can easily bend to maintain conformal attachment on the abdomen. Wireless wearable device is suitable for long term monitoring. Noise reducing algorithm is useful in noisy clinical environments.
2022, Kutsumi [111]	Prototype smartphone application to record BS using built-in microphone with automatic analyzation of BS.	BS recorded with built-in microphone of Apple iPhone 7 using the BS recording application. Annotated BS segments were analyzed using CNN and LSTM models.	The CNN model was superior and recognized BS with moderate accuracy (88.9%) with data recorded from a smartphone.

6. Discussion

Bowel sounds have a promising potential as a non-invasive diagnostic modality and management aids are needed in practice to establish patient-friendly, cost-effective care. We reviewed previous studies to understand how bowel sounds are produced, evaluate the need of bowel sound auscultation or recording in clinical practice, and the future of phonoenterogram in healthcare. Studies explained that bowel sound production are scarce with varied theories. Some studies [12–14] link bowel sounds to gut motility, whereas others [39,40] believe it to be due to the transfer of energy between luminal contents. Collectively, the production of bowel sounds could be due to a combination of luminal contents [34], amount of luminal air [33], type of contractions [13], and the myoelectrical activity of the intestine [40]. Physiology-focused studies are required to establish a definite origin.

Despite limited knowledge on the genesis of bowel sounds, phonoenterograms have been applied in various conditions such as intestinal obstruction [57], irritable bowel syndrome [17,25,48,61,75], acute gastrointestinal conditions [24], inflammatory bowel disease [61], diverticular disease [61], bowel polyps [61], postoperative ileus [27], critical care [64], sepsis [66], ascites [63], diabetes mellitus [28,29], neurodegenerative disorders [30], neonatal care [83] and hypertrophic pyloric stenosis [31]. A recent systematic review [19] concluded that computerized analysis of bowel sounds shows promise in the field of diagnostic and prognostic gastroenterology. When integrated with engineering knowledge to create a standardized recording and analysis device this could turn into a powerful technology in the field of gastroenterology.

Auscultation of bowel sounds has been in practice since the time of Hippocrates [12]. This ancient practice was later studied by multiple researchers but had limited usability due to interference of surrounding medium air, with long duration of recordings ultimately leading to erroneous results [71,87–89,91,92,97]. Subsequently, the use of procedures such as endoscopy, colonoscopy and manometry increased and are widely employed today. Despite their high accuracy rate, they pose the risk of perforation which can be life-threatening [11]. Thus, there is a need for an inexpensive, non-invasive, patient-friendly alternative for bedside diagnosis of common gastrointestinal conditions.

A phonoenterogram has the potential to revolutionize clinical practice. Research should be focused on building a system that not only records bowel sounds efficiently but also interprets the results accurately. Such a system could eliminate the factor of human error and inter-personal variability involved with the auscultation of bowel sounds. Using this system, a large database for normal and pathological bowel sounds could be created to increase the accuracy of computerized interpretation. This data set can also be used for food evaluation technology, which developing value-added foods based on an individual's constitution, predisposing conditions and bowel activity [87]. In the future, a digital system capable of recording bowel sounds remotely would be helpful in the monitoring and diagnosis of bed-bound critical patients, and older adults unable to visit the clinic. In addition, a model for self-diagnosis of irritable bowel syndrome could help diagnose this chronic functional motility disorder early and reduce the mental and financial strain on the affected population and the healthcare system.

Digital Phonoenterography Using Microwave-Based Systems: Future Perspectives

Tomomasa et al. first proposed the relationship between migrating motor complex (MMC) and bowel sounds (BS), suggesting that the sound index synchronizes with the MMC cycle, and BS can potentially be a biomarker for clinical use [40]. However, as the current sensors have various limitations, as discussed above, a novel technique is needed that can effectively measure BS with a phonoenterogram (PEG). Electromagnetic (EM) based sensors have been explored in medicine for continuous vital monitoring. Most of these applications have been used in detecting heart sounds [134]. Microwave energy has recently gained attention, and its applications in healthcare are tremendous, including diagnostic and therapeutic methods [135]. Microwaves are non-ionizing EM waves and are helpful in the development of new treatments and biosensor diagnostics [136].

EM detects audible signals as the reflected radiation from the vibrating object has amplitude modulation representing the vibration. Kumar developed a microwave acoustic detection system to detect vibrating signals by speech through a wall [137]. Researchers have also developed non-contact microwave radar sensors for structural vibration monitoring. With significant advancements and focused radiation beams, microwave technology is used to create auditory radars for vocal signal detection [138]. Lin et al. developed a coherent homodyne demodulator to detect the radar signal reflected from vibrating vocal cords of human subjects. These measured signals are consistent with acoustic signals and have a variety of potential medical applications [139]. Therefore, microwave energy can be used to create wireless sensing applications to detect internal body sounds. Wireless microwave acoustic sensors have been developed and used in various industries, but their application in health remains unexplored [140,141].

Liu. S et al. summarized the theories and applications of electromagnetic acoustic (EMA) techniques in biomedical applications [142]. They found that electromagnetic and acoustic techniques are superior to conventional ultrasound techniques as they have better tolerance to sound speed variation than ultrasonic propagation. Although these studies have shown potential applications, EMA is yet to be applied clinically. Hui et al. [143] demonstrated the UHF microwave technique to retrieve heart sounds. They created a microwave near-field coherent sensor that adapted a radio frequency identification (RFID) tag and compared it to the conventional acoustic stethoscope, which showed similar heart sound content and can be used as a biometric parameter. This can also be used for diagnostic purposes regardless of the ambient noise level [143]. These results suggest the potential design of microwave acoustic PEG sensor for high fidelity data capturing of BS. AI assisted acoustic sensor designs using novel metamaterials offer huge promise for digital phonoenterography using microwave telemetry system.

Biomedical telemetry is extensively employed in the ambulatory monitoring of physiological data such as heart rate, blood pressure, oxygen saturation and respiratory rate [144–147]. The use of microwave energy to monitor vital signs is gaining popularity. Continuous wave radar has been used to monitor heart rate and blood pressure. Various antenna design developments helped improve the use of microwaves in telemetry [148]. Most conventional monitoring systems use inductive transmission for data transfer and device recharge, with problems with high power requirements and biocompatibility. However, high-frequency (~400 MHz) microwave devices with small implantable antennas can serve the same purpose with better battery life and compatibility. Therefore, a microwave telemetry system can complement the digital phonoenterography system design for efficient wireless transmission. Figure 3 [37] depicts an implementation example for digital phonoenterography using microwave systems and its potential impact.

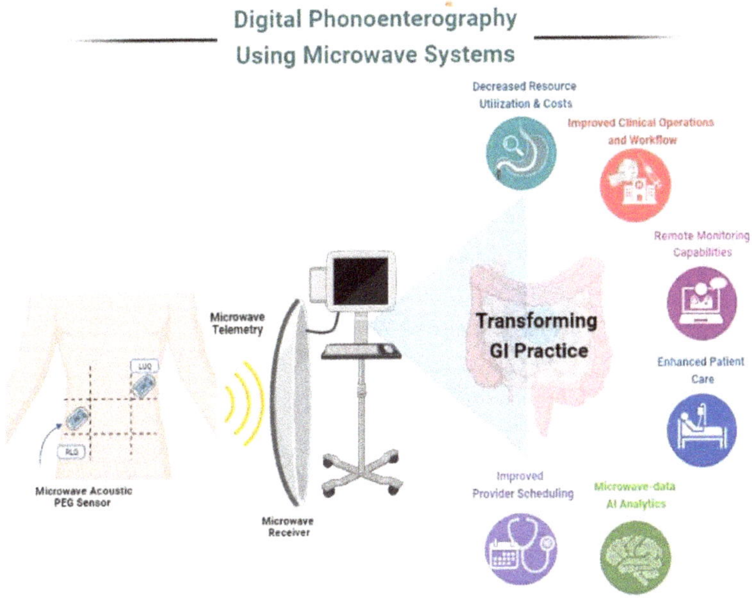

Figure 3. Pictorial representation of digital phonoenterography using microwave systems.

Novel microwave-based acoustic PEG sensors will pave the way for the accurate capturing of bowel sounds. Data transmission using microwave telemetry may employ AI in both PEG data mining and interpretation as well as in the design of a computer-aided decision support system for the accurate diagnosis of GI diseases. Digital phonoenterography assisted with microwave-based systems can positively impact practice operations as well as enhance patient care. With an efficient system in place, healthcare providers can appreciate its impact in terms of reduced resource utilization, lowered operational costs, improved provider scheduling and workflows, remote digital health monitoring as well as an opportunity for data analytics using AI with microwave data to optimize these utilities.

Future research is warranted on the design of novel AI-assisted microwave acoustic sensors specific to the application of interest for digital phonoenterography. Novel AI-assisted metamaterial designs and frequency selective surfaces for microwave acoustic sensors offer huge promise to propel this field. AI-assisted microwave telemetry system design is needed to provide noise free phonoenterography data transmission for reliable diagnosis. Overall, it is evident that the non-invasive diagnosis of GI diseases is warranted, with novel AI-assisted microwave tools that can impact GI practice and patient care. This review provides new insights and directions for practicing digital gastroenterology using a microwave based phonoenterography system.

7. Conclusions

Preliminary studies show promising results in the usefulness of bowel sounds in GI practice, though more research is warranted. Research related to the origin of normal bowel sounds as well as the pathophysiology of abnormal bowel sounds is needed to effectively translate acoustic features into clinical practice. The recording and analysis of bowel sounds shows tremendous potential for creating a device that is accessible, patient-friendly, cost-effective and, most importantly, devoid of any risk factors that are associated with radiation or intervention. Microwave-based digital phonoenterography offers a huge opportunity to impact both GI practice as well as patient care. Future research should focus on the design of novel AI-assisted microwave acoustic sensors and telemetry system designs.

Author Contributions: R.R. and S.P.A. defined the review scope, context and purpose of the study. D.N.D., V.G.C., X.J.W., C.A.A., K.G. and A.J.R. provided clinical perspectives and expertise for the study. R.R., A.K., P.M., A.K.S., K.A., A.R., K.G. and A.Y. conducted a literature review and drafted the manuscript. S.P.A., R.R. and A.R. conceived and crafted the illustrative figures. D.N.D., V.G.C., X.J.W., C.A.A., A.J.R. and S.P.A. provided consulting and performed a critical review of the manuscript. R.R., A.K., A.R. and S.P.A. performed the cleaning and organization of the manuscript. S.P.A. provided conceptualization, supervision and project administration. All authors have read and agreed to the published version of the manuscript.

Funding: This research received no external funding.

Institutional Review Board Statement: Not applicable.

Informed Consent Statement: Not applicable.

Data Availability Statement: The review was based on publicly available academic literature databases.

Acknowledgments: This work was supported by the Advanced Analytics and Practice Innovation unit for Artificial Intelligence and Informatics research within the Department of Medicine, Mayo Clinic, Rochester, MN USA. This work was also supported by the GIH Division for the GIH Artificial Intelligence Laboratory (GAIL) and Microwave Engineering and Imaging Laboratory (MEIL), Department of Medicine, Mayo Clinic, Rochester, MN USA.

Conflicts of Interest: The authors declare no conflict of interest.

References

1. Sperber, A.D.; Bangdiwala, S.I.; Drossman, D.A.; Ghoshal, U.C.; Simren, M.; Tack, J.; Whitehead, W.E.; Dumitrascu, D.L.; Fang, X.; Fukudo, S. Worldwide prevalence and burden of functional gastrointestinal disorders, results of Rome Foundation Global Study. *Gastroenterology* **2021**, *160*, 99–114.e113. [CrossRef] [PubMed]
2. Horwitz, B.J.; Fisher, R.S. The irritable bowel syndrome. *N. Engl. J. Med.* **2001**, *344*, 1846–1850. [CrossRef]
3. Saha, L. Irritable bowel syndrome: Pathogenesis, diagnosis, treatment, and evidence-based medicine. *World J. Gastroenterol. WJG* **2014**, *20*, 6759. [CrossRef] [PubMed]
4. Defrees, D.N.; Bailey, J. Irritable bowel syndrome: Epidemiology, pathophysiology, diagnosis, and treatment. *Prim. Care Clin. Off. Pract.* **2017**, *44*, 655–671. [CrossRef] [PubMed]
5. Harnsberger, C.R.; Maykel, J.A.; Alavi, K. Postoperative ileus. *Clin. Colon Rectal Surg.* **2019**, *32*, 166–170. [CrossRef]
6. Gu, Y.; Lim, H.J.; Moser, M.A. How useful are bowel sounds in assessing the abdomen? *Dig. Surg.* **2010**, *27*, 422–426. [CrossRef]
7. Van Bree, S.; Prins, M.; Juffermans, N. Auscultation for bowel sounds in patients with ileus: An outdated practice in the ICU? *Neth. J. Crit. Care* **2018**, *26*, 142–146.
8. Jackson, P.G.; Raiji, M.T. Evaluation and management of intestinal obstruction. *Am. Fam. Physician* **2011**, *83*, 159–165.
9. Gergely, M.; Deepak, P. Tools for the Diagnosis and Management of Crohn's Disease. *Gastroenterol. Clin. N. Am.* **2022**, *51*, 213–239. [CrossRef]
10. Peery, A.F.; Crockett, S.D.; Murphy, C.C.; Jensen, E.T.; Kim, H.P.; Egberg, M.D.; Lund, J.L.; Moon, A.M.; Pate, V.; Barnes, E.L. Burden and cost of gastrointestinal, liver, and pancreatic diseases in the United States: Update 2021. *Gastroenterology* **2022**, *162*, 621–644. [CrossRef]
11. Kavic, S.M.; Basson, M.D. Complications of endoscopy. *Am. J. Surg.* **2001**, *181*, 319–332. [CrossRef] [PubMed]

12. Cannon, W.B. Auscultation of the rhythmic sounds produced by the stomach and intestines. *Am. J. Physiol.-Leg. Content* **1905**, *14*, 339–353. [CrossRef]
13. Du Plessis, D. Clinical observations on intestinal motility. *South Afr. Med. J.* **1954**, *28*, 27–33.
14. Milton, G. Normal bowel sounds. *Med. J. Aust.* **1958**, *2*, 490–493. [CrossRef]
15. Baid, H. A critical review of auscultating bowel sounds. *Br. J. Nurs.* **2009**, *18*, 1125–1129. [CrossRef]
16. Watson, W.C.; Knox, E.C. Phonoenterography: The recording and analysis of bowel sounds. *Gut* **1967**, *8*, 88–94. [CrossRef]
17. Craine, B.L.; Silpa, M.; O'Toole, C.J. Computerized auscultation applied to irritable bowel syndrome. *Dig. Dis. Sci.* **1999**, *44*, 1887–1892. [CrossRef] [PubMed]
18. Safronov, B.; Shakhova, S.; Polyatykina, O.; Nazarov, S. Computer phonoenterography in the assessment of the motor-evacuatory function of the gastrointestinal tract in healthy children. *Hum. Physiol.* **2006**, *32*, 122–124. [CrossRef]
19. Inderjeeth, A.-J.; Webberley, K.M.; Muir, J.; Marshall, B.J. The potential of computerised analysis of bowel sounds for diagnosis of gastrointestinal conditions: A systematic. *Syst. Rev.* **2018**, *7*, 124. [CrossRef] [PubMed]
20. Nowak, J.K.; Nowak, R.; Radzikowski, K.; Grulkowski, I.; Walkowiak, J. Automated bowel sound analysis: An overview. *Sensors* **2021**, *21*, 5294. [CrossRef]
21. Wang, G.; Yang, Y.; Chen, S.; Fu, J.; Wu, D.; Yang, A.; Ma, Y.; Feng, X. Flexible dual-channel digital auscultation patch with active noise reduction for bowel sound monitoring and application. *IEEE J. Biomed. Health Inform.* **2022**, *26*, 2951–2962. [CrossRef] [PubMed]
22. Zhao, K.; Feng, S.; Jiang, H.; Wang, Z.; Chen, P.; Zhu, B.; Duan, X. A Binarized CNN-based Bowel Sound Recognition Algorithm with Time-domain Histogram Features for Wearable Healthcare Systems. *IEEE Trans. Circuits Syst. II Express Briefs* **2021**, *69*, 629–633. [CrossRef]
23. Ching, S.S.; Tan, Y.K. Spectral analysis of bowel sounds in intestinal obstruction using an electronic stethoscope. *World J. Gastroenterol. WJG* **2012**, *18*, 4585. [CrossRef] [PubMed]
24. Arnbjörnsson, E.; Bengmark, S. Auscultation of Bowel Sounds in Patients with Suspected Acute Appendicitis–an Aid in the Diagnosis? *Eur. Surg. Res.* **1983**, *15*, 24–27. [CrossRef]
25. Craine, B.L.; Silpa, M.L.; O'Toole, C.J. Enterotachogram analysis to distinguish irritable bowel syndrome from Crohn's disease. *Dig. Dis. Sci.* **2001**, *46*, 1974–1979. [CrossRef]
26. Liatsos, C.; Hadjileontiadis, L.J.; Mavrogiannis, C.; Patch, D.; Panas, S.M.; Burroughs, A.K. Bowel sounds analysis: A novel noninvasive method for diagnosis of small-volume ascites. *Dig. Dis. Sci.* **2003**, *48*, 1630–1636. [CrossRef]
27. Kaneshiro, M.; Kaiser, W.; Pourmorady, J.; Fleshner, P.; Russell, M.; Zaghiyan, K.; Lin, A.; Martinez, B.; Patel, A.; Nguyen, A. Postoperative gastrointestinal telemetry with an acoustic biosensor predicts ileus vs. uneventful GI recovery. *J. Gastrointest. Surg.* **2016**, *20*, 132–139. [CrossRef]
28. Al Mamun, K.A.; McFarlane, N. Integrated real time bowel sound detector for artificial pancreas systems. *Sens. Bio-Sens. Res.* **2016**, *7*, 84–89. [CrossRef]
29. Mamun, K.; McFarlane, N. Live Demonstration: Portable Bowel Sound Idenfication System. In Proceedings of the 2018 IEEE International Symposium on Circuits and Systems (ISCAS), Florence, Italy, 27–30 May 2018.
30. Ozawa, T.; Saji, E.; Yajima, R.; Onodera, O.; Nishizawa, M. Reduced bowel sounds in Parkinson's disease and multiple system atrophy patients. *Clin. Auton. Res.* **2011**, *21*, 181–184. [CrossRef]
31. Tomomasa, T.; Takahashi, A.; Nako, Y.; Kaneko, H.; Tabata, M.; Tsuchida, Y.; Morikawa, A. Analysis of gastrointestinal sounds in infants with pyloric stenosis before and after pyloromyotomy. *Pediatrics* **1999**, *104*, e60. [CrossRef]
32. Vasseur, C.; Devroede, G.; Dalle, D.; Van Houtte, N.; Bastin, E.; Thibault, R. Postprandial bowel sounds. *IEEE Trans. Biomed. Eng.* **1975**, 443–448. [CrossRef]
33. Wilson, S.R.; Burns, P.N.; Wilkinson, L.M.; Simpson, D.H.; Muradali, D. Gas at abdominal US: Appearance, relevance, and analysis of artifacts. *Radiology* **1999**, *210*, 113–123. [CrossRef] [PubMed]
34. Politzer, J.-P.; Devroede, G.; Vasseur, C.; Gerard, J.; Thibault, R. The genesis of bowel sounds: Influence of viscus and gastrointestinal content. *Gastroenterology* **1976**, *71*, 282–285. [CrossRef] [PubMed]
35. Farrar, J.T.; Ingelfinger, F.J. Gastrointestinal motility as revealed by study of abdominal sounds. *Gastroenterology* **1955**, *29*, 789–802. [CrossRef] [PubMed]
36. Liu, C.J.; Huang, S.C.; Chen, H.I. Oscillating gas bubbles as the origin of bowel sounds: A combined acoustic and imaging study. *Chin. J. Physiol* **2010**, *53*, 245–253. [CrossRef]
37. BioRender. Created with BioRender.com. BioRender: Toronto, ON, Canada, 2021. Available online: https://biorender.com/ (accessed on 31 December 2022).
38. Elliott, T.; Barclay-Smith, E. Antiperistalsis and other muscular activities of the colon. *J. Physiol.* **1904**, *31*, 272. [CrossRef]
39. Drake, A.; Franklin, N.; Schrock, J.W.; Jones, R.A. Auscultation of Bowel Sounds and Ultrasound of Peristalsis Are Neither Compartmentalized Nor Correlated. *Cureus* **2021**, *13*, 14982. [CrossRef]
40. Tomomasa, T.; Morikawa, A.; Sandler, R.H.; Mansy, H.A.; Koneko, H.; Masahiko, T.; Hyman, P.E.; Itoh, Z. Gastrointestinal sounds and migrating motor complex in fasted humans. *Am. J. Gastroenterol.* **1999**, *94*, 374–381. [CrossRef]
41. Deane, A.; Chapman, M.J.; Fraser, R.J.; Bryant, L.K.; Burgstad, C.; Nguyen, N.Q. Mechanisms underlying feed intolerance in the critically ill: Implications for treatment. *World J. Gastroenterol. WJG* **2007**, *13*, 3909. [CrossRef]

42. Tsai, C.-F.; Wu, T.-J.; Chao, Y.-M. Labview based bowel-sounds monitoring system in realtime. In Proceedings of the 2011 International Conference on Machine Learning and Cybernetics, Guilin, China, 10–13 July 2011; pp. 1815–1818.
43. Griffith, G.; Owen, G.; Kirkman, S.; Shields, R. Measurement of rate of gastric emptying using chromium-51. *Lancet* **1966**, *1*, 1244–1245. [CrossRef]
44. Roth, J.L.A. The symptom patterns of gaseousness. *Ann. New York Acad. Sci.* **1968**, *150*, 109–126. [CrossRef] [PubMed]
45. Ellis, H. BORBORYGMI. In *French's Index of Differential Diagnosis*; Elsevier: Amsterdam, The Netherlands, 1979; p. 111.
46. Adams, B. The measurement of intestinal sounds in man and their relationship to serum 5-hydroxytryptamine. *Gut* **1961**, *2*, 246–251. [CrossRef] [PubMed]
47. Martin, D.C.; Beckloff, G.L.; Arnold, J.D.; Gitomer, S. Bowel sound quantitation to evaluate drugs on gastrointestinal motor activity. *J. Clin. Pharmacol. New Drugs* **1971**, *11*, 42–45. [CrossRef]
48. Emoto, T.; Shono, K.; Abeyratne, U.R.; Okahisa, T.; Yano, H.; Akutagawa, M.; Konaka, S.; Kinouchi, Y. ARMA-based spectral bandwidth for evaluation of bowel motility by the analysis of bowel sounds. *Physiol. Meas.* **2013**, *34*, 925. [CrossRef] [PubMed]
49. Kaufman, P.N.; Krevsky, B.; Malmud, L.S.; Maurer, A.H.; Somers, M.B.; Siegel, J.A.; Fisher, R.S. Role of opiate receptors in the regulation of colonic transit. *Gastroenterology* **1988**, *94*, 1351–1356. [CrossRef]
50. Cali, R.L.; Meade, P.G.; Swanson, M.S.; Freeman, C. Effect of morphine and incision length on bowel function after colectomy. *Dis. Colon Rectum* **2000**, *43*, 163–168. [CrossRef]
51. Horiyama, K.; Emoto, T.; Haraguchi, T.; Uebanso, T.; Naito, Y.; Gyobu, T.; Kanemoto, K.; Inobe, J.; Sano, A.; Akutagawa, M. Bowel sound-based features to investigate the effect of coffee and soda on gastrointestinal motility. *Biomed. Signal Process. Control.* **2021**, *66*, 102425. [CrossRef]
52. Brown, S.; Cann, P.; Read, N. Effect of coffee on distal colon function. *Gut* **1990**, *31*, 450–453. [CrossRef]
53. Dessirier, J.-M.; Simons, C.T.; Carstens, M.I.; O'Mahony, M.; Carstens, E. Psychophysical and neurobiological evidence that the oral sensation elicited by carbonated water is of chemogenic origin. *Chem. Senses* **2000**, *25*, 277–284. [CrossRef]
54. Holtmann, G.; Enck, P. Stress and gastrointestinal motility in humans: A review of the literature. *Neurogastroenterol. Motil.* **1991**, *3*, 245–254. [CrossRef]
55. Cappell, M.S.; Batke, M. Mechanical obstruction of the small bowel and colon. *Med. Clin. N. Am.* **2008**, *92*, 575–597. [CrossRef] [PubMed]
56. Bhat, S. *Intestinal Obstruction*; Jaypee brothers: New Delhi, India, 2016.
57. Yoshino, H.; Abe, Y.; Yoshino, T.; Ohsato, K. Clinical application of spectral analysis of bowel sounds in intestinal obstruction. *Dis. Colon Rectum* **1990**, *33*, 753–757. [CrossRef] [PubMed]
58. Gade, J.; Kruse, P.; Andersen, O.T.; Pedersen, S.B.; Boesby, S. Physicians' abdominal auscultation: A multi-rater agreement study. *Scand. J. Gastroenterol.* **1998**, *33*, 773–777. [PubMed]
59. Stevens, N.C. Auscultation of the Abdomen: An Aid to Diagnosis. *New Engl. J. Med.* **1934**, *211*, 108–110. [CrossRef]
60. Hobson, T.; Rosenman, L.D. Acute appendicitis—When is it right to be wrong? *Am. J. Surg* **1964**, *108*, 306–312. [CrossRef]
61. Hadjileontiadis, L.; Kontakos, T.; Liatsos, C.; Mavrogiannis, C.; Rokkas, T.; Panas, S. Enhancement of the diagnostic character of bowel sounds using higher-order crossings. In Proceedings of the First Joint BMES/EMBS Conference, 1999 IEEE Engineering in Medicine and Biology 21st Annual Conference and the 1999 Annual Fall Meeting of the Biomedical Engineering Society, Atlanta, GA, USA, 13–16 October 1999; Volume 2, p. 1027.
62. Yuki, M.; Adachi, K.; Fujishiro, H.; Uchida, Y.; Miyaoka, Y.; Yoshino, N.; Yuki, T.; Ono, M.; Kinoshita, Y. Is a computerized bowel sound auscultation system useful for the detection of increased bowel motility. *Am. J. Gastroenterol.* **2002**, *97*, 1846–1848. [CrossRef]
63. Goldberg, B.B.; Goodman, G.A.; Clearfield, H.R. Evaluation of ascites by ultrasound. *Radiology* **1970**, *96*, 15–22. [CrossRef]
64. Wang, G.; Wang, M.; Liu, H.; Zhao, S.; Liu, L.; Wang, W. Changes in bowel sounds of inpatients undergoing general anesthesia. *BioMedical Eng. OnLine* **2020**, *19*, 60. [CrossRef]
65. Spiegel, B.M.; Kaneshiro, M.; Russell, M.M.; Lin, A.; Patel, A.; Tashjian, V.C.; Zegarski, V.; Singh, D.; Cohen, S.E.; Reid, M.W. Validation of an acoustic gastrointestinal surveillance biosensor for postoperative ileus. *J. Gastrointest. Surg.* **2014**, *18*, 1795–1803. [CrossRef]
66. Goto, J.; Matsuda, K.; Harii, N.; Moriguchi, T.; Yanagisawa, M.; Sakata, O. Usefulness of a real-time bowel sound analysis system in patients with severe sepsis (pilot study). *J. Artif. Organs* **2015**, *18*, 86–91. [CrossRef]
67. Li, B.; Wang, J.-R.; Ma, Y.-L. Bowel sounds and monitoring gastrointestinal motility in critically ill patients. *Clin. Nurse Spec.* **2012**, *26*, 29–34. [CrossRef]
68. Shelly, M.; Church, J. Bowel sounds during intermittent positive pressure. *Anaesthesia* **1987**, *42*, 207–209. [CrossRef] [PubMed]
69. Read, T.E.; Brozovich, M.; Andujar, J.E.; Ricciardi, R.; Caushaj, P.F. Bowel sounds are not associated with flatus, bowel movement, or tolerance of oral intake in patients after major abdominal surgery. *Dis. Colon Rectum* **2017**, *60*, 608–613. [CrossRef] [PubMed]
70. Massey, R.L. Return of bowel sounds indicating an end of postoperative ileus: Is it time to cease this long-standing nursing tradition? *Medsurg Nurs.* **2012**, *21*, 146.
71. Van Bree, S.; Bemelman, W.; Hollmann, M.; Bennink, R.; Boeckxstaens, G. Auscultation of bowel sounds to assess intestinal motility? *Neurogastroenterol. Motil.* **2015**, *27*, 105–106.

72. Deane, A.M.; Ali Abdelhamid, Y.; Plummer, M.P.; Fetterplace, K.; Moore, C.; Reintam Blaser, A. Are classic bedside exam findings required to initiate enteral nutrition in critically ill patients: Emphasis on bowel sounds and abdominal distension. *Nutr. Clin. Pract.* **2021**, *36*, 67–75. [CrossRef]
73. Du, X.; Allwood, G.; Webberley, K.M.; Inderjeeth, A.-J.; Osseiran, A.; Marshall, B.J. Noninvasive diagnosis of irritable bowel syndrome via bowel sound features: Proof of concept. *Clin. Transl. Gastroenterol.* **2019**, *10*, e00017. [CrossRef] [PubMed]
74. Campbell, F.; Storey, B.; Cullen, P.; Cuschieri, A. Surface vibration analysis (SVA): A new non-invasive monitor of gastrointestinal activity. *Gut* **1989**, *30*, 39–45. [CrossRef]
75. Craine, B.L.; Silpa, M.L.; O'toole, C.J. Two-dimensional positional mapping of gastrointestinal sounds in control and functional bowel syndrome patients. *Dig. Dis. Sci.* **2002**, *47*, 1290–1296. [CrossRef]
76. Papatheodorou, K.; Banach, M.; Bekiari, E.; Rizzo, M.; Edmonds, M. Complications of Diabetes 2017. *J. Diabetes Res.* **2018**, *2018*, 3086167. [CrossRef]
77. Yamaguchi, K.; Yamaguchi, T.; Odaka, T.; Saisho, H. Evaluation of gastrointestinal motility by computerized analysis of abdominal auscultation findings. *J. Gastroenterol. Hepatol.* **2006**, *21*, 510–514. [CrossRef] [PubMed]
78. Breton, M.; Farret, A.; Bruttomesso, D.; Anderson, S.; Magni, L.; Patek, S.; Dalla Man, C.; Place, J.; Demartini, S.; Del Favero, S.; et al. Fully integrated artificial pancreas in type 1 diabetes: Modular closed-loop glucose control maintains near normoglycemia. *Diabetes* **2012**, *61*, 2230–2237. [CrossRef]
79. Harvey, R.A.; Wang, Y.; Grosman, B.; Percival, M.W.; Bevier, W.; Finan, D.A.; Zisser, H.; Seborg, D.E.; Jovanovic, L.; Doyle, F.J.; et al. Quest for the artificial pancreas: Combining technology with treatment. *IEEE Eng. Med. Biol. Mag.* **2010**, *29*, 53–62. [CrossRef] [PubMed]
80. Doyle, F.J.; Huyett, L.M.; Lee, J.B.; Zisser, H.C.; Kerr, D.; Dassau, E. Response to comment on Doyle et al. Closed-loop artificial pancreas systems: Engineering the algorithms. Diabetes Care 2014;37:1191–1197. *Diabetes Care* **2014**, *37*, e228. [CrossRef]
81. Benarroch, E.; Schmeichel, A.; Sandroni, P.; Low, P.; Parisi, J. Involvement of vagal autonomic nuclei in multiple system atrophy and Lewy body disease. *Neurology* **2006**, *66*, 378–383. [CrossRef] [PubMed]
82. Hill, J.M.; Maloney, A.; Stephens, K.; Adrezin, R.; Eisenfeld, L. Stethoscope for monitoring neonatal abdominal sounds. *Proc. IAJC-IJME Int. Conf.* **2008**, *9*, 5–11.
83. Hill, J.M.; Regan, M.S.; Adrezin, R.S.; Eisenfeld, L. System for recording the bowel sounds of premature infants. *Front. Biomed. Devices* **2008**, *48337*, 37–38.
84. Sitaula, C.; He, J.; Priyadarshi, A.; Tracy, M.; Kavehei, O.; Hinder, M.; Withana, A.; McEwan, A.; Marzbanrad, F. Neonatal bowel sound detection using convolutional neural network and Laplace hidden semi-Markov model. *IEEE/ACM Trans. Audio Speech Lang. Process.* **2022**, *30*, 1853–1864. [CrossRef]
85. Mansy, H.; Sandler, R. Choice of operating parameters in heart sound removal from bowel sounds using adaptive filtering. In Proceedings of the 19th Annual International Conference of the IEEE Engineering in Medicine and Biology Society.'Magnificent Milestones and Emerging Opportunities in Medical Engineering'(Cat. No. 97CH36136), Chicago, IL, USA, 30 October–2 November 1997; pp. 1398–1401.
86. Mansy, H.A.; Sandler, R.H. Bowel-sound signal enhancement using adaptive filtering. *IEEE Eng. Med. Biol. Mag.* **1997**, *16*, 105–117. [CrossRef]
87. Sakata, O.; Suzuki, Y.; Matsuda, K.; Satake, T. Temporal changes in occurrence frequency of bowel sounds both in fasting state and after eating. *J. Artif. Organs* **2013**, *16*, 83–90. [CrossRef]
88. Kim, K.S.; Seo, J.H.; Ryu, S.H.; Kim, M.H.; Song, C.G. Estimation algorithm of the bowel motility based on regression analysis of the jitter and shimmer of bowel sounds. *Comput. Methods Programs Biomed.* **2011**, *104*, 426–434. [CrossRef] [PubMed]
89. Kim, K.-S.; Seo, J.-H.; Song, C.-G. Non-invasive algorithm for bowel motility estimation using a back-propagation neural network model of bowel sounds. *Biomed. Eng. Online* **2011**, *10*, 69. [CrossRef]
90. Ulusar, U.D.; Canpolat, M.; Yaprak, M.; Kazanir, S.; Ogunc, G. Real-time monitoring for recovery of gastrointestinal tract motility detection after abdominal surgery. In Proceedings of the 2013 7th International Conference on Application of Information and Communication Technologies, Azerbaijan, Baku, 23–25 October 2013; pp. 1–4.
91. Sato, R.; Emoto, T.; Gojima, Y.; Akutagawa, M. Automatic bowel motility evaluation technique for noncontact sound recordings. *Appl. Sci.* **2018**, *8*, 999. [CrossRef]
92. Emoto, T.; Abeyratne, U.R.; Gojima, Y.; Nanba, K.; Sogabe, M.; Okahisa, T.; Akutagawa, M.; Konaka, S.; Kinouchi, Y. Evaluation of human bowel motility using non-contact microphones. *Biomed. Phys. Eng. Express* **2016**, *2*, 045012. [CrossRef]
93. Grenier, M.-C.; Gagnon, K.R.; Genest, J.; Durand, J.; Durand, L.-G. Clinical comparison of acoustic and electronic stethoscopes and design of a new electronic stethoscope. *Am. J. Cardiol.* **1998**, *81 5*, 653–656. [CrossRef]
94. Bray, D.; Reilly, R.; Haskin, L.; McCormack, B. Assessing motility through abdominal sound monitoring. In Proceedings of the 19th Annual International Conference of the IEEE Engineering in Medicine and Biology Society. 'Magnificent Milestones and Emerging Opportunities in Medical Engineering' (Cat. No. 97CH36136), Chicago, IL, USA, 30 October–2 November 1997; pp. 2398–2400.
95. Zaborski, D.; Halczak, M.; Grzesiak, W.; Modrzejewski, A. Recording and analysis of bowel sounds. *Euroasian J. Hepato-Gastroenterol.* **2015**, *5*, 67. [CrossRef] [PubMed]
96. Felder, S.; Margel, D.; Murrell, Z.; Fleshner, P. Usefulness of bowel sound auscultation: A prospective evaluation. *J. Surg. Educ.* **2014**, *71*, 768–773. [CrossRef]

97. Lu, Q.; Yadid-Pecht, O.; Sadowski, D.; Mintchev, M.P. Acoustic and intraluminal ultrasonic technologies in the diagnosis of diseases in gastrointestinal tract: A review. *Engineering* **2013**, *5*, 73–77. [CrossRef]
98. Wang, N.; Testa, A.; Marshall, B.J. Development of a bowel sound detector adapted to demonstrate the effect of food intake. *Biomed. Eng. Online* **2022**, *21*, 1. [CrossRef]
99. Bickley, L.S.; Szilagyi, P.G.; Bates, B. *Bates' Guide to Physical Examination and History Taking*; Lippincott Williams & Wilkins: Philadelphia, PA, USA, 2009.
100. Kahan, S. *Signs and Symptoms*, 2nd ed.; Lippincott Williams and Wilkins: Philadelphia, PA, USA, 2009.
101. Talley, N.J. *Clinical Examination: A Systemic Guide to Physical Diagnosis*, 5th ed.; Churchill Livingstone Elsevier: London, UK, 2006.
102. Seidel, H.M. *Mosby's Guide to Physical Examination*; Elsevier: Amsterdam, The Netherlands, 2010.
103. Rushforth, H. *Assessment Made Incredibly Easy!* Lippincott Williams & Wilkins: London, UK, 2009.
104. Epstein, O. *The Abdomen- Clinical Examination*, 4th ed.; Mosby, Elsevier: Maryland Heights, MO, USA, 2008; pp. 186–225.
105. Cox, C.; Steggall, M. A step– by-step guide to performing a complete abdominal examination. *Gastrointest. Nurs.* **2009**, *7*, 10–17. [CrossRef]
106. Evans, M.M.; Evans, M.; Lashinski, K.; Franklin, A. Assessing the abdomen. *Nursing2020* **2009**, *39*, 12. [CrossRef] [PubMed]
107. Mehta, M. Assessing the abdomen. *Nursing* **2003**, *33*, 54–55. [CrossRef]
108. Vizioli, L.H.; Winckler, F.D.; da Luz, L.C.; Marques, G.K.; Callegari-Jacques, S.M.; Fornari, F. Abdominal Palpation Does Not Modify the Number of Bowel Sounds in Healthy Volunteers and Gastrointestinal Outpatients. *Am. J. Med. Sci.* **2020**, *360*, 378–382. [CrossRef] [PubMed]
109. Ranta, R.; Louis-Dorr, V.; Heinrich, C.; Wolf, D.; Guillemin, F. Towards an acoustic map of abdominal activity. In Proceedings of the 25th Annual International Conference of the IEEE Engineering in Medicine and Biology Society (IEEE Cat. No. 03CH37439), Cancun, Mexico, 17–21 September 2003; pp. 2769–2772.
110. Ranta, R.; Louis-Dorr, V.; Heinrich, C.; Wolf, D.; Guillemin, F. Principal component analysis and interpretation of bowel sounds. In Proceedings of the 26th Annual International Conference of the IEEE Engineering in Medicine and Biology Society, San Francisco, CA, USA, 1–5 September 2004; pp. 227–230.
111. Kutsumi, Y.; Kanegawa, N.; Zeida, M.; Matsubara, H.; Murayama, N. Automated Bowel Sound and Motility Analysis with CNN Using a Smartphone. *Sensors* **2023**, *23*, 407. [CrossRef] [PubMed]
112. Georgoulis, B. Bowel Sounds. *J. R. Soc. Med.* **1967**, *60*, 917–920. [CrossRef]
113. Radnitz, C.L.; Blanchard, E.B. Bowel sound biofeedback as a treatment for irritable bowel syndrome. *Biofeedback Self-Regul.* **1988**, *13*, 169–179. [CrossRef]
114. Hadjileontiadis, L.J.; Panas, S.M. On modeling impulsive bioacoustic signals with symmetric spl alpha/-stable distributions: Application in discontinuous adventitious lung sounds and explosive bowel sounds. In Proceedings of the 20th Annual International Conference of the IEEE Engineering in Medicine and Biology Society. Vol.20 Biomedical Engineering Towards the Year 2000 and Beyond (Cat. No.98CH36286), Hong Kong, China, 1 November 1998; Volume 11, pp. 13–16.
115. Sugrue, M.; Redfern, M. Computerized phonoenterography: The clinical investigation of a new system. *J. Clin. Gastroenterol.* **1994**, *18*, 139–144. [CrossRef]
116. Hadjileontiadis, L.J.; Liatsos, C.N.; Mavrogiannis, C.C.; Rokkas, T.A.; Panas, S.M. Enhancement of bowel sounds by wavelet-based filtering. *IEEE Trans. Biomed. Eng.* **2000**, *47*, 876–886. [CrossRef]
117. Ranta, R.; Heinrich, C.; Louis-Dorr, V.; Wolf, D.; Guillemin, F. Wavelet-based bowel sounds denoising, segmentation and characterization. In Proceedings of the 23rd Annual International Conference of the IEEE Engineering in Medicine and Biology Society, Istanbul, Turkey, 25–28 October 2001; pp. 1903–1906.
118. Hadjileontiadis, L.J.; Rekanos, I.T. Enhancement of explosive bowel sounds using kurtosis-based filtering. In Proceedings of the 25th Annual International Conference of the IEEE Engineering in Medicine and Biology Society (IEEE Cat. No. 03CH37439), Cancun, Mexico, 17–21 September 2003; pp. 2479–2482.
119. Hadjileontiadis, L.J.; Rekanos, I.T. Detection of explosive lung and bowel sounds by means of fractal dimension. *IEEE Signal Process. Lett.* **2003**, *10*, 311–314. [CrossRef]
120. Hadjileontiadis, L.J. Wavelet-based enhancement of lung and bowel sounds using fractal dimension thresholding-Part II: Application results. *IEEE Trans. Biomed. Eng.* **2005**, *52*, 1050–1064. [CrossRef]
121. Dimoulas, C.; Kalliris, G.; Papanikolaou, G.; Petridis, V.; Kalampakas, A. Bowel-sound pattern analysis using wavelets and neural networks with application to long-term, unsupervised, gastrointestinal motility monitoring. *Expert Syst. Appl.* **2008**, *34*, 26–41. [CrossRef]
122. Lin, B.-S.; Sheu, M.-J.; Chuang, C.-C.; Tseng, K.-C.; Chen, J.-Y. Enhancing bowel sounds by using a higher order statistics-based radial basis function network. *IEEE J. Biomed. Health Inform.* **2013**, *17*, 675–680. [CrossRef] [PubMed]
123. Mamun, K.A.A.; Habib, M.H.U.; McFarlane, N.; Paul, N. A low power integrated bowel sound measurement system. *Conf. Rec. IEEE Instrum. Meas. Technol. Conf.* **2015**, *2015*, 779–783. [CrossRef]
124. Zhou, L.; Sun, Y.; Hua, S.; Li, Z.; Hao, D.; Hu, Y. Identification of bowel sound signal with spectral entropy method. In Proceedings of the 2015 12th IEEE International Conference on Electronic Measurement & Instruments (ICEMI), Qingdao, China, 16–18 July 2015; pp. 798–802.
125. Sheu, M.-J.; Lin, P.-Y.; Chen, J.-Y.; Lee, C.-C.; Lin, B.-S. Higher-order-statistics-based fractal dimension for noisy bowel sound detection. *IEEE Signal Process. Lett.* **2014**, *22*, 789–793. [CrossRef]

126. Yin, Y.; Yang, W.; Jiang, H.; Wang, Z. Bowel sound based digestion state recognition using artificial neural network. In Proceedings of the 2015 IEEE Biomedical Circuits and Systems Conference (BioCAS), Atlanta, GA, USA, 22–24 October 2015; pp. 1–4.
127. Liu, J.; Yin, Y.; Jiang, H.; Kan, H.; Zhang, Z.; Chen, P.; Zhu, B.; Wang, Z. Bowel sound detection based on MFCC feature and LSTM neural network. In Proceedings of the 2018 IEEE Biomedical Circuits and Systems Conference (BioCAS), Cleveland, OH, USA, 17–19 October 2018; pp. 1–4.
128. Kölle, K.; Aftab, M.F.; Andersson, L.E.; Fougner, A.L.; Stavdahl, Ø. Data driven filtering of bowel sounds using multivariate empirical mode decomposition. *Biomed. Eng. Online* **2019**, *18*, 28. [CrossRef] [PubMed]
129. Kodani, K.; Sakata, O. Automatic Bowel Sound Detection under Cloth Rubbing Noise. In Proceedings of the 2020 IEEE Region 10 Conference (Tencon), Osaka, Japan, 16–19 November 2020; pp. 779–784.
130. Zhao, K.; Jiang, H.; Yuan, T.; Zhang, C.; Jia, W.; Wang, Z. A CNN Based Human Bowel Sound Segment Recognition Algorithm with Reduced Computation Complexity for Wearable Healthcare System. In Proceedings of the 2020 IEEE International Symposium on Circuits and Systems (ISCAS), Seville, Spain, 12–14 October 2020; pp. 1–5.
131. Zheng, X.; Zhang, C.; Chen, P.; Zhao, K.; Jiang, H.; Jiang, Z.; Pan, H.; Wang, Z.; Jia, W. A CRNN System for Sound Event Detection Based on Gastrointestinal Sound Dataset Collected by Wearable Auscultation Devices. *IEEE Access* **2020**, *8*, 157892–157905. [CrossRef]
132. Namikawa, T.; Yamaguchi, S.; Fujisawa, K.; Ogawa, M.; Iwabu, J.; Munekage, M.; Uemura, S.; Maeda, H.; Kitagawa, H.; Kobayashi, M. Real-time bowel sound analysis using newly developed device in patients undergoing gastric surgery for gastric tumor. *JGH Open.* **2021**, *5*, 454–458. [CrossRef]
133. Ficek, J.; Radzikowski, K.; Nowak, J.K.; Yoshie, O.; Walkowiak, J.; Nowak, R. Analysis of Gastrointestinal Acoustic Activity Using Deep Neural Networks. *Sensors* **2021**, *21*, 7602. [CrossRef]
134. Will, C.; Shi, K.; Schellenberger, S.; Steigleder, T.; Michler, F.; Fuchs, J.; Weigel, R.; Ostgathe, C.; Koelpin, A. Radar-based heart sound detection. *Sci. Rep.* **2018**, *8*, 1–14. [CrossRef]
135. Rosen, A. Microwave Applications in Medicine in the USA-a Short Overview. In Proceedings of the 1991 21st European Microwave Conference, Stuttgart, Germany, 9–12 September 1991; pp. 139–149.
136. Gartshore, A.; Kidd, M.; Joshi, L.T. Applications of microwave energy in medicine. *Biosensors* **2021**, *11*, 96. [CrossRef]
137. Kumar, R. Remote Acoustic Detection System Using Microwave Signals. 2006. Available online: https://www.researchgate.net/publication/230807188_Remote_Acoustic_Detection_System_using_Microwave_Signals (accessed on 31 December 2022).
138. Li, C.; Peng, Z.; Huang, T.-Y.; Fan, T.; Wang, F.-K.; Horng, T.-S.; Munoz-Ferreras, J.-M.; Gomez-Garcia, R.; Ran, L.; Lin, J. A review on recent progress of portable short-range noncontact microwave radar systems. *IEEE Trans. Microw. Theory Tech.* **2017**, *65*, 1692–1706. [CrossRef]
139. Lin, C.-S.; Chang, S.-F.; Chang, C.-C.; Lin, C.-C. Microwave human vocal vibration signal detection based on Doppler radar technology. *IEEE Trans. Microw. Theory Tech.* **2010**, *58*, 2299–2306.
140. Pereira da Cunha, M. *Wireless Microwave Acoustic Sensor System for Condition Monitoring in Power Plant Environments*; University of Maine: Orono, ME, USA, 2017.
141. Maskay, A.; Da Cunha, M.P. High temperature static strain microwave acoustic sensor. In Proceedings of the 2016 IEEE International Ultrasonics Symposium (IUS), Tours, France, 18–21 September 2016; pp. 1–4.
142. Liu, S.; Zhang, R.; Zheng, Z.; Zheng, Y. Electromagnetic–acoustic sensing for biomedical applications. *Sensors* **2018**, *18*, 3203. [CrossRef] [PubMed]
143. Hui, X.; Sharma, P.; Kan, E.C. Microwave stethoscope for heart sound by near-field coherent sensing. In Proceedings of the 2019 IEEE MTT-S International Microwave Symposium (IMS), Boston, MA, USA, 2–7 June 2019; pp. 365–368.
144. Orphanidou, C.; Clifton, D.; Khan, S.; Smith, M.; Feldmar, J.; Tarassenko, L. Telemetry-based vital sign monitoring for ambulatory hospital patients. In Proceedings of the 2009 Annual International Conference of the IEEE Engineering in Medicine and Biology Society, Minneapolis, Minnesota, 3–6 September 2009; pp. 4650–4653.
145. Polk, T.; Walker, W.; Hande, A.; Bhatia, D. Wireless telemetry for oxygen saturation measurements. In Proceedings of the 2006 IEEE Biomedical Circuits and Systems Conference, Nara, Japan, 17–19 October 2019; pp. 174–177.
146. Zulkifli, N.S.A.; Harun, F.C.; Azahar, N. Centralized heart rate monitoring telemetry system using ZigBee wireless sensor network. In Proceedings of the 2012 IEEE-EMBS International Conference on Biomedical and Health Informatics, Hong Kong, China, 5–7 January 2012; pp. 265–268.
147. Budinger, T.F. Biomonitoring with wireless communications. *Annu. Rev. Biomed. Eng.* **2003**, *5*, 383–412. [CrossRef] [PubMed]
148. Sinharay, A.; Das, R.; Seth, S. A novel microwave measurement technique for non-contact vital sign monitoring. In Proceedings of the 2018 IEEE SENSORS, New Delhi, India, 28–31 October 2018; pp. 1–4.

MDPI
St. Alban-Anlage 66
4052 Basel
Switzerland
www.mdpi.com

Sensors Editorial Office
E-mail: sensors@mdpi.com
www.mdpi.com/journal/sensors